中华典籍英译赏析

主编：万 华 冯 奇

编委：(按姓氏拼音排序)
　　　段梦梦　高　源　蒋婷婷
　　　米法利　王　斌　谢漪珊
　　　张　玲

上海大学出版社
·上海·

图书在版编目(CIP)数据

中华典籍英译赏析 / 万华，冯奇主编. —上海：
上海大学出版社，2021.3(2021.9重印)
ISBN 978-7-5671-3967-1

Ⅰ. ①中… Ⅱ. ①万… ②冯… Ⅲ. ①古籍—英语—翻译—研究 Ⅳ. ①H315.9

中国版本图书馆CIP数据核字(2021)第029116号

策　划　许家骏
责任编辑　王悦生
助理编辑　王　俊　潘　鸣
封面设计　柯国富
技术编辑　金　鑫　钱宇坤

中华典籍英译赏析

万　华　冯　奇　主编

上海大学出版社出版发行
(上海市上大路99号　邮政编码200444)
(http://www.shupress.cn　发行热线 021-66135112)
出版人　戴骏豪

*

南京展望文化发展有限公司排版
上海普顺印刷包装有限公司印刷　各地新华书店经销
开本 787mm×1092mm　1/16　印张 22.25　字数 474千
2021年3月第1版　2021年9月第2次印刷
ISBN 978-7-5671-3967-1/H·383　定价 88.00元

版权所有　侵权必究
如发现本书有印装质量问题请与印刷厂质量科联系
联系电话：021-36522998

序 Preface

　　典籍是用汉字记载的、历代各领域的权威性著作,中华典籍是中国历史的见证和中华文化的重要载体,蕴含着中华民族特有的精神价值、思维方式、想象力和文化意识,体现着中华民族的生命力和创造力。在经济全球化的今天,传播中华文化是增强文化软实力、让更多外国人了解中国的历史与未来的重要途径。而典籍作为人类文化多元系统的一个组成部分,积极参与到世界文化交流中去成为一种必然趋势。因此,作为向海外传播中华文化的桥梁,典籍翻译也就具有重要的意义。

　　广义的中华典籍不仅涵盖儒家文化,还包括道家文化和佛家文化,以及法家和名家;不仅有先秦的典籍,还有先秦之后的典籍,像程朱理学、陆王心学,均颇具精彩内容。

　　东西交流源远流长。13世纪意大利人马可·波罗等人来到中国,并撰有游记传世,介绍中国文化和东方智慧。1590年,西班牙教士高母羡(Juan Cobo)翻译了一本辑录箴言的启蒙读物——《明心宝鉴》(*Precious Mirror of the Clear Heart*),这是中国文学译成欧洲文字的第一本书,属真正意义的典籍翻译。明清之际,西方天主教士陆续来华,为中国文化西传掀开了新的一页,然而,由于语言文化障碍等种种原因,这个时期的典籍翻译仅仅用于交流,没有留下完整译本。纵观历史,典籍外译历经5次高潮,即两汉至唐宋的译经时期、明末清初的科技翻译时期、新中国成立初期到"文革"之前的文学翻译时期、"文革"期间的政治翻译时期、20世纪70年代至今翻译在各个领域全面开花的时期。中西译者两支队伍都在进行中华典籍英译,相互交流,使典籍英译的数量和质量有了更大提高。当然,我国的台湾和香港地区也印行过大量中国古典文学著作的英译和论著。

　　早期的中华典籍外译的主力军是来华的基督传教士,他们以典籍译介为主,对初始汉学的创立和"中华风"的流行起了重要的作用。其中有利玛窦(Matteo Ricci)的《四书译本》等,金尼阁(Nicolas Trigault)译注的《大秦景教碑》等,郭纳爵(Ignatius da Costa)翻译的《大学》《论语》等,柏应理(Philippe Couplet)翻译的《西文四书解》,马若瑟(Joseph de Prémare)翻译的《书经》《尚书》《诗经》以及《赵氏孤儿》等。

　　自18世纪以来,中华典籍英译发展迅速。英国威廉·琼斯(William Jones)翻译了

《诗经》若干片段；英国德庇时（John Francis Davis）译《好逑传》（Hao Ch'iu Chuan）等明清小说与元杂剧《汉宫秋》（The Sorrows of Han）等；英国第一代汉学家代表人物翟理斯（Herbert Allen Giles），编译了《中国文学瑰宝》（Gems of Chinese Literature），并撰写《中国文学史》（A History of Chinese Literature）；英国第二代最优秀的汉学家、擅长诗歌翻译的亚瑟·韦利（Arthur Waley）完成了《诗经》《楚辞》《唐诗》《三字经》等的翻译；英国第三代汉学家戴维·霍克斯（David Hawks）翻译的《红楼梦》闻名遐迩；美国白之（Cyril Birch）译有《牡丹亭》；英国闵福德（John Minford）翻译《红楼梦》（后四十回）、《孙子兵法》、金庸武侠小说《鹿鼎记》，以及编著《含英咀华集》（Classical Chinese Literature: An Anthology of Translations）。这些汉学家的中华典籍英译为中国文化传播作出了巨大的贡献。

除了众多西方汉学家的倾情巨献，英美的出版机构对中国文化的传播也功不可没。近代以来，英国共有100余家外国出版机构印行过中国古典文学的书籍，总数达200余种。牛津和剑桥出版过的中国古典文学的书籍分别约40种、20种。近400年来，英国有关中国古典文学的书籍出版了300余种，博士论文30余篇。由于历史原因，美国在中国典籍翻译上起步较晚，起于20世纪，但现有书籍和博士论文却也有1 000余种。最突出的是宇文所安（Stephen Owen）编译的《中国文学作品选：从先秦到1911》（An Anthology of Chinese Literature: Beginnings to 1911）、《中国文论：英译与评论》（Readings in Chinese Literary Thought）等。

除了英、美两国之外，新加坡、菲律宾、爱尔兰、加拿大、新西兰、澳大利亚、南非等国家均有中国古典文学英译本问世。其中，新加坡、加拿大和澳大利亚在数量上领先。还有部分非英语国家对中华典籍进行了翻译，尤其以荷兰、瑞典、印度、法国和日本出版的中国古典文学译作数量最多。

国内学者从事中华典籍翻译起步较晚，发展呈不平衡、不稳定状态。晚清民初时期有辜鸿铭英译《论语》和《中庸》等，另外苏曼殊英译古诗110首，其中取自《诗经》的篇目有60首，唐代李白、杜甫等诗50首。20世纪20年代—40年代典籍英译数量较少，主要有林语堂翻译的《墨子》《镜花缘》《老残游记》《古文小品选译》《老子之智慧》《庄子》《中国著名诗文选读》《英译重编传奇小说》等，贺敬瞻翻译的《聊斋志异》，杨宪益与戴乃迭翻译的《老残游记》，林文庆翻译的《离骚》，刘师舜翻译的《二十年目睹之怪现状》，朱湘翻译的《今古奇观》。

新中国成立后，在中国共产党的领导下，中华典籍英译受到前所未有的重视。杨宪益（Hsien-i Yang）和戴乃迭（Gladys Yang）共同翻译《红楼梦》《楚辞》《魏晋南北朝小说选》《史记选》《唐代传奇选》《宋明平话选》《儒林外史》《关汉卿杂剧》《长生殿》《聊斋选》《古代寓言选》等，共上千万字。许渊冲的诗词翻译包括《诗经》《楚辞》《汉魏六朝诗一百五十首》《唐诗三百首》《宋词三百首》《元曲三百首》《李白诗选》《苏东坡词选》《李煜词选》《西厢记》《元明清诗一百五十首》等。

同时，中国政府对典籍英译给予了极大的支持，1949—1966年间，外文出版社和新世界出版社出版了《离骚》《诗经选》《中国古代寓言选》《杜甫诗歌选》《白居易诗歌选》《水浒传》《儒林外史》《聊斋志异》等多种古典文学翻译作品。

中国改革开放以来，典籍翻译进入蓬勃发展期，多种丛书相继出版，例如，新闻出版署直接领导的《大中华文库》英译本、湖南人民出版社出版的《汉英对照中国古典名著丛书》、山东友谊出版社出版的《儒学经典译丛》、外文出版社的《古诗苑汉英译丛》和《经典的回声》等，外语教学与研究出版社和中国文学出版社联合出版的《朝花惜拾：汉英对照中国文学书系》《英汉对照中国文学宝库古代文学系列》，江苏教育出版社翻译的《中国古典文学走向世界丛书》，上海外语教育出版社出版《外教社中国文化汉外对照丛书》等，还有辽宁教育出版社的《诗经》，苏州大学出版社的《吴歌精华》《评弹精华》《昆曲精华》和《苏剧精华》等。

哪里有实践，哪里就有理论。21世纪的初始，中国陆续出现了更多的典籍翻译研究组织，如"中国英汉语比较研究会"增设了"典籍英译专业委员会"，截至2019年，共召开11届"全国典籍翻译学术研讨会"；2001年，汕头大学建立了"典籍英译研究中心"；2003年，大连理工大学成立了"大连理工大学典籍英译研究所"；2011年，原"全国典籍英译研究会"更名为"中国典籍英译研究会"；2018年，"国学双语研究会"成立，致力于包括典籍翻译在内的各种中华文化传播活动。南开大学、四川大学、苏州大学、大连理工大学等多所高校相继招收了典籍英译研究方向硕士、博士研究生。2009年7月27日，国家汉办宣布，将组织海内外相关领域学者共同翻译堪称"中国儒家文化原点"的"五经"，并首先推出英译本。

实践出真知，学者们从不同的角度在翻译实践中理性归纳翻译原则和翻译策略。许渊冲先生总结了中国古典诗歌翻译中"三美"原则：音美、意美、形美。潘文国为翻译古代哲理名言语录制定了"明白、晓畅、简洁"的标准。王宏印在强调翻译策略时提出：(1)关键术语的"综合性注释"作为译文正文的必要补充；(2)英文基本术语对应于阐释须明确有序；(3)句子须求语义明晰而行文晓畅；(4)篇章层次可做必要的调整以求适合性；(5)译文应关注不同文体和表达功能的体现；(6)在知识可靠的基础上讲究艺术性和诗学功能。

汪榕培以自己的翻译实践为基础，总结了典籍英译的总体标准是"传神达意"，建议根据典籍英译的对象和目的采取两种基本策略：(1)学术性翻译，即读者对象是研究汉学的汉学家，在翻译原文之处还需旁征博引，解释典故，考释出处，这种翻译突出的是译文的叙述价值和文化价值；(2)普及性翻译，即面对普通读者大众，注重文笔的生动传神，注重可读性、大众化。前者可采取适当异化的翻译策略，后者可以采取适当归化的翻译策略。当然，译者的文化取向往往决定其翻译策略的选择。赵彦春在《诗经》《道德经》《论语》《庄子》《三字经》《弟子规》《千字文》《李白诗歌全集》《王维诗歌全集》等国学经典文献的翻译实践中，为重铸经典，求斯道极轨，概论出了"以诗译诗，以经译经"的准则。从语言的本质属性出发,赵彦春提出,形神兼备是诗歌翻译的最高境界和最基本的要求。"形"是"神"的导航者,"神"是"形"的主管人,缺其一端,其结局都必定是形散而神离的。总之,典籍英译标准的制定不仅与原作内容、风格、文本类型和原作者的意图密切相关,还要考虑文化、社会现实、翻译目的、读者需求等因素。译者的选择应以是否恰当为依据,在尽量贴近原文和满足读者的阅读需求之间寻找平衡。

纵观中西文化交流史,在漫长的"西学东渐"的过程中,中国文化一直是被动接受。中国要发展,必须加强文化传播交流。把中华典籍翻译为英文、介绍给世界各国人民,是文化传播不可或缺的环节。在世界多极化、文化多元化和全球一体化的今天,国际交流日益深入,须大力继承和发展中华民族的优秀传统文化,让世界真正了解中国。因此,典籍英译的意义不言而喻。正如卓振英所指出的"对于弘扬民族文化、促进东西方文化融合、保持中国固有的文化身份来说,典籍英译有着十分重大的现实意义"。

本书的主要内容自 2015 年起,一直用于上海大学翻译专业研究生"中华典籍英译"课程的教学中,效果良好。上海大学 2015 级翻译硕士研究生白莲、高源、李华倩、刘洁、宋亚丽、孙婧乐、田婷、张浏芳等参与了本书的前期资料的收集工作,感谢她们的付出。本书的出版还得到了上海市教委、上海震旦职业学院 3D 思想政治工作创新项目的大力支持,在此,表示衷心的感谢!

冯 奇

2020 年 7 月 31 日

目 录
Contents

第一课 《诗经》译介赏析 ·· 1

第二课 《三字经》译介赏析 ·· 32

第三课 《论语》译介赏析 ·· 69

第四课 《道德经》译介赏析 ·· 101

第五课 《庄子》译介赏析 ·· 116

第六课 《孙子兵法》译介赏析 ·· 133

第七课 唐诗译介赏析 ··· 177

第八课 宋词译介赏析 ··· 194

第九课 《楚辞》译介赏析 ·· 212

第十课 《红楼梦》译介赏析 ·· 230

第十一课 《西游记》评介赏析 ·· 257

第十二课 《三国演义》评介赏析 ······································ 271

第十三课 《水浒传》评介赏析 ·· 285

第十四课 《黄帝内经》译介赏析 ······································ 307

参考答案 ··· 325

第一课
《诗经》译介赏析

> 《诗经》是中国第一部诗歌总集,成书的时间大概在公元前6世纪左右,与《书》《礼》《乐》《易》《春秋》合称为"六经"。
>
> 《诗经》收集了自西周初年至春秋时期500多年的305篇诗歌。内容上分为风、雅、颂三部分。风、雅、颂,是《诗经》的体裁,也是《诗经》作品分类的主要依据。其中"风"是地方民歌,有十五国风,共160首;"雅"主要是朝廷乐歌,分大雅和小雅,共105篇;"颂"主要是宗庙乐歌,有40首。《诗经》在词语层面表现为叠字、重言、双声、迭韵,比如"关关、夭夭、灼灼、依依、霏霏、迟迟、载渴载饥、悠哉悠哉、窈窕"等等。在句子层面表现为四字格为主,言简意赅,音韵合谐,节奏齐整,加之迭章手法,使诗歌首首有韵,有一唱三叹之感,并有视觉美感。《诗经》的修辞手法有"赋""比""兴"三种。"赋"就是铺陈(敷陈其事而直言之也),"比"就是类比(以彼物比此物也),"兴"就是启发(先言它物以引起所咏之词也)。"风""雅""颂"和修辞手法"赋""比""兴"合称《诗经》的"六义"。《诗经》对中国文学产生了巨大影响,是后人效仿的典范。

一、翻译简介

迄今为止,《诗经》翻译已经有了三百多年的历史,世界上几乎每一种主要文字都已经有了《诗经》译本。比较广为人知的翻译《诗经》的国内学者有许渊冲、汪榕培、戴乃迭和杨宪益等人,国外也有很多人翻译过《诗经》,比如理雅各(James Legge),庞德(Ezra Pound),亚瑟·韦利(Arthur Waley),等等。

二、书名翻译

不同的译者对《诗经》的书名以及重点的词语有着不同的翻译,光书名《诗经》的翻译就有很多种。翻译大家许渊冲把它译作"the book of poetry",James Legge 将其译作"the She King",此外它也常被译为 classic of poetry/Shijing/Shih-ching/Odes/Poetry。以下的翻译分别来自许渊冲和 James Legge。

国风　book of songs/lessons from the states
小雅　book of odes/minor odes of the kingdom
大雅　book of epics/greater odes of the kingdom
颂　　book of hymns/odes of the temple and the altar
周南　songs collected south of the capital/the odes of Chow and the south
召南　songs collected south of Shao/the odes of Shaou and the south
鹿鸣　first decade of odes/the decade of Luh Ming
商颂　Hymns of Shang/the sacrificial odes of Shang

三、特殊概念的翻译

诗歌语言是音韵协调的语言,无韵不成诗,音韵乃诗歌之灵魂。音韵是传递诗情、表现意义的中介,是重要的音美因素。诗的音韵美,是诗人内在情感的显现。诗歌语言的音乐性诉诸诗的节奏和韵律。一首好诗首先应是音韵协调,具有音乐的美感,可以使读者获得和谐的听觉审美满足。无论汉诗还是英诗,都借助韵律实现诗歌的审美功能。汉英语音系统差异较大,汉英诗歌在音韵表现和安排上有所不同:汉诗的音乐性主要表现为四声变化、节奏和用韵;英诗则主要表现为轻重音、节奏和用韵。诗的翻译不应只追求语言的对等,还应转换原诗的韵律美。可以说,传达原诗的音韵协调之美是诗歌翻译者的首要任务。优秀的译者会意识到韵脚对原诗的重要性,经常用"rhyme"来使译文押韵。在下文的例子中,用许渊冲的译文(简称"许译")和理雅各的译文(简称"理译")进行分析。

例1:以许渊冲翻译的《关雎》为例。

Cooing and Wooing

By riverside a pair
Of turtledoves are cooing;
There is a good maiden fair
Whom a young man is wooing.

Water flows left and <u>right</u>

Of cresses here and <u>there</u>;

The youth yearns day and <u>night</u>

For the maiden so <u>fair</u>.

His yearning grows so <u>strong</u>,

He cannot fall <u>asleep</u>,

But tosses all night <u>long</u>,

<u>So deep in love, so deep</u>!

Now gather left and <u>right</u>

Cress long or short and <u>tender</u>!

O lute, play music <u>light</u>

For the fiancée so <u>slender</u>!

Feast friends at left and <u>right</u>

On cresses cooked <u>tender</u>!

O bells and drums, <u>delight</u>

The bride so sweet and <u>slender</u>!

评析：可以看出，译文既形象地再现了原诗的意义，画线部分又以明快清丽的节奏和韵脚重现了原诗的韵律之美。韵体翻译使得意韵相谐，形神兼备，音意结合，因而在听觉效果上超过非韵体，造就了音乐美。

例2：死生契阔，与子成说。执子之手，<u>与子偕老</u>。——《诗经·邶风·击鼓》

许译：

  Meet or part, live or die;

  We made oath, you and I.

  Give me your hand I'll hold

  And <u>live with me till old</u>!

理译：

  For life or for death, however separated,

  To our wives we pledged our word.

  We held their hands;

  <u>We were to grow old together</u> with them.

评析：《诗经》诗句多为四言句，语言具有音乐美，简而不竭。在"与子偕老"一句的翻译上，许译和理译均表达出了"与你一起老去"的意思，但就译文的形式上，理译偏向于散体，许译则在传达意思的同时保留了原文的韵体的形式，"die"和"I"、"hold"和"old"形成偶韵，句式工整对仗，读来朗朗上口。

例3：今夕何夕,见此良人。子兮子兮,如此良人何!——《诗经·唐风·绸缪》

许译：

What evening's coming round
For me to find my bridegroom here!
O he is here! O he is here!
What shall I not do with my dear!

理译：

This evening is what evening,
That I see this good man?
O me! O me!
That I should get a good man like this!

评析：正确的理解是诗歌翻译的前提,此句中许译和理译对"良人"的概念有不同的理解。许译将其理解为"新郎",而理译将其理解为"好人"。根据前一句"绸缪束薪,三星在天"可以判断,诗中所写的时间为十月,而当时以仲春为婚期,而非十月,因此对"良人"更为精确的理解应为"未婚夫"。

例4：它山之石,可以攻玉。——《诗经·小雅·鹤鸣》

许译：

Stones from another hill
May be used to polish gem.

理译：

The stones of those hills,
May be used to polish gems.

评析：原句的意思是"别的山上面的石头坚硬,可以琢磨玉器。"在此句的翻译上,许译和理译都忠实地传达了原文的含义。

例5：皇矣上帝,临下有赫。监观四方,求民之莫。——《诗经·大雅·皇矣》

许译：

O God is great!
He saw our state,
Surveyed our land,
Saw how people did stand.

理译：

Great is God,
Beholding this lower world in majesty.
He surveyed the four quarters (of the kingdom),
Seeking for some one to give settlement to the people.

评析：此句的意思是"天帝伟大而又辉煌，洞察人间慧目明亮。监察观照天地四方，发现民间疾苦灾殃。"这是一首叙述周王先祖功德的颂诗，是周部族多篇开国史诗之一。《毛诗序》："《皇矣》，美周也。天监代殷莫若周，周世世修德莫若文王。"在传达原文意思的同时，与理译相比，许译在形式上采用偶韵，语言简而不俗，更为贴近原文。

例6：作为文化概念的"勺药"。

维士与女，伊其相谑，赠之以<u>勺药</u>。——《诗经·郑风·溱洧》

许译：

　　Playing together then,
　　They have a happy hour;
　　Each gives the other <u>peony flower</u>.

理译：

　　So the gentlemen and ladies.
　　Make sport together,
　　Presenting one another with <u>small peonies</u>.

评析："芍药（勺药）"是中国六大名花之一，其英文解释为"Chinese herbaceous peony"。许译采用"peony flower"，可以看出，译者的用意是为了与"hour"形成押韵，使得译文句式工整。

例7：作为普通语的词语"乐"。

参差荇菜，左右芼之。窈窕淑女，钟鼓<u>乐</u>之。——《诗经·周南·关雎》

许译：

　　Feast friends at left and right
　　On cresses cooked tender!
　　O bells and drums, <u>delight</u>
　　The bride so sweet and slender!

理译：

　　Here long, there short, is the duckweed;
　　On the left, on the right, we cook and present it.
　　The modest, retiring, virtuous, young lady:
　　With bells and drums let us show our <u>delight</u> in her.

评析：在原文中，"乐"是一个动词，指的是"使……快乐"，译成英文时，许译和理译都将其译为名词"delight"。值得注意的是，许译中"delight"与第一行的"right"构成押韵，译文形成 abab 韵式，做到了"译诗如诗"。

例8：比喻。

温温恭人，<u>如</u>集于木。惴惴小心，<u>如</u>临于谷。战战兢兢，<u>如</u>履薄冰。——《诗经·小雅·小宛》

许译：

> Precarious, ill at ease,
> As if perched on trees;
> Careful lest I should ail
> On the brink of a vale;
> I tremble twice or thrice
> As treading on thin ice.

理译：

> We must be mild, and humble,
> As if we were perched on trees.
> We must be anxious and careful,
> As if we were on the brink of a valley.
> We must be apprehensive and cautious,
> As if we were treading upon thin ice.

评析：原文中"如集于木""如临于谷""如履薄冰"均是表示比喻的概念。许译的特点是押韵而简洁。理译在处理三个"如……"时均采用"As if ..."的句式，整体上形成排比句，加强了译文的气势。

例9：拟人。

昔我往矣，杨柳依依。今我来思，雨雪霏霏。——《诗经·小雅·采薇》

许译：

> When I left here,
> Willows shed tear.
> I come back now,
> Snow bends the bough.

理译：

> At first, when we set out,
> The willows were fresh and green;
> Now, when we shall be returning,
> The snow will be falling in clouds.

亚瑟·韦利（Arthur Waley）译：

> Long ago, when we started,
> The willows spread their shade.
> Now that we turn back
> The snow flakes fly.

庞德（Ezra Pound）译：

> Willows were green when we set out,

it's blowin' an' snowin' as we go

评析：许译忠实地表达了原文的情境，"Willows shed tear"，不但将杨柳拟人化，而且赋予其人的多情，生动地再现当时战士们出征的场景。虽然 Waley 的译文也采用了拟人手法，接近了原诗的风格，但是在体现原诗诗人借物抒情方面，仍逊色于许渊冲的译文。

四、译文对比赏析

1. 经典句子

(1)　　　　死生契阔，与子成说。
　　　　　　执子之手，与子偕老。

　　　　　　　　　　　　　　　　《诗经·邶风·击鼓》

(1)　　　　Meet or part, live or die;
　　　　　　We made oath, you and I.
　　　　　　Give me your hand I'll hold
　　　　　　And live with me till old!

　　　　　　　　　　　　　　　　（许渊冲译）

　　　　　　For life or for death, however separated,
　　　　　　To our wives we pledged our word.
　　　　　　We held their hands;
　　　　　　We were to grow old together with them.

　　　　　　　　　　　　　　　　（Tr. James Legge）

(2)　　　　知我者，谓我心忧；
　　　　　　不知我者，谓我何求。
　　　　　　悠悠苍天，此何人哉？

　　　　　　　　　　　　　　　　《诗经·王风·黍离》

(2)　　　　Those who know me will say
　　　　　　My heart is sad and bleak;
　　　　　　Those who don't know me may
　　　　　　Ask me for what I seek.
　　　　　　O boundless azure sky,
　　　　　　Who's ruined the land and why?

　　　　　　　　　　　　　　　　（许渊冲译）

Those who knew me,

Said I was sad at heart.

Those who did not know me,

Said I was seeking for something.

O thou distant and azure Heaven!

By what man was this (brought about)?

(Tr. James Legge)

(3) 维士与女,

伊其相谑,

赠之以勺药。

《诗经·郑风·溱洧》

(3) Playing together then,

They have a happy hour;

Each gives the other peony flower.

(许渊冲译)

So the gentlemen and ladies.

Make sport together,

Presenting one another with small peonies.

(James Legge 译)

(4) 不狩不猎,胡瞻尔庭有县狟兮?

彼君子兮,不素餐兮!

《诗经·魏风·伐檀》

(4) How can those who nor hunt nor chase

Have in their courtyard badgers of each race?

Those lords are good

Who do not need work for food!

(许渊冲译)

You do not follow the chase;

How do we see the badgers hanging up in your courtyards?

O that superior man!

He would not eat the bread of idleness!

(Tr. James Legge)

(5)　　今夕何夕,见此良人。
　　　　子兮子兮,如此良人何!

《诗经·唐风·绸缪》

(5)　　What evening's coming round
　　　　For me to find my bridegroom here!
　　　　O he is here! O he is here!
　　　　What shall I not do with my dear!

（许渊冲译）

　　　　This evening is what evening,
　　　　That I see this good man?
　　　　O me! O me!
　　　　That I should get a good man like this!

(Tr. James Legge)

(6)　　悠悠苍天,曷其有极?

《诗经·唐风·鸨羽》

(6)　　O gods in boundless, endless sky,
　　　　Can all this end before I die?

（许渊冲译）

　　　　O thou distant and azure Heaven!
　　　　When shall (our service) have an end?

(Tr. James Legge)

(7)　　昔我往矣,杨柳依依。
　　　　今我来思,雨雪霏霏。
　　　　行道迟迟,载渴载饥。
　　　　我心伤悲,莫知我哀。

《诗经·小雅·采薇》

(7)　　When I left here,
　　　　Willows shed tear.
　　　　I come back now.
　　　　Snow bends the bough.
　　　　Long, long the way;
　　　　Hard, hard the day.

Hunger and thirst

Press me the worst.

My grief o'erflows.

Who knows? Who knows?

（许渊冲译）

At first, when we set out,

The willows were fresh and green;

Now, when we shall be returning,

The snow will be falling in clouds.

Long and tedious will be our marching;

We shall hunger; we shall thirst.

Our hearts are wounded with grief,

And no one knows our sadness.

(Tr. James Legge)

Long ago, when we started,

The willows spread their shade.

Now that we turn back

The snow flakes fly.

The march before us is long,

We are thirsty and hungry,

Our hearts are stricken with sorrow,

But no one listens to our plaint.

(Tr. Arthur Waley)

Willows were green when we set out,

It's blowin' an' snowin' as we go

Down this road, muddy and slow,

Hungry and thirsty and blue a doubt

(no one feels half of what we know).

(Tr. Ezra Pound)

(8) 它山之石，可以攻玉。

《诗经·小雅·鹤鸣》

(8) Stones from another hill

May be used to polish gem.

(许渊冲译)

The stones of those hills,
May be used to polish gems.

(Tr. James Legge)

(9) 温温恭人，如集于木。
惴惴小心，如临于谷。
战战兢兢，如履薄冰。

《诗经·小雅·小宛》

(9) Precarious, ill at ease,
As if perched on trees;
Careful lest I should ail
On the brink of a vale;
I tremble twice or thrice
As treading on thin ice.

(许渊冲译)

We must be mild, and humble,
As if we were perched on trees.
We must be anxious and careful,
As if we were on the brink of a valley.
We must be apprehensive and cautious,
As if we were treading upon thin ice.

(Tr. James Legge)

(10) 皇矣上帝，临下有赫。
监观四方，求民之莫。

《诗经·大雅·皇矣》

(10) O God is great!
He saw our state,
Surveyed our land,
Saw how people did stand.

(许渊冲译)

Great is God,

Beholding this lower world in majesty.
He surveyed the four quarters (of the kingdom),
Seeking for some one to give settlement to the people.

(Tr. James Legge)

2. 经典段落

(1) 　　　　　　　　诗经·周南·关雎

关关雎鸠,在河之洲。
窈窕淑女,君子好逑。

参差荇菜,左右流之。
窈窕淑女,寤寐求之。

求之不得,寤寐思服。
悠哉悠哉,辗转反侧。

参差荇菜,左右采之。
窈窕淑女,琴瑟友之。

参差荇菜,左右芼之。
窈窕淑女,钟鼓乐之。

(1) 　　　　　　　　Cooing and Wooing

By riverside a pair
Of turtledoves are cooing;
There's a good maiden fair
Whom a young man is wooing.

Water flows left and right
Of cress long here, short there;
The youth yearns day and night
For the good maiden fair.

His yearning grows so strong,
He cannot fall asleep,
But tosses all night long,
So deep in love, so deep!

Now gather left and right
Cress long or short and tender!
O lute, play music light

For the fiancée so slender!

Feast friends at left and right
On cresses cooked tender!
O bells and drums, delight
The bride so sweet and slender!

(许渊冲译)

Kwan ts'eu

Kwan kwan go the ospreys,
On the islet in the river.
The modest, retiring, virtuous, young lady: —
For our prince a good mate she.

Here long, there short, is the duckweed,
To the left, to the right, borne about by the current.
The modest, retiring, virtuous, young lady: —
Waking and sleeping, he sought her.

He sought her and found her not,
And waking and sleeping he thought about her.
Long he thought; oh! Long and anxiously;
On his side, on his back, he turned, and back again.

Here long, there short, is the duckweed;
On the left, on the right, we gather it,
The modest, retiring, virtuous, young lady: —
With lutes, small and large, let us give her friendly welcome.

Here long, there short, is the duckweed;
On the left, on the right, we cook and present it.
The modest, retiring, virtuous, young lady: —
With bells and drums let us show our delight in her.

(Tr. James Legge)

(2) **诗经·邶风·式微**

式微式微,胡不归?
微君之故,胡为乎中露?

式微式微,胡不归?

微君之躬，胡为乎泥中？

(2) **Toilers**

It's near dusk, lo!

Why not home go?

Sire, it's for you

We're wet with dew.

It's near dusk, lo!

Why not home go?

For you, O sire,

We toil in mire.

（许渊冲译）

Shih we

Reduced! Reduced!

Why not return?

If it were not for your sake, O prince,

How should we be thus exposed to the dew?

Reduced! Reduced!

Why not return?

If it were not for your person, O prince,

How should we be here in the mire?

(Tr. James Legge)

(3) **诗经·邶风·静女**

静女其姝，

俟我于城隅。

爱而不见，

搔首踟蹰。

静女其娈，

贻我彤管。

彤管有炜，

说怿女美。

自牧归荑，

洵美且异。

匪女之为美，

美人之贻。

(3) **A Shepherdess**

A maiden mute and tall

Trysts me at corner wall.

I can find her nowhere,

Perplexed, I scratch my hair.

The maiden fair and mute

Gives me a grass-made lute.

The lute makes rosy light

And brings me high delight.

Coming back from the mead,

She gives me a rare reed,

Lovely not for it's rare,

It's the gift of the fair.

（许渊冲译）

Tsing neu

How lovely is the retiring girl!

She was to await me at a corner of the wall.

Loving and not seeing her,

I scratch my head, and am in perplexity.

How handsome is the retiring girl!

She presented to me a red tube.

Bright is the red tube; —

I delight in the beauty of the girl.

From the pasture lands she gave a shoot of the white grass,

Truly elegant and rare.

It is not you, O grass, that are elegant; —

You are the gift of an elegant girl.

（Tr. James Legge）

(4) 诗经·卫风·氓

氓之蚩蚩，抱布贸丝。

匪来贸丝，来即我谋。
送子涉淇，至于顿丘。
匪我愆期，子无良媒。
将子无怒，秋以为期。

乘彼垝垣，以望复关。
不见复关，泣涕涟涟。
既见复关，载笑载言。
尔卜尔筮，体无咎言。
以尔车来，以我贿迁。

桑之未落，其叶沃若。
于嗟鸠兮，无食桑葚！
于嗟女兮，无与士耽！
士之耽兮，犹可说也；
女之耽兮，不可说也。

桑之落矣，其黄而陨。
自我徂尔，三岁食贫。
淇水汤汤，渐车帷裳。
女也不爽，士贰其行。
士也罔极，二三其德！

三岁为妇，靡室劳矣。
夙兴夜寐，靡有朝矣！
言既遂矣，至于暴矣。
兄弟不知，咥其笑矣。
静言思之，躬自悼矣！

及尔偕老，老使我怨。
淇则有岸，隰则有泮。
总角之宴，言笑晏晏。
信誓旦旦，不思其反。
反是不思，亦已焉哉！

(4) **A Faithless Man**

A man seemed free from guile,
In trade he wore a smile,
He'd barter cloth for thread;

No, to me he'd be wed.
We went across the ford;
I'd not give him my word.
I said by hillside green,
"You have no go-between.
Try to find one, I pray.
In autumn be the day!"

I climbed the wall to wait
To see him pass the gate.
I did not see him pass;
My tears streamed down, alas!
I saw him passing by,
I'd laugh with joy and cry.
Both reed and tortoise shell.
Foretold all would be well.
"Come with your cart," I said.
"To you I will be wed."

How fresh were mulberries
With their fruits on the trees!
Beware, O turtledove,
Eat not the fruits you love,
For they'll intoxicate.
Do not repent too late!
Man may do what they will,
He can atone it still.
The wrong a woman's done
No man will e'er condone.

The mulberries appear
With yellow leaves and sear.
'er since he married me,
I've shared his poverty.
Desert'd, from him I part,
The flood has wet my cart.
I have done nothing wrong;

He changes all along.
He's fickle to excess,
Capricious, pitiless.

Three years I was his wife
And led a toilsome life.
ach day I early rose,
And late I sought repose.
He thought it not enough
And began to become rough
My brothers did not know,
Their jeers at me would go.
Mutely I ruminate
And then deplore my fate.

I'd live with him in vain;
I had cause to complain.
I love the ford of yore
And the wide rivershore.
When we were girl and boy,
We'd talk and laugh with joy.
He pledged to me his troth
Could he forget his oath?
He's forgot what he swore.
Should I say any more?

(许渊冲译)

Mang

A simple-looking lad you were,
Carrying cloth to exchange it for silk.
(But) you came not so to purchase silk; —
You came to make proposals to me.
I convoyed you through the K'e,
As far as Tun-k'ew.
'It is not I,' (I said), 'who would protract the time;
But you have had no good go-between.

I pray you be not angry,
And let autumn be the time.'

I ascended that ruinous wall,
To look towards Fuh-kwan;
And when I saw (you) not (coming from) it;
My tears flowed in streams.
When I did see (you coming from) Fuh-kwan,
I laughed and I spoke.
You had consulted, (you said), the tortoise-shell and the reeds,
And there was nothing unfavourable in their response.
'Then come,' (I said), 'with your carriage,
And I will remove with my goods.'

Before the mulberry tree has shed its leaves,
How rich and glossy are they!
Ah! thou dove,
Eat not its fruit (to excess).
Ah! thou young lady,
Seek no licentious pleasure with a gentleman.
When a gentleman indulges in such pleasure,
Something may still be said for him;
When a lady does so,
Nothing can be said for her.

When the mulberry tree sheds its leaves,
They fall yellow on the ground.
Since I went with you,
Three years have I eaten of your poverty;
And (now) the full waters of the Qi,
Wet the curtains of my carriage.
There has been no difference in me,
But you have been double in your ways.
It is you, Sir, who transgress the right,
Thus changeable in your conduct.

For three years I was your wife,

And thought nothing of my toil in your house.

I rose early and went to sleep late,

Not intermitting my labours for a morning.

Thus (on my part) our contract was fulfilled,

But you have behaved thus cruelly.

My brothers will not know (all this),

And will only laugh at me.

Silently I think of it,

And bemoan myself.

I was to grow old with you;—

Old, you give me cause for sad repining.

The K'e has its banks,

And the marsh has its shores.

In the pleasant time of my girlhood, with my hair simply gathered in a knot,

Harmoniously we talked and laughed.

Clearly were we sworn to good faith,

And I did not think the engagement would be broken.

That it would be broken I did not think,

And now it must be all over!

(Tr. James Legge)

(5) 　　　　　诗经·卫风·木瓜

投我以木瓜，

报之以琼琚。

匪报也，

永以为好也！

投我以木桃，

报之以琼瑶。

匪报也，

永以为好也！

投我以木李，

报之以琼玖。

匪报也，

永以为好也！

(5) **Gifts**

She throws a quince to me,
I give her a green jade
Not in return, you see,
But to show acquaintance made.

She throws a peach to me,
I give her a white jade
Not in return, you see,
But to show friendship made.

She throws a plum to me,
I give her jasper fair
Not in return, you see,
But to show love fore'er.

(许渊冲译)

Muh kwa

There was presented to me a papaya,
And I returned for it a beautiful keu-gem;
Not as a return for it,
But that our friendship might be lasting.

There was presented to me a peach,
And I returned for it a beautiful yaou-gem;
Not as a return for it,
But that our friendship might be lasting.

There was presented to me a plum,
And I returned for it a beautiful këw-gem;
Not as a return for it,
But that our friendship might be lasting.

(Tr. James Legge)

(6) 诗经·郑风·子衿

青青子衿,
悠悠我心。
纵我不往,

子宁不嗣音？

青青子佩，

悠悠我思。

纵我不往，

子宁不来？

挑兮达兮，

在城阙兮，

一日不见，

如三月兮。

(6) **To a Scholar**

Student with collar blue,

How much I long for you!

Though to see you I am not free,

O why don't you send word to me?

Student with belt-stone blue,

How long I think of you!

Though to see you I am not free,

O why don't you come to see me?

I'm pacing up and down

On the wall of the town.

When to see you I am not free,

One day seems like three months to me.

（许渊冲译）

Tsze k'in

O you, with the blue collar,

Prolonged is the anxiety of my heart.

Although I do not go (to you),

Why do you not continue your messages (to me)?

O you with the blue (strings to your) girdle-gems,

Long, long do I think of you.

Although I do not go (to you),

Why do you not come (to me)?

How volatile are you and dissipated,

By the look-out tower on the wall!
One day without the sight of you,
Is like three months.

(Tr. James Legge)

(7) 诗经·秦风·蒹葭

蒹葭苍苍,白露为霜。
所谓伊人,在水一方,
溯洄从之,道阻且长。
溯游从之,宛在水中央。

蒹葭凄凄,白露未晞。
所谓伊人,在水之湄。
溯洄从之,道阻且跻。
溯游从之,宛在水中坻。

蒹葭采采,白露未已。
所谓伊人,在水之涘。
溯洄从之,道阻且右。
溯游从之,宛在水中沚。

(7) **Where Is She?**

The reeds grow green;
Frosted dew-drops gleam.
Where was she seen?
Beyond the stream.
Upstream I go;
The way's so long.
And downstream, lo!
She's thereamong.

The reeds turn white,
Dew not yet dried.
Where's she so bright?
On the other side.
Upstream I go;
Hard is the way.
And downstream.lo!

She's far away.

The reeds still there,
With frost dews blend.
Where's she so fair?
At river's end.
Upstream I go;
The way does wind.
And downstream, lo!
She's far behind.

（许渊冲译）

Këen këa

The reeds and rushes are deeply green,
And the white dew is turned into hoarfrost.
The man of whom I think
Is somewhere about the water.
I go up the stream in quest of him,
But the way is difficult and long.
I go down the stream in quest of him,
And lo! he is right in the midst of the water.

The reeds and rushes are luxuriant,
And the white dew is not yet dry.
The man of whom I think
Is on the margin of the water.
I go up the stream in quest of him,
But the way is difficult and steep.
I go down the stream in quest of him,
And lo! he is on the islet in the midst of the water.

The reeds and rushes are abundant,
And the white dew is not yet ceased.
The man of whom I think
Is on the bank of the river.
I go up the stream in quest of him,
But the way is difficult and turns to the right.

I go down the stream in quest of him,
And lo！he is on the island in the midst of the water.

(Tr. James Legge)

The Reed

Green, green the reed,
Dew and frost gleam.
Where's she I need?
Beyond the stream.
Upstream I go,
The way is long.
Downstream I go,
She's thereamong.

White, white the reed,
Dew not yet dried.
Where's she I need?
On the other side.
Upstream I go,
Hard is the way.
Downstream I go,
She's far away.

Bright, bright the reed,
Dew and frost blend.
Where's she I need?
At river's end.
Upstream I go,
The way does wind.
Downstream I go,
She's far behind.

(杨宪益、戴乃迭译)

（8） 诗经·秦风·无衣

岂曰无衣？
与子同袍。
王于兴师，

修我戈矛。

与子同仇!

岂曰无衣?

与子同泽。

王于兴师,

修我矛戟。

与子偕作!

岂曰无衣?

与子同裳。

王于兴师,

修我甲兵。

与子偕行!

(8)　　　　　　　**Comradeship**

　　　　　　Are you not battle-drest?

　　　　　　Let's share the plate for breast!

　　　　　　We shall go up the line.

　　　　　　Let's make our lances shine!

　　　　　　Your foe is mine.

　　　　　　Are you not battle-drest?

　　　　　　Let's share the coat and vest!

　　　　　　We shall go up the line.

　　　　　　Let's make our halberds shine!

　　　　　　Your job is mine.

　　　　　　Are you not battle-drest?

　　　　　　Let's share the kilt and the rest!

　　　　　　We shall go up the line.

　　　　　　Let's make our armor shine!

　　　　　　And march your hand in mine!

(许渊冲译)

Woo e

How shall it be said that you have no clothes?

I will share my long robes with you.

The king is raising his forces;

I will prepare my lance and spear,
And will be your comrade.

How shall it be said that you have no clothes?
I will share my under clothes with you.
The king is raising his forces;
I will prepare my spear and lance,
And will take the field with you.

How shall it be said that you have no clothes?
I will share my lower garments with you.
The king is raising his forces;
I will prepare my buffcoat and sharp weapons,
And will march along with you.

(Tr. James Legge)

3. 译文比读：不同译本的语言特点
(1) 译本情况

前面的章节选取了多个《诗经》译本，但最常出现的译文是19世纪英国汉学家理雅各（James Legge）和中国翻译大家许渊冲的译文。理雅各的译文从头到尾都体现忠实与拘谨；美国诗人、翻译家庞德（Ezra Pound）的译文总以再创造的形式出现；许渊冲的译文一韵到底，追求音、形、意三美兼具。译者对于韵脚的处理手段大同小异，从本质上说，分为用韵与不用韵两种。本课所选译本的外国译者有理雅各、庞德以及20世纪英国汉学家亚瑟·韦利，中国译者有著名翻译家杨宪益、戴乃迭、许渊冲、汪榕培。译诗形式分为散体和诗体。两者一般都是分行的，其主要区别在于后者强调用韵及格律。

(2) 译本讨论

下面我们将结合《小雅·采薇》的不同译本来分析讨论译者的翻译风格和特点。

原文：

昔我往矣，杨柳依依。
今我来思，雨雪霏霏。
行道迟迟，载渴载饥。
我心伤悲，莫知我哀．

译文：

When I left here,
Willows shed tear.

I come back now.
Snow bends the bough.
Long, long the way;
Hard, hard the day.
Hunger and thirst
Press me the worst.
My grief o'erflows.
Who knows? Who knows?

(许渊冲译)

At first, when we set out,
The willows were fresh and green;
Now, when we shall be returning,
The snow will be falling in clouds.
Long and tedious will be our marching;
We shall hunger; we shall thirst.
Our hearts are wounded with grief,
And no one knows our sadness.

(Tr. James Legge)

Long ago, when we started,
The willows spread their shade.
Now that we turn back
The snow flakes fly.
The march before us is long,
We are thirsty and hungry,
Our hearts are stricken with sorrow,
But no one listens to our plaint.

(Tr. Arthur Waley)

Willows were green when we set out,
it's blowin' an' snowin' as we go
down this road, muddy and slow,
hungry and thirsty and blue a doubt
(no one feels half of what we know)

(Tr. Ezara Pound)

原文结构紧凑,用自然景观描述了羁旅天涯的哀伤心情,寓情于景,托物言志。首先以庞德的译文为例,"it's blowin' an' snowin' as we go"用词凝练、意象鲜明,用 blowin' an' snowin' 替代了 blowing and snowing 节奏感强,对应于原文结构紧凑的特点;用具象思维再现了原文的韵味和风格,传达了原文的语体色彩。王东波认为:"庞德的译作是西方作者的风格。他打破了原作的形式,使其译作更适合西方人的口味,同时也在更大程度上的贴近原文。他成功地抓住了原作的意境而且使其英文作品更容易让西方读者接受。"

通观各篇译文,它们基本上都忠实地表达了原诗的内容,但是在抒发情感和表达意境方面仍有很大差异。首先原诗前四句交代了时间更替是由"昔"而"今",因此翻译成英文时,时态应该切换于过去和现在之间,而理雅各的译文却用了一系列将来进行时代替一般现在时(以 will be, shall be 等为标志),虽然书面色彩更浓,文风也更优雅,但是却稍有矫揉造作之嫌。从这点来说,韦利和许渊冲把握得不错。在意象的描摹上,比如杨柳的"依依"之貌,理雅各翻译成"The willows were fresh and green",的确表达出了当时阳春三月杨柳青青的景象,但流于平淡的描述,意境不够优美;而韦利将该句译为"The willows spread their shade",拟人的手法不禁让我们联想到郁郁葱葱的柳树舒展开来、遮阴大地的美丽图景。虽然,韦利的译文也采用了拟人手法,接近了原诗的风格,但是在体现原诗诗人借物抒情方面,仍逊色于许渊冲的译文(以下简称许译)。许译更加忠实地表达了原文的情境,"Willows shed tears",不但将杨柳拟人化,而且赋予其人的多情,生动地再现当时战士们出征的场景。

若从"韵体翻译"(或称"诗体")和"无韵体翻译"(也称"散体"或"散文式")来区分,四位译者中理雅各和亚瑟·韦利的译文是无韵的,庞德的译文是自由式的,而许渊冲的译文则一路用韵,在神形皆似方面达到了很高的境界。

此外,理雅各的英译诗在内容上一贯极其忠实,但基本上是分行写出的散文,既无节奏,也未用韵脚,因此构不成抑扬顿挫的诗歌韵律。韦利的译文也没有运用韵律,每个诗行的音步也无法一致。按他的说法,译诗用韵不可避免地要产生因声损义,所以他的要求就是准确地表达原诗的意义,因此他的英译文其实也就是散文。但是,《诗经》英译无论如何不能回避的问题是:如果译出的诗不能传达出原诗的韵味,就没有感染力,那么再忠实也欠可读性,因而就很难被认定为是成功的翻译。这样的风格已缺少了《诗经》的原汁原味,因为诗歌成了散文。虽然个别也有可取之处,但从总体上来说,由于无韵,原诗的意象丧失殆尽,优美形式也荡然无存。这样一来,译文可能因难以记诵而不易流传,缺乏生命力。

庞德的翻译是自由式的,套用了译入语的民族形式,跟原文不太贴切,给人感觉是译者自己的创作。但他的译诗由于用韵恰当,旨趣离原文不远,符合英美读者的口味,因此也自成一家。

许渊冲先生译诗一路用韵,在保持原诗的形象、意思和旨趣方面都无懈可击:每行四个音节,与原诗相同,双行押韵,声美形美兼具,乃译诗精品。在他看来,译诗如不传达原诗的音美,就不可能产生和原诗相似的效果;相反,用韵的音美有时反而有助于传达原诗的意美。也就是说,用韵虽然可能因声损义,但不用韵则一定损义,用韵损义的程度反比不用韵小。也许正是藉于这样的理论才产生了其三美兼具的作品。

五、课后练习

1. 分析题

(1) 试分析"悠悠苍天,曷其有极"在许渊冲和理雅各的译本中是如何体现原文的句式的。

(2)《诗经·卫风·木瓜》原文用了赋比兴哪种手法?译文的行文结构有何特点?

2. 实训题

翻译以下诗歌。

(1) **诗经·周南·芣苢**

采采芣苢,薄言采之。
采采芣苢,薄言有之。

采采芣苢,薄言掇之。
采采芣苢,薄言捋之。

采采芣苢,薄言袺之。
采采芣苢,薄言襭之。

(2) **诗经·鄘风·柏舟**

汎彼柏舟,在彼中河。
髧彼两髦、实维我仪。
之死矢靡它。
母也天只、不谅人只。

汎彼柏舟,在彼河侧。
髧彼两髦、实维我特。
之死矢靡慝。
母也天只、不谅人只。

3. 思考题

(1) 你最喜欢的《诗经》译文是哪篇?为什么?

(2) 试着列举诗歌的翻译和其他文学作品的翻译有哪些异同。

(3) 试分析一篇诗歌翻译文本的优点和缺点。

(4) 诗歌翻译是否是一种改写？为什么？
(5) 作为译者，自译自校重要吗？为什么要请人校对译稿？
(6) 除了韵脚的使用，《诗经》译文还可以如何体现韵律美？
(7) 诗歌翻译有哪些基本特点？
(8) 举例说明直译和死译有哪些区别？
(9) 如何限制译者主体性的过度发挥？
(10) 音译应遵循什么原则？

六、参考文献

[1] 刘晓晖.既远且近的悖论——阐释间距与文学典籍翻译创生[J].天津外国语大学学报,2015,22(4)：24-29.

[2] 王东波.语际翻译与文化翻译——兼论中国传统典籍翻译策略[J].山东大学学报(哲学社会科学版),2007(4)：118-121.

[3] 王秀梅译注.诗经[M].北京：中华书局,2015.

第二课
《三字经》译介赏析

> 《三字经》是中国三大国学启蒙读物之一,被视为"蒙学第一书",是中华民族珍贵的文化遗产。全书共分为六个部分,每一部分有一中心。内容上至天文,下达地理,涵盖历史变迁,表达人伦道德、哲学义理,是一部高度浓缩的中国文化史。正所谓,"熟读《三字经》,可知千古事"。书中取材典范,将中国传统文化中的文学经典、历史故事、民间传说、名物常识等娓娓道来,深入浅出地教授"仁、义、诚、敬、孝"的做人做事之理,被誉为国学中的"袖里《通鉴纲目》"。
>
> 格式上,《三字经》三字一句,四句一组,大都韵文,短小精悍,读来琅琅上口,如同歌谣。其文笔流畅自然,朴实无华,情真意切,深入浅出,数百年来对中华民族的精神与文化有着深刻的影响。

一、翻译简介

《三字经》的翻译史已达四百多年。首个西文译本诞生于明万历十年(1582),译者为意大利的耶稣会士罗明坚(Michele Ruggieri),译文为拉丁文。罗明坚的译本带动了《三字经》拉丁文译事浪潮,为后来的传教士们找到一条学习汉语的途径。十八九世纪教会学校多以《三字经》等作为初学中文的识字课本。此后,《三字经》更被译成英、俄、德、法、日、韩等多种文字。

《三字经》因其特殊格式和韵律以及丰富的文化内涵,英译并非易事,甚至有评论家称其为"天使不敢涉足的地方"。首先,汉字整齐划一,英文单词却长短不齐,如何译出原文三字一行之形态,此为难点之一;其次,原文四句一节,双句押韵,如何译出原文韵式,此为难点之二;再者,原文蕴含了丰富深厚的中国特色文化,如何译出其文化内涵,此为难点之三。

英译《三字经》肇始于传教士马礼逊(Robert Morrison),1812年出版于伦敦。如今,英译版已有16个译本。其中,影响力最大的当属国外译者翟理斯(Herbert Allen Giles)的阐释性散体译本和国内译者赵彦春的三词格偶韵体译本。翟理斯译本是在参考并批判分析前人翻译的基础之上而成,他曾直言要"译出比前人更好的译本"。赵彦春译本是在深挖原典基础上的独辟蹊径,被网友和媒体誉为"有史以来最美汉英翻译"。

二、书名翻译

《三字经》书名英译主要有以下几种:

Robert Morrison(1812):The Three-Character Classic

E. C. Bridgman(1835):Trimetrical Classic

Solomon Caesar Malan(1856):The Three-Fold San-Tsze-King or the Triliteral Classic of China

Stanislas Julien(1864):Three Character Classic

Herbert Allen Giles(1900):The San Tzu Ching or Three Character Classic

梁卓尧(1995):New Three Character Verses

王宝童(2008):The Triword Primer

赵彦春(2014):The Three Word Primer

《三字经》的"经",译为classic(经典)不难理解。但王宝童和赵彦春皆译为Primer,其意为初级读本、识字课本。《三字经》本为古代儿童启蒙读本,此译法倒也传达出原典性质。

三、特殊概念的翻译

《三字经》原文蕴含了丰富深厚的中国特色文化,在此,分析翟理斯(以下简称"翟译")和赵彦春(以下简称"赵译")两位译者对特殊概念的处理方式,希冀为译者带来一定启示。

例1:国风

翟译:

Kuo Feng

赵译:

Psalm

评析:《国风》是《诗经》的一部分,内含了西周初年至春秋中叶各诸侯国的民间歌曲,反映了当时中国劳动人民的真实生活,表达了他们对剥削压迫的不平和对美好生活的向往。

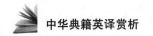

翟将其音译为 Kuo Feng,并在后文中提到,此为"the four sections of the Book of Poetry",既保留了中国文化的异质性,也让读者在后文的解释中明白《国风》是一本书的一部分。

赵采取归化策略,译为 Psalm,字典解释为 a song or poem praising God, especially in the Bible(《圣经》中的圣咏、赞美诗)。《国风》并不涉及宗教,更非对上帝的咏叹,所以从意思上看,此词在此并不贴切。

例2:三纲(君臣义、父子亲、夫妇顺)

翟译:

The Three Bonds

the obligation between sovereign and subject

the love between father and child

the harmony between husband and wife

赵译:

Three tenets

Subject Lord obeys

Child Father reveres

Wife Man endears

评析:"三纲"为中国儒家文化思想之一,指的是"君臣义、父子亲、夫妇顺"。意即,君主以身作则,臣民遵从君主;父为垂范,子女遵从父亲;夫为表率,妻子顺从丈夫:在此,强调的是双方各安其分的序列关系。

翟理斯的"三纲"用"Three Bonds"。"bond"含义为联系,字典中的解释为 something that forms a connection between people or groups。翟理斯在此将"三纲"理解为人与人或人与组织间的一种稳固联系,在一定程度上体现了社会秩序关系。"君臣义",翟译为"the obligation between sovereign and subject"。其中,"obligation"意为职责、义务,即 the state of being faced to do something because it is your duty or because of a law;sovereign 意为君主;subject 意为臣民。翟的译法,体现了君臣双方之间的关系:君须为臣作表率,臣须为君尽忠则。"父子亲",翟译为 the love between father and child,说明了父母和子女之间相亲相爱的关系。"夫妇顺",翟译为 the harmony between husband and wife,正体现了夫妻相处之景。整体说来,翟理斯的翻译,诠释出了"三纲"的内涵。

赵彦春的"三纲"译为 Three tenets。"tenet"意为原则、信条。三纲是君臣、父子、夫妻之间当遵守的一定原则,从此层面看,含义是对的。"君臣义""父子亲""夫妇顺",赵的翻译是 SVO(主谓宾)结构,分别译为"Subject lord obeys",意即臣当遵从君主;"Child Father reveres",意为孩子当遵从父亲;"Wife man endears",意为妻子敬慕丈夫。赵对三纲具体内容的翻译简洁明了,且三字一句,与原典形式一致,但却只是道出了关系中一方的做法,"三纲"的含义在此未全部展示出来。

例3:五常(仁、义、礼、智、信)

翟译：

Five virtues (charity of heart, duty towards one's neighbor, propriety, wisdom, and truth)

赵译：

Constants Five (grace, justice, courtesy, wisdom, and fidelity)

评析：

儒家思想中的"五常"，即"仁、义、礼、智、信"。仁以爱人为核心；义为天下合宜之理；强调公正的态度；礼教导人为人处事时须合乎礼仪规范；智是以智慧的眼光看待事物，勿被表面所迷惑；信指待人接物须注重诚信。

翟将"五常"译为 five virtues，意即五种美德。"仁"译为 charity，字典意为 kindness and sympathy towards other people, especially when you are judging them。由此可知，在此选择 charity 是贴合原文的。"义"译为 duty towards one's neighbor，意即对身边人的责任与义务，在一定程度上体现了道义之心。"礼"译为 propriety，词典解释为 moral and social behavior that is considered to be correct and acceptable(得体的举止行为)；the rules of correct behavior(行为规范)。可见，翟理斯将"礼"的基本含义都表达出来了。"智"译为 wisdom，字典解释为 the ability to make sensible decisions and give good advice because of the experience and knowledge that you have(基于已有的经验和学问从而可做明智决定的能力)；the knowledge that a society or culture has gained over a long period of time(社会或文化长期积累的知识学问)。wisdom 一词准确传递出了"智"的含义。"信"译为 truth，意为真实、真理，原文中诚实守信的含义并未表现出来。

赵将"五常"译为 Constants Five，字表意为五种常量，而良好的社会秩序正是源于这五种品质，这与原文的思想颇为贴切。赵将"仁"译为 grace，其字典解释为 the kindness that God shows towards the human race，侧重上帝对人类的恩慈，原文想表达的人与人之间相处的宽厚爱人待人之意并未体现出来。"义"译为 justice，字典解释为 the quality of being fair or reasonable 公正合理，贴切表达了原文中公道公义的态度。"礼"译为 courtesy，字典解释为 polite behavior and respect for other people(礼貌谦恭)，未能深层次表现出"礼"作为一种社会礼仪规范来规约人行为的含义。"智"，同译为 wisdom，与原文贴切。"信"译为 fidelity，意为 the quality of being loyal to somebody or something(忠诚)，符合原文诚实守信之意。

四、译文对比赏析

1. 经典句子

例1：　　　　人之初，

　　　　　　　性本善。

性相近，
习相远。

翟译：

Man at their birth are naturally good.

Their natures are much the same;

their habits become widely different.

赵译：

Man on earth

Good at birth.

The same nature

Varies on nurture.

评析： 此为《三字经》开篇第一节，人性本善、当重教化的思想统领全文。

翟理斯的英译是长句结构，侧重解释语义，这便于西方读者理解《三字经》想要表达的内容和意思。但最明显的不足在于，不是工整对仗的三字一句，没有协调的韵律，未能体现原文的经典行文特征。在用词方面，"相近"译为 much the same，意为"蛮像的"，与原文的"近"想要表达的意思有点距离。"习"在此译为 habits，亦有不妥。原文的"习"意为后天一切习染，包括教育和社会环境的影响，而 habits，意为"习惯"，将原文所指范围缩小了。翻译既须传达原味的意思，也当体现原文的风格。

赵译本，三字一行，采用 aabb 韵式，每个字皆为单音节，短小精悍。其中 on earth 和 at birth 皆为介词短语，且押韵；在选词上，"性"译为 nature，"习"译为 nurture（意为后天培育，意合原文），二词不仅尾音相同，音节亦同，读来朗朗上口，如诵儿歌。

例2：

马牛羊，

鸡犬豕。

此六畜，

人所饲。

翟译：

The horse, the ox, the sheep,

The fowl, the dog, and the pig.

These six animals

are those which men keep.

赵译：

Horses, sheep, cows,

Chickens, dogs, sows.

These six breeds

A husbandman feeds.

评析：翟理斯这段译文颇为工整，每种动物名称前皆加了定冠词"the"，使得译文颇有节奏感；且"the+名词单数"的形式可指某一类事物，与原文全称概念吻合。

赵的译文，依然是三字句结构，形意皆逼近原文。赵以名词复数形式指代此类动物，且在顺序上有所调整。原文"马牛羊"对应成"horses, sheep, cows"。在此，cows 和 sows（猪）音节相同，且成韵脚，韵律和谐。下一句中，赵将"人"的概念细化成 husbandman，意即农夫，更加明确了所指，将原文意思更精确地传递出来。

2. 经典段落

  人之初，
  性本善。
  性相近，
  习相远。

Men at their birth,
are naturally good.
Their natures are much the same;
their habits become widely different.

（Tr. Herbert Giles）

Man on earth,
Good at birth.
The same nature
Varies on nurture.

（赵彦春译）

  苟不教，
  性乃迁。
  教之道，
  贵以专。

If follishly there is no teaching
the nature will deteriorate.
The right way in teaching,
is to attach the utmost importance in thoroughness.

（Tr. Herbert Giles）

With no education,
There'd be aberration.

To teach well,
You deeply dwell.

（赵彦春译）

昔孟母，
择邻处，
子不学，
断机杼。

Of old, the mother of Mencius
chose a neighborhood
and when her child would not learn,
she broke the shuttle from the loom.

(Tr. Herbert Giles)

Then Mencius' mother
Chose her neighbor.
At Mencius sloth,
She cut th' cloth.

（赵彦春译）

窦燕山，
有义方，
教五子，
名俱扬。

Tou of the Swallow Hills
had the right method
He taught five son,
each of whom raised the family reputation.

(Tr. Herbert Giles)

Dough by name
Fulfilled his aim.
His five sons
Became famous ones.

（赵彦春译）

养不教，
父之过。
教不严，
师之惰。

To feed without teaching,
is the father's fault.
To teach without severity,
is the teacher's laziness.

(Tr. Herbert Giles)

What's a father?
A good teacher.
What's a teacher?
A strict preacher.

（赵彦春译）

子不学，
非所宜。
幼不学，
老何为？

If the child does not learn,
this is not as it should be.
If he does not learn while young,
what will he be when old ?

(Tr. Herbert Giles)

An unschooled child
Will grow wild.
A young loafer,
An old loser!

（赵彦春译）

玉不琢，
不成器。
人不学，
不知义。

If jade is not polished,
it cannot become a thing of use.
If a man does not learn,
he cannot know his duty towards his neighbor.

(Tr. Herbert Giles)

No jade crude,
Shows craft good.
Unless you learn,
Brute you'll turn.

（赵彦春译）

为人子，
方少时，
亲师友，
习礼仪。
He who is the son of a man,
when he is young,
should attach himself to his teachers and friends
and practice ceremonial usages.

(Tr. Herbert Giles)

Son of man,
Mature you can.
Teacher or peer,
Hold them dear.

（赵彦春译）

香九龄，
能温席。
孝于亲，
所当执。
Hsiang, at nine years of age,
could warm (his parents') bed.
Filial piety towards parents,

is that to which we should hold fast.

(Tr. Herbert Giles)

Hsiang, at nine,
Warmed bedding fine,
Follow this one,
This filial son.

（赵彦春译）

融四岁，
能让梨。
弟于长，
宜先知。

Jung, at four years of age,
could yield the (bigger) pears.
To hehave as a younger brother towards elders,
is one of the first things to know.

(Tr. Herbert Giles)

Aged four years,
Rong proffered pears.
Bear in mind
Fraternally be kind.

（赵彦春译）

首孝悌，
次见闻，
知某数，
识某文。

Begin with filial piety and fraternal love,
and then see and hear.
Learn to count,
and learn to read.

(Tr. Herbert Giles)

Stress piety more
Than your lore.

Learn some numeracy,
Know some literacy.

（赵彦春译）

一而十,
十而百,
百而千,
千而万。

units and tens,
tens and hundreds,
hundreds and thousands,
thousands and then tens of thousands.

(Tr. Herbert Giles)

One to ten,
A hundred then,
One thousand more,
Ten thousand afore.

（赵彦春译）

三才者,
天地人。
三光者,
日月星。

The three forces,
are Heaven, Earth and Man.
The Three Luminaries,
are the sun, the moon and the stars.

(Tr. Herbert Giles)

Tri-vitals, of worth:
Man, heaven, earth;
Tri-lights, a boon:
Sun, stars, moon.

（赵彦春译）

三纲者，
君臣义。
父子亲，
夫妇顺。
The three bonds,
are the obligation between sovereign and subject,
the love between father and child,
the harmony between husband and wife.

（Tr. Herbert Giles）

Three tenets always:
Subject Lord obeys;
Child Father reveres;
Wife Man endears.

（赵彦春译）

曰春夏，
曰秋冬，
此四时，
运不穷。
We speak of spring and summer,
we speak of autumn and winter,
These four seasons,
revolve without ceasing.

（Tr. Herbert Giles）

Spring and summer,
Autumn and winter.
These four seasons
Cycle with reasons.

（赵彦春译）

曰南北，
曰西东，
此四方，
应乎中。

We speak of North and South,

we speak of East and West,

These four points,

respond to the requirements of the centre.

(Tr. Herbert Giles)

South, north, west,

'N east, we quest.

These four ways

Upon center gaze.

（赵彦春译）

曰水火，

木金土，

此五行，

本乎数。

We speak of water, fire,

wood, metal and earth.

These five elements,

have their origin in number.

(Tr. Herbert Giles)

Water, fire, behold,

Earth, wood, gold.

These five materials

Accord to numerals.

（赵彦春译）

曰仁义，

礼智信，

此五常，

不容紊。

We speak of charity of heart and of duty towards one's neighbour,

of propriety, of wisdom, and of truth.

These five virtues

admit of no compromise.

(Tr. Herbert Giles)

Grace, justice, courtesy
Wisdom, and fidelity
Good order derive
From Constants Five.

（赵彦春译）

稻粱菽，
麦黍稷，
此六谷，
人所食。

Rice, spiked, millet, pulse,
Wheat, glutinous millet, and common millet,
These six grains
are those which men eat.

(Tr. Herbert Giles)

Rice, sorghum, beans,
Wheat, millet, corns.
These crops main
Our life sustain.

（赵彦春译）

马牛羊，
鸡犬豕，
此六畜，
人所饲。

The horse, the ox, the sheep,
the fowl, the dog, and the pig.
These six animals
are those which men keep.

(Tr. Herbert Giles)

Horses, sheep, cows,
Chickens, dogs, sows.

These six breeds

A husbandman feeds.

（赵彦春译）

曰喜怒，
曰哀惧，
爱恶欲，
七情具。

We speak of joy, of anger,
We speak of pity, of fear,
Of love, of hate, and of desire.
These are the seven passions.

（Tr. Herbert Giles）

Say anger, gladness,
Say fear, sadness,
Hate, greed, love.
Seven feelings above.

（赵彦春译）

匏土革，
木石金，
丝与竹，
乃八音。

The gourd, earthenware, skin
wood, stone, metal,
silk and bamboo,
yield the eight musical sounds.

（Tr. Herbert Giles）

Gourd, leather, clay,
Wood we play,
Stone, metal, bamboo,
And string, too.

（赵彦春译）

高曾祖,
父而身,
身而子,
子而孙。

Great great grandfather, great grandfather, grandfather,
father and self,
self and son,
son and grandson.

(Tr. Herbert Giles)

Grand, great-grand, great-great-grand,
Father, myself, and
Children, and grandchildren
All are kinsmen.

(赵彦春译)

自子孙,
至玄曾,
乃九族,
人之伦。

From son and grandson,
on to great grandson and great great grandson.
These are the nine agnates,
constituting the kinships of man.

(Tr. Herbert Giles)

Now great-grand, and
His son, great-great-grand.
There're generations nine,
A genealogical line.

(赵彦春译)

父子恩,
夫妇从。
兄则友,
弟则恭。

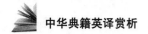

Affection between father and child,
harmony between husband and wife,
friendliness on the part of elder brothers,
respectfulness on the part of younger brothers.

（Tr. Herbert Giles）

Father loves son;
Man-wife is one.
Brothers are bland,
Hand in hand.

（赵彦春译）

长幼序，
友与朋。
君则敬，
臣则忠。

Precedence between elders and youngers,
as between friend and friend.
respect on the part of the sovereign,
loyalty on the part of the subject.

（Tr. Herbert Giles）

Senior to young,
The ethical rung.
Lord loves subjects,
And enjoys respects.

（赵彦春译）

凡训蒙，
须讲究，
详训诂，
明句读。

In the education of the young,
there should be explanation and elucidation,
careful teaching of the interpretations of commentators,

and due attention to paragraphs and sentences.

(Tr. Herbert Giles)

While you teach,
Do deeply reach.
Go with explanation,
And guide punctuation.

（赵彦春译）

为学者，
必有初，
小学终，
至四书。
Those who are learners,
must have a beginning.
The Little Learning finished,
they proceed to the four books.

(Tr. Herbert Giles)

To further learn,
You now turn
From school nooks
To Four Books.

（赵彦春译）

论语者，
二十篇，
群弟子，
记善言。
There is the Lun Yu (discourse or Analects),
in twenty sections.
In this, the various disciples,
have recorded the wise sayings of Confucius.

(Tr. Herbert Giles)

Analects — the lections
Has twenty sections.

Confucius and disciples
Gave off sparkles.

（赵彦春译）

孟子者，
七篇止，
讲道德，
说仁义。

The works of Mencius,
are comprised in seven sections.
These explain the way and the exemplifications thereof,
and expound clarity and duty towards one's neighbor.

(Tr. Herbert Giles)

Mencius, the sutras,
Has seven chapters.
These are counsels
Of virtues 'nd morals.

（赵彦春译）

作中庸，
乃孔伋，
中不偏，
庸不易。

The Chung Yung was written,
by the pen of Tzu-su;
Chung (the middle) being that which does not lean toward any side,
Yung (the course) being that which cannot be changed.

(Tr. Herbert Giles)

The Golden Mean,
All kept between.
Kong Jih, the scholar
Is its author.

（赵彦春译）

作大学，
乃曾子，
自修齐，
至平治。
He who wrote the Great Learning
was the philosopher Tseng.
Beginning with cultivation of the individual and ordering of the family,
it goes on to government of one's own State and tranquillisation of the Empire.

（Tr. Herbert Giles）

Great Learning, great,
Tsengcius did create:
From personal perfection
To national progression.

（赵彦春译）

孝经通，
四书熟，
如六经，
始可读。
When the Classic of Filial Piety is mastered,
and the Four books are known by heart,
the next step is to the Six classics,
which may now be studied.

（Tr. Herbert Giles）

Piety learned ahead,
Four Books fully-read,
Six Classics now,
You should plough.

（赵彦春译）

诗书易，
礼春秋，
号六经，
当讲求。

The Books of Poetry, of History and of Changes.

the Rites of Chou Dynasty, the book of Rites, and the Spring and Autumn Annals

are called the Six Classics

which should be carefully explained and analyzed.

(Tr. Herbert Giles)

History, *Changes*, *Odes*,
Books of altitudes.
Spring 'n Fall, *Rituals*
Books for perusals.

（赵彦春译）

有连山，

有归藏，

有周易，

三易详。

There is the Lien Shan System,

there is the Kuei tsang

and there is the system of Changes of the Chou Dynasty,

such are the three systems which elucidate the changes.

(Tr. Herbert Giles)

Book of Ranges,
Book of Changes,
Book of Retreat,
Detailed and great.

（赵彦春译）

有典谟，

有训诰。

有誓命，

书之奥。

There are the Regulations and the Counsels,

the Instruction, the Announcements,

the Oaths, the Charges,

these are the profundities of the

Book of History.

(Tr. Herbert Giles)

Canons, duties, plans,
Edicts, and bans,
And imperial mandates,
Are *History*'s aggregates.

（赵彦春译）

我周公，
作周礼。
著六官，
存治体。
Our Duke of Chou,
drew up the Ritual of the Chou Dynasty,
in which he set forth the duties of the six classes of officials,
and thus gave a settled form to the government.

(Tr. Herbert Giles)

Th' Prince of Chough
Did *Rites* bestow,
Regimen he designed
And government defined.

（赵彦春译）

大小戴，
注礼记。
述圣言，
礼乐备。
The Elder and the Younger Tai
wrote commentaries on the Book of Rites.
They published the holy words,
and Ceremonies and Music were set in order.

(Tr. Herbert Giles)

The Days supplied
Protocols well clarified,

And paraphrased adages

Of those sages.

（赵彦春译）

曰国风，

曰雅颂。

号四诗，

当讽咏。

We speak of the Kuo Feng,

we speak of the Ya and the Sung.

These are the four sections of the Book of Poetry,

which should be hummed over and over.

(Tr. Herbert Giles)

The Psalms, say,

The Chants, say,

And those airs

Of various affairs.

（赵彦春译）

诗既亡，

春秋作。

寓褒贬，

别善恶。

When odes ceased to be made,

the Spring and Autumn Annals were produced.

These Annals contain praise and blame,

and distinguish the good from the bad.

(Tr. Herbert Giles)

When *Poems* perished,

Spring 'n Fall flourished,

Flogging what's lewd,

Praising what's good.

（赵彦春译）

三传者，
有公羊，
有左氏，
有谷梁。
The three commentaries upon the above
include that of Kung-Yang,
that of Tso
and that of Ku-Liang.

(Tr. Herbert Giles)

Companion authors three:
Zuo Qiu-ming, and he
Who was Gongyang,
And another, Goo Liang.

（赵彦春译）

经既明，
方读子。
撮其要，
记其事。
When the classics were understood,
then the writings of the various philosophers should be read.
Pick out the important points in each,
and take a note of all facts.

(Tr. Herbert Giles)

Classics well read,
Study sophists ahead.
Make a list,
Get the gist.

（赵彦春译）

五子者，
有荀扬。
文中子，
及老庄。

The five chief philosophers,
are Hsun, Yang,
Wen Chung Tzu
Lao Tzu, and Chung Tzu.

(Tr. Herbert Giles)

Five sophists then
Were great men:
Hsun, Wenchung, Yang,
Laocius and Chuang.

(赵彦春译)

经子通,
读诸史。
考世系,
知终始。

When the classics and the philosophers are mastered,
the various histories should then be read,
and the genealogical connections should be examined,
so that the end of one dynasty and the beginning of the next be known.

(Tr. Herbert Giles)

After finishing these
Read histories please.
Do study genealogy
And know causality.

(赵彦春译)

自羲农,
至黄帝。
号三皇,
居上世。

From Fu Hsi and Shen Nung.
on to the Yellow Emperor,
these are called the Three Rulers.

who lived in the early ages.

(Tr. Herbert Giles)

The legendary Fooshee,
Shennong and Huangdee
Were great forefathers,
Esteemed Three Emperors.

（赵彦春译）

唐有虞，
号二帝。
相揖逊，
称盛世。

T'ang and Yu-Yu
are called the Two Emperors.
They abdicated one after the other,
and their was called the Golden Age.

(Tr. Herbert Giles)

Yao and You-yuh,
Called Grandees Two.
They demised throne,
A heyday known.

（赵彦春译）

夏有禹，
商有汤。
周文武，
称三王。

The Hsia dynasty had Yu;
the Shang dynasty had T'ang;
the Chou dynasty had Wen and Wu;
these are called the Three Kings.

(Tr. Herbert Giles)

Hsiah, Shang, Chough,
Three dynasties, lo.

Yuh，Tang，Wuh，
Three kings true.

（赵彦春译）

夏传子，
家天下。
四百载，
迁夏社。

Under the Hsia dynasty，the throne was inherited from father to son，
making a family possession of the empire.
After four hundred years，
the Imperial sacrifice passed from the House of Hsia.

（Tr. Herbert Giles）

Yuh，heredity begun，
Throned his son.
Four centuries passed
Seeing Hsiah's last.

（赵彦春译）

汤伐夏，
国号商。
六百载，
至纣亡。

T'ang the Completer destroyed the Hsia Dynasty
and the dynastic title became Shang.
The line lasted for six hundred years，
ending with Chou Hsin.

（Tr. Herbert Giles）

The Conqueror Tang
Founded Kingdom Shang.
Six centuries' elapse
Ere Chow's collapse.

（赵彦春译）

周武王,
始诛纣。
八百载,
最长久。

King Wu of the Chou Dynasty

finally slew Chou Hsin.

His line lasted for eight hundred years,

the longest dynasty of all.

(Tr. Herbert Giles)

Wuh of Chough

Triumphed over Chow.

Eight centuries' gain,

Chough's longest reign.

(赵彦春译)

周辙东,
王纲坠。
逞干戈,
尚游说。

When the Chous made tracks eastwards,

the feudal bond slackened;

the arbitrament of spear and shields prevailed;

and peripatetic politicians were held in high esteem.

(Tr. Herbert Giles)

Chough moved east,

And controlled least.

There arose militance;

Valued was eloquence.

(赵彦春译)

始春秋,
终战国。
五霸强,
七雄出。

This period began with the Spring and Autumn Epoch
and ended with that of the Warring States.
Next, the Five Chieftains domineered,
and the Seven Martial States came to the front.

(Tr. Herbert Giles)

Spring 'n Fall began,
Warring States then.
Five Lords strived!
Seven Powers thrived!

（赵彦春译）

嬴秦氏，
始兼并。
传二世，
楚汉争。

Then the House of Chin, descended from the Ying clan,
finally united all the states under one sway.
The thrown was transmitted to Erh Shih,
upon which followed the struggle between the Ch'u and the Han states.

(Tr. Herbert Giles)

Emperor the First
Other states burst.
Generations but two,
Arose Han 'n Chuh.

（赵彦春译）

高祖兴，
汉业建。
至孝平，
王莽篡。

Then Kao Tsu arose,
and the House of Han was established.
When we come to the reign of Hsiao P'ing,

Wang Mang usurped the throne.

（Tr. Herbert Giles）

Liu Bang almighty ran;
Arose Great Han.
Hsiao Ping was slayed;
So Wang Mang swayed.

（赵彦春译）

读史者，
考实录。
通古今，
若亲目。

Ye who read history

must study the Annals,

whereby you will understand ancient and modern events,

as though having seen them with your own eyes.

（Tr. Herbert Giles）

As past's explored,
Check every record.
You'll know how
Then became now.

（赵彦春译）

口而诵，
心而惟。
朝于斯，
夕于斯。

Recite them with the mouth,

and ponder over them in your hearts.

Do this in the morning;

do this in the evening.

（Tr. Herbert Giles）

Read and think
And pieces link

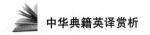

From early morning
To late evening.

（赵彦春译）

昔仲尼，
师项橐。
古圣贤，
尚勤学。

Of old, Confucius,
took Hsiang T'o for his teacher.
The inspired men and sages of old,
studied diligently nevertheless.

(Tr. Herbert Giles)

Confucius, of yore
Studied, studied more,
From Tuo learned,
As he yearned.

（赵彦春译）

赵中令，
读鲁论。
彼既仕，
学且勤。

Chao, President of the Council,
studied the Lu test of the Lun Yu.
He, when already an official
Studied, and moreover with diligence.

(Tr. Herbert Giles)

Chao Puh of Song
Read *Analects* long.
This premier crack
Was never slack.

（赵彦春译）

披蒲编，
削竹简。
彼无书，
且知勉。

One opened out rushes and plaited them together;
another scraped tablets of bamboo.
These men had no books,
but they knew how to make an effort.

(Tr. Herbert Giles)

With cattail tips!
With bamboo slips!
None they possessed,
Persisting with zest.

（赵彦春译）

头悬梁，
锥刺股。
彼不教，
自勤苦。

One tied his head to the beam above him;
another pricked his thigh with an awl.
They were not taught,
but toiled hard of their own accord.

(Tr. Herbert Giles)

Head hung high!
Needled his thigh!
Not pushed, they
Kept working away.

（赵彦春译）

如囊萤，
如映雪。
家虽贫，
学不辍。

63

Then we have one who put fireflies in a bag,
and again another who used the white glare from snow.
Although their families were poor,
these men studied unceasingly.

(Tr. Herbert Giles)

With fireworms bright!
With snow white!
Poor, having none,
They studied on.

（赵彦春译）

如负薪。
如挂角，
身虽劳，
犹苦卓。
Again, there was one who carried fuel,
and another who used horns and pegs.
Although they toiled with their bodies,
they were nevertheless remarkable for their application.

(Tr. Herbert Giles)

With fuel's borne!
Book on horn!
They, making time,
Employed their prime.

（赵彦春译）

犬守夜，
鸡司晨。
苟不学，
曷为人？
The dog keeps guard by night;
the cock proclaims the dawn.
If foolishly you do not study,

how can you become men?

(Tr. Herbert Giles)

Dogs thieves bite;
Cocks dawn invite.
Unless you learn,
Inhuman you'll turn.

（赵彦春译）

蚕吐丝，
蜂酿蜜。
人不学，
不如物。
The silkworm produced silk,
the bee makes honey.
If a man does not learn,
he is not equal to the brutes.

(Tr. Herbert Giles)

Silkworms silk educe;
Bees honey produce.
Such you learn,
Or receive spurn.

（赵彦春译）

幼而学，
壮而行。
上致君，
下泽民。
Learn while young,
and when grown up apply what you have learned,
influencing the sovereign above;
benefiting the people below.

(Tr. Herbert Giles)

Learn when young;
Act while strong.

Benefit each one
Under the sun.

（赵彦春译）

扬名声，
显父母。
光于前，
裕于后。

Make a name for yourselves,
and glority your father and mother,
shed lustre on your ancestors,
enrich your posterity.

(Tr. Herbert Giles)

Carve your name
And parents' name.
Ancestors you glorify,
Offspring you dignify.

（赵彦春译）

人遗子，
金满籝。
我教子，
惟一经。

Men bequeath to their children
coffers of gold；
I teach you children
only this one book.

(Tr. Herbert Giles)

For children hold
Silver and gold?
My only bequest：
Learn your best.

（赵彦春译）

勤有功，
戏无益。
戒之哉，
宜勉力。

Diligence has its reward;
play has no advantages.
Oh，be on your guard,
and put forth your strength.

(Tr. Herbert Giles)

Good is diligence;
Poor is negligence.
Trials you breast，
Work with zest.

（赵彦春译）

3. 比读感悟：

《三字经》是儿童启蒙读物，既有丰富的教育思想，更有精彩的咏诵体验。

整体而言，翟理斯译本基本是逐字翻译，过于拘泥文字，行文铺陈冗长。为了易于理解，他也加入了自己的阐释，但因对源文化理解的缺失，出现了些微误译。表面看这是为了追求文字忠实，然而舍弃原文经典行文特征，则是对原文的大不忠实。《三字经》作为中国古典蒙文的代表之一，无论其三字韵文格特点，还是丰富的思想内涵，都是中国符号的一种象征。

赵彦春忠实原典文风，在翻译时更灵活多变，如微调原文顺序、将内容适当加工整合，全篇"三字格"结构、aabb 韵式，无论是表意，还是音节，抑或押韵，皆丝丝入扣，形神兼顾。杨炳钧教授曾评价赵译本：目的明确、意境极高；对仗工整、韵律得到；用词精妙、锦上添花、语言简洁、美感不失；比照名译、更胜一筹；注释独特、促进理解。

比较分析翟和赵的译本，也给了我们诸多启示：翻译并非文字间的简单转换，更须注意的是文化价值、思想内涵的传播，应当灵活使用翻译策略，将原著的形神之美悉皆译出。

五、练习与思考

1. 分析题

(1) 找出原文所含的典故翻译，比较分析翟理斯和赵彦春译本的区别。

(2) 结合《三字经》中任一段译文，分析两译本在形美、音美和意美上有否体现或缺憾。

2. 实训题

翻译以下段落。

（1）　　　　　　　　　光武兴，

为东汉。

四百年，

终于献。

（2）　　　　　　　　　魏蜀吴，

争汉鼎。

号三国，

迄两晋。

3. 思考题

（1）意合的汉语向形合的英译转化时，须注意哪些因素？可结合实例分析。

（2）你喜欢哪个译本的翻译，为什么？

六、参考文献

［1］　Giles，H. A. Elementary Chinese：San Tzu Ching［M］. Shanghai：Messrs. Kelly & Walsh，Ltd，1900.

［2］　赵彦春.英韵三字经［M］.北京：光明日报出版社，2014.

［3］　乐爱国.儒家"三纲五常"的本义、演变及其辨正——以朱熹理学的诠释为中［J］.学习与实践，2018(12)：119‐128.

［4］　于婷.《三字经》英译本比较研究——以翟里斯和赵彦春两个英译本为例［D］.呼和浩特：内蒙古大学，2016.

［5］　韩东方.中国传统蒙学读物《三字经》的对外传播研究［D］.太原：山西大学，2016.

第三课
《论语》译介赏析

> 《论语》是记载孔子及其弟子言行的记实性语录体散文,是孔子和弟子之间教学、谈论的片断,集中体现了孔子的政治主张、伦理思想、道德观念及教育原则等。它不仅对中国的经学史、学术史产生了深刻的影响,而且对中国的政治、经济、思想、教育、文化乃至人们的日常生活都产生了巨大的影响,其博大精深的内容影响了中国两千多年的文明史。《论语》语言简洁明快,全书共20篇,总计1万多字,记言最多的《季氏将伐颛臾》章,不过279字。《论语》不是文献资料的编撰,故口语化,自然亲切。《论语》综合运用排比、反问、比喻、映衬、对比、对偶、顶真等多种修辞手法,句式丰富多彩,表达多样,语气音韵和谐,节奏鲜明。《论语》包含成语、格言、警句,在内容上主要涵盖了道德、政治、人格,集中体现了孔子"仁"的主张,而"仁"的观点也是儒家思想的精髓。

一、翻译简介

《论语》第一个译本是利玛窦(Matteo Ricci)译成的拉丁文译本,后被意大利、比利时、法国的耶稣会士和英国的新教传教士不断重译。迄今,共有58个正式英译本。译本纵览如下:

1	Joshua Marshman, 1809. The Works of Confucius. Serampore: Mission Press. (《论语》在英语世界的第一个译本)
2	David Collie, 1828. Lun Yu (Dialogues) in the Chinese Classical Work Commonly Called Four Books. Malacea: Mission Press.

(续表)

3	James Legge, 1861. Confucian Analects in the Chinese Classics. Hong Kong: The Author; London: Tiubner & Co. (《中国经典》英译本,包括《论语》英译)
4	T. F. Wade, 1869. The Lun Yǔ: Being Utterances of Kung Tzu, Known to the Western World as Confucius. London: s.n.
5	William Jennings, 1895. The Confucian Analects: A Translation. London: George Routledge and Sons.
6	Ku Hung-ming（辜鸿铭）, 1898. The Discourses and Sayings of Confucius: A New Special Translation Illustrated with Quotations from Goethe and Other Writers. Shanghai: Kelly and Walsh, Ltd.
7	Lionel Giles, 1907. The Sayings of Confucius: A New Translation of the Greater Part of the Confucian Analects. London: J. Murray.
8	Leonard J. Lyall, 1909. The Sayings of Confucius. London: Longmans.
9	William E. Soothill, 1910. The Analects of Confucius. Yokohama: The Fukuin Printing Company.
10	Arthur Waley, 1938. The Analects of Confucius. London: George Allen & Unwin; New York: Macmillan Company.
11	林语堂, 1938. Aphorisms of Confucius, in The Wisdom of Confucius. New York: The Modern Library.
12	E. R. Hughes, 1942. Part I & II in Chinese Philosophy in Classical Times. London: J. M. Dent & Sons.
13	Ezra Pound, 1951. The Analects, in Confucius: the Great Digest, the Unwobbling Pivot, the Analects. New York: New Directions Publishing Corporation.
14	James R. Ware, 1955. The Sayings of Confucius. New York: The New American Library of World Literature.
15	Wing-tsit Chan, 1963. The Humanism of Confucius. in A Source Book in Chinese Philosophy. Princeton: Princeton University Press.
16	Chu Chai & Winberg Chai, 1965. The Confucian Analects, or Lun Yu. in The Sacred Books of Confucius, and Other Confucian Classics. New York: University Books.
17	Lawrance Faucett, 1978. The Sayings of Confucius: A New Translation of the Analects Based Closely on the Meaning and Frequency of the Chinese Characters. San Diego: Faucett.
18	D. C. Lau（刘殿爵）, 1979. The Analects (Lun yu). Harmondsworth; New York: Penguin Books.
19	Shis-chuan Chen（程石泉）, 1986. The Confucian Analects: A New Translation of the Corrected Text of Lun Yu. 台北: 黎明文化事业公司.
20	Cheng Lin（郑麐 lín）, 1987. The Analects of Confucius, in The Four Books: Confucian Classics. 中国台湾: 中国学典馆.
21	Goh Beng Choo, 1989. The Sayings of Confucius: The Message of the Benevolent. Singapore: Asiapac.

(续表)

22	Iren Bloom, 1990. Confucius and the Analects, in Wm. Theodore de Bary & Irene Bloom (eds.) Sources of Chinese Tradition (Vol. I). New York: Columbia University Press.
23	John B. Khu et al, 1991. The Confucian Bible. Book 1, Analects: the non-theocentric code for concerned humans. Manila: Granhill Corporation.
24	李天辰,孔凡富,佟光武,任国生,1991.论语(汉英对照读本).济南:山东大学出版社.
25	Thomas Cleary, 1992. The Essential Confucius: the Heart of Confucius' Teachings in Authentic I-ching Order. New York: Harper San Francisco.
26	鲍时祥(今译),老安英,1992.论语(汉英对照本).济南:山东友谊书社.
27	梅仁毅,1992.论语.北京:和平出版社.
28	Raymond Dawson, 1993. The Analects. Oxford: Oxford University Press.
29	杨伯峻,吴树平(今译),潘富恩,温少霞,1993.论语今译(汉英对照).济南:齐鲁出版社.
30	蔡希勤(译注),赖波,夏玉和(译),1994.论语.北京:华语教学出版社.
31	Brian Bruya, 1996. Confucius Speaks: Words to Live By. New York: Anchor Books.
32	Jack Cai & Emma Yu, 1997. The Analects of Confucius: A Standard Version with a Chinese Study Text. AmeriCD-Rom Publishing Company.
33	Chichung Huang, 1997. The Analects of Confucius. New York & Oxford: Oxford University Press.
34	Simon Leys. 1997. The Analects of Confucius. New York: W. W. Norton.
35	王福林,1997.论语详注及英译.上海:世界图书出版公司.
36	Roger T. Ames & Henry Rosemond, Jr. 1998. The Analects of Confucius: A Philosophical Translation. New York: Ballantine Pub. Group.
37	E. Bruce Brooks & A. Taeko Brooks, 1998. Original Analects: Sayings of Confucius and His Successors. New York: Columbia University Press.
38	David Hinton, 1998. The Analects. Washington D. C.: Counterpoint.
39	丁往道,1998.孔子语录一百则(汉英对照).北京:中国对外翻译公司.
40	David H. Li(李祥甫),1999. Analects of Confucius: A New-Millenium Bilingual Edition. Bethesta Md.: Premier Publishing Company.
41	Adam Sia, 2000. The Complete Analects of Confucius. Singapore: Asiapac.
42	徐志刚,2001.论语精选综译(中、英、日).济南:济南出版社.
43	Edward Gilman Slingerland, 2003. Confucius Analects: with Selections from Traditional Commentaries. Indianapolis: Hackett Publishing Company.
44	Charles Muller, 2004. The Analects of Confucius. www.acmuller.net/con-dao/analects.html.
45	Tom Te-wu Ma(马德武),2004.孔子说(汉英对照).上海:上海世界图书出版公司.
46	冯大建(编注),王健、李盈、谢琰,2004.论语百则.天津:南开大学出版社.

(续表)

47	Robert Eno, 2005. The Analects of Confucius. www.indiana.edu/-p374/Analects-374.pdf.
48	金沛霖、李亚斯,2005.孔子语录.北京：中国文联出版社.
49	彭子游,2005.论语英译.沈阳：万卷出版公司.
50	许渊冲,2005. Confucius Modernized.北京：高等教育出版社.
51	洪青皎,2006.论语精译(汉英对照).哈尔滨：黑龙江教育出版社.
52	Burton Watson, 2007. The Analects of Confucius. New York：Columbia University Press.
53	（日）谷学,2007.全球论语(中英日对照读本).上海：上海译文出版社.
54	李军峰(编),管晓霞(译),2008.孔子语录.济南：山东友谊出版社.
55	王正文,2008.孔子名言精选.上海：上海外语教育出版社.
56	候信杰、孙红宴(点校)、张晓文、孔艳英,2008.论语全译.济南：齐鲁书社.
57	周春才(插图),Paul White(译),2008. The Illustrated Book of THE ANALECTS.北京：新世界出版社.
58	赵彦春,2019.英韵三字经.北京：光明日报出版社.

二、书名翻译

《论语》的书名翻译有很多，比如：

1	The Works of Confucius（《论语》在英语世界的第一个译本）
2	Lun Yu (Dialogues) in the Chinese Classical Work Commonly Called Four Books
3	Confucian Analects in the Chinese Classics （《中国经典》英译本,包括《论语》英译）
4	The Lun Yǔ：Being Utterances of Kung Tzu, Known to the Western World as Confucius
5	The Confucian Analects
6	The Discourses and Sayings of Confucius：A New Special Translation Illustrated with Quotations from Goethe and Other Writers
7	The Sayings of Confucius
8	The Analects of Confucius
9	Aphorisms of Confucius, in The Wisdom of Confucius
10	Part I & II in Chinese Philosophy in Classical Times
11	The Analects, in Confucius：the Great Digest, the Unwobbling Pivot, the Analects
12	The Humanism of Confucius

(续表)

13	The Confucian Analects, or Lun Yu. in The Sacred Books of Confucius, and Other Confucian Classics
14	The Analects (Lun yu)
15	The Sayings of Confucius: The Message of the Benevolent
16	Confucius and the Analects, in Wm
17	The Confucian Bible. Book 1, Analects: the non-theocentric code for concerned humans
18	The Essential Confucius: the Heart of Confucius' Teachings in Authentic I-ching Order
19	Confucius Speaks: Words to Live By
20	Original Analects: Sayings of Confucius and His Successors
21	The Analects
22	Analects of Confucius: A New-Millenium Bilingual Edition
23	The Complete Analects of Confucius
24	Confucius Analects: with Selections from Traditional Commentaries
25	Confucius Modernized: Thus The Master Spoke

三、特殊概念的翻译

1. 基本概念

（1）基本概念的翻译与分析

例1：孔子、公、子。

译文：Confucius, Lord, -cius。

评析：除了音译之外，《论语》的多数译者分别采用 Duke 和 Viscount 来对译"公"和"子"。比如，Arthur Waley、James Legge、Chichung Huang、许渊冲等都将"晋文公""齐桓公"中的"公"译作 Duke，将"微子"中的"子"译作 Viscount。在中国古代，"公"和"子"的称呼可分别归入爵位和行政两大体系。爵位的"公"和"子"可分指公爵和子爵，而行政体系的"公"和"子"却只是尊称。据此，汉语的"公"和"子"都是多义词。这两个词看似简单，其理解历来都是有争议的。汉语的"公"确有"公爵"的意思，《礼记·王制》有云："王者之制禄爵，公、侯、伯、子、男，凡五等。"

"公"是古代五等爵位中的第一等。从这个角度看，译作 Duke 也无可厚非。然而，"公"并非一定是公爵。晋文公和齐桓公分别是春秋时期晋国第 22 位和齐国第 15 位国君，但他们都是侯爵而非公爵。可能是考虑到"公"指称的复杂性，辜鸿铭在权衡利弊后则选用了 prince of a certain state（某国的君王）来表达，意义相当于尼可罗·马基雅维利著名的《君主论》中的"君主"。赵彦春的译本使用概念范围同样宽泛的 Lord 统一对译"公",在外延上可以涵盖各种身份,包括爵位与尊称的概念范围,避免了"公"被误解和误译的可能。

春秋战国时期,"子"是一个重要的概念,它既可以是一个独立的词,也可以是一个能产性很高的语素。"夫子"曾是一个尊称,用来称呼当时的朝廷官员,相当于"阁下"或者英语的 Your Excellency/His Excellency。因为孔子担任过鲁国大司寇的职位,所以被人尊称为"孔夫子"。"孔夫子"的译名 Confucius 是通过译为拉丁语进入英语的。拉丁语是典型的综合语,词法是语法的重要部分,其词汇意义须通过词尾的形态变化来表达。根据拉丁语的构词原理,表示名称的词语需要进行词性变位方能成立,即译文需在音译 Confuci 的基础上,增加-us 的后缀才能成为一个名称。罗马史诗和戏剧的创始人安德罗尼柯(Livius Andronicus),古罗马历史剧作家涅维乌斯(Gnaeus Naevius),古代最有影响的拉丁诗人、罗马文学之父恩尼乌斯(Quintus Ennius)等拉丁语名字中都带有-us 的后缀。同理,"孟子"根据拉丁语的构词法译成了 Mencius。

既然"孔子"和"孟子"的译名 Confucius 和 Mencius 在西方已经约定俗成,那么通过类推,"微子"可以译作 Weicius。为顺应既有的生成原理,赵彦春根据英语的造词规律进行相应处理,以现有的 Confucius、Mencius 为基础,创造性地将"子"统一译为-cius,不仅保持了原则和译法一致,而且使名字中的尊称得到还原和显化。如此看来,赵彦春将"微子""有子""崔子""季康子""曾子""陈文子"等当中的"子"统一译作-cius,是在仿拟 Confucius 和 Mencius 的译名,从而建立起了原文表达与译文表达的对应关系。如此处理避开了各种争议带来的问题,并且将汉语原文中的统一说法保留到英语译文中去。孔子的原名是孔丘,"孔子"是"孔夫子"的缩写,"夫子"是对老人家的尊称。因此 Master Confucius 是孔夫子的英译,其中 Con = 孔,fu = 夫,ci = 子。

例2:天、德、士。

译文:

天:Heaven;

德:Moral Power;

士:Knight。

(Tr. Arthur Waley)

评析:通过这种方式,将中国文化纳入西方的思想构架之中,目的是便于理解,易于接受。"德"在《论语》中是一个概念,译成"moral power"则成了两个概念。

例3:道。

关于"道"的翻译可以归纳为三种:

① 音译(如:Tao、Dao、Tau 等);

② 直译(如:Way、Road、Path 等);

③ 改译(如:Logos、Providence、Divine Law 等)。

评析： 尽管上述三种译法已经约定俗成，它们都从不同的侧面强调了"道"的内涵，也各有一定的道理，但从发生学的角度看，却都有这样或那样的缺陷。比如：音译割裂了中西文化一体性，并割裂了音义之间的联系，多数直译和改译也存在没有深入中西对比而随意比附等问题。汉语"道"的原始概念义是"道路""坦途"，之后语义逐渐扩展为"道理"，用以表达事物的规律性。尽管"道"的确切定义不易把握，后世还是将古人关于"道"的讨论进行归纳并概括，总结出三个层面的意思：① 宇宙万物产生和发展的总根源，或者说是世界的本原(本体)；② 自然规律，或者说世界的本质或世界之所以然，也即世界面貌的决定力量；③ 人类社会的一种规则、法则。

赵彦春的译本中将"道"译作"Word"。就宇宙论而言，东西方哲学是近似的，都是"有生于无"或"道成肉身"，"Word"和"道"同是造物主或是同一造物主。要理解"Word"与"道"的各种关系，还须从"Word"的词源说起。历时地看，"Word"源于拉丁语词根 vVr 的构造，其中小写字母 v 代表一个词的首字母，大写的 V 代表该词的第二个字母为元音，r 代表词的第三个字母。这一构造的原始意义为 penis, ver, originally man, or the genital organ of a man, symbolizing strength or truth, hence the words having to do with strength or truth。

由于历时音变，v 产生了 w 的变体，ver 的原始构型成为印欧语系的词根 wer-，进入古英语和中世纪英语后继而演变成了 word，与荷兰语的 woord，德语的 Wort，古诺斯语(Old Norse)的 orth 和哥特语(Gothic)的 waurd 同源，都与古普鲁士语(OPruss)的 wirds，拉丁语的 verbum(word)和立陶宛语的 vardas(name)有亲缘关系。拉丁语 Verbum 中的-um 其实是词尾屈折变化的结果，表明该词是一个中性名词、主格、第二格变式。

词源表明，"word"这个词最初的意思是阴茎，转喻为"生"。巧合，"道"有着相似的含义：道生一，一生二，二生三，三生万物。在《圣经》"约翰福音"第一节提到的"Word"，就是指上帝的创世之言，即道生万物。《圣经》詹姆士王译本(King James Version of *the Bible*)里说：In the beginning was the Word, and the Word was with God, and the Word was God（太初有道，道与上帝同在，道就是上帝）。

综上，"Word"的本义是"生殖器"，转喻为"生"。"道"亦是"生"。这是"Word"与"道"的第一层关系。"Word"与"道"的第二层关系是，拉丁语 Verbum 符合 vVr 的结构构造，而 Verbum 的确切含义是 the Word of God，即"神谕"。由于历时音变的缘故，拉丁语的 v 逐渐变成了 w，在意义和渊源上对应了英语的 Word。由此，Word 转义为言语、话语；"道"本身也是言语、话语。真可谓全方位对应。

对比"道"和"Word"的意义，可以进一步建立它们在概念上的对应关系。大写的"Word"属于通名转化为专名的现象。比如各类词典对"Word"的解释是：Word 乃是 Word of God 的缩写形式(陆谷孙《英汉大辞典》)，*The New Oxford Dictionary of English* 直接写成 the Word (of God)，并参见 Logos，在意义上相当于 Bible or part of it, title of Christ，或 Logos (*The Concise Oxford Dictionary*)。据 *Longman Modern English*

Dictionary，the Word 解释为 God incarnate in Jesus Christ (Christian theol.)，或者 the Bible as the revelation of God (Christian theol.)。*Longman Dictionary of Contemporary English* 将其解释为：the religious ideas and messages in the Bible. Word，the Word：The Scriptures；Christ as the Logos。

由于多重的对应关系，用"Word"对译"道"在具体翻译中的优势才能较好地显现出来。比如，在翻译《道德经》"道可道，非常道"这句千古名言时，Witter Bynner 给出的译文是：Existence is beyond the power of Words；Arthur Waley 的译文是：The Way that can be told of is not an Unvarying Way；许渊冲教授的译文是：The divine law is not a common law；而赵译则是：The Word that can be worded is not the Word per se。"道"是一个形式，表达多个意义；"Word"亦是一个形式，表达多个意义。所以，赵译表义准确，词义和词性兼顾。

例 4：德。

原文：

子曰：德不孤，必有邻。

译文：

利斯：The Master said, Virtue is not solitary; it always has neighbors.

白牧之、白妙子：The Master said, virtue is not solitary; it must have neighbors.

评析：利斯理解的"德"具有改造功能(transformative power)，可以吸引人们自动靠近；白牧之、白妙子强调的"德"具有社会特征(social character)，不能孤立存在。

例 5：仁。

译文：常见的英译有：benevolence/benevolent（如许渊冲、D. C. Lau），humanity/humane（如丁往道），love/kindness/Humanity〔Jen〕（如 Charles Chai Ch'u, Winsburg Chai），humaneness（如 Raymond Dawson），humaneness（如 Khu Brothers），virtue/virtuous（如 James Legge、Joshua Marshman、David Collie、William Edward Soothill），true/perfect virtue（如 James Legge），Good/Goodness（如 Arthur Waley、Edward Slingerland 等），full manhood（如 Ezra Pound），moral character（如辜鸿铭），manhood-at-its-best/men-at-their best（如 James Roland Ware），human-heartedness……

评析："仁"在孔子的思想体系中居于十分重要的地位，在全文的出现频率最高，达109次之多。作为一种最高的道德理想以及所有道德的总和，"仁"的内涵意义丰富，其理解和翻译自然是多种多样。

由于文化和思维的差异，解释性翻译在任何译本中都不能避免，但原文信息的准确度和语体对应上难免有所损失。在各种译文中，最常见且在语义和语体上认可度最高的当属以词译词的 benevolence/benevolent 和 humanity/humane。要确定对应程度，还须从原文的概念范围着手。

对 humanity 和 benevolence 做一个简要的语义分析即可知道这两个词与汉语的

"仁"有根本的联系。*Webster's Dictionary of Synonyms* 将 humane 和 benevolent 同时列入 charitable 的同义场,并用来作为 kind 的定义词。

要分析汉语"仁"的构型才能还原其本来面目。"仁"的基本含义是"爱人"。所谓"仁者爱人"就是这个意思。Raymond Dawson 和 Chichung Huang 都从字形训诂的角度,讨论了"仁"译为 huamaneness 和 humanity 的合理性。无论语义、训诂、构词还是释经,赵译选择"humanity"作为"仁"这一词义上的对等选项都是恰如其分的。

例6:君子、小人。

在处理这对概念的时候有三种译法:

① 一词多译:在不同的场合采用不同的译法,如 James Legge 将"君子"分别译作 superior man/moral man/scholar man/superiors/man in a superior situation/man of high station,并将"小人"分别译作 mean man/small man/inferiors/one of the lower people/servant/man of low station。辜鸿铭使用了 wise and good man、wise man、gentleman、good man、ruler、man/men、highly educated、polite、moral man、scholar、great man 作为"君子"的对应概念,并使用 fool 和 petty minded man 作为"小人"的对应概念。显然,译文隔断了原文统一形态表述的内在联系。

② 同词对译:即模拟汉语将一个表达式中的两个概念统一到一个表达方式中,如 Arthur Waley 将其分别译作 gentleman 和 commoner;William Edward Soothill 将"君子"和"小人"分别译作 the higher type of man 和 common herd;Roger T. Ames 和 Henry Rosemont, Jr.的译文是 exemplary persons 和 petty person;James Roland Ware 使用的是 Great Man 和 Petty Man;E. Bruce Brooks & A. Tacko Brooks 的译文是 gentleman 和 little man;程石泉使用了 gentleman 和 inferior man。这种译法的机制值得提倡,但实际译文基本上是在译文中使用短语来对译原文的概念词,降低了文化概念词在篇章中的地位。

③ 音译+解释:Robert Eno 采用了音译"junzi"和"xiaoren"并使用 "true prince"作为对"junzi",和 a petty man、the small man 作为对"xiaoren"的解释。音译最大的问题是割裂了语音与语义的天然联系,而解释性话语在普通话语中有一定的可操作性,但作为"君子"和"小人"的对应语言单位,却不合适。

评析:"君子"和"小人"是相对立的。在《论语》中,"君子"有两个主要定义:有道德修养的人和地位高的人;而"小人"可以指"无德之人"或"普通老百姓"。

以上部分译文在概念对应上失配也是显而易见的。毕竟"小人"是一种道德和社会评价,而 small man、little man、fool 等译法很难让人第一反应就得出道德和社会身份的联想。赵彦春将"君子"译作 gentleman,将"小人"译作 flunky,可谓恰如其分。先看 flunky 这一译法。与译界现行的 small man、little man、fool 等译法相比,其优点在哪里呢?首先我们可以从词典的定义来评判译文与原文的语义对应程度。*The New Oxford Dictionary of English* 对 flunky 的定义是:chiefly derogatory a liveried manservant or footman, a person who performs relatively menial tasks for someone else, especially obsequiously。从 derogatory、manservant、footman、menial tasks、obsequiously 的关键定义词可见,它们要么明示了指称对象的社会地位,要么暗示了对指称对象的道德评价,同时包涵了"无德之人"或"普通老百姓"的关键义素,可谓语义趋近。其次,flunky 以词译词,这种译法和 gentleman 的译法在语言单位上更加对应,反映了译者为还原原文所做的努力。

例7:礼。

译文:proprieties

评析:字典上对 propriety 的定义是:

① a. 单数:conformity to conventional standards of behavior or morality;

   b. 复数:socially correct usages or behaviors.

② The quality of being proper; appropriateness.

解释:

你想看、想听、想说、想动这些行为,若不符合礼的规定,就别看、别听、别说、别动。至于你想看、想听、想说、想动的对象(那些事)是否违背礼,那可不一定。

许多情况下,那些事儿本身并不违背礼,但由特定的人去看、去听、去说、或去做,却不符合礼的规定。

例8:文、质。

原文:

子曰:质胜文则野,文胜质则史。文质彬彬,然后君子。

译文:

1) Arthur Waley 译:The Master said, when natural substance prevails over ornamentation, you get the boorishness of the rustic. When ornamentation prevails over natural substance, you get the pedantry of the scribe. Only when ornament and substance are duly blended do you get the true gentleman.

2) 王福林译:Confucius said, "If a person's nature of humaneness exceeds its external manifestation, he will be rustic. If its external manifestation exceeds a person's nature of humaneness, he'll be ostentatious. If they are harmoniously blended, he'll be a real superior person."

3) 丁往道译:Confucius said, "He who knows more simplicity than refinement is a rude man, he who shows more refinement than simplicity is like an office clerk. Only the proper blending of these two qualities makes a gentleman."

评析:"质"和"文"各有两种解释:

① 质:a)"质朴",b)"内在品质"。

② 文:a)"文采",b)"外部修饰"。

一般的理解是"质"与"文"不可偏废,既不能流于粗野,亦不能失于虚浮。既反对"巧言令色",亦反对"言之无文",要求"文""质"兼备,两者结合,和谐统一。

例9:天命。

评析:"天命"大多数人局限于字面,把它译为:the biddings of Heaven。

林戊荪则译为:mandate of Heaven(上天的指令)/my position in the universe/way of Heaven。

理雅各、刘殿爵译为:the decrees of Heaven / the laws of Heaven / the orders of Heaven。

辜鸿铭译为:the truth in religion。

李天辰(1999)将"天命"改译为:the rules in the universe / the objective laws of nature。

(2) 其他基本概念的翻译

儒家思想

① 儒学,儒教 Confucianism

② 孔子 Confucius

③ 中庸 the way of medium (cf. Golden Means)

④ 中和 harmony（zhonghe）

⑤ 孝顺 to show filial obedience

⑥ 孝悌 behave well towards one's parents and elder brothers

⑦ 孝子 dutiful son

⑧ 家长 family head

⑨ 三纲:君为臣纲,父为子纲,夫为妻纲

three cardinal guides: ruler guides subject, father guides son, husband guides wife

⑩ 五常:仁、义、理、智、信

five constant virtues: benevolence (humanity), righteousness, propriety, wisdom and fidelity

⑪ 八股文 eight legged essays

⑫ 多子多福 the more sons; children, the more blessing/great happiness

⑬ 养儿防老 raising sons to support one in one's old age

⑭ 孔子庙 Confucian temple

⑮ 义,礼,智,信,忠,恕,孝,悌 rightness, propriety, wisdom, trustworthiness, loyalty, reciprocity, filial piety, brotherly love

⑯ 学而优则仕

a good scholar can become an official; he who excels in study can follow an official career.

⑰ 三字经 three character scripture

⑱ 儒家文化 Confucian culture

求知求学

① 有教无类。

In teaching there should be no distinction of classes.

② 当仁，不让于师。

When it comes to benevolence, one need not give precedence even to his teacher.

③ 学而时习之，不亦说乎？

Is it not pleasant to learn with a constant perseverance and application?

④ 温故而知新，可以为师矣。

If a man keeps cherishing his old knowledge, so as continually to be acquiring new, he may be a teacher of others.

⑤ 学而不思则罔，思而不学则殆。

Learning without thought is labor lost; thought without learning is perilous.

⑥ 敏而好学，不耻下问。

He was of an active nature and yet fond of learning, and he was not ashamed to ask and learn of his inferiors.

⑦ 十室之邑，必有忠信，如丘者焉，不如丘之好学也。

In a hamlet of ten families, there may be found one honorable and sincere as I am, but not so fond of learning.

⑧ 知之者，不如好之者，好之者，不如乐之者。

They who know the truth are not equal to those who love it, and they who love it are not equal to those who delight in it.

⑨ 默而识之，学而不厌，诲人不倦，何有于我哉？

The silent treasuring up of knowledge; learning without satiety; and instructing others without being wearied which one of these things belongs to me?

⑩ 我非生而知之者，好古，敏以求之者也。

I am not one who was born in the possession of knowledge; I am one who is fond of antiquity, and earnest in seeking it there.

⑪ 三人行，必有我师焉。择其善者而从之，其不善者而改之。

When I walk along with two others, they may serve me as my teachers. I will select their good qualities and follow them, their bad qualities and avoid them.

⑫ 学如不及，犹恐失之。

Learn as if you could not reach your object, and were always fearing also lest you should lose it.

为政以德

① 君君,臣臣,父父,子子。

There is government, when the prince is prince, and the minister is minister; when the father is father, and the son is son.

② 子为政,焉用杀;子欲善,而民善矣。君子之德风,小人之德草,草上之风必偃。

In carrying on your government, why should you use killing at all? Let your evinced desires be for what is good, and the people will be good. The relation between superiors and inferiors is like that between the wind and the grass. The grass must bend, when the wind blows across it.

③ 举直错诸枉,能使枉者直。

Employ the upright and put aside all the crooked; in this way the crooked can be made to be upright.

④ 先有司,赦小过,举贤才。

Employ various officers, pardon small faults, and raise to office men of virtue and talents.

⑤ 名不正,则言不顺;言不顺,则事不成;事不成,则礼乐不兴;礼乐不兴,则刑罚不中;刑罚不中,则民无所措手足。

If names be not correct, language is not in accordance with the truth of things. If language be not in accordance with the truth of things, affairs cannot be carried on to success. When affairs cannot be carried on to success, proprieties and music will not flourish. When proprieties and music do not flourish, punishments will not be properly awarded. When punishments are not properly awarded, the people do not know how to move hand or foot.

⑥ 如有王者,必世而后仁。

If a truly royal ruler were to arise, it would still require a generation, and then virtue would prevail.

⑦ 行己有耻,使于四方,不辱君命,可谓士矣。

He who in his conduct of himself maintains a sense of shame, and when sent to any quarter will not disgrace his princes commission, deserves to be called an officer.

⑧ 以不教民战,是谓弃之。

To lead an uninstructed people to war is to throw them away.

⑨ 不在其位,不谋其政。

He who is not in any particular office, has nothing to do with plans for the administration of its duties.

⑩ 上好礼,则民易使也。

When rulers love to observe the rules of propriety, the people respond readily to the calls on the service.

2. 翻译方法对比分析

（1）句法变异

原文：雍也仁而不佞。

译文：

Legge：Yung is truly virtuous, but he is not ready with his tongue.

辜鸿铭：He is a good moral man, but he is not a man of ready wit.

Waley：Jan Yung is Good, but he is a poor talker.

吴国珍：Ran Yong is benevolent but not eloquent.

评析：Legge 的译本为小句复合体：属性由形容词词组体现。

辜鸿铭的译本为小句复合体：属性由名词词组体现。

Waley 的译本为小句复合体：属性分别由形容词词组和名词词组体现简单小句。

吴国珍的译本属性由形容词词组复合体体现。

（2）理解

原文：子贡曰："如有博施于民而能济众，如何？可谓仁乎？"子曰："何事于仁？必也圣乎！尧、舜其犹病诸！夫仁者，己欲立而立人，己欲达而达人。能近取譬，可谓仁之方也。"（《论语·雍也》）

译文：

Arthur Waley 译：Tzu-kung said, If a ruler not only conferred wide benefits upon the common people, but also compassed the salvation of the whole nation, what would you say of him? Surely, you would call him Good? The Master said, It would no longer be a matter of 'Good'. He would without doubt be a Divine Sage. Even Yao and Shun could hardly criticize him. As for Goodness — you yourself desire rank and standing, then help others to get rank and standing. You want to turn your own merits to account; then help others to turn theirs to account — in fact, the ability to take one's own feelings as a guide — that is the sort of thing that lies in the direction of Goodness.

丁往道译：Zigong asked, "What would you say about a person who gives extensive relief to the common people and helps many men? Can he be called a humane person?" Confucius answered, "He is more than a humane man — he must be a sage! Even Yao and Shun may not have done so much. A humane person is one who helps others to be established when he wishes to be established himself, and helps others to be successful when he wishes to be successful himself. To start from one's own desires can be said to be a way of practicing humanity."

评析：病：不足。

诸:虚词,尧舜等这么道德高尚的圣人都会感到有所不及。

丁往道的译本准确无误,通俗易懂。Arthur Waley 的译本语言流畅,颇具文气,但有失于忠:"病诸""立"和"达"译走了样。

(3) 理解与表达

例1: 子曰:"举直错诸枉,能使枉者直。"(《论语·颜渊》)

译文:

1) Arthur Waley 译:The Master said, "By raising the straight and putting them on top of the crooked, he can make the crooked straight."

2) 王福林译:Confucius said, "Single out and employ the upright and put aside the wicked. Thus the wicked can be made upright."

3) 丁往道译:The master continued, "Putting the upright above the crooked could help to make the crooked straight."

评析: "举直错诸枉"是个典故:把直的东西放到弯曲的东西上面,弯曲的东西就自然变直了,指人才选准用好了,就能促进国家、民族的兴旺和事业的发展;反之则会加速国家、民族的朽亡和事业的衰败。

译例 1 翻译是 sense,译例 2 翻译是 reference,均用复合句。译例 3 为简单句。

例2: 子曰:"吾十有五而志于学,三十而立,四十而不惑,五十而知天命,六十而耳顺,七十而从心所欲,不逾矩。"(《论语·为政》)

译文:

王福林译:Confucius said, "At fifteen I set my mind on learning. At thirty I acted on the proprieties. At forty I could make a clear distinction between benevolence and non-benevolence. At fifty I came to know the existence of the heavenly principles. At sixty, the heavenly principles were not offensive to my ears. At seventy I could do whatever I wished to without going beyond the heavenly principles."

丁往道译:Confucius said, "At fifteen I made up my mind to study, at thirty I was established, at forty I was no longer perplexed, at fifty I understood the will of Heaven, at sixty I listened to everything without feeling unhappy, at seventy I followed all my desires and none of them was against the norms."

评析: 丁往道的译本忠实原文、译义到位、简洁流畅、了无冗词、通俗易懂。

(4) 信息补偿

原文:

子见南子,子路不说。夫子矢之曰:"予所否者,天厌之!天厌之!"

译文:

Lau 译:The Master went to see Nan Tzu. Tzu-lu was displeased. The Master swore, 'If I have done anything improper, may Heaven's curse be on me, may Heaven's curse be on me！'

Watson 译：The Master had an audience with Nanzi. Zilu was not pleased. Confucius swore an oath, saying, If I have done anything wrong, may Heaven cast me aside! May Heaven cast me aside!

Legge 译：The Master having visited Nanzi，Zilu was displeased，on which the Master swore, saying, "Wherein I have done improperly, may Heaven reject me, may Heaven reject me!"

许渊冲译：When Zi Lu was displeased with the Master's visit to the beautiful but ill-famed Princess Nan Zi, the Master swore, "If I had done anything wrong, may Heaven reject me! May Heaven reject me!"

评析：南子指卫灵公夫人，把持着当日卫国的政治，而且有不正当的行为，名声不好。《史记·孔子世家》对"子见南子"的情况有生动的描述。

所：如果，假若。假设连词，但只用于誓词中。详阎若璩《四书释地》。

该句原文的意思是孔子去和南子相见，子路不高兴。孔子发誓道："我假若不对的话，天厌弃我罢！天厌弃我罢！"

Watson 对南子进行了注释："The wife of Duke Ling of Wei, notorious for her adulterous conduct, which is why Zilu disapproved of the meeting".

Legge 也进行了注释：Confucius vindicates himself for visiting the unworthy Nan-tsze. Nan-tsze was the wife of the duke of Wei, and half-sister of prince Chao, mentioned in chap. XIV. Her lewd character was well known, and hence Tsze-lu was displeased, thinking an interview with her was disgraceful to the Master. Great pains are taken to explain the incident. 'Nan-tsze,' says one, 'sought the interview from the stirrings of her natural conscience.' 'It was a rule,' says another, 'that stranger officers in a State should visit the prince's wife.' 'Nan-tsze,' argues a third, 'had all influence with her husband, and Confucius wished to get currency by her means for his doctrine.' Whether 矢 is to be understood in the sense of 'to swear,' = 誓, or 'to make a declaration,' = 陈, is much debated. Evidently the thing is an oath, or solemn protestation against the suspicions of Tsze-lu.

许渊冲对译本增加了 the beautiful but ill-famed，作为信息补偿。

3. 问题与点评

（1）问题一：与白话文相左

例1：父母唯其疾之忧。

白话：做子女的，唯恐父母亲有病，经常以此为忧。

译文：A good child should behave in such a way that the parents have no anxiety about the child, except concerning his health.

评析：回译成汉语是"好孩子的举止应该让父母只担心他的身体状况而别无他忧"。译文和白话注释不符：译者自行其是，不按白话释义转换信息。

例2：曾子曰："吾日三省吾身：为人谋而不忠乎？与朋友交而不信乎？传不习乎？"

白话：曾子说："我每天多次反省自己：为别人谋划办事，尽了心没有？和朋友交往，有没有不诚实的地方？学到的东西复习了吗？"

译文：Zeng Zi said, "Each day I examine myself on these three points: In doing things for others, have I failed to do all that I could? In my interactions with friends, have I been untrustworthy? And have I failed to practise what I have learned?"

评析：回译成汉语是"我每天在以下三件事上反省自己"以及最后一句与白话内容相去甚远。三省是多次反省的意思。

（2）问题二：过度依赖白话文

例：曾子曰："慎终追远，民德归厚矣。"

白话：曾子说："当父母过世了以后，做子女的人应当恭敬地办理丧葬事宜，并祭祀祖先。如此社会上的民风便会笃厚了。"

译文：Zengzi said: "When a parent passes away, children should perform the funeral rites with respect, and offer sacrifice to ancestors. In doing so, morality in society will be increased."

评析：完全依赖白话文解释，导致译文啰嗦冗繁。

（3）问题三：粗制滥造

例：子曰："君子不重则不威，学则不固。主忠信。无友不如己者。过则勿惮改。"

译文：Confucius said, "If a man is not grave, he will not call forth any veneration, and his learning will not be solid. First and foremost he must learn to be faithfulness and truthfulness. Don't make friends not as good as himself. When he has faults, do not fear to correct them."

评析：译文过于贴近字面，"Don't make friends not as good as himself. When he has faults, do not fear to correct them"一句译得较为随意。

（4）问题四：不尊重先前译者的知识产权，"继承"方式生硬、机械

例：子曰："先进于礼乐，野人也。后进于礼乐，君子也。如用之，则吾从先进。"

译文：

魏鲁南译：Chapter XI The Pioneers ...

"The first ones to have formulated the rites and music are called crude; those later, Great Men. When it is a question of drawing upon rites and music, I follow the work of the pioneers."

洪青皎译：Chapter XI The Pioneers

The Master said,"The common people can take office only till they have learned rites and music. The sons of officials can take office first and then learn rites and music later on. If I were to appoint someone, I should be on the side of those who take up their studies first."

David Hinton 译：XI. Studies begin

The Master said:"Those whose studies begin with Ritual and music are commoners ...."

黄继忠(Chichung Huang)译：Book XI.XIAN JIN (Those Who First Entered)

The Master said:"Those who first entered into the rituals and music were rustics：..."

评析：译本存在对前人译本生硬挪用的痕迹。

四、译文对比赏析

1.《论语》篇名翻译

《论语》共20篇，因为每篇都涉及诸多方面，篇名与内容没有直接的逻辑关系，所以很难以一个标题简单概括其要旨。因此，每篇都是以第一章的前两个或前三个字作为篇名。不同译本对篇名的处理如下：

原　文	许渊冲/辜鸿铭	Arthur Waley	Chichung Huang	赵彦春
学而第一	Chapter I	Book One	Book One XUE ER（To Learn Something And）	Isn't It
为政第二	Chapter II	Book Two	Book Two WEI ZHENG（He Who Conducts Government）	Governing
八佾第三	Chapter II	Book Three	Book Three BA YI（Eight Rows of Dancers）	Eight Rows
里仁第四	Chapter IV	Book Four	Book Four LI REN（To Live among Men of Humanity）	Neighborhood
公冶长第五	Chapter V	Book Five	Book Five GONG-YE CHANG	Kungyech'ang
雍也第六	Chapter VI	Book Six	Book Six YONG YE（Yong）	Ranyung
述而第七	Chapter VII	Book Seven	Book Seven SHU ER（I Transmit and）	Retelling But
泰伯第八	Chapter VIII	Book Eight	Book Eight TAI-BO	T'aipo
子罕第九	Chapter IX	Book Nine	Book Nine ZI HAN（The Master Seldom）	Confucius Seldom
乡党第十	Chapter X	Book Ten	Book Ten XIANG DANG（In His Native Place）	His Hometown

(续表)

原　文	许渊冲/辜鸿铭	Arthur Waley	Chichung Huang	赵彦春
先进第十一	Chapter XI	Book Eleven	Book Eleven XIAN JIN (Those Who First Entered)	Those Who
颜渊第十二	Chapter XII	Book Twelve	Book Twelve YAN YUAN	Yanhui
子路第十三	Chapter XIII	Book Thirteen	Book Thirteen ZI-LU	Chongyu
宪问第十四	Chapter XIV	Book Fourteen	Book Fourteen XIAN WEN (Xian Asked)	To Yuanhsian
卫灵公第十五	Chapter XV	Book Fifteen	Book Fifteen WEI LING GONG (Duke Ling of Wei)	Lord Ling of Watch
季氏第十六	Chapter XVI	Book Sixteen	Book Sixteen JI SHI	The Chi's
阳货第十七	Chapter XVII	Book Seventeen	Book Seventeen YANG HUO	Yanghuo
微子第十八	Chapter XVIII	Book Eighteen	Book Eighteen WEI ZI (The Viscount of Wei)	Weicius
子张第十九	Chapter XIX	Book Nineteen	Book Nineteen ZI-ZHANG	Tsuchang
尧曰第二十	Chapter XX	Book Twenty	Book Twenty YAO YUE (Yao Said)	Yao Said

篇名翻译点评：或许是因为篇名与内容的关系不好理解，许渊冲、辜鸿铭和 Arthur Waley 采用了避而不译的策略，以序数的方法表示。这种译法起到了排序的作用，便于普通读者认知，但缺点是没有还原篇名的原本设计。Chichung Huang 的译文则采用音译加英语解释的方式，如将"学而"和"八佾"分别处理为 XUE ER（To Learn Something And）和 BA YI（Eight Rows of Dancers），这也不符合原作的设计，且行文过于冗长，失之于经典的简练。

赵彦春显然领会了原作的设计意图，根据《论语》各篇篇名的生成方式是取每一篇的前两三个字作为篇名的原则，他把第一篇的篇名"学而"译作 Isn't it? 把"八佾"译作 Eight Rows。赵教授在翻译篇名时采用了原文的设计方法。这是赵教授为还原经典原貌并寻求忠实与对应所做的努力。

2. 经典段落

2.1　学而第一

（1）子曰："学而时习之，不亦说乎？有朋自远方来，不亦乐乎？人不知而不愠，不亦君子乎？"

（1）The Master said, To learn and at due times to repeat what one has learnt, is that not after all a pleasure? That friend should come to one from afar, is this not after all delightful? To remain unsoured even though one's merits are unrecognized by others is that not after all what is expected of a gentleman?

(2) 有子曰:"其为人也孝悌,而好犯上者,鲜矣;不好犯上,而好作乱者,未之有也。君子务本,本立而道生。孝悌也者,其为人之本与?"

(2) Master You said, "Those who in private life behave well towards their parents and their elder brothers, in public life seldom show a disposition to resist the authority of their superiors. And as for such men starting a revolution, no instance of it has ever occurred. It is upon the trunk that a gentleman works. When that is firmly set up, the Way grows. And surely proper behavior towards parents and elder brothers is the trunk of Goodness?"

(3) 子曰:"巧言令色,鲜矣仁。"

(3) The Master said, "Clever talk and a pretentious manner are seldom found in the Good."

(4) 曾子曰:"吾日三省吾身。为人谋而不忠乎?与朋友交而不信乎?传不习乎?"

(4) Master Zeng said, "Every day I examine myself on these three points: in acting on behalf of others, have I always been loyal to their interests? In intercourse with my friends, have I always been true to my word? Have I failed to repeat the precepts that have been handed down to me?"

(5) 子曰:"道千乘之国,敬事而信,节用而爱人,使民以时。"

(5) The Master said, "A country of a thousand war-chariots cannot be administered unless the ruler attends strictly to business, punctually observes his promises, is economical in expenditure, shows affection towards his subjects in general, and uses the labor of the peasantry only at the proper times of year."

(6) 子曰:"弟子入则孝,出则悌,谨而信,泛爱众而亲仁。行有余力,则以学文。"

(6) The Master said, "A young man's duty is to behave well to his parents at home and to his elders abroad, to be cautious in giving promises and punctual in keeping them, to have kindly feelings towards everyone, but seek the intimacy of the Good. If, when all that is done, he has any energy to spare, then let him study the polite arts."

(7) 子夏曰:"贤贤易色;事父母能竭其力;事君,能致其身;与朋友交,言而有信。虽曰未学,吾必谓之学矣。"

(7) Zixia said, "A man who

Treats his betters as betters,

Wears an air of respect,

Who into serving father and mother

Knows how to put his whole strength,

Who in the service of his prince will lay down his life,

Who in intercourse with friends is true to his word —

Others may say of him that he still lacks education, but I for my part should certainly call him an educated man."

(8) 子曰:"君子不重则不威,学则不固。主忠信。无友不如己者。过则勿惮改。"
(8) The Master said, "If a gentleman is frivolous, he will loss the respect of his inferiors and lack firm ground upon which to build his education. First and foremost he must learn to be faithful to his superiors, to keep promises, to refuse the friendship of all who are not like him. And if he finds he has made a mistake, then he must not be afraid of admitting the fact and amending his ways."

(9) 曾子曰:"慎终追远,民德归厚矣。"
(9) Master Zeng said, "When proper respect towards the dead is shown at the End and continued after they are far away the moral force of a people has reached its highest point."

(10) 子禽问于子贡曰:"夫子至于是邦也,必闻其政,求之与? 抑与之与?"子贡曰:"夫子温、良、恭、俭、让以得之。夫子之求之也,其诸异乎人之求之与?"
(10) Ziqin in said to Zigong, "When our Master arrives in a fresh country he always manages to finds out about its policy. Does he do this by asking questions, or do people tell him of their own accord?" Zigong said, "Our Master gets things by being cordial, frank, courteous, temperate, and deferential. That is our Master's way of enquiring — a very different matter, certainly, from the way in which enquiries are generally made."

(11) 子曰:"父在观其志,父没观其行,三年无改于父之道,可谓孝矣。"
(11) The Master said, "While a man's father is alive, you can only see his intentions; it is when his father dies that you discover whether or not he is capable of carrying them out. If for the whole three years of mourning he manages to carry on the household exactly as in his father's day, then he is a good son indeed."

(12) 有子曰:"礼之用,和为贵。先王之道斯为美;小大由之,有所不行,知和而和,不以礼节之,亦不可行也。"

(12) Master You said, "In the usages of ritual it is harmony that is prized; the Way of the Former Kings from this got its beauty. Both small matters and great depend upon it. If things go amiss, he who knows the harmony will be able to attune them. But if harmony will be able to attune them. But if harmony itself is not modulated by ritual, things will still go amiss."

(13) 有子曰:"信近于义,言可复也。恭近于礼,远耻辱也。因不失其亲,亦可宗也。"

(13) Master You said,

"In your promises cleave to what is right,

And you will be able to fulfill your word.

In your obeisance cleave to ritual,

And you will keep dishonor at bay.

Marry one who has not betrayed her own kin,

And you may safely present her to your ancestors."

(14) 子曰:"君子食无求饱,居无求安,敏于事而慎于言,就有道而正焉,可谓好学也已。"

(14) The Master said, "A gentleman who never goes on eating till he is sated, who does not demand comfort in his home, who is diligent in business and cautious in speech, who associates with those that possess the Way and thereby corrects his own faults — such a one may indeed be said to have a taste for learning."

(15) 子贡曰:"贫而无谄,富而无骄,何如?"子曰:"可也。未若贫而乐道,富而好礼者也。"子贡曰:"《诗》云:'如切如磋!如琢如磨',其斯之谓与?"子曰:"赐也!始可与言《诗》已矣,告诸往而知来者。"

(15) Zigong said, "'Poor without cadging, rich without swagger.' What of that?" The Master said, "Not bad. But better still, 'Poor, yet delighting in the Way; rich, yet a student of ritual.'" Zigong said, "The saying of the Songs,

As thing cut, as thing filed,

As thing chiseled, as thing polished

refers, I suppose, to what you have just said?" The Master said, "Ci, now I can really begin to talk to you about the Songs, for when I allude to sayings of the past, you see what bearing they have on what was to come after."

(16) 子曰:"不患人之不已知,患不知人也。"

(16) The Master said, "(The good man) does not grieve that other people do not recognize his merits. His only anxiety is lest he should fail to recognize theirs."

2.2　为政第二

本篇主要内容涉及孔子"为政以德"的思想,如何谋求官职和从政为官的基本原则,学习与思考的关系,孔子本人学习和修养的过程,温故而知新的学习方法,以及对孝、悌等道德范畴的进一步阐述。

(1) 子曰:"为政以德,譬如北辰,居其所而众星共之。"

(1) The Master said, "He who rules by moral force (*de*) is like the pole star, which remains in its place while all the lesser stars do homage to it."

(2) 子曰:"《诗》三百,一言以蔽之,曰:'思无邪。'"

(2) The Master said, "If out of the three hundred *Songs* I had to take one phrase to cover all my teaching, I would say 'Let there be no evil in your thoughts.'"

(3) 子曰:"道之以政,齐之以刑,民免而无耻;道之以德,齐之以礼,有耻且格。"

(3) The Master said, "Govern the people by regulations, keep order among them by chastisements, and they will flee from you, and lose all self-respect. Govern them by moral force, keep order among them by ritual and they will keep their self-respect and come to you of their own accord."

(4) 子曰:"吾十有五而志于学,三十而立,四十而不惑,五十而知天命,六十而耳顺,七十而从心所欲,不逾矩。"

(4) The Master said, "At fifteen I set my heart upon learning. At thirty, I had planted my feet firm upon the gound. At forty, I no longer suffered from perplexities. At fifty, I knew what the biddings of Heaven were. At sixty, I heard them with docile ear. At seventy, I could follow the dictates of my own heart; for what I desired no longer overstepped the boundaries of right."

(5) 孟懿子问孝,子曰:"无违。"樊迟御,子告之曰:"孟孙问孝于我,我对曰无违。"樊迟曰:"何谓也。"子曰:"生,事之以礼;死,葬之以礼,祭之以礼。"

(5) Meng Yi asked about the treatment of parents. The Master said, "Never disobey!" When Fan Chi was driving his carriage for him, the Master said, "Meng asked me about the treatment of parents and I said, 'Never disobey!'" Fan Chi said, "In what sense did you mean it?" The Master said, "While they are alive, serve them

according to ritual. When they die, bury them according to ritual and sacrifice to them according to ritual."

(6) 孟武伯问孝,子曰:"父母唯其疾之忧。"

(6) Meng Wu asked about the treatment of parents. The Master said, "Behave in such a way that your father and mother have no anxiety about you, except concerning your health."

(7) 子游问孝,子曰:"今之孝者,是谓能养。至于犬马,皆能有养,不敬,何以别乎?"

(7) Ziyou asked about the treatment of parents. The Master said, "'Filial sons' nowadays are people who see to it that their parents get enough to eat. But even dogs and horses are cared for to that extent. If there is no feeling of respect, wherein lies the difference?"

(8) 子夏问孝,子曰:"色难。有事,弟子服其劳;有酒食,先生馔,曾是以为孝乎?"

(8) Zixia asked about the treatment of parents. The Master said, "It is the demeanor that is difficult. Filial piety does not consist merely in young people undertaking the hard work, when anything has to be done, or serving their elders first with wine and food. It is something much more than that."

(9) 子曰:"吾与回信,终日不违如愚。退而省其私,亦足以发,回也不愚。"

(9) The Master said, "I can talk to Yan Hui a whole day without his ever differing from me. One would think he was stupid. But if I enquire into his private conduct when he is not with me I find that is fully demonstrates what I have taught him. No, Hui is by no means stupid."

(10) 子曰:"视其所以,观其所由,察其所安,人焉廋哉?人焉廋哉?"

(10) The Master said, "Look closely into his aims, observe the means by which he pursues them, and discover what brings him content — and can the man's real worth remain hidden from you, can it remain hidden from you?"

(11) 子曰:"温故而知新,可以为师矣。"

(11) The Master said, "He who by reanimating the Old can gain the knowledge of the New is fit to be a teacher."

(12) 子曰:"君子不器。"

(12) The Master said, "A gentleman is not an implement."

(13) 子贡问君子,子曰:"先行其言而后从之。"

(13) Zigong asked about the true gentleman. The Master said, "He does not preach what he practices till he has practiced what he preaches."

(14) 子曰:"君子周而不比,小人比而不周。"

(14) The Master said, "A gentleman can see a question from all sides without bias. The small man is biased and can see a question only from one side."

(15) 子曰:"学而不思则罔,思而不学则殆。"

(15) The Master said, "He who learns but does not think, is lost. He who thinks but does not learn is in great danger."

(16) 子曰:"攻乎异端,斯害也已。"

(16) The Master said, "He who sets to work upon a different strand destroys the whole fabric."

(17) 子曰:"由,诲女知之乎? 知之为知之,不知为不知,是知也。"

(17) The Master said, "You, shall I teach you what knowledge is? When you know a thing, to recognize that you know it, and when you do not know a thing, to recognize that you do not know it. That is knowledge."

(18) 子张学干禄,子曰:"多闻阙疑,慎言其余,则寡尤;多见阙殆,慎行其余,则寡悔。言寡尤,行寡悔,禄在其中矣。"

(18) Zizhang was studying the *Song Han-lu*. The Master said, "Hear much, but maintains silence as regards doubtful points and be cautious in speaking of the rest; then you will seldom get into trouble. See much, but ignore what it is dangerous to have seen, and be cautious in acting upon the rest; then you will seldom want to undo your acts. He who seldom gets into trouble about what he has said and seldom does anything that he afterwards wishes he had not done, will be sure incidentally to get his reward."

(19) 哀公问曰:"何为则民服?"孔子对曰:"举直错诸枉,则民服;举枉错诸直,则民不服。"

(19) Duke Ai asked, "What can I do in order to get the support of the common people?" Master Kong replied, "If you 'raise up the straight and set them on top of the crooked,' the commoners will support you. But if you raise the crooked and set them on top of the straight, the commoners will not support you."

(20) 季康子问:"使民敬、忠以劝,如之何?"子曰:"临之以庄,则敬;孝慈,则忠;举善而教不能,则民劝。"

(20) Ji Kang asked whether there were any form of encouragement by which he could induce the common people to be respectful and loyal. The Master said, "Approach them with dignity, and they will respect you. Show piety towards your parents and kindness towards your children, and they will be loyal to you. Promote those who are worthy, train those who are incompetent; that is the best form of encouragement."

(21) 或谓孔子曰:"子奚不为政?"子曰:"《书》云:'孝乎惟孝,友于兄弟。'施于有政,是亦为政,奚其为为政?"

(21) Someone, when talking to Master K'ung, said, How is it that you are not in the public service? The Master said, "The *Books* says: 'Be filial, only be filial and friendly towards your brothers, and you will be contributing to government.' There are other sorts of service quite different from what you mean by service."

(22) 子曰:"人而无信,不知其可也。大车无輗,小车无軏,其何以行之哉?"

(22) The Master said, "I do not see what use a man can be put to, whose word cannot be trusted. How can a wagon be made to go if it has no yoke-bar or a carriage, if it has no collar-bar?"

(23) 子张问:"十世可知也?"子曰:"殷因于夏礼,所损益可知也。周因于殷礼,所损益可知也。其或继周者,虽百世可知也。"

(23) Zizhang asked whether the state of things ten generations hence could be foretold. The Master said, "We know in what ways the Yin modified ritual when they followed upon the Hsia. We know in what ways the Zhou modified ritual when they followed upon the Yin. And hence we can foretell what the successors of Zhou will be like, even supposing they do not appear till a hundred generations from now."

(24) 子曰:"非其鬼而祭之,谄也。见义不为,无勇也。"

(24) The Master said, "Just as to sacrifice to ancestors other than one's own is

presumption, so to see what is right and not do it is cowardice."

2.3 里仁第四

本篇主要内容涉及义与利的关系问题、个人的道德修养问题、孝敬父母的问题以及君子与小人的区别。这一篇包括了儒家的若干重要范畴、原则和理论,对后世都产生过较大影响。

(1) 子曰:"里仁为美。择不处仁,焉得知!"

(1) The Master said, "It is Goodness that gives to a neighborhood its beauty. One who is free to choose, yet does not prefer to dwell among the Good — how can he be accorded the name of wise?"

(2) 子曰:"不仁者,不可以久处约,不可以长处乐。仁者安仁,知者利仁。"

(2) The Master said, "Without Goodness a man

Cannot for long endure adversity,

Cannot for long enjoy prosperity.

The Good Man rests content with Goodness; he that is merely wise pursues Goodness in the belief that it pays to do so."

(3) 子曰:"唯仁者能好人,能恶人。"

(4) 子曰:"苟志于仁矣,无恶也。"

(3,4) Of the adage "Only a Good Man knows how to like people, knows how to dislike them," the Master said, "He whose heart is in the smallest degree set upon Goodness will dislike no one."

(5) 子曰:"富与贵,是人之所欲也,不以其道得之,不处也;贫与贱,是人之所恶也,不以其道得之,不去也。君子去仁,恶乎成名?君子无终食之间违仁,造次必于是,颠沛必于是。"

(5) Wealth and rank are what every man desires; but if they can only be retained to the detriment of the Way he professes, he must relinquish them. Poverty and obscurity are what every man detests; but if they can only be avoided to the detriment of the Way he professes, he must accept them. The gentleman who ever parts company with Goodness does not fulfill that name. Never for a moment does a gentleman quit the way of Goodness. He is never so harried but that he cleaves to this; never so tottering but that he cleaves to this.

(6) 子曰:"我未见好仁者,恶不仁者。好仁者,无以尚之;恶不仁者,其为仁矣,不使不仁者加乎其身。有能一日用其力于仁矣乎？我未见力不足者。盖有之矣，我未之见也。"

(6) The Master said, "I for my part have never yet seen one who really cared for Goodness, nor one who really abhorred wickedness. One who really cared for Goodness would never let any other consideration come first. One who abhorred wickedness would be so constantly doing Good that wickedness would never have a chance to get at him. Has anyone ever managed to do Good with his whole might even as long as the space of a single day? I think not. Yet I for my part have never seen anyone give up such an attempt because he had not the strength to go on. It may well have happened, but I for my part have never seen it."

(7) 子曰："人之过也，各于其党。观过，斯知仁矣。"

(7) The master said, "Every man's faults belong to a set. If one looks out for faults it is only as a means of recognizing Goodness."

(8) 子曰："朝闻道，夕死可矣。"

(8) The Master said, "In the morning, hear the Way; in the evening, die content!"

(9) 子曰："士志于道，而耻恶衣恶食者，未足与议也。"

(9) The Master said, "A Knight whose heart is set upon the Way, but who is ashamed of wearing shabby clothes and eating coarse food, is not worth calling into counsel."

(10) 子曰："君子之于天下也，无适也，无莫也，义之与比。"

(10) The Master said, "A gentleman in his dealings with the world has neither enmities nor affections; but wherever he sees Right he ranges himself beside it."

(11) 子曰："君子怀德，小人怀土。君子怀刑，小人怀惠。"

(11) The Master said, "Where gentlemen set their hearts upon moral force (*tê*) the commoners set theirs upon the soil. Where gentlemen think only of punishment, the commoners think only of exemptions."

(12) 子曰："放于利而行，多怨。"

(12) The Master said, "Those whose measures are dictated by mere expediency will arouse continual discontent."

(13) 子曰:"能以礼让为国乎,何有？不能以礼让为国,如礼何?"

(13) The Master said, "If it is really possible to govern countries by ritual and yielding, there is no more to be said. But if it is not really possible, of what use is ritual?"

(14) 子曰:"不患无位,患所以立。不患莫己知,求为可知也。"

(14) The master said, "He does not mind being in office; all he minds about is whether he has qualities that entitle him to office. He does not mind failing to get recognition; he is too busy doing the things that entitle him to recognition."

(15) 子曰:"参乎,吾道一以贯之。"曾子曰:"唯。"子出,门人问曰:"何谓也?"曾子曰:"夫子之道,忠恕而已矣。"

(15) The Master said, Shen! My Way has one (thread) that runs right through it. Master Zeng said, Yes. When the Master had gone out, the disciples asked, saying What did he mean? Master Zeng said, "Our Master's Way is simple this: Loyalty, consideration."

(16) 子曰:"君子喻于义,小人喻于利。"

(16) The Master said, "A gentleman takes as much trouble to discover what is right as lesser men take to discover what will pay."

(17) 子曰:"见贤思齐焉,见不贤而内自省也。"

(17) The Master said, "In the presence of a good man, think all the time how you may learn to equal him. In the presence of a bad man, turn your gaze within!"

(18) 子曰:"事父母,几谏,见志不从,又敬不违,劳而不怨。"

(18) The Master said, "In serving his father and mother a man may gently remonstrate with them. But if he sees that he has failed to change their opinion, he should resume an attitude of deference and not thwart them; may feel discouraged, but not resentful."

(19) 子曰:"父母在,不远游,游必有方。"

(19) The Master said, "While father and mother are alive, a good son does not wander far afield; or if he does so, goes only where he has said he was going."

（20）子曰："三年无改于父之道，可谓孝矣。"

(20) The Master said, "If for the whole three years of mourning a son manages to carry on the household exactly as in his father's day, then he is a good son indeed."

（21）子曰："父母之年，不可不知也。一则以喜，一则以惧。"

(21) The Master said, "It is always better for a man to know the age of his parents. In one case such knowledge will be a comfort to him; in the other, it will fill him with a salutary dread."

（22）子曰："古者言之不出，耻躬之不逮也。"

(22) The Master said, "In old days a man kept a hold on his words, fearing the disgrace that would ensue should be himself fail to keep pace with them."

（23）子曰："以约失之者鲜矣。"

(23) The Master said, "Those who err on the side of strictness are few indeed!"

（24）子曰："君子欲讷于言而敏于行。"

(24) The Master said, "A gentleman covets the reputation of being slow in word but prompt in deed."

（25）子曰："德不孤，必有邻。"

(25) The Master said, "Moral force (*tê*) never dwells in solitude; it will always bring neighbors."

（26）子游曰："事君数，斯辱矣。朋友数，斯疏矣。"

(26) Ziyou said, "In the service of one's prince repeated scolding can only lead to loss of favor; in friendship, it can only lead to estrangement."

五、练习与思考

1. 分析题

（1）结合比读体悟，分析《论语》翻译的风格和特点。

（2）结合全译及似律，分析在《论语》的翻译过程中形似、意似和风格似何者更重要。

2. 实训题

翻译以下段落。

先 进 篇

(1) 子曰:"先进于礼乐,野人也;后进于礼乐,君子也。如用之,则吾从先进。"

(2) 子曰:"从我于陈、蔡者,皆不及门也。德行:颜渊,闵子骞,冉伯牛,仲弓。言语:宰我,子贡。政事:冉有,季路。文学:子游,子夏。"

(3) 子曰:"回也非助我者也,于吾言无所不说。"

(4) 子曰:"孝哉闵子骞!人不间于其父母昆弟之言。"

(5) 南容三复白圭,孔子以其兄之子妻之。

(6) 季康子问:"弟子孰为好学?"孔子对曰:"有颜回者好学,不幸短命死矣,今也则亡。"

(7) 颜渊死,颜路请子之车以为之椁。子曰:"才不才,亦各言其子也。鲤也死,有棺而无椁,吾不徒行以为之椁。以吾从大夫之后,不可徒行也。"

(8) 颜渊死。子曰:"噫!天丧予!天丧予!"

(9) 颜渊死,子哭之恸,从者曰:"子恸矣!"曰:"有恸乎?非夫人之为恸而谁为?"

(10) 颜渊死,门人欲厚葬之,子曰:"不可。"门人厚葬之,子曰:"回也视予犹父也,予不得视犹子也。非我也,夫二三子也!"

(11) 季路问事鬼神,子曰:"未能事人,焉能事鬼?"曰:"敢问死。"曰:"未知生,焉知死?"

(12) 闵子侍侧,訚訚如也;子路,行行如也;冉有、子贡,侃侃如也。子乐。"若由也,不得其死然。"

(13) 鲁人为长府,闵子骞曰:"仍旧贯如之何?何必改作?"子曰:"夫人不言,言必有中。"

(14) 子曰:"由之瑟奚为于丘之门?"门人不敬子路,子曰:"由也升堂矣,未入于室也。"

(15) 子贡问:"师与商也孰贤?"子曰:"师也过,商也不及。"曰:"然则师愈与?"子曰:"过犹不及。"

(16) 季氏富于周公,而求也为之聚敛而附益之。子曰:"非吾徒也,小子鸣鼓而攻之可也。"

(17) 柴也愚,参也鲁,师也辟,由也喭。

(18) 子曰:"回也其庶乎,屡空。赐不受命而货殖焉,亿则屡中。"

(19) 子张问善人之道,子曰:"不践迹,亦不入于室。"

(20) 子曰:"论笃是与,君子者乎,色庄者乎?"

3. 思考题

(1)《论语》翻译有哪些基本要求?

(2) 译文比读中的三个译本,你更倾向于哪个?

(3) 除了译文比读中的三个译本,还有哪些著名的《论语》译本?
(4) 外国语学院毕业的学生如何才能更好地从事典籍翻译工作?
(5) 《论语》这类古代哲学论著在翻译时遇到最大的问题是什么?
(6) 如何处理古代哲学翻译中遇到的问题?
(7) 如何做到全译的形似、意似、风格似?
(8) 淡化法在什么情况下用得比较多?
(9) 深化法在什么情况下用得比较多?
(10) 作为笔译专业的学生,你认为推广《论语》这样的典籍还需要做些什么?

六、参考文献

[1] 李天辰.《论语》英译体会点滴[J].外语教学,1999(02):39-41.
[2] 张政,胡文潇.《论语》中"天"的英译探析[J].中国翻译,2015(06):92-96.
[3] 杨伯峻.论语译注[M].北京:中华书局,2009.

第四课
《道德经》译介赏析

> 《道德经》据传是春秋时期老子之作,是中国历史上首部完整的哲学著作,是道家哲学思想的活水源头,被誉为"万经之王",更被外国友人称为"东方智慧的结晶"。《道德经》文本以哲学意义之"道德"为纲目,论述修身、养生、治国、用兵之要,探讨天之道、地之道、人之道,短短五千言,微言大义,一语万端。
>
> 《道德经》不仅以其宏阔的思想维度、玄远的哲学义理影响着中国文化、思想史,更以其独到的语言特色屹立于哲学著述、诗文创作之林。书中语言体现了先秦时期由诗到文的过渡:既有诗的韵律和齐整,又有散文的铺陈和灵活。全篇语势上,由缓入急,又以长句收尾,舒张有致,气势浑圆;句式上,常是上下两句并列,多用设问和否定,字数同等,结构相同,各句既独立表意,又相互联系、集中表旨;表达上,多采用比兴,并以大量排比、比喻进行铺陈,成汪洋之势。

一、翻译简介

《道德经》是有史以来译成外文版本最多、海外发行量最大的中国经典。据联合国教科文组织统计,《道德经》是除《圣经》之外被译成外国文字发行量最多的文化名著。老子布的"道",不仅被视作中国人的文化宝库,更被视作全人类的精神财富。

早在7世纪的唐朝,玄奘等人便将《道德经》译成梵文。自16世纪始,这部经典更是被不断地译成各种外文译本。据统计,到目前为止,其外文译本已有600多种,涉及语言30多种,其中英译本近200种。《道德经》的大规模英译,经历了三次浪潮。第一次是19世纪60年代到20世纪初。1868年英籍传教士湛约翰(John Chalmers)翻译的《道德经》

在伦敦出版,由此拉开了《道德经》英译的序幕。其中,传教士理雅各(James Legge)的译本是当时最流行的版本。这一时期译者多为传教士,译作的基督教色彩颇为浓厚。第二个时期是20世纪30年代到60年代初,贯穿二战及战后初期,西方社会面临严重的社会危机,希冀从东方智慧中找到答案。这一时期的英译本主要从跨文化比较的角度挖掘老子思想,以作为对西方思想的批判。如英国汉学家亚瑟·韦利(Arthur Waley)将原作放到中国整体文化思想体系中去考察,多用解释性语言,并含大量注释。胡子霖的译本也在这一时期问世,这是首个国人英译本,《道德经》英译由此走出了西方学者话语垄断的时代。第三次浪潮是20世纪70年代初至今。1973年长沙马王堆汉墓出土帛书《道德经》甲乙本,在全球范围内形成"老子热",由此形成了第三次译事高峰。这一时期的英译,更加注重文化差异,译作也更为准确客观。

二、书名翻译

《道德经》译名在三次翻译高峰期,呈现出不同特征,整体来说,第一个时期,多是解释性翻译;第二个时期,多是解释性翻译和威妥玛式拼音音译;第三个时期,多是汉语拼音音译。例如:

第一个时期:

John Chalmers (1868): The Speculations on Metaphysics, Policy and Morality of "The Old Philosopher", Lau-Tsze

James Legge (1891): The Texts of Taoism

Alexander George Gardiner (1895): Lao-Tsze, the Great Thinker: with a Translation of His Thoughts on Nature and Manifestations of God

Paul Carus (1913): The Canon of Reason and Virtue: Being Lao-Tze's Tao Teh King

第二个时期:

Arthur Waley (1934): The Way and Its Power: A Study of Tao Te Ching and Its Place in Chinese Thought

胡子霖 (Hu Tse ling) (1936): Lao Tsu: Tao Teh Ching

林语堂 (Lin Yutang) (1948): The Wisdom of Laotse

Archie J. Bahm (1958): Tao Teh King: Interpreted as Nature and Intelligence

第三个时期:

Robert G. Henricks (1989): Lao-tzu Te-tao Ching: A New Translation Based on the Recently Discovered Ma-wang-tui Texts

Wang Rongpei & William Puffenberger (1991): Lao Tse

辜正坤 (Gu Zhengkun) (1993): The Book of Tao and Teh

Roger T. Ames & David L. Hall (2003): Daodejing "Making This Life Significant":

A Philosophical Translation

书名《道德经》的核心是高度抽象的"道德"一词。一般认为,"道"为"德"之根源,"德"为"道"之表现;道与德一体一用,体用不二。《道德经》书名译法众多,主要有以下特征:首先,很多译者试图将名称具体化,加入了很多阐释,致使书名冗长;其次,在前期译者多用基督教词汇,如多用 God(上帝)、canon(圣典,神所启示的书籍)、way(上帝指明的通向彼岸世界的光明大道)等。再者,"道"被采用最多的译法,为直译"Way"和音译 Dao/Tao。Way 为宗教术语,但并非根植于西方哲学概念,因而常被理解成一般的"方式、方法",由此,便不能充分表达"道"的深刻内涵。因此,长期以来,此译法颇受争议。因很难在译入语中找到能表达出此概念的对应词,此后,译者便直接用音译法来翻译书名,理雅各是使用"Tao"第一人,之后越来越多的人开始使用"Tao"。如今,"Tao"已被收录于牛津词典中,成了特有的中国文化词。

三、特殊概念的翻译

《道德经》作为中国古代哲学经典巨著,蕴含着大量精辟、富有深意的语言。这些特殊文化概念词成为翻译的一大难点。分析不同译者的不同处理方式,可为读者带来一定启示。以下以 Legge、Waley 和辜正坤译本为例。

例1:天地不仁,以万物为刍狗。

Legge 译:

Heaven and earth do not act from (the impulse of) any wish to be benevolent; they deal with all things as the dogs of grass are dealt with. (note)

Waley 译:

Heaven and Earth are ruthless;
To them the Ten Thousand Things are but as straw dogs. (note)

辜正坤译:

Heaven and Earth are not merciful,
They treat all things as straw dogs. (note)

评析:"刍狗"是古代祭祀时用草扎成的狗。在祭祀前,大家对刍狗很重视,不可随意触碰;祭祀结束后,就扔之不管了。所以,也比喻为贵贱一体的东西。Legge 将其译为 the dog of grass,并通过注释补偿:The grass-dogs were made of straw tied up in the shape of dogs, and used in praying for rain; and afterwards, when the sacrifice was over, were thrown aside and left uncared for. Heaven and earth and the sages dealt so with all things and with the people; but the illustration does not seem a happy one. Legge 的解释,让读者一目了然,到底刍狗为何,用此比喻的用意为何。但在这里,需注意,刍狗是用来祭祀、求福,此解释说是用来"求雨",显然将范围窄化了,不够准确。Waley 亦通过

注释加以说明：The straw dogs are for the occasion of sacrifice, when it is finished, they are abandoned. The analogy shows they receive no particular favour and are easily forgotten ... Some scholars explain this sentence as treating people as straws, certainly they are mistaken. 同样，辜正坤亦加注释，Straw dogs: a kind of offering used by Chinese ancients for the purpose of sacrifice ceremony, usually discarded and trampled upon at the end of the ceremony. 对此句话的理解，一直以来有两种观念：一种认为这表达了天地的公平和无为，因为天地看待万物是一样的，没有特别偏爱谁，一切随其自然发展；另一种认为，这句话想说天地不标榜、不叫嚷自己仁爱，它对待万物如同刍狗一样，并不要求你真的作出牺牲去祭祀，所以这是天地无言、不求回报、真正仁爱的表现。

原文中的民族文化信息，翻译时用加注可以让读者更好地理解。然而，注释到何种程度，这是需要注意的。Legge 和 Waley 的注释无疑加入了自己的理解（主要是第一种观念）。辜正坤的注释则只是告诉大家刍狗是什么，未说整体比喻在此的用意，如此便为读者留有更多的思考空间。

例2：天地相合，以降甘露，民莫之令而自均。

Legge 译：

Heaven and Earth (under its guidance) unite together and send down the sweet dew, which, without the direction of men, reaches equally everywhere as of its own accord.

Waley 译：

Heaven-and-earth would conspire

To send Sweet Dew,

Without law or compulsion, men would dwell in harmony.

林语堂译：

And the sweet rain falls,

Beyond the command of men,

Yet evenly upon all.

评析：甘露是中国古代文化中一种很神圣的物质，在传说中为晶莹剔透的珠状物，会于晨曦时出现在植物上。天降甘露则象征吉祥。

Legge 和 Waley 皆将其译为 sweet dew，不同的是，Waley 将其二词大写，以示其异于普通名词，暗示读者：这在原文化中有着特殊含义。林语堂则直接译成 sweet rain。显然，"露"并非 rain（雨水），译词与原文有差异，但这种归化策略，在一定程度上，却也让读者更容易理解文本。

例3：知其雄，守其雌。

Legge 译：

Who knows his manhood's strength

Yet still his female feebleness maintains.

Waley 译：

He who knows the male, yet cleaves to what is female.

辜正坤译：

Though knowing what is <u>masculine</u>,

You are ready to play <u>the role of female</u>.

评析："雌"与"雄"实为一组对应词，在此指的是两种不同的状态，并非单指性别上的差异。而真正圆融的状态，则如原文所说——"知其雄，守其雌"，是雌雄一体，刚中有柔，能屈能伸。"雌"指柔与弱，"雄"指刚与强。Waley 直接译成 female（女性）和 male（男性），将意义窄化，未能准确输出原文内涵。辜正坤则将"雄"译为 masculine，字典解释为：have qualities such as strength or confidence which are considered typical of men（有力量，有信心，有男子气概的）；"雌"则稍微做了解释，用 the role of female 代替。如此，意义传达更精确。Legge 同是采用直译加解释的方式揭示了二词隐含的意义，即男性的刚强和女性的柔弱。

例4：胜而不美，而美之者，是乐杀人。夫乐杀人者，则不可得志于天下矣。吉事尚左，凶事尚右。偏将军居左，上将军居右。言以丧礼处之。杀人之众，以悲哀泣之。战胜，以丧礼处之。

Waley 译：

For to think them lovely means to delight in them, and to delight in them means to delight in the slaughter of men. And he who delights in the slaughter of men will never get what he looks for out of those that dwell under heaven. A host that has slain men is received with grief and mourning; he that has conquered in battle is received with rites of mourning.

许渊冲译：

Victory should not be glorified. To glorify it is to take delight in killing. Those delighted in killing cannot do what they will in the world. Good omen keeps to the left, and evil omen to the right. A lieutenant general keeps to the left, and a full general to the right as in the funeral service. The heavier the casualties, the deeper the mourning should be. Even a victory should be celebrated in funeral ceremony.

辜正坤译：

He who glorifies the victory is one who takes delight in killing. He who takes delight in killing can never be successful in winning the empire. On occasion of auspicious celebration the left is favoured; On occasions of mourning the right is favoured. A lieutenant's position is on the left; A general's position is on the right. That is to say, mourning rites should be observed in military operations. War brings about heavy casualties, So one should take part in with deep sorrow. When winning the victory, victors should treat the dead by observing the rites of mourning.

评析：中国古代的尚左与尚右观念，有着丰富的社会性内容和文化内涵。这一段解释了中国古代在什么情况下尊"左"，又在何条件下尊"右"。在古代中国，左为阳，右为阴。老子说，"上将军居右"、"君子居则贵左，用兵则贵右"，是在强调要严肃审慎地对待战争，即使迫不得已有了战争，对于阵亡之人也要给予最大的同情与尊重，故则尊为"右"。

这一文化概念，在西方社会是缺省的。Waley 在翻译时，对于"吉事尚左，凶事尚右。偏将军居左，上将军居右"这句，略过未译。许渊冲和辜正坤则是更尊重原文，表达出了尚左和尚右的概念，且逻辑顺畅，不会给读者造成理解困难。

四、译文对比赏析

1. 经典段落

道可道，非常道；名可名，非常名。

无名，天地之始；有名，万物之母。

故常无欲，以观其妙；常有欲，以观其徼。此两者，同出而异名，同谓之玄。

玄之又玄，众妙之门。

Waley 译：

The Way that can be told of is not an Unvarying Way;

The names that can be named are not unvarying names.

It was from the Nameless that Heaven and Earth sprang;

The named is but the mother that rears the ten

thousand creatures, each after its kind.

Truly, Only he that rids himself forever of desire can see the Secret Essences;

He that has never rid himself of desire can see only the Outcomes.

These two things issued from the same mould, but nevertheless are different in name.

This 'same mould' we can but call the Mystery,

Or rather the 'Darker than any Mystery',

The Doorway whence issued all Secret Essences.

Legge 译：

The Tao that can be trodden is not the enduring and unchanging Tao. The name that can be named is not the enduring and unchanging name.

(Conceived of as) having no name, it is the Originator of heaven and earth; (conceived of as) having a name, it is the Mother of all things.

Always without desire we must be found,

If its deep mystery we would sound;
But if desire always within us be,
Its outer fringe is all that we shall see.
Under these two aspects, it is really the same; but as development takes place, it receives the different names. Together we call them the Mystery. Where the Mystery is the deepest is the gate of all that is subtle and wonderful.

许渊冲译：
The divine law may be spoken of,
but it is not the common law.
Things may be named,
but names are not the things.
In the beginning heaven and earth are nameless,
When named, all things become known.
So we should be free from desires
in order to understand the internal
mystery of the divine law;
and we should have desires
in order to observe its external
manifestations.
Internal mystery and external manifestations
come from the same origin,
but have different names,
They may be called essence.
The essential of the essence
is the key to the understanding of all mysteries.

辜正坤译：
The Tao that can be expressed in words
Is not the true and eternal Tao;
The name that can be uttered in words
Is not the true and eternal name.
The word Nothingness may be used
to designate the beginning of Heaven and Earth;
The word Existence (Being) may be used
to designate the mother of all things.

Hence one should gain an insight into the subtley
of Tao by observing Nothingness,
and should gain an insight into the beginning
Of Tao by observing
Existence (Being).
These two things, Nothingness and Existence,
Are of the same origin but different in name.
They are extremely profound in depth
Serving as the door of myriad secret beings.

Mitchell 译:
The tao that can be told
is not the eternal Tao
The name that can be named
is not the eternal Name.
The unnamable is the eternally real.
Naming is the origin
Of all particular things.
Free from desire, you realize the mystery.
Caught in desire, you see only the manifestations.
Yet mystery and manifestations
arise from the same source.
This source is called darkness.
Darkness within darkness,
The gateway to all understanding.

道冲而用之,或不盈。
渊兮,似万物之宗。
挫其锐,解其纷,和其光,同其尘。
湛兮,似或存。
吾不知谁之子,象帝之先。

Waley 译:
The Way is like an empty vessel
That yet may be drawn from
Without ever needing to be filled.

It is bottomless; the very progenitor of all things in the world.
In it all sharpness is blunted,
All tangles untied,
All glare tempered,
All dust smoothed.
It is like a deep pool that never dries.
Was it too the child of something else? We cannot tell.
But as a substanceless image it existed before the Ancestor.

Legge 译：

The Tao is (like) the emptiness of a vessel; and in our employment of it we must be on our guard against all fullness. How deep and unfathomable it is, as if it were the Honoured Ancestor of all things!

We should blunt our sharp point, and unravel the complications of things; we should attemper our brightness, and bring ourselves into agreement with the obscurity of others. How pure and still the Tao is, as if it would ever so continue!

I do not know whose son it is. It might appear to have been before God.

许渊冲译：

The divine law is formless,
its use is inexhaustible.
It is endless,
whence come all things
where the sharp is blunted,
the knots are united,
the glare is softened,
all look like dust.
Apparent,
it seems to exist.
I do not know when it came;
it seems to exist before God.

辜正坤译：

Tao is invisibly empty,
But its use is extremely plentiful.
It is profound like the originator of all things.

It shows no sharpness,

stays away from entanglements,

glows with veiled radiance,

mingles with dust.

It is formless and invisible,

but indeed exists.

I do not know where it comes from

It seems to have appeared

before the existence of God.

Mitchell 译：

The Tao is like a well:

used but never used up.

It is like the eternal void:

filled with infinite possibilities.

It is hidden but always present.

I don't know who gave birth to it.

It is older than God.

孔德之容，为道是从。道之为物，惟恍惟惚。惚兮恍兮，其中有象；恍兮惚兮，其中有物；窈兮冥兮，其中有精；其精甚真，其中有信。

Waley 译：

Such the scope of the All-pervading Power

That it alone can act through the Way

For the Way is a thing impalpable, incommensurable

Incommensurable, impalpable.

Yet latent in it are forms;

Impalpable, incommensurable

Yet within it there are entities.

Shadowy it is and dim;

Yet within it there is a force,

A force that though rarefied

Is none the less efficacious.

Legge 译：

The grandest forms of active force

From Tao come, their only source.
Who can of Tao the nature tell?
Our sight it flies, our touch as well.
Eluding sight, eluding touch,
The forms of things all in it crouch;
Eluding touch, eluding sight,
There are their semblances, all right.
Profound it is, dark and obscure;
Things' essences all there endure.
Those essences the truth enfold
Of what, when seen, shall then be told.
Now it is so; it was so of old.

许渊冲译：

The content of great virtue

conforms to the divine law.

The divine law is something

which seems to be and not to be.

What seems to exist and does not exist?

It is the image.

What seems not to exist but exists?

It is the image of something.

What seems deep and dark?

It is the essence.

The essence is very true,

for we believe in it.

辜正坤译：

The forms of the great Teh (virtue)

Exclusively depend on Tao.

Tao as a thing

Is vague and indefinite

Vague and indefinite,

It presents images;

Indefinite and vague,

It embodies substance

Distant and dark,

It embraces semen-like essence

The essence is a genuine existence

That can be tested as true.

Mitchell 译：

The Master keeps her mind

always at one with the Tao;

that is what gives her her radiance.

The Tao is ungraspable.

How can her mind be at one with it?

Because she doesn't cling to ideas.

The Tao is dark and unfathomable.

How can it make her radiant?

Because she lets it.

Since before time and space were,

the Tao is.

It is beyond is and is not.

How do I know this is true?

I look inside myself and see.

持而盈之，不如其已；揣而锐之，不可长保。
金玉满堂，莫之能守。富贵而骄，自遗其咎。
功遂身退，天之道也！

Waley 译：

Stretch a bow to the very full,

And you will wish you had stopped in time;

Temper a sword-edge to its very sharpest,

And you will find it soon grows dull.

When bronze and jade fill your hall.

It can no longer be guarded.

Wealth and place breed insolence.

That brings ruin in its train.

When your work is done, then withdraw!

Such is Heaven's Way.

Legge 译：

It is better to leave a vessel unfilled, than to attempt to carry it when it is full. If you keep feeling a point that has been sharpened, the point cannot long preserve its sharpness.

When gold and jade fill the hall, their possessor cannot keep them safe. When wealth and honours lead to arrogancy, this brings its evil on itself. When the work is done, and one's name is becoming distinguished, to withdraw into obscurity is the way of Heaven.

许渊冲译：

Don't hold your fill
but refrain from excess.
A whetted and sharpened sword
cannot be sharp for ever.
A houseful of gold and jade
cannot be safeguarded.
Arrogance of wealth and power
will bring ruin.
Withdrawal after success
conforms to the divine law.

辜正坤译：

One should stop in due time
Rather than fill it to the brim.
When a point is whittled too sharp,
Its sharpness cannot remain long.
When a hall is full of gold and jade,
Nobody can keep them long;
When a man of wealth and rank is arrogant,
He is looking for a calamity upon himself.
When one succeeds and subsequently retires,
He follows the true way of Heaven.

Mitchell 译：

Fill your bowl to the brim
and it will spill.
Keep sharpening your knife

and it will blunt.
Chase after money and security
and your heart will never unclench.
Care about people's approval
and you will be their prisoner.
Do your work, then step back.
The only path to serenity.

五、练习与思考

1. 分析题
（1）分析比较 Waley、Legge、Mitchell，许渊冲和辜正坤五个译本，各自是何特征。
（2）以上各译本用了什么翻译策略和手段，具体体现在哪里？

2. 实训题
翻译以下段落。
（1）　　　　　　　　明白四达，
　　　　　　　　　　能无知乎？
　　　　　　　　　　生而畜之，
　　　　　　　　　　生而不有，
　　　　　　　　　　为而不恃，
　　　　　　　　　　长而不宰，
　　　　　　　　　　是谓玄德。
（2）　　　　　　　　致虚极，守静笃。
　　　　　　　　　　万物并作，
　　　　　　　　　　吾以观复。
　　　　　　　　　　夫物芸芸，
　　　　　　　　　　各复归其根。
　　　　　　　　　　归根曰静，
　　　　　　　　　　是曰复命。
　　　　　　　　　　复命曰常，
　　　　　　　　　　知常曰明。

3. 思考题
（1）哲学著作翻译要注意哪些方面的问题？

（2）《道德经》的各个译本对文化词语是如何处理的？

（3）你喜欢哪位译者的译本？为什么？

六、参考文献

［1］ James Legge. Tao Te Ching［M］. New York：Dover Publications Inc.，1997.

［2］ Stephen Mitchell. Tao Te Ching［M］. New York：Harper Perennial，1994.

［3］ Waley Arthur. TAO TE CHING［M］.北京：外语教学与研究出版社，1999.

［4］ 许渊冲.Laws Divine and Human［M］.北京：五洲传播出版社，2018.

［5］ 林语堂.Wisdom of Laotse［M］.南京：江苏人民出版社，2014.

［6］ 辜正坤.The Book of Tao and Teh［M］.北京：中国对外翻译出版公司，2006.

［7］ 张玥.道德经文化负载词的英译研究［D］.济南：山东大学，2012.

第五课
《庄子》译介赏析

> 《庄子》又称《南华经》，系庄周及其后学所撰。庄子（约前369—前286），名周，曾受号南华仙人，战国时期蒙（今河南商丘东北）人。曾做过漆园吏，后厌恶仕途，隐居著述，是先秦道家学派的代表人物。
>
> 《庄子》约成书于先秦时期。《汉书·艺文志》著录五十二篇，今本三十三篇。其中内篇七，外篇十五，杂篇十一。全书以"寓言""重言""卮言"为主要表现形式，继承老子学说而倡导相对主义，蔑视礼法权贵而倡言逍遥自由，内篇的《齐物论》《逍遥游》和《大宗师》集中反映了此种哲学思想。《庄子》行文汪洋恣肆，瑰丽诡谲，意出尘外，乃先秦诸子文章的典范之作。

一、翻译简介

《庄子》的翻译史超过了千年。早在四五世纪时，《庄子》就随同大量的汉籍经朝鲜半岛流传至日本；在汉唐时期，《庄子》已传播到今越南境内；19世纪下半叶，越来越频繁的中西交流，促使《庄子》出现在欧洲。最初，英国的传教士巴尔福（Balfour）于1881年翻译了《庄子》的相关内容，以 *The Divine Classic of Nan-Hua: Being the Works of Chuang Tsze, Taoist Philosopher. With an Excursus, and Copious Annotations in English and Chinese*（《南华真经：道家哲学家庄子的著作》）为名出版。1889年，翟理斯（Herbert A. Giles）翻译出版了《庄子》的第一本英文全译本：*Chuang Tzu: Mystic, Moralist, and Social Reformer*（《庄子：神秘家、道德家以及社会改革家》）。此后，华滋生（Burton Watson）的 *The Complete Works of Zhuangzi*（《庄子全书》）被公认为是较好的英译本。

国内学者也对《庄子》做了大量翻译。冯友兰的 *Chuang-Tzu: A New Selected Translation with an Exposition of the Philosophy of Kuo Hsiang* 于 1933 年出版,林语堂的选译本 *Chuang-Tzu* 于 1942 年出版,汪榕培借鉴现有的各种英文全译本和选译本译出的 *Zhuang zi*,于 1999 年被收入《大中华文库》出版。

至今,《庄子》已被翻译成英、法、德、芬、日、韩、俄、越等多种译本。译本有全译、节译、编译三种形式。其中,编译主要是学者出于研究目的,将其中的篇章按自己的理解重新归类排序,以供后来学者参考,例如,葛瑞汉(Graham)的 *Chuang-tzǔ: The Seven Inner Chapters and other writings from the book Chuang-tzǔ*(《庄子:内七篇及其他部分篇章》)。

二、书名翻译

《庄子》一书包含内篇七篇,外篇十五,杂篇十一,共计三十三篇。对其书名的翻译一般沿用威妥玛式拼音:Chuang-Tzu。但是,对其中各篇篇名的翻译,则有多种方法。理雅各(James Legge)、冯友兰等比较注重传译《庄子》一书的哲学内涵,而华滋生、葛瑞汉、汪榕培等则兼顾其哲学内涵和文学特点。

因译者的翻译目的、角度和侧重点不同,采取的翻译策略也不尽相同。有的几乎是逐字翻译(如理雅各),有的过于自由甚至改变原文的格局(如葛瑞汉),有的通顺流畅、通俗易懂(如华滋生),有的灵活处理、可读性强(如汪榕培)。

以下选取冯友兰、华滋生两位学者的内篇篇名的译法进行对比:

篇　名	冯友兰译文	华滋生译文
《逍遥游》	The Happy Excursion	Free and Easy Wandering
《齐物论》	On the Equality of Things	Discussion on Making All Things Equal
《养生主》	The Fundamentals for the Cultivation of Life	The Secret of Caring For Life
《人间世》	The Human World	In the World of Men
《德充符》	The Evidence of Virtue Complete	The Sign of Virtue Complete
《大宗师》	The Great Teacher	The Great and Venerable Teacher
《应帝王》	The Philosophy-King	Fit for Emperors and Kings

三、特殊概念的翻译

1. 阴阳

葛瑞汉译:the energies of Yin and Yang

迈尔(Victor H. Mair)译：yin and yang breath

评析："阴""阳"作为哲学概念本身蕴含着极为深厚的文化意义,哲学意义和文化信息的传递也就不会那么直接和简单,这也是翻译文化性的充分体现。

2. 彭祖

冯友兰译：Peng Tsu was the one specially renowned until the present day for his length of life.（脚注：Peng Tsu is said to be a man of the Shang Dynasty, who lived as long as 800 years.）

华滋生译：Yet Pengzu alone is famous today for having lived a long time，...（脚注：He is said to have lived to an incredible old age.）

评析：彭祖何人？只译其名似乎不能令读者通晓其内涵,两位译者采用加注法为译语读者扫清障碍,方便读者的理解。

3. 机

南郭子綦隐机而坐,仰天而嘘,荅焉似丧其耦。

冯友兰译：Nan Kuo Tzu Chi sat leaning on a table. He looked to heaven and breathed gently, seeming to be in a trance and unconscious of his body.

华滋生译：Ziqi of South Wall sat leaning on his armrest, staring up at the sky and breathing — vacant and far away, as though he'd lost his companion.

评析："机"同"几",指小型的矮桌,是战国时期人们日常坐卧家具之一种,常见搭配有"机案"（案桌：table）、"机杖"（几案与手杖：table and cane）、"机筵"（几案和坐席：table and mat）以及"机榻"（几案与床榻：table and bed）。冯译"table"一词大致传达此文化特指项,但混同于一般桌子;华译"armrest",虽易理解,却有误译之嫌。

4. 南面

我欲伐宗、脍、胥敖,南面而不释然。

冯友兰译：Ever since I have been on the throne, I have not been able to put them out of my mind.

华滋生译：Even as I sit on my throne, this thought nags at me.

评析：古代以坐北朝南为尊位,故天子、诸侯见群臣,皆面南而坐。帝位面朝南,故代称帝位。由于英语的 facing south 没有这一特殊含义,不像 way 可以表示"道"那样,所以翻译时不得不舍弃形象,他们不约而同采取意译传达其旨。

四、译文对比赏析

1.《庄子·内篇·逍遥游第一》
THE HAPPY EXCURSION

(1) 北冥有鱼,其名为鲲。鲲之大,不知其几千里也。化而为鸟,其名为鹏。鹏之背,不知其几千里也。怒而飞,其翼若垂天之云。是鸟也,海运则将徙于南冥。南冥者,天池也。

(1) In the Northern Ocean, there is a fish, by the name of *kun*, which is many thousand *li* in size. This fish metamorphoses into a bird by the name of *peng*, whose back is many thousand *li* in breadth. When the bird rouses itself and flies, its wings obscure the sky like clouds. When this bird moves itself in the sea, it is preparing to start for the Southern Ocean, the Celestial Lake.

(冯友兰 译)

In the northern darkness there is a fish and his name is Kun. The Kun is so huge I don't know how many thousand *li* he measures. He changes and becomes a bird whose name is Peng. The back of the Peng measures I don't know how many thousand *li* across, and when he rises up and flies off, his wings are like clouds all over the sky. When the sea begins to move, this bird sets off for the southern darkness, which is the Lake of Heaven.

(华滋生 译)

(2)《齐谐》者,志怪者也。《谐》之言曰:"鹏之徙于南冥也,水击三千里,抟扶摇而上者九万里,去以六月息者也。"野马也,尘埃也,生物之以息相吹也。天之苍苍,其正色邪?其远而无所至极邪?其视下也,亦若是则已矣。且夫水之积也不厚,则其负大舟也无力。覆杯水于坳堂之上,则芥为之舟;置杯焉则胶,水浅而舟大也。风之积也不厚,则其负大翼也无力。故九万里,则风斯在下矣,而后乃今培风;背负青天而莫之夭阏者,而后乃今将图南。

(2) A man named Chi Hsieh, who recorded novel occurrences, said: "When the *peng* is moving to the Southern Ocean, it flaps along the water for three thousand *li*. Then it ascends on a whirlwind up to a height of ninety thousand *li*, for a flight of six months' duration." There is the wandering air; there are the motes; there are living things that blow one against another with their breath. We do not know whether the blueness of the sky is its original color or is simply caused by its infinite height. When the *peng* sees the earth from above, just as we see the sky from below, it will stop

rising and begin to fly to the south. Without sufficient depth, the water would not be able to float a large boat. Upset a cup of water into a small hole, and a mustard seed will be the boat. Try to float the cup, and it will stick, because the water is shallow and the vessel is large. Without sufficient density, the wind would not be able to support the large wings. Therefore, when the *peng* ascends to the height of ninety thousand *li*, the wind is all beneath it. Then, with the blue sky above, and no obstacle on the way, it mounts upon the wind and starts for the south.

(冯友兰译)

The *Universal Harmony* records various wonders, and it says: "When the Peng journeys to the southern darkness, the waters are roiled for three thousand *li*. He beats the whirlwind and rises ninety thousand *li*, setting off on the sixth-month gale." Wavering heat, bits of dust, living things blown about by the wind — the sky looks very blue. Is that its real color, or is it because it is so far away and has no end? When the bird looks down, all he sees is blue too. If water is not piled up deep enough, it won't have the strength to bear up a big boat. Pour a cup of water into a hollow in the floor, and bits of trash will sail on it like boats. But set the cup there, and it will stick fast, for the water is too shallow and the boat too large. If wind is not piled up deep enough, it won't have the strength to bear up great wings. Therefore when the Peng rises ninety thousand *li*, he must have the wind under him like that. Only then can he mount on the back of the wind, shoulder the blue sky, and nothing can hinder or block him. Only then can he set his eyes to the south.

(华滋生译)

(3) 蜩与学鸠笑之曰:"我决起而飞,抢榆枋,时则不至,而控于地而已矣。奚以之九万里而南为?"适莽苍者,三飡而反,腹犹果然;适百里者,宿舂粮;适千里者,三月聚粮。之二虫又何知!

(3) A cicada and a young dove laugh at the *peng*, saying: "When we make an effort, we fly up to the trees. Sometimes, not able to reach, we fall to the ground midway. What is the use of going up ninety thousand *li* in order to start for the south?" He who goes to the grassy suburbs, taking enough food for three meals with him, comes back with his stomach as full as when he started. But he who travels a hundred *li* must grind flour enough for a night's halt. And he who travels a thousand *li* must supply himself with provisions for 3 months. What do these two creatures know?

(冯友兰译)

The cicada and the little dove laugh at this, saying, "When we make an effort and fly up, we can get as far as the elm or the sapanwood tree, but sometimes we don't make it and just fall down on the ground. Now how is anyone going to go ninety thousand *li* to the south!" If you go off to the green woods nearby, you can take along food for three meals and come back with your stomach as full as ever. If you are going a hundred *li*, you must grind your grain the night before; and if you are going a thousand *li*, you must start getting the provisions together three months in advance. What do these two creatures understand?

（华滋生译）

(4) 小知不及大知，小年不及大年。奚以知其然也？朝菌不知晦朔，蟪蛄不知春秋，此小年也。楚之南有冥灵者，以五百岁为春，五百岁为秋；上古有大椿者，以八千岁为春，八千岁为秋，此大年也。而彭祖乃今以久特闻，众人匹之，不亦悲乎！

(4) Small knowledge is not to be compared with the great nor a short life to a long one. How do we know that this is so? The morning mushroom knows not the end and the beginning of a month. The chrysalis knows not the alternation of spring and autumn. These are instances of short life. In the south of the Chu state, there is Ming-ling, whose spring is 500 years and whose autumn is equally long. In high antiquity, there was Ta-chun, whose spring was 800 years and whose autumn was equally long. Peng Tsu was the one specially renowned until the present day for his length of life. If all men were to match him, would they not be miserable?

（冯友兰译）

Little understanding cannot come up to great understanding; the short-lived cannot come up to the long-lived. How do I know this is so? The morning mushroom knows nothing of twilight and dawn; the summer cicada knows nothing of spring and autumn. They are the short-lived. South of Chu there is a caterpillar that counts five hundred years as one spring and five hundred years as one autumn. Long, long ago there was a great rose of Sharon that counted eight thousand years as one spring and eight thousand years as one autumn. They are the long-lived. Yet Pengzu alone is famous today for having lived a long time, and everybody tries to ape him. Isn't it pitiful!

（华滋生译）

(5) 汤之问棘也是已。穷发之北，有冥海者，天池也。有鱼焉，其广数千里，未有知其修者，其名为鲲。有鸟焉，其名为鹏。背若太山，翼若垂天之云。抟扶摇羊角而上者九万里，绝云气，负青天，然后图南，且适南冥也。斥鴳笑之曰："彼且奚适也！我腾跃而上，不过数仞而下，翱翔蓬蒿之间，此亦飞之至也。而彼且奚适也。"此小大之辩也。

(5) In the question put by Tang to Chi, there was a similar statement: In the barren north, there is a sea, the Celestial Lake. In it there is a fish, several thousand *li* in breadth, and no one knows how many *li* in length. Its name is the *Kun*. There is also a bird, named the *peng*, with a back like Mount Tai, and wings like clouds across the sky. Upon a whirlwind it soars up to a height of ninety thousand *li*. Beyond the clouds and atmosphere, with the blue sky above it, it then directs its flight to the south, and thus proceeds to the ocean there. "A quail laughs at it, saying: 'Where is that bird going? I spring up with a bound, and when I have reached not more than a few yards I come down again. I just fly about among the brushwood and the bushes. This is also the perfection of flying. Where is that bird going?" This is the difference between the great and the small.

（冯友兰译）

Among the questions of Tang to Qi we find the same thing. In the bald and barren north, there is a dark sea, the Lake of Heaven. In it is a fish that is several thousand *li* across, and no one knows how long. His name is Kun. There is also a bird there, named Peng, with a back like Mount Tai and wings like clouds filling the sky. He beats the whirlwind, leaps into the air, and rises up ninety thousand *li*, cutting through the clouds and mist, shouldering the blue sky, and then he turns his eyes south and prepares to journey to the southern darkness. The little quail laughs at him, saying, "Where does he think *he's* going? I give a great leap and fly up, but I never get more than ten or twelve yards before I come down fluttering among the weeds and brambles. And that's the best kind of flying, anyway! Where does he think *he's* going?" Such is the difference between big and little.

（华滋生译）

(6) 故夫知效一官，行比一乡，德合一君，而征一国者，其自视也亦若此矣。而宋荣子犹然笑之。且举世而誉之而不加劝，举世而非之而不加沮，定乎内外之分，辩乎荣辱之境。斯已矣。彼其于世，未数数然也。虽然，犹有未树也。

(6) There are some men whose knowledge is sufficient for the duties of some office. There are some men whose conduct will secure unity in some district. There are some men whose virtue befits him for a ruler. There are some men whose ability wins credit in the country. In their opinion of themselves, they are just like what is mentioned

above. Yet Sung Tzu laughed at it. If the whole world should admire him, he would not be encouraged thereby, nor if the whole world should blame him would he thereby be discouraged. He held fast the difference between the internal and the external. He marked distinctly the boundary of honor and disgrace. This was the best of him. In the world such a man is rare, yet there is still something which he did not establish.

（冯友兰译）

Therefore a man who has wisdom enough to fill one office effectively, good conduct enough to impress one community, virtue enough to please one ruler, or talent enough to be called into service in one state, has the same kind of self-pride as these little creatures. Sung Rongzi would certainly burst out laughing at such a man. The whole world could praise Sung Rongzi and it wouldn't make him exert himself; the whole world could condemn him and it wouldn't make him mope. He drew a clear line between the internal and the external, and recognized the boundaries of true glory and disgrace. But that was all. As far as the world went, he didn't fret and worry, but there was still ground he left unturned.

（华滋生译）

（7）夫列子御风而行，泠然善也。旬有五日而后反。彼于致福者，未数数然也。此虽免乎行，犹有所待者也。若夫乘天地之正，而御六气之辩，以游无穷者，彼且恶乎待哉！故曰：至人无己，神人无功，圣人无名。

（7）Lieh Tzu could ride upon the wind and pursue his way, in a refreshing and good manner, returning after fifteen days. Among those who attained happiness, such a man is rare. Yet, although he was able to dispense with walking, he still had to depend upon something. But suppose there is one who chariots on the normality of the universe, rides on the transformation of the six elements and thus makes excursion into the infinite, what has he to depend upon? Therefore, it is said that the perfect man has no self; the spiritual man has no achievement; the true sage has no name.

（冯友兰译）

Lieh Tzu could ride the wind and go soaring around with cool and breezy skill, but after fifteen days he came back to earth. As far as the search for good fortune went, he didn't fret and worry. He escaped the trouble of walking, but he still had to depend on something to get around. If he had only mounted on the truth of Heaven and Earth, ridden the changes of the six breaths, and thus wandered through the boundless, then what would he have had to depend on? Therefore I say, the Perfect Man has no self;

the Holy Man has no merit; the Sage has no fame.

（华滋生译）

2.《庄子·内篇·齐物论第二》
ON THE EQUALITY OF THINGS

《齐物论》是《庄子》的又一代表篇目。"齐物论"包含齐物与齐论两个意思。庄子认为世界万物包括人的品性和感情，看起来是千差万别的，但归根结底却又是齐一的，这就是"齐物"。庄子还认为人们的各种看法和观点，看起来也是千差万别的，但世间万物是齐一的，言论归根结底也应是齐一的，没有所谓是非和不同，这就是"齐论"。"齐物"和"齐论"合在一起便是本篇的主旨。

（1）南郭子綦隐机而坐，仰天而嘘，荅焉似丧其耦。颜成子游立侍乎前，曰："何居乎？形固可使如槁木，而心固可使如死灰乎？今之隐机者，非昔之隐机者也。"子綦曰："偃，不亦善乎，而问之也！今者吾丧我，汝知之乎？女闻人籁，而未闻地籁，女闻地籁，而未闻天籁夫！"子游曰："敢问其方。"子綦曰："夫大块噫气，其名为风。是唯无作，作则万窍怒呺。而独不闻之翏翏乎？山林之畏佳，大木百围之窍穴，似鼻，似口，似耳，似枅，似圈，似臼，似洼者，似污者；激者，謞者，叱者，吸者，叫者，譹者，宎者，咬者，前者唱于而随者唱喁。泠风则小和，飘风则大和，厉风济，则众窍为虚。而独不见之调调之刁刁乎？"子游曰："地籁则众窍是已，人籁则比竹是已，敢问天籁。"子綦曰："夫吹万不同，而使其自己也，咸其自取，怒者其谁邪？"

（1）Nan Kuo Tzu Chi sat leaning on a table. He looked to heaven and breathed gently, seeming to be in a trance, and unconscious of his body. Yen Cheng Tzu Yu, who was in attendance on him, said: "what is this? Can the body become thus like dry wood, and the mind like dead ashes? The man leaning on the table is not he who was here before." "Yen," said Tzu Chi, "your question is very good. Just now, I lost myself, do you understand? You may have heard the music of man, but not the music of earth; you may have heard the music of earth, but not the music of heaven." "I venture," said Tzu Yu, "to ask from you a general description of these." "The breath of the universe," said Tzu Chi, "is called the wind. At times, it is inactive. When it is active, angry sounds come from every aperture. Have you not heard the growing roar? The imposing appearance of mountain forest, the apertures and cavities in huge trees many a span in girth: these are like nostrils, like mouth, like ears, like beam sockets, like goblets, like mortars, like pools, like puddles. The wind goes rushing into them, making the sounds of rushing water, of whizzing arrows, of scolding, of breathing, of shouting, of crying, of deep wailing, of moaning agony. Some sounds are shrill, some deep. Gentle winds produce minor harmonies; violent winds, major ones. When the fierce gusts pass away, all the apertures are empty and still. Have you not seen the bending and quivering of the branches and leaves?" "The music of earth," Tzu Yu said, "consists of sounds produced on the various apertures; the music of man, of sounds produced on pipes and flutes. I venture to ask of what consists the music of heaven." "The winds as they blow," said Tzu Chi, "differ in thousands of ways, yet all are self-produced. Why should there be any other agency to excite them?"

(冯友兰译)

Ziqi south wall sat leaning on his armrest, staring up at the sky and breathing — vacant and far away, as though he'd lost his companion. Yan Cheng Ziyou, who was standing by his side in attendance, said, "What is this? Can you really make the body like a withered tree and the mind like dead ashes? The man leaning on the armrest now is not the one who leaned on it before!" Ziqi said, "You do well to ask the question, Yan. Now I have lost myself. Do you understand that? You hear the piping of men, but you haven't heard the piping of earth. Or if you've heard the piping of earth, you haven't heard the piping of Heaven!" Ziyou, "May I venture to ask what this means?" Ziqi said, "The Great Clod belches out breath, and its name is wind. So long as it doesn't come forth, nothing happens. But when it does, then ten thousand hollows begin crying wildly. Can't you hear them, long drawn out? In the mountain forests that lash and sway, there are huge trees a hundred spans around with hollows and openings like noses, like mouths, like ears, like jugs, like cups, like mortars, like rifts, like ruts. They roar like waves, whistle like arrows, screech, gasp, cry, wail, moan, and howl, those in the lead calling out *yeee*!, those behind calling out *yuuu*! In a gentle breeze they answer faintly, but in a full gale the chorus is gigantic. And when the fierce wind has passed on, then all the hollows are empty again. Have you never seen the tossing and trembling that goes on?" Ziyou said, "By the piping of earth, then, you mean simply [the sound of] these hollows, and by the piping of man, [the sound of] flutes and whistles. But may I ask about the piping of Heaven?" Ziqi said, "Blowing on the ten thousand things in a different way, so that each can be itself — all take what they want for themselves, but who does the sounding?"

(华滋生译)

(2) 大知闲闲,小知间间;大言炎炎,小言詹詹。其寐也魂交,其觉也形开;与接为搆,日以心斗。缦者,窖者,密者。小恐惴惴,大恐缦缦。其发若机栝,其司是非之谓也;其留如诅盟,其守胜之谓也;其杀若秋冬,以言其日消也;其溺之所为之,不可使复之也;其厌也如缄,以言其老洫也。近死之心,莫使复阳也。喜怒哀乐,虑叹变慹,姚佚启态;乐出虚,蒸成菌。日夜相代乎前,而莫知其所萌。已乎,已乎! 旦暮得此,其所由以生乎!

(2) Great knowledge is wide and comprehensive; small knowledge is partial and restricted. Great speech is rich and powerful; small speech is merely so much talk. When people sleep, there is confusion of soul; When awake, there is movement of body. In the association of men with men, there are plotting and scheming, and daily there is striving of mind with mind. There are indecisions, concealments and reservations. Small apprehensions cause restless distress; great apprehensions cause endless fear. The mind of some flies forth, like a javelin, the arbiter of right and wrong. The mind of others remains firm, like a solemn covenanter, the guardian of rights secured. The mind of some fails like decay in autumn and winter. The mind of others is sunk in sensuous pleasure and cannot come back. The mind of yet others has fixed habits like an old drain; it is near to death and cannot be restored to vigor. Joy and anger, sorrow and pleasure, anxiety and regret, fickleness and determination, vehemence and indolence, indulgence and extravagance, these come like music sounding from an empty tube or mushrooms springing out of warmth and moisture. Daily and nightly they alternate within us, but we cannot tell whence they spring. Can we expect in a moment to find out how they are produced?

(冯友兰译)

Great understanding is broad and unhurried; little understanding is cramped and busy. Great words are clear and limpid; little words are shrill and quarrelsome. In sleep, men's spirits go visiting; in waking hours, their bodies hustle. With everything they meet they become entangled. Day after day they use their minds in strife, sometimes grandiose, sometimes sly, sometimes petty. Their little fears are mean and trembly; their great fears are stunned and overwhelming. They bound off like an arrow or a crossbow pellet, certain that they are the arbiters of right and wrong. They cling to their position as though they had sworn before the gods, sure that they are holding on to victory. They fade like fall and winter — such is the way they dwindle day by day. They drown in what they do — you cannot make them turn back. They grow dark, as though sealed with seals — such are the excesses of their old age. And when their minds draw near to death, nothing can restore them to the light. Joy, anger, grief, delight, worry, regret, fickleness, inflexibility, modesty, willfulness, candor, insolence — music from empty holes, mushrooms springing up in dampness, day and night replacing each other before us, and no one knows where they sprout from. Let it be! Let it be! [It is enough that] morning and evening we have them, and they are the means by which we live.

（华滋生译）

（3）非彼无我，非我无所取。是亦近矣，而不知其所为使。若有真宰，而特不得其眹。可行已信，而不见其形，有情而无形。百骸、九窍、六藏，赅而存焉，吾谁与为亲？汝皆说之乎？其有私焉？如是皆有为臣妾乎？其臣妾不足以相治乎？其递相为君臣乎？其有真君存焉！如求得其情与不得，无益损乎其真。一受其成形，不亡以待尽，与物相刃相靡，其行尽如驰，而莫之能止，不亦悲乎！终身役役，而不见其成功；苶然疲役，而不知其所归，可不哀邪！人谓之不死，奚益！其形化，其心与之然，可不谓大哀乎？人之生也，固若是芒乎？其我独芒，而人亦有不芒者乎？夫随其成心而师之，谁独且无师乎？奚必知代，而心自取者有之，愚者与有焉。未成乎心而有是非，是今日适越而昔至也。是以无有为有。无有为有，虽有神禹，且不能知，吾独且奈何哉！

(3) If there is no other, there will be no I. If there is no I, there will be none to make distinctions. This seems to be true. But what causes these varieties? It might seem to be true. But what causes these varieties? It might seem as if there would be a real Lord, but there is no indication of His existence. One may believe that He exists, but we do not see His form. He may have reality, but no form. The hundred parts of the human body, with its nine openings, and six viscera, all are complete in their places. Which shall I prefer? Do you like them all equally? Or do you like some more than others? Are they all servants? Are these servants unable to control each other, but need another as ruler? Do they become rulers and servants in turn? Is there any true ruler other than themselves? Regarding these questions, whether we can obtain true answers or not, it matters but little to the reality of the ruler (if there is one). When once we have received the bodily form complete, its parts do not fail to perform their functions till the end comes. In conflict with things or in harmony with them, they pursue their course with the speed of a galloping horse which cannot ba stopped; is it not deplorable? To be constantly toiling all the time of one's life, without seeing the fruit of one's labour, and to be weary and worn out, without knowing where one is going to; is it not lamentable? Man may say, there is immortality. But what is the use of this saying? When the body is decomposed, so with it is the spirit. Can it not be called very deplorable? Is the life of man, indeed, so ignorant? Am I the only one who is ignorant, but are there others who are not?

（冯友兰译）

Without them we would not exist; without us, they would have nothing to take hold of. This comes close to the matter. But I do not know what makes them the way they are. It would seem as though they have some True Master, and yet I find no trace of him. He can act — that is certain. Yet I cannot see his form. He has identity but no form. The hundred joints, the nine openings, the six organs, all come together and exist here [as my body]. But which part should I feel closest to? I should delight in all parts, you say? But there must be one I ought to favor more. If not, are they all of them mere servants? But if they are all servants, then how can they keep order among themselves? Or do they take turns being lord and servant? It would seem as though there must be some True Lord among them. But whether or not I succeed in discovering his identity, it neither adds to nor detracts from his Truth. Once a man receives this fixed bodily form, he holds on to it, waiting for the end. Sometimes clashing with things, sometimes bending before them, he runs his course like a galloping steed, and nothing can stop him. Is he not pathetic? Sweating and laboring to the end of his days and never seeing his accomplishment, utterly exhausting himself and never knowing where to look for rest — can you help pitying him? I'm not dead yet! he says, but what good is that? His body decays, his mind follows it — can you deny that this is a great sorrow? Man's life has always been a muddle like this. How could I be the only muddled one, and other men not muddled?

(华滋生译)

（4）夫言非吹也，言者有言，其所言者特未定也。果有言邪？其未尝有言邪？其以为异于鷇音，亦有辨乎？其无辨乎？道恶乎隐而有真伪？言恶乎隐而有是非？道恶乎往而不存？言恶乎存而不可？道隐于小成，言隐于荣华。故有儒墨之是非，以是其所非而非其所是。欲是其所非而非其所是，则莫若以明。

（4）If men are to be guided by opinions, who will not have such a guide? Not only those who know the alternations of right and wrong and choose between them have opinions; the fools have theirs too. The case in which there are no opinions, while yet a distinction is made between right and wrong, is as inconceivable as that one goes to Yueh today, but arrived there yesterday. That is to make what is not is. How to make what is not is, even holy Yu could not know. How can I do it? Speech is not merely the blowing of winds. It is intending to say something. But what it is intending to say is not absolutely established. Is there really such a thing as speech? Is there really no such thing as speech? Someone considers speech as different from the chirping of young birds. But is there any distinction between them, or is there no distinction? How is *Tao* obscured that there should be a distinction between true and false? How is speech obscured that there should be a distinction between right and wrong? Where is *Tao* not present? Where is speech not appropriate? *Tao* is obscured by partiality. Speech is obscured by eloquence. The result is the affirmations and denials of the Confucianists and Mohists, the one regarding as right what the other regards as wrong, and regarding as wrong what the other regards as right. If we are to affirm what these two schools both deny, and to deny what they both affirm, there is nothing better than to use the light of reason.

(冯友兰译)

If a man follows the mind given him and makes it his teacher, then who can be without a teacher? Why must you comprehend the process of change and form your mind on that basis before you can have a teacher? Even an idiot has his teacher. But to fail to abide by this mind and still insist on your rights and wrongs — this is like saying that you set off for Yue today and got there yesterday. This is to claim that what doesn't exist exists. If you claim that what doesn't exist exists, then even the holy sage Yu couldn't understand you, much less a person like me! Words are not just wind. Words have something to say. But if what they have to say is not fixed, then do they really say something? Or do they say nothing? People suppose that words are different from the peeps of baby birds, but is there any difference, or isn't there? What does the Way rely on, that we have true and false? What do words rely on, that we have right and wrong? How can the Way go away and not exist? How can words exist and not be acceptable? When the Way relies on little accomplishments and words rely on vain show, then we have the rights and wrongs of the Confucians and the Mohists. What one calls right, the other calls wrong; what one calls wrong, the other calls right. But if we want to right their wrongs and wrong their rights, then the best thing to use is clarity.

(华滋生译)

(5) 物无非彼,物无非是。自彼则不见,自知则知之。故曰彼出于是,是亦因彼。彼是方生之说也,虽然,方生方死,方死方生;方可方不可,方不可方可;因是因非,因非因是。是以圣人不由,而照之于天,亦因是也。是亦彼也,彼亦是也。彼亦一是非,此亦一是非,果且有彼是乎哉? 果且无彼是乎哉? 彼是莫得其偶,谓之道枢。枢始得其环中,以应无穷。是亦一无穷,非亦一无穷也,故曰莫若以明。以指喻指之非指,不若以非指喻指之非指也;以马喻马之非马,不若以非马喻马之非马也。天地一指也,万物一马也。

(5) Everything is "that" (another thing's other); everything is "this" (its own

self). Things do not know that they are another's "that"; they only know that they are "this". The "that" and the "this" produce each other. Nevertheless, when there is life, there is death, and when there is death, there is life. When there is possibility, there is impossibility, and when there is impossibility, there is possibility. Because there is right, there is wrong. Because there is wrong, there is right. On account of this fact, the sages do not take this way, but see things in the light of Heaven. The "this" is also "that". The "that" is also "this". The "that" has a system of right and wrong. The "this" also has a system of right and wrong. Is there really a distinction between "that" and "this"? Or is there really no distinction between "that" and "this"? That the "that" and the "this" cease to be opposites is the very essence of *Tao*. Only the essence, an axis as it were, is the center of the circle responding to the endless changes. The right is an endless change. The wrong is also an endless change. Therefore, it is said that there is nothing better than to use the light of reason. To take fingers in illustration of fingers as not being fingers is not so good as to take non-fingers in illustration of fingers as not being fingers. To take a white horse in illustration of horses as not being horses is not so good as to take non-horse in illustration of horses as not being horses. The universe is a finger; all things are a horse.

（冯友兰译）

Everything has its "that", everything has its "this". From the point of view of "that", you cannot see it; but through understanding, you can know it. So I say, "that" comes out of "this", and "this" depends on "that" — which is to say that "this" and "that" give birth to each other. But where there is birth, there must be death; where there is death, there must be birth. Where there is acceptability, there must be unacceptability; where there is unacceptability, there must be acceptability. Where there is recognition of right, there must be recognition of wrong; where there is recognition of wrong, there must be recognition of right. Therefore the sage does not proceed in such a way but illuminates all in the light of Heaven. He, too, recognizes a "this" but a "this" that is also "that", a "that" that is also "this". His "that" has both a right and a wrong in it; his "this", too, has both a right and a wrong in it. So, in fact, does he still have a "this" and "that"? Or does he, in fact, no longer have a "this" and "that"? A state in which "this" and "that" no longer find their opposites is called the hinge of the Way. When the hinge is fitted into the socket, it can respond endlessly. Its right then is a single endlessness, and its wrong, too, is a single endlessness. So I say, the best thing to use is clarity. To use an attribute to show that attributes are not attributes is not as good as using a nonattribute to show that attributes are not attributes. To use a horse to show that a horse is not a horse is not as good as using a non-horse to show that a horse is not a horse; Heaven and earth are one attribute; the ten thousand things are one horse.

（华滋生译）

五、练习与思考

1. 分析题

分析上文《逍遥游》和《齐物论》两篇译文的翻译手段，试比较冯友兰译本与华滋生译本的区别。

2. 实训题

翻译以下段落。

内篇　养生主第三

吾生也有涯，而知也无涯。以有涯随无涯，殆已；已而为知者，殆而已矣。为善无近名，为恶无近刑。缘督以为经，可以保身，可以全生，可以养亲，可以尽年。

庖丁为文惠君解牛，手之所触，肩之所倚，足之所履，膝之所踦，砉然响然，奏刀騞然，莫不中音，合于桑林之舞，乃中经首之会。

文惠君曰："嘻，善哉！技盖至此乎？"庖丁释刀对曰："臣之所好者，道也，进乎技矣。始臣之解牛之时，所见无非牛者。三年之后，未尝见全牛也。方今之时，臣以神遇而不以目视，官知止而神欲行，依乎天理，批大郤，导大窾，因其固然。技经肯綮之未尝，而况大軱乎！良庖岁更刀，割也；族庖月更刀，折也。今臣之刀十九年矣，所解数千牛矣，而刀刃若新发于硎。彼节者有间，而刀刃者无厚；以无厚入有间，恢恢乎其于游刃必有余地矣，是以十九年而刀刃若新发于硎。虽然，每至于族，吾见其难为，怵然为戒，视为止，行为迟，动刀甚微，謋然已解，如土委地，提刀而立，为之四顾，为之踌躇满志，善刀而藏之。"文惠君曰："善哉！吾闻庖丁之言，得养生焉。"

公文轩见右师而惊曰："是何人也，恶乎介也？天与，其人与？"曰："天也，非人也。天之生是使独也，人之貌有与也。以是知其天也，非人也。"泽雉十步一啄，百步一饮，不蕲畜乎樊中。神虽王，不善也。

老聃死，秦失吊之，三号而出。弟子曰："非夫子之友邪？"曰："然。""然则吊焉若此，可乎？"曰："然。始也吾以为其人也，而今非也。向吾入而吊焉，有老者哭之，如哭其子；少者哭之，如哭其母。彼其所以会之，必有不蕲言而言，不蕲哭而哭者。是遁天倍情，忘其所受，古者谓之遁天之刑。适来，夫子时也；适去，夫子顺也。安时而处顺，哀乐不能入也，古者谓是帝之县解。"

指穷于为薪,火传也,不知其尽也。

3. 思考题
(1) 文言文翻译要注意哪些方面?
(2)《庄子》的两个译本对于文化词语是如何翻译的?
(3) 你喜欢哪位译者的译本?为什么?

六、参考文献

[1] Fung Yu-lan. Chuang Tzu: A Selected Translation with an Exposition of the Philosophy of Kuo Hsiang[M]. Beijing and Heidelberg: Foreign Language Teaching and Research Publishing Co., Ltd and Springer-Verlag Berlin Heidelberg, 2016.

[2] Burton Watson, The Complete Works of Chuang Tzu[M]. New York: Columbia University Press, 2013.

[3] 刘妍.西行漫记:《庄子》在英美的翻译[J].海外英语,2017(14):97-98.

[4] 张爱民.《庄子》在国外的版本注本及译本[J].枣庄学院学报,2008(4):18-22.

[5] 袁思琪.《庄子》英译及其在英语世界的传播[J].海外英语,2016(19):143-145.

[6] 洪琪.浅谈《庄子·内篇》篇名翻译[J].湖北教育学院学报,2007(11):127-129.

[7] 高深.国外《庄子》版本概述[J].出版发行研究,2016(8):86-89.

第六课
《孙子兵法》译介赏析

《孙子兵法》又称《孙武兵法》《吴孙子兵法》《孙子兵书》《孙武兵书》等,为春秋末年的齐国人孙武所著。全书包括计篇、作战篇、谋攻篇、形篇、势篇、虚实篇、军争篇、九变篇、行军篇、地形篇、九地篇、火攻篇、用间篇,分为上、中、下三卷,共有十三篇,故又名《兵法十三篇》。全书虽然只有五千九百多字,但它的价值却备受推崇,对中国古代军事实践起过极其重要的指导作用。《孙子兵法》不仅是中国古代兵学的杰出代表和中国优秀传统文化的重要组成部分,也是世界上最古老的一部伟大的军事著作,被西方学者誉为"兵学圣典"和公认的最具深远影响的三大兵书之一。其内容博大精深,思想精邃富赡,逻辑缜密严谨。它的影响早已超出了军事范畴,而成为指导政治、经济、外交等方面的经典,被翻译成英、俄、德、日等二十多种语言文字,不少国家的军校把它列为必修教材。

正是由于《孙子兵法》的重要地位,这部经典之作已经有国外和国内译者翻译的许多个英文译本,其中比较有影响的译者有 E. F. Calthrop(1905)、Lionel Giles(1910)、Samuel B. Griffith(1963)、袁士槟(1987)、Thomas Cleary(1988)、J. H. Huang(1993)、林戊荪(1994)、Gary Gagliardi(1999)、John Minford(2002)等。

一、翻译简介

作为中华军事典籍,《孙子兵法》已被翻译成种几十种语言,根据屠国元等整理,《孙子兵法》自1905年到2010年间共产生了33个译本。

第一阶段(1905—1910)共产生2个译本。一部是由 E. F. Calthrop 1905 年翻译出版、1908 年修改后再版的译本：*The Book of War: The Military Classic of the Far East*。另一部是 Lionel Giles 于 1910 年在清代孙星衍的《孙子十家注》基础上，重译出版的 *Sun Tzu on the Art of War: The Oldest Military Treatise in the World*。

第二阶段(1943—1969)共产生 6 个译本。E. Machell-Cox(1943)和 A. L. Sadler(1947)分别翻译了一个节译本。Cox 的译本名为 *Principles of War*，Sadler 的译本名为 *The Military Classic of China*。1945 年台北世界图书有限公司出版的郑麐主译的《兵法——约公元前 510 年成书的军事指南》英译本是第一部由华人主译的译本。1963 年台湾学者葛振先(Chen-Sien Ko)的汉英对照版 *The Art of War* 在台北出版，但发行量有限。同年，牛津大学出版了由美国海军陆战队准将 Samuel Griffith 翻译、英国著名战略学家 Liddell Hart 作序的 *The Art of War*，被列入联合国教科文组织的中国代表作翻译丛书，因而取代了 Giles 译本在西方的统治地位，成为经久不衰的畅销书并被确定为权威译本。1969 年，唐子长在台湾编译出版了《孙子重编》(*Principles of Conflict*)，该书中英对照，并配有插图，但发行量有限，影响并不大。

第三阶段(1983—1988)共产生了 4 个译本。1983 年 James Clavell 作序并编订再版了 Giles 的译本，该译本曾被 10 次印刷，影响甚大。1987 年，袁士槟教授翻译出版了陶汉章将军所著的《孙子兵法概论》，该译本汉英对照。1988 年，R. L. Wing 和 Thomas Cleary 的译本先后出版。

第四阶段(1991—2010)是《孙子兵法》英译的高潮期，短短 20 年间，共产生了 21 个译本。1993 年，美国汉学家 Roger T. Ames 以 1972 年在山东临沂出土的西汉简本《孙子》为底本，翻译出版了《孙子兵法：第一个含有银雀山新发现竹简本的英译本》(*The Art of Warfare: the First English Translation Incorporating the Recently Discovered Yin Chueh Shang Text*)。同年，Ralph D. Sawyer 在参考了北京大学李零教授和中国军事科学院吴如嵩教授科研成果的基础上，翻译出版了《武经七书》英译本——《古代中国的七部军事经典》，其中就有《孙子兵法》[*The Art of War* (*History and Warfare*)]。1999 年，Gary Gagliardi 出版了《兵法：孙子之言》(*The Art of War: In Sun Tzu's Own Words*)。2002 年汉学家 John Minford 的英译本出版。同年，iUniverse Star Inc.出版了 Tarver 的 *The Art of War — Sun Tzu's Classic in Plain English with Sun Pin's The Art of Warfare*。还是 2002 这一年，American Denma Translation Group 历时 10 年，翻译出版了《孙子兵法》的英译本 *Sun Tzu's Art of War*，采用了异化的翻译策略。2007 年，汉学家 Victor H. Mair 出版了新版的《孙子兵法》，其特点也是努力忠实原文结构和文本格式。同年，罗志野的《孙子兵法》英汉对照版问世，其译文质量上乘，被列入中译经典文库。2009 年 Minford 翻译的 *The Art of War* 由 Penguin Group 再版。2010 年，Gray 翻译出版了《孙子的智慧》，同年 Trout Lake Media 出版了 *The Art of War* 的音频版。这一阶段的一个特色是，华人译者人数多，其中包括台湾的罗顺德(1991)、大陆翻译家林戊荪(1994)和罗志野(2007)、新加坡的黄昭虎(Chow-Hou Wee)(2003)等。

二、书名翻译

《孙子兵法》的书名翻译多种，比如：

1	The Book of War: The Military Classic of the Far East
2	Sun Tzu on the Art of War: The Oldest Military Treatise in the World
3	Principles of War
4	The Military Classic of China
5	The Art of War
6	Principles of Conflict
7	The Art of Warfare: the First English Translation Incorporating the Recently Discovered Yin Chueh Shang Text
8	The Art of War (History and Warfare)
9	The Art of War: In Sun Tzu's Own Words
10	The Art of War — Sun Tzu's Classic in Plain English with Sun Pin's The Art of Warfare
11	Sun Tzu's Art of War

三、特殊概念的翻译

词汇是语言的建筑材料，也是语言的基本单位，因而词义是各级语义的基础。在词义准确的前提下，短语、句子才可能与原文趋近。中国是个具有上下五千年历史的文明古国，传统文化博大精深，字词的内涵往往特别丰富。比如在不同的领域，汉语的"天"会有不同的含义和译法。作为中华典籍中的一个重要概念，"天"在《老子》中一共出现了14次，表现为一种道。如"人法地，地法天，天法道，道法自然"。老子的"天"是自然之天。"天"在《孙子兵法》中，也出现了14次。在孙子看来，"天者，阴阳，寒暑，时制也。"也即是说，"天"其实就是白天，黑夜，阴雨，晴天和四时季节。"天时地利人和"都是决定战争胜负的重要因素。在现有的译本中，常见的译法有音译 Tian（如袁士槟等），直译 Heaven（如Calthrop、Giles 等）、意译 Nature（如）、weather（如 Griffith、Cleary、袁士槟等）和直译+音译 heaven(tian)（如林戊荪等）四大类。每一种译法都有各自趋近原文的依据。对于英语学习者来说，知道如何用目标语言输出本国文化是势在必行的任务。众所周知，涉及中国传统文化的词汇有很多，在正式开始学习课文之前，有必要了解一些传统文化的词汇的英文解释。一般认为，儒释道是中国文化的三大支柱。来源于这些领域的文化概念的词在典籍中十分普遍。

以下我们将以部分文化词为例，对比袁士槟先生和林戊荪先生对同一汉语文化概念的不同处理：

原文	袁士槟的译法	林戊荪的译法
道	Politics	The way（dao 道）
天	Weather	Heaven（tian 天）
地	Terrain	Earth（di 地）
将	The commander	Command（jiang 将）
法	Doctrine	Rules and regulations（fa 法）
奇	The extraordinary（forces）	Qi tactic（qi 奇）
正	The normal（forces）	Zheng tactic（zheng 正）
通	Accessible	Tong（通）— that which is accessible
挂	Entangling	Gua（挂）— that which enmeshes
支	Temporising	Zhi（支）— that which is disadvantageous to both sides
隘	Having narrow passes	Ai（隘）— that which is narrow and precipitous
险	Precipitous	Xian（险）— that which is hazardous
远	Distant	Yuan（远）— that which is distant
散	Dispersive	Dispersive（san 散）
轻	Frontier	Marginal（qing 轻）
争	Key	Contested（zheng 争）
交	Open	Open（jiao 交）
衢	Focal	Focal（qu 衢）
重	Serious	Critical（zhong 重）
圮	Difficult	Difficult（pi 圮）
围	Encircled	Beleaguered（wei 围）
死	Desperate	Deadly（si 死）

四、译文对比赏析

《孙子兵法》中有很多经典的句子和段落，译成英文之后不同版本的语言特点各不相同。其英译本为数众多，良莠不齐而又各有千秋。我们这里选取了国内比较常见的林戊荪和袁士槟的译本来做对比赏析。

1. 经典句子

(1) 孙子曰：兵者，国之大事，死生之地，存亡之道，不可不察也。——《孙子兵法·计篇》

［注］孙子说：战争是国家的大事，是军队生死之所在，国家存亡之所在，不能不认真考察。

（1）War is a matter of vital importance to the state; a matter of life or death, the road either to survival or to ruin. Hence, it is imperative that it be studied thoroughly.

— *Estimates*   （袁士槟译）

Sunzi said: War is a question of vital importance to the state, a matter of life and death, the road to survival or ruin. Hence, it is a subject which calls for careful study.

— *Making Assessments*   （林戊荪译）

Sun Tzu said: What is war? It may be described as one of the most important affairs to the state. It is the ground of death or life of both soldiers and people, and the way that governs the survival or the ruin of the state. So we must deliberately examine and study it.

Way: in ancient Chinese language "way" means law, principle or reason.

（罗志野译）

Sun Tzu said: the art of war is of vital importance to the State. It is a matter of life and death, a road either to safety or to ruin. Hence it is a subject of inquiry which can on no account be neglected.

（Tr. Lionel Giles）

Sun Tzu said: War is a matter of vital importance to the state; the province of life or death; the road to survival or to ruin. It is mandatory that it be thoroughly studied.

（Tr. Samuel B. Griffith）

> War is
> A grave affair of state;
> It is a place of life and death,
> A road
> To survival and extinction,
> A matter
> To be pondered carefully.

（Tr. John Minford）

(2) 夫未战而庙算胜者，得算多也；未战而庙算不胜者，得算少也。多算胜，少算不

胜,而况于无算乎! 吾以此观之,胜负见矣。——《孙子兵法·计篇》

(2) Now the general who wins a battle makes many calculations in his temple where the battle is fought. The general who loses a battle makes but few calculations beforehand. Thus do many calculation lead to victory and few calculations to defeat: how much more no calculation at all! It is by attention to this point that I can foresee who is likely to win or lose.

(Tr. Lionel Giles)

Now, if the estimates made before a battle indicate victory, it is because careful calculations show that your conditions are more favorable than those of your enemy; if they indicate defeat, it is because careful calculations show that favorable conditions for a battle are fewer. With more careful calculations, one can win; with less, one cannot. How much less chance of victory has one who makes no calculations at all! By this means, one can foresee the outcome of a battle.

— *Estimates* （袁士槟译）

He who makes full assessment of the situation at the prewar council meeting in the temple (translator's note: an ancient Chinese practice) is more likely to win.

He who makes insufficient assessment of the situation at this meeting is less likely to win. This being the case, what chances has he of winning if he makes no assessment at all? With my assessment method, I can forecast who is likely to emerge as victor.

— *Making Assessments* （林戊荪译）

It gives a general greater advantage to win to make military decisions in the temple before fighting a battle, and less advantage if he makes no military decision in the temple before doing battle.

Make military decision in the temple: Doing battle is a matter of vital importance to the nation. The generals must hold a ceremony for military actions and forecasting the outcome of war.

（罗志野译）

(3) 故兵贵胜,不贵久。——《孙子兵法·作战篇》

(3) Hence, what is valued in war is victory, not prolonged operations.

— *Waging War* （袁士槟译）

So, what is important in war is quick victory, not prolonged operations.

— *Waging War* （林戊荪译）

(4) 故知胜有五：知可以战与不可以战者胜；识众寡之用者胜；上下同欲者胜；以虞待不虞者胜；将能而君不御者胜。——《孙子兵法·谋攻篇》

"众寡"的两个译者的理解和译法相去甚远，但都有依据，陶汉章对原文的解释是："善于根据敌对双方兵力对比的众寡情况，正确采用不同的战法。"即"众寡"指敌军力量的多少。

郭化若的解释是"众，指大军队；寡，指小部队。懂得指挥大兵团也懂得指挥小部队的就会胜利。"吴如嵩的解释是"懂得多兵和少兵的不同用法的能胜利。"

(4) Thus, there are five points in which victory may be predicted：

1 He who knows when he can fight and when he cannot will be victorious.

2 He who understands how to fight in accordance with the strength of antagonistic forces will be victorious.

3 He whose ranks are united in purpose will be victorious.

4 He who is well prepared and lies in wait for an enemy who is not well prepared will be victorious.

5 He whose generals are able and not interfered with by the sovereign will be victorious.

—*Offensive Strategy* （袁士槟译）

Therefore, there are five factors to consider in anticipating which side will win, namely：

The side which knows when to fight and when not to will win；

The side which knows the difference between commanding a large army and a small army will win；

The side which has unity of purpose among its officers and men will win；

The side which engages enemy troops that are unprepared with preparedness on its own part will win； and

The side which has a capable commander who is free of interference from the sovereign will win.

—*Attacking by Stratagem* （林戊荪译）

(5) 故曰：知彼知己，百战不殆；不知彼而知己，一胜一负；不知彼，不知己，每战必殆。——《孙子兵法·谋攻篇》

(5) Therefore, I say: Know the enemy and know yourself; in a hundred battles, you will never be defeated. When you are ignorant of the enemy but know yourself, your chances of winning or losing are equal. If ignorant both of your enemy and of

yourself, you are sure to be defeated in every battle.

— *Offensive Strategy* （袁士槟译）

Therefore I say: Know your enemy and know yourself and you can fight a hundred battles without peril. If you are ignorant of the enemy and know only yourself, you will stand equal chances of winning and losing. If you know neither the enemy nor yourself, you are bound to be defeated in every battle.

— *Attacking by Stratagem* （林戊荪译）

(6) 不可胜在己,可胜在敌。故善战者,能为不可胜,不能使敌之必可胜。故曰：胜可知,而不可为。——《孙子兵法·形篇》

(6) Invincibility depends on oneself, but the enemy's vulnerability on himself. It follows that those skilled in war can make themselves invincible but cannot cause an enemy to be certainly vulnerable. Therefore, it can be said that, one may know how to win, but cannot necessarily do so.

— *Dispositions* （袁士槟译）

Invulnerability depends on one's own efforts, whereas victory over the enemy depends on the latter's negligence. It follows that those skilled in warfare can make themselves invincible but they cannot be sure of victory over the enemy. Therefore it is said that victory can be anticipated but it cannot be forced.

— *Disposition*（*xing* 形） （林戊荪译）

(7) 出其所不趋,趋其所不意。行千里而不劳者,行于无人之地也。——《孙子兵法·虚实篇》

(7) Appear at places which he is unable to rescue; move swiftly in a direction where you are least expected. That you may march a thousand li without tiring yourself is because you travel where there is no enemy.

— *Void and Actuality* （袁士槟译）

All this is possible because you appear at places the enemy cannot come to the rescue of and least expects you. That you may march a thousand li without tiring yourself is because you are passing through territory where there is no enemy to stop you.

— *Weaknesses and Strengths*（*xu shi* 虚实） （林戊荪译）

(8) 故用兵之法,无恃其不来,恃吾有以待也;无恃其不攻,恃吾有所不可攻也。——

《孙子兵法·九变篇》

［注］孙子说：用兵的法则，不用寄希望于敌人不来，而要依靠自己做好充分的准备；不要寄希望于敌人不进攻，而要依靠自己拥有力量，使敌人无法进攻。

（8）It is a doctrine of war not to assume the enemy will not come but rather to rely on one's readiness to meet him, and not to presume that he will not attack but rather to make oneself invincible.

— *The nine Variables*　　　　　　　　　　　　　　　　　　　（袁士槟译）

Hence, it is a rule in war that you must not count on the enemy not coming, but always be ready for him; that you must not count on the enemy not attacking, but make yourself so strong that you are invincible.

— *Varying the Tactics*　　　　　　　　　　　　　　　　　　　（林戊荪译）

It is a doctrine of war not to assume the enemy will not come but rather to rely on one's readiness to meet him, and not to presume that he will not attack but rather to make oneself invincible.

（袁士槟译）

It is a rule in war that you must not count on the enemy not coming, but always be ready for him; that you must not count on the enemy not attacking but make oneself so strong that you are invincible.

（林戊荪译）

（9）视卒如婴儿，故可与之赴深溪；视卒如爱子，故可与之俱死。厚而不能使，爱而不能令，乱而不能治，譬若骄子，不可用也。——《孙子兵法·地形篇》

（9）A general regards his men as infants who will march with him into the deepest valleys. He treats them as his own beloved sons and they will stand by him unto death. If a general indulges his men but is unable to employ them, if he loves them but cannot enforce his commands, if the men are disorderly and he is unable to control them, they may be compared to spoiled children, and are useless.

— *Terrain*　　　　　　　　　　　　　　　　　　　　　　　　（袁士槟译）

Because he cares for his soldiers as if they were infants, they will follow him through the greatest dangers. Because he loves his soldiers as if they were his own sons, they will stand by him even unto death. However, if the commander indulges his troops to the point he cannot use them, if he dotes on them to the point he cannot enforce his orders, if his troops are disorderly and he is unable to control them, they will be like spoiled children and useless.

— *The Terrain* （林戊荪译）

(10) 故知兵者，动而不迷，举而不穷。故曰：知彼知己，胜乃不殆；知天知地，胜乃不穷。——《孙子兵法·地形篇》

(10) Therefore, when those experienced in war move, they are never bewildered; when they act, their resources are limitless. And therefore, I say: know the enemy, know yourself; your victory will never be endangered. Know the ground, know the weather; your victory will then be complete.

— *Terrain* （袁士槟译）

Therefore, it is said: Know your enemy and know yourself, victory will not be at risk; know both heaven and earth, and victory will be complete.

— *The Terrain* （林戊荪译）

(11) 将听吾计，用之必胜，留之；将不听吾计，用之必败，去之。——《孙子兵法·计篇》

(11) The general that hearkens to my counsel and acts upon it, will conquer: let such a one be retained in command! The general that hearkens not to my counsel nor acts upon it, will suffer defeat: let such a one be dismissed.

(Tr. Lionel Giles)

If a general who heeds my strategy is employed, he is sure to win. Retain him. When one who refuses to listen to my strategy is employed he is certain to be defeated. Dismiss him.

(Tr. Samuel B. Griffith)

The commanders who follow these stratagems of mine will surely win, and I shall, therefore, stay with them; otherwise, they will definitely lose, I shall leave.

（陈炳富译）

The general who heeds my counsel is sure to win. Such a general should be retained in command. One who ignores my counsel is certain to be defeated, such a one should be dismissed.

（袁士槟译）

The general who employs my assessment methods is bound to win; I shall therefore stay with him. The general who does not heed my words will certainly lose; I shall leave him.

(林戊荪译)

> Heed my plan,
> Employ me,
> And victory is surely yours;
> I will stay.
> Do not heed my plan,
> And even if you did employ me,
> You would surely be defeated;
> I will depart.

(Tr. John Minford)

(12) 凡用兵之法，驰车千驷，革车千乘，带甲十万，千里馈粮。——《孙子兵法·作战篇》

(12) Generally, operations of war require one thousand fast four-horse chariots, one thousand four-horse wagons covered in leather, and one hundred thousand mailed troops.

(Tr. Samuel B. Griffith)

Launching a war will usually involve thousands of chariots, thousands of vehicles loaded with gear and supplies, and a hundred thousand soldiers with food sufficient for a thousand miles march.

(陈炳富译)

(13)（故智将务食于敌,）食敌一钟,当吾二十钟,食敌一石,当吾二十石（或苤秆一石,当吾二十石）。——《孙子兵法·作战篇》

(13)（Hence a wise general makes a point of foraging on the enemy.）One cartload of the enemy's provisions is equivalent to twenty of one's own, and likewise a single picul of his provender is equivalent to twenty of one's own store.

(Tr. Lionel Giles)

(Hence a wise general sees to it that his troops feed on the enemy,) for one zhong of the enemy's provisions is equivalent to twenty of one's own and one shi of the enemy's fodder to twenty shi of one's own.

(袁士槟译)

Hence a wise commander should strive to get provisions in the enemy state. The consumption of one zhong of food from the enemy is equivalent to twenty zhong from his own land; and the consumption of one dan of enemy fodder to twenty dan of his.

Zhong: ancient Chinese unit of dry measure for food; dan: ancient Chinese unit of dry measure for grain.

（罗志野译）

One bushel of the enemy's provisions is worth twenty of our own, one picul of fodder is worth twenty of our own.

(Tr. Sonshi)

One zhong of grains obtained from local area is equal to twenty zhong from the home country; one dan of fodder in the conquered area is equal to twenty dan from the domestic store.

（潘嘉芬、刘瑞芳译）

> One peck
> Of enemy provisions
> Is worth twenty
> Carried from home;
> One picul
> Of enemy fodder
> Is worth twenty
> Carried from home.

(Tr. John Minford)

（14）凡先处战地而待敌者佚，后处战地而趋战者劳。——《孙子兵法·虚实篇》

(14) Whoever is the first in the field and awaits the coming of the enemy, will be fresh for the fight; whoever is the second in the field and has to hasten to battle will arrive exhausted.

(Tr. Lionel Giles)

Generally, he who occupies the field of battle first and awaits his enemy is at ease; he who comes later to the scene and rushes into the fight is weary.

(Tr. Samuel Griffith)

Generally he who occupies the field of battle first and awaits his enemy is rested and prepared; he who comes late to the scene and hastens into battle is weary and passive.

（袁士槟译）

Generally, he who first occupies the field of battle and awaits his enemy is rested and prepared; he who comes later to the scene and hastens into battle is weary and passive.

(林戊荪译)

One who takes position first at the battleground and awaits the enemy is at ease. One who takes position later at the battleground and hastens to do battle is at labor

(Tr. Denma)

(15) 微乎微乎，至于无形；神乎神乎，至于无声。故能为敌之司命。——《孙子兵法·虚实篇》

(15) O divine art of subtlety and secrecy! Through you we learn to be invisible, through you inaudible.

(Tr. Lionel Giles)

Subtle and insubstantial, the expert leaves no trace; divinely mysterious, he is inaudible.

(Tr. Samuel Griffith)

  Subtle! Subtle!
  They become formless.
  Mysterious! Mysterious!
  They become soundless.
  Therefore, they are masters of the enemy's fate.

(Tr. Sonshi)

How subtle and insubstantial, that the expert leaves no trace. How divinely mysterious, that he is inaudible. Thus, he is the master of his enemy's fate.

(潘嘉芬、刘瑞芳译)

How subtle and insubstantial, that the expert leaves no trace. How divinely mysterious, that he is inaudible.

(袁士槟译)

So subtle is the expert that he leaves no trace, so mysterious he makes no sound. Thus, he becomes the arbiter of his enemy's fate.

(林戊荪译)

(16) 纷纷纭纭，斗乱而不可乱也；浑浑沌沌，形圆而不可败也。——《孙子兵法·势篇》

(16) Amid the turmoil and tumult of the battle, there may be seeming disorder at all; amid confusion and chaos, your array may be without head or tail, yet it will be proof against defeat.

(Tr. Lionel Giles)

In the tumult and uproar, the battle seems chaotic, but there must be no disorder in one's own troops. The battlefield may seem in confusion and chaos, but one's array must be in good order.

(袁士槟译)

Amidst the chaos of men and horses locked in battle beneath waving banners, there must be no disorder in command.

(林戊荪译)

In the tumult of battle, the struggle may seem pell-mell, but there is no disorder; In the confusion of the melee, the battle array may seem topsy-turvy, but defeat is out of the question.

(Tr. John Minford)

(17) 凡此五者，将莫不闻，知之者胜，不知者不胜。——《孙子兵法·计篇》

(17) These five heads should be familiar to every general. He who knows them will be victorious; he who knows them not will lose.

(Tr. Lionel Giles)

These five fundamental factors are familiar to every general. Those who master them win and those who do not are defeated.

(袁士槟译)

There is no general who has not heard of these five factors. Yet it is he who masters them that wins and he who does not that loses.

(林戊荪译)

(18) 攻其不备，出其不意。——《孙子兵法·计篇》

(18) Attack him where he is unprepared. Appear where you are not expected.

(Tr. Lionel Giles)

Attack him where he is least prepared. Take action when he least expects you.

(林戊荪译)

(19) 故经之以五事,校之以计,而索其情。一曰道,二曰天,三曰地,四曰将,五曰法。——《孙子兵法·计篇》

(19) The art of war, then, is governed by five constant factors, to be taken into account in one's deliberation when seeking to determine the conditions obtaining in the field. These are: 1) moral law, 2) Heaven, 3) Earth, 4) the Commander, 5) Method and Discipline.

(Tr. Lionel Giles)

The first of these factors is moral influence; the second, weather; the third, terrain; the fourth, command; and the fifth, doctrine.

(Tr. Griffith)

To assess the outcome of a war, we need to examine the belligerent parties and compare them in terms of the following five fundamental factors: The first is the way (dao 道), the second, heaven (tian 天), the third, earth (di 地), the fourth, command (jiang 将), the fifth, rules and regulations (fa 法).

(林戊荪译)

(20) 夫未战而庙算胜者,得算多也;未战而庙算不胜者,得算少也。——《孙子兵法·计篇》

(20) Now the general who wins a battle makes many calculations in his temple ere the battle is fought. The general who loses a battle makes but few calculations beforehand.

(Tr. Lionel Giles)

Now, if the estimates made before a battle indicate victory, it is because careful calculations show that your conditions are more favorable than those of your enemies; if they indicate defeat, it is because careful calculations show that favorable conditions for a battle are fewer.

(袁士槟译)

Now if the estimates made in temple before hostilities indicate victory it is because calculations show one's strength to be superior to that of his enemy; if they indicate defeat, it is because indications show that one is inferior.

(Tr. Samuel B. Griffith)

He who makes full assessment of the situation at the prewar council meeting in the temple (translator's note: an ancient Chinese practice) is more likely to win. He who makes insufficient assessment of the situation at this meeting is less likely to win.

(林戊荪译)

(21) 天者,阴阳,寒暑,时制也。——《孙子兵法·计篇》
(21) Heaven signifies night and day, cold and heat, times and seasons.

(Tr. Lionel Giles)

By weather, I mean the interaction of natural forces; the effects of winter's cold and summer's heat and the conduct of military operations in accordance with the seasons.

(Tr. Samuel B. Griffith)

Heaven is Yin and Yang, cold and hot, the cycle of seasons.

(Tr. John Minford)

Heaven encompasses yin and yang, cold and heat, and the constraints of the seasons.

(Tr. Ralph D. Sawyer)

Heaven comprises yin and yang, cold and heat, the ordering of time.

(Tr. Victor Mair)

Weather signifies night and day, cold and heat, fine days and rain, and change of seasons.

(袁士槟译)

By "heaven", I mean the effects of night and day, of good and bad weather, of winter's cold and summer's heat; in short, the conduct of military operations in accordance with the changes of natural forces.

(林戊荪译)

(22) 日者,月在箕、壁、翼、轸也;凡在此四宿者,风起之日也。——《孙子兵法·火攻篇》
(22) The special days are those when the moon is in the constellations of the Sieve, the Wall, the Wing, or the Cross-bar; for these four are all days of rising wind.

(Tr. Lionel Giles)

  The proper days are
  When the moon is in
  Sagittarius,
  Pegasus,
  Crater,
  Corvus.

>These are the
>Four constellations
>Of rising wind.

(Tr. John Minford)

The days when the moon passes through the constellations of the Winnowing Basket, the Wall, the Wings and the Chariot Platform are the best for launching a fire attack because those are generally the days when the winds rise.

(林戊荪译)

(23) 地者,(简本补:高下)远近、险易、广狭、死生也。——《孙子兵法·计篇》

(23) Earth comprises distances, high and low, great and small; danger and security, open ground and narrow passes; the chances of life and death.

(Tr. Lionel Giles)

Terrain means distances, and refers to whether the ground is traversed with ease or difficulty and to whether it is open or constricted, and influences your chances of life and death.

(袁士槟译)

By "earth", I mean distance, whether it is great of small; the terrain, whether it is treacherous or secure; the land, whether it is open or constricted; the place, whether it portends life or death.

(林戊荪译)

>Earth is
>Height and depth,
>Distance and proximity,
>Ease and danger,
>Open and confined ground,
>Life and death.

(Tr. John Minford)

(24) 故举秋毫不为多力,见日月不为明目,闻雷霆不为聪耳。——《孙子兵法·形篇》

(24) To lift an autumn down requires no great strength; to distinguish between the sun and moon is no test of vision; to hear the thunderclap is no indication of acute hearing.

[Note] Chang Yu: By 'autumn down' Sun Tzu means rabbits' down, which on the coming of autumn is extremely light.

(Tr. Samuel B. Griffith)

To lift an autumn hair is no sign of strength; To see the sun and moon is no sign of sharp sight. To hear thunder is no sign of quick ear.

(Tr. Lionel Giles)

For to lift an autumn down requires no great strength, to distinguish between the sun and moon is no test of vision.

（袁士槟译）

It is like lifting a strand of animal hair in autumn. (translator's note: Animal hair is very fine and light in autumn), which is no sign of strength.

（林戊荪译）

Thus lifting an autumn hair does not mean great strength. Seeing the sun and the moon does not mean a clear eye. Hearing thunder does not mean a keen ear.

(Tr. Denma)

（25）故胜兵若以镒称铢，败兵若以铢称镒。——《孙子兵法·形篇》

（25）The army that conquers as against the army destined to defeat is as a beam against a feather in the scales.

(Tr. Calthrop)

Therefore a victorious army is like a pound compared to a gram, a defeated army is like a gram compared to a pound.

(Tr. Cleary)

Thus a victorious army is a hundredweight balanced against a grain; a defeated army as a grain balanced against a hundredweight.

(Tr. Samuel B. Griffith)

A victorious army is like a ton against an ounce; a defeated army is like an ounce against a ton!

(Tr. Sonshi)

Thus, a victorious army is as one yi (an ancient Chinese weight, approximately equivalent to 24 ounces) balanced against a grain, and a defeated army is as a grain balanced against one yi.

（袁士槟译）

Thus, a victorious army has full advantage over its enemy, just like putting 500 grains against one grain; the opposite is true with an army doomed to defeat, like putting one against 500.

(林戊荪译)

Therefore, a victorious army is as one yi balanced against a grain, and a defeated army is as a grain balanced against one yi.

(潘嘉芬、刘瑞芳译)

A victorious army is like one yi balanced against one zhu while a defeated army is like one zhu balanced against one yi.

yi: an ancient Chinese unit of weight, one yi is 24 liang (1 yi = 50 grammes); zhu: an ancient Chinese unit of weight, one zhu is equal to 1/24 liang.

(罗志野译)

Therefore, a winning Strategy is like a pound balanced against an ounce, while a losing Strategy is like an ounce balanced against a pound.

(Tr. R. L. Wing)

(26) 胜者之战民也,若决积水于千仞之溪者,形也。——《孙子兵法·形篇》

(26) The onrush of a conquering force is like the bursting of pent-up waters into chasm a thousand fathoms deep.

(Tr. Lionel Giles)

It is because of disposition that a victorious general is able to make his soldiers fight with effect of pent-up waters which, suddenly released, plunge into a bottomless abyss.

(袁士槟译)

So great is the disparity of strength that a victorious army goes into battle with the force of an onrushing torrent which, when suddenly released, plunges into a chasm a thousand fathoms deep.

(林戊荪译)

The former has an obvious advantage over the latter. A general who will certainly win commands his men to fight with a force like the bursting of pent-up waters pouring down from a stream ten thousand feet high. This is the disposition of actual military strength.

(罗志野译)

(27) 故政举之日，夷关折符，无通其使，厉于廊庙之上，以诛其事。——《孙子兵法·九地篇》

(27) On the day that you take up your command, block the frontier passes, destroy the official tallies, and stop the passage of all emissaries. Be stern in the council chamber so that you may control the situation.

(Tr. Lionel Giles)

For this reason, on the day the course of war is to be decided, close off the passes, destroy the official tallies and forbid the passage of enemy emissaries. Discuss the plans secretly and finalize your strategy in the ancestral temple.

(林戊荪译)

(28) 诸侯自战其地者，为散地。——《孙子兵法·九地篇》

(28) When a chieftain is fighting in his own territory, it is dispersive ground.

(Tr. Lionel Giles)

When the battle is fought within the territory of one's own state, it is a region that makes for the dispersion of his troops.

(林戊荪译)

(29) 昔殷之兴也，伊挚在夏；周之兴也，吕牙在殷。——《孙子兵法·用间篇》

(29) Of old, the rise of the Yin dynasty was due to I Chih who had served under the Hsia. Likewise, the rise of the Chou dynasty was due to Lu Ya who had served under the Yin.

(Tr. Lionel Giles)

In ancient time, Yi Zhi, who had served the Xia Dynasty, was instrumental in the rise of the Yin (Shang) Dynasty over Xia. Likewise, Lu Ya, who had served the Yin Dynasty, had much to do with the rise of the succeeding Zhou Dynasty.

(林戊荪译)

(30) 三军之众，可使必受敌而无败者，奇正是也。——《孙子兵法·势篇》

(30) To ensure that your whole host may withstand the brunt of the enemy's attack and remain unshaken — this is effected by maneuvers direct and indirect.

(Tr. Lionel Giles)

Making the armies able to take on opponents without being defeated is a matter of unorthodox and orthodox methods.

(Tr. Cleary)

That the army is certain to sustain the enemy's attack without suffering defeat is due to operations of the extraordinary and the normal forces.

(袁士槟译)

Thanks to the combined use of qi（奇）and zheng（正）tactics, the army is able to withstand the onslaught of the enemy forces.

Note: Qi and zheng, as military terminology used in ancient China, are a pair of opposites. Generally, qi denotes the use of unusual and unexpected methods, of sudden, surprise attacks, of flanking movements in military operations; while zheng denotes the use of normal and regular methods, of frontal attacks and defensive moves in military operations.

(林戊荪译)

(31) 故善战者,致人而不致于人。——《孙子兵法·虚实篇》

(31) Therefore those skilled in warfare move the enemy, and are not moved by the enemy.

(Tr. Sonshi)

And, therefore, one skilled in war brings the enemy to the field of battle and is not brought there by him.

(潘嘉芬、刘瑞芳译)

(32) 故用兵之法：十则围之,五则攻之,倍则战之,敌则能分之,少则能守之,不若则避之。——《孙子兵法·谋攻篇》

(32) Generally in warfare:

If ten times of the enemy's strength, surround them; if five times, attack them; if double, divide them; if equal, be able to fight them; if fewer, be able to evade them; if weaker, be able to avoid them.

(Tr. Sonshi)

Consequently, the art of using troops is this: when ten to enemy's one, surround him. When five times his strength, attack him. When double his strength, engage him. If equally matched, be capable of dividing him. If less in number, be capable of defending yourself. If in all respects unfavorable, be capable of eluding him.

(潘嘉芬、刘瑞芳译)

Consequently, the art of using troops is this: when you outnumber the enemy ten to one, surround him; when five to one, attack him; when two to one, divide him; and if equally matched, stand up to him.(tr.: Another version of the text reads:"when two to one, stand up to him; if equally matched, divide him.") If you are fewer than the enemy in number, retreat. If you are no match for him, try to elude him. For no matter how stubbornly a small force may fight, it must in the end succumb to greater strength and fall captive to it.

（林戊荪译）

(33) 掠乡分众,廓地分利,悬权而动。——《孙子兵法·军争篇》

解读：掳掠乡邑,要分兵掠取；扩张疆土,要分兵扼守。权衡形势利害与得失,然后决定行动。

(33) When you plunder the countryside, divide the wealth among your troops. When you expand your territory, divide up and hold places of advantage. Calculate the situation, and then move.

(Tr. Sonshi)

When you plunder the countryside, divide your forces. When you conquer territory, defend strategic points. Weigh the situation before you move.

（潘嘉芬、刘瑞芳译）

When plundering the countryside, divide your forces; when extending your territory, distribute them to hold key points. Weigh the pros and cons before moving into action.

（林戊荪译）

(34) 谆谆翕翕,徐言人言者,失众也。——《孙子兵法·行军篇》

李筌注："谆谆翕翕,窃语貌。"张预注："谆谆,语也。翕翕,聚也。"

全句意为：（敌将）低声同部下讲话的,是失去人心的表现。

(34) If troops constantly gather in small groups and whisper together, he has lost his men.

(Tr. Sonshi)

When the general speaks in meek and subservient tone to his subordinates, he has lost the support of his men.

（潘嘉芬、刘瑞芳译）

When the enemy commander speaks to his subordinates in a meek and halting voice, he has lost their confidence.

（林戊荪译）

（35）道者，令民与上同意者也，故可以与之死，可以与之生，而不畏危（简本为：民勿诡也）。——《孙子兵法·计篇》

[注] 道的含义就是使全国人民，意志统一，精神集中，人民和政府才能同心协力，同生死，共患难，不怕牺牲。

(35) The Moral Law causes the people to be in complete accord with their ruler, so that they will follow him regardless of their lives, undismayed by any danger/without the slightest disloyalty.

(Tr. Lionel Giles)

Politics means the thing which causes the people to be in harmony with their ruler so that they will follow him in disregard of their lives and without fear of any danger.

（袁士槟译）

By "the way", I mean moral influence, or that which causes people to think in line with their sovereign so that they will follow him through every vicissitude, whether to live or to die, without fear of mortal peril.

（林戊荪译）

（36）故杀敌者，怒也；取敌之利者，货也。——《孙子兵法·作战篇》

(36) Now in order to kill the enemy, our men must be roused to anger; that there may be advantage from defeating the enemy, they must have their rewards.

(Tr. Lionel Giles)

In order to make the soldiers courageous in overcoming the enemy, they must be roused to anger. In order to capture more booty from the enemy, soldiers must have their rewards.

（袁士槟译）

In order to embolden your men to annihilate the enemy, you must boost their morale; in order to encourage your men to seize the enemy provisions, you must give them material rewards.

（林戊荪译）

（37）主孰有道？将孰有能？——《孙子兵法·计篇》

(37) Which of the two sovereigns is imbued with the Moral Law? Which of the two generals has most ability?

(Tr. Lionel Giles)

Which ruler is wise and more able? Which commander is more talented?

（袁士槟译）

(38) 吾以此知胜负矣。——《孙子兵法·计篇》

(38) By means of these seven considerations I can forecast victory or defeat.

(Tr. Lionel Giles)

By means of these seven elements, I shall be able to forecast which side will be victorious and which will be defeated.

（袁士槟译）

(39) 不得操事者,七十万家。——《孙子兵法·用间篇》

(39) As many as seven hundred thousand families will be impeded in their labor.

(Tr. Lionel Giles)

And the farm work of seven hundred thousand households will be disrupted.[In ancient China, eight families comprised a community. When a family sent a man to the army, the remaining seven contributed to its support. Thus, when an army of one hundred thousand was raised, those unable to attend fully to their own ploughing and sowing amounted to seven hundred thousand households.]

（袁士槟译）

(40) 众树动者,来也；众草多障者,疑也。——《孙子兵法·行军篇》

(40) Movement amongst trees of a forest shows that the enemy is advancing. The appearance of a number of screens in the the midst of thick grass means that the enemy wants to make us suspicious.

(Tr. Lionel Giles)

When the trees are seen to move, it means the enemy is advancing. When many screens have been placed in the undergrowth, it is for the purpose of deception.

（袁士槟译）

(41) 声不过五,五声之变,不可胜听也。色不过五,五色之变,不可胜观也。味不过

五,五味之变,不可胜尝也。——《孙子兵法·势篇》

[注]五声:宫商角徵羽;五色:青黄赤白黑;五味:酸咸辛苦甘。

(41) There are five notes; but by combinations, innumerable harmonies are produced. There are but five colours; but if we mix them, the shades are infinite. There are five tastes, but if we mix them, there are more flavours than the palate can distinguish. (Note: The five cardinal tastes are acridity, bitterness, sourness, sweetness and saline taste.)

(Tr. Calthrop)

The musical notes are only five in number, but their combination gives rise to so numerous melodies that one cannot hear them all. The primary colours are only five in number, but their combinations are so infinite that one cannot visualize them all. The flavours are only five in number, but their blends are so various that one cannot taste them all.

(袁士槟译)

There are only five musical notes, but their varied combinations bring about melodies more pleasing and wonderful than ever heard. There are only five basic colours, but their variations and blending produce colours more beautiful and splendid than ever seen. There are only five cardinal tastes, but their mixture yields flavour more delicious and savoury than ever tasted.

In ancient China, the people considered that there were five musical notes, namely: gong, shang, jue, zhi and yu; five basic colours, namely: blue, yellow, red, white and black; and five cardinal tastes, namely: sour, salty, pungent, bitter and sweet.

(罗志野译)

(42) 昔殷之兴也,伊挚在夏;周之兴也,吕牙在殷。——《孙子兵法·用间篇》

(42) In old times, the rise of the Shang Dynasty was due to Yi Zhi, who had served under the Xia, and likewise the rise of the Zhou Dynasty was due to Lu Ya, who had served under the Yin.

(袁士槟译)

In ancient history, the rise of Yin was due to Yi Zhi, who was former minister of Xia; and the rise of the Zhou Dynasty was due to Jiang Zhiya, the former minister of Shang.

(罗志野译)

(43) 无邀正正之旗,勿击堂堂之阵,此治变者也。——《孙子兵法·军争篇》

(43) To refrain from intercepting an enemy whose banners are in perfect order,

to refrain from attacking an army drawn up in calm and confident array: — this is the art of studying the circumstances.

(Tr. Lionel Giles)

Do not engage well-ordered pennants. Do not strike imposing formations. This is ordering transformation.

(Tr. Denma)

(44) 利而诱之,乱而取之,实而备之,强而避之,怒而挠之,卑而骄之,佚而劳之,亲而离之。——《孙子兵法·计篇》

(44) Offer the enemy a bait to lure him; feign disorder and strike him. When he concentrates, prepare against him; where he is strong, avoid him. Anger his general and confuse him. Pretend inferiority and encourage his arrogance. Keep him under a strain and wear him down. When he is united, divide him.

(Tr. Griffith)

Hold out baits to entice the enemy. Feign disorder and crush him. If he is in superior strength, evade him. If your opponent is of choleric temper, seek to irritate him. Pretend to be weak, that he may grow arrogant. If he is taking his ease, give him no rest.

(Tr. Lionel Giles)

Thus when he seeks advantage, lure him. When he is in chaos, take him. When he is substantial, prepare against him. When he is strong, avoid him. When he is wrathful, harass him. When he is humble, make him proud. When he is at ease, make him labor. When he is in kinship, separate him.

(Tr. Denma)

When the enemy is greedy for gains hand out a bait to lure him; when he is in disorder, attack and overcome him; when he boasts substantial strength, be doubly prepared against him; and when he is formidable, evade him. If he is given to anger, provoke him. If he is timid and careful, encourage his arrogance.

(林戊荪译)

(45) 乱生于治,怯生于勇,弱生于强。治乱,数也;勇怯,势也;强弱,形也。——《孙子兵法·势篇》

(45) Simulated disorder postulates perfect discipline; simulated fear postulates courage; simulated weakness postulates strength. Hiding order beneath the cloak of

disorder is simply a question of subdivision; concealing courage under a show of timidity presupposes a fund of latent energy; masking strength with weakness is to be effected by tactical dispositions.

（Tr. Lionel Giles）

Chaos is born from order. Cowardice is born from bravery. Weakness is born from strength. Order and chaos are a matter of counting. Bravery and cowardice are a matter of shih. Strength and weakness are a matter of form.

（Tr. Denma）

（46）故兵闻拙速，未睹巧之久也。——《孙子兵法·作战篇》

（46）While we have heard of stupid haste in war, we have not yet seen a clever operation that was prolonged.

（袁士槟译）

While we have heard of blundering in seeking swift decisions in war, we have yet to see a smart operation that drags on endlessly.

（林戊荪译）

（47）取用于国，因粮于敌。——《孙子兵法·作战篇》

（47）They carry military equipment from the homeland, but rely on the enemy for provisions.

（袁士槟译）

They obtain their military supplies from home but commandeer provisions from the enemy territory.

（林戊荪译）

（48）力屈、财殚，中原内虚于家。——《孙子兵法·作战篇》

（48）With this loss of wealth and exhaustion of strength the households in the country will be extremely poor.

（袁士槟译）

With military strength thus depleted and wealth consumed, the people's homes will be stripped bare.

（林戊荪译）

(49) 鸷鸟之疾，至于毁折者，节也。——《孙子兵法·势篇》

(49) When the strike of a hawk breaks the body of its prey, it is because of timing.

（袁士槟译）

When falcons strike and destroy their prey, it is because of perfect timing.

（林戊荪译）

(50) 斗众如斗寡。《孙子兵法·势篇》

(50) And to direct a large force is the same as to direct a few men.

（袁士槟译）

There is no difference between commanding a large army and a small one.

（林戊荪译）

(51) 故小敌之坚，大敌之擒也。——《孙子兵法·谋攻篇》

[注] 据褚良才解释："小"和"大"都是使动词，表示"使敌小则坚""使敌大则擒"的意思。故译文有误。

(51) For a small force is but booty for one more powerful if it fights recklessly.

（袁士槟译）

For no matter how stubbornly a small force may fight, it must in the end succumb to greater strength and fall captive to it.

（林戊荪译）

(52) 不知三军之事而同三军之政者，则军士惑矣。——《孙子兵法·谋攻篇》

(52) When ignorant of military affairs, to interfere in their administration. This causes officers to be perplexed.

（袁士槟译）

He interferes with the administration of the army when he is ignorant of its internal affairs, thus causing confusion among the officers and men.

（林戊荪译）

(53) 地形有通者，有挂者，有支者，有隘者，有险者，有远者。——《孙子兵法·地形篇》

(53) Sun Tzu said: Ground may be classified according to its nature as accessible, entrapping, indecisive, constricted, precipitous, and distant.

（Tr. Samuel B. Griffith）

Master Sun said: There are different forms of terrain:
> Accessible terrain,
> Entangling terrain,
> Deadlock terrain,
> Enclosed terrain,
> Precipitous terrain,
> Distant terrain.

（Tr. John Minford）

Ground may be classified according to its nature as accessible, entangling, temporising, precipitous, distant, or having narrow passes.

（袁士槟译）

There are the following six terrains: tong — that which is accessible; gua — that which enmeshes, zhi — that which is disadvantageous to both sides; ai — that which is narrow and precipitous; xian — that which is hazardous; and yuan — that which is distant.

（林戊荪译）

（54）善守者，藏于九地之下；善攻者，动于九天之上。——《孙子兵法·形篇》

（54）Those who are skilled in defence, hide themselves under the ninefold earth; [in ancient China, the number nine was used to signify the highest number] Those in attack flash force as from above the ninefold heavens.

（袁士槟译）

He who is skilled in defense positions his forces in place as safe and in accessible as in the depth of the earth, whereas he who is skilled in attack strikes as from the highest reaches of heaven.

（林戊荪译）

（55）非人之将也，非主之佐也，非胜之主也。——《孙子兵法·用间篇》

（55）Such a man is no general, no good assistant to his sovereign, and such a sovereign no master of victory.

（袁士槟译）

Such a person is no commander worthy of his soldiers, no counselor worthy of his sovereign, no master of victory.

（林戊荪译）

(56) 兵非益多也，惟无武进，足以并立，料敌，取人而已。——《孙子兵法·行军篇》

［注］"取人"有不同的理解：是"取胜于敌"？还是"任用贤将"？学术界没有定论。

(56) In war, numbers alone confer no advantage. It is sufficient if you do not advance relying on sheer military power. If you estimate the enemy situation correctly and then concentrate your strength to overcome the enemy, there is no more to it than this.

（袁士槟译）

The strength of an army does not lie in mere numbers. Do not advance recklessly. So long as you can concentrate your own forces, have a clear picture of the enemy's situation and secure the full support of your men, that is sufficient.

（林戊荪译）

(57) 兵者，国之大事，死生之地，存亡之道，不可不察也。——《孙子兵法·计篇》

(57) War is a matter of vital importance to the state; the province of life and death, the road to survival or ruin. It is mandatory that it be thoroughly studied.

（Tr. Griffith）

Military action is important to the nation — it is the ground of death and life, the path of survival and destruction, so it is imperative to examine it.

（Tr. Thomas Cleary）

War is
A grave affair of state;
It is a place
Of life and death,
A road
To survival and extinction,
A matter
To be pondered carefully.

（Tr. John Minford）

War is a matter of vital importance to the state; a matter of life or death, the road either to survival or to ruin. Hence, it is imperative that it be studied thoroughly.

（袁士槟译）

War is a matter of vital importance to the state, a matter of life and death, the road to survival or ruin. Hence, it is a subject which calls for careful study.

（林戊荪译）

(58) 故经之以五事，较之以计，而索其情。一曰道，二曰天，三曰地，四曰将，五曰法。——《孙子兵法·计篇》

(58) The first of these factors is moral influence, the second, weather, the third, terrain, the fourth, command, and the fifth, doctrine.

(Tr. Samuel Griffith)

(The art of war is, then, governed by five constant factors, to be taken into account in one's deliberations, when seeking to determine the conditions obtaining in the field.) These are (1) the Moral Law; (2) Heaven; (3) Earth; (4) the Commander; (5) Method and Discipline.

(Tr. Lionel Giles)

Therefore measure in terms of five things, use these assessments to make comparisons, and thus find out what the conditions are. The five things are the way, the weather, the terrain, the leadership, and discipline.

(Tr. Thomas Leary)

  There are Five Fundamentals
  For this deliberation,
  For the making of comparison
  And the assessing of the conditions;
  The Way,
  Heaven,
  Earth,
  Command,
  Discipline.

(Tr. John Minford)

(Therefore, appraise it in terms of the five fundamental factors and make comparisons of the various conditions of the antagonistic sides in order to ascertain the results of a war.) The first of these factors is politics; the second one, weather; the third, terrain; the fourth, commanders; and the fifth, doctrine.

（袁士槟译）

(1) morality; (2) heaven; (3) land; (4) the commander and; (5) discipline.

（陈炳富译）

(59) 是故朝气锐，昼气惰，暮气归。——《孙子兵法·军争篇》

(59) Now a soldier's spirit is keenest in the morning; by noonday it has begun to flag; and in the evening his mind is bent only on returning to camp. Notes: Always provided, I suppose, that he has had breakfast. And at the battle of the Trebia, the Romans were foolishly allowed to fight fasting, whereas Hannibal's men had breakfasted at their leisure.

(Tr. Lionel Giles)

During the early morning spirits are keen, during the day they flag, and in the evening thoughts turn toward home. Notes: Mei Yao-chen (梅尧臣) says that "morning" "day" "evening" represent the phases of a long campaign.

(Tr. Samuel B. Griffith)

At the beginning of a campaign, soldier's morale is high, after a while it begins to flag and in the end it is gone.

(林戊荪译)

2. 经典段落
(1) 故经之以五事，校之以计而索其情：一曰道，二曰天，三曰地，四曰将，五曰法。道者，令民与上同意也，故可以与之死，可以与之生，而不畏危。天者，阴阳、寒暑、时制也。地者，远近、险易、广狭、死生也。将者，智、信、仁、勇、严也。法者，曲制、官道、主用也。

——《孙子兵法·计篇》

(1) Therefore, appraise it in terms of the five fundamental factors and make comparisons of the various conditions of the antagonistic sides in order to ascertain the results of a war. The first of these factors is politics; the second, weather; the third, terrain; the fourth, the commander; and the fifth, doctrine. Politics means the thing which causes the people to be in harmony with their ruler so that they will follow him in disregard of their lives and without fear of any danger. Weather signifies night and day, cold and heat, fine days and rain, and change of seasons. Terrain means distances, and refers to whether the ground is traversed with ease or difficulty and to whether it is open or constricted, and influences your chances of life or death. The commander stands for the general's qualities of wisdom, sincerity, benevolence, courage, and strictness. Doctrine is to be understood as the organization of the army, the gradations of rank among the officers, the regulations of supply routes, and the provision of military materials to the army.

— *Estimates*

(袁士槟译)

To assess the outcome of a war, we need to examine the belligerent parties and compare them in terms of the following five fundamental factors:

The first is the way (dao 道); the second, heaven (tian 天); the third, earth (di 地); the fourth, command (jiang 将); and the fifth, rules and regulations (fa 法).

By "the way", I mean moral influence, or that which causes the people to think in line with their sovereign so that they will follow him through every vicissitude, whether to live or to die, without fear of moral peril.

By "heaven", I mean the effects of night and day, of good and bad weather, of winter's cold and summer's heat; in short, the conduct of military operations in accordance with the changes of natural forces.

By "earth", I mean distance, whether it is great or small; the terrain, whether it is treacherous or secure; the land, whether it is open or constricted; and the place, whether it portends life or death.

By "command", I mean the wisdom, trustworthiness, benevolence, courage and firmness of the commander.

By "rules and regulations", I mean the principles guiding the organization of army units, the appointment and administration of officers and the management of military supplies and expenditures.

— *Making Assessments* （林戊荪译）

(2) 孙子曰：凡用兵之法，全国为上，破国次之；全军为上，破军次之；全旅为上，破旅次之；全卒为上，破卒次之；全伍为上，破伍次之。是故百战百胜，非善之善者也；不战而屈人之兵，善之善者也。

——《孙子兵法·谋攻篇》

(2) Generally, in war the best policy is to take a state intact; to ruin it is inferior to this. To capture the enemy's entire army is better than to destroy it; to take intact a regiment, a company, or a squad is better than to destroy them. [Regiment, company, and squad are lu, zu, and wu in Chinese. In ancient China, five hundred soldiers made up a lu, one hundred a zu, and five a wu.] For to win one hundred victories in one hundred battles is not the acme of skill. To subdue the enemy without fighting is the supreme excellence.

— *Offensive Strategy* （袁士槟译）

Sunzi said: Generally in war, the best policy is to take the enemy state whole and intact, to destroy it is not. To have the enemy's army surrender in its entirety is better than to crush it; likewise, to take a battalion, a company or a five-man squad intact is better than to destroy it. Therefore, to fight a hundred battles and win each and every one of them is not the wisest thing to do. To break the enemy's resistance without fighting is.

— *Attacking by Stratagem* （林戊荪译）

(3) 微乎微乎，至于无形；神乎神乎，至于无声。故能为敌之司命。进而不可御者，冲其虚也；退而不可追者，速而不可及也。故我欲战，敌虽高垒深沟，不得不与我战者，攻其所必救也；我不欲战，画地而守之，敌不得与我战者，乖其所之也。

——《孙子兵法·虚实篇》

(3) How subtle and insubstantial, that the expert leaves no trace. How divinely mysterious, that he is inaudible. Thus, he is master of his enemy's fate. His offensive will be irresistible if he makes for his enemy's weak positions; he cannot be overtaken when he withdraws if he moves swiftly. When I wish to give battle, my enemy, even though protected by high walls and deep moats, cannot help but engage me, for I attack a position he must relieve. When I wish to avoid battle, I may defend myself simply be drawing a line on the ground; the enemy will be unable to attack me because I divert him from going where he wishes.

— *Void and Actuality* （袁士槟译）

So subtle is the expert that he leaves no trace, so mysterious that he makes no sound. Thus, he becomes the arbiter of his enemy's fate. His advance is irresistible because he plunges into his enemy's weak position; and his withdrawal cannot be overtaken because it is so swift. Thus, when we wish to give battle, the enemy cannot but leave his position to engage us even though he is safe behind high walls and deep moats, because we attack a position he must rescue. When we wish to avoid battle, we may simply draw a line on the ground by way of defense and the enemy cannot engage us because we have diverted him to a different target.

— *Weaknesses and Strengths*（*xu shi* 虚实） （林戊荪译）

(4) 夫兵形象水，水之形，避高而趋下，兵之形，避实而击虚。水因地而制流，兵因敌而制胜。故兵无常势，水无常形，能因敌变化而取胜者，谓之神。故五行无常胜，四时无常位，日有短长，月有死生。

——《孙子兵法·虚实篇》

(4) Now, an army may be likened to water, for just as flowing water avoids the heights and hastens to the lowlands, so an army should avoid strength and strike

weakness. And as water shapes its flow in accordance with the ground, so an army manages its victory in accordance with the situation of the enemy. And as water has no constant form, there are in warfare no constant conditions. Thus, one able to win the victory by modifying his tactics in accordance with the enemy situation may be said to be divine. Of the five elements [water, fire, metal, wood, and earth], none is always predominant; of the four seasons, none lasts forever; of the days, some are long and some short, and the moon waxes and wanes. That is also the law of employing troops.

— *Void and Actuality*　　　　　　　　　　　　　　　　　　　（袁士槟译）

Now the law governing military operations is as that governing the flow water, which always evades high points, choosing lower ones instead. To operate the army successfully, we must avoid the enemy's strong points and seek out his weak points. As the water changes its course in accordance with the contours of the terrain, so a warrior changes his tactics in accordance with the enemy's changing situation. There is no fixed pattern in the use of tactics in war, just as there is no constant course in the flow of water. He who wins modifies his tactics in accordance with the changing enemy situation and this works miracles. None of the five elements of nature（wuxing 五行）is ever predonimant, and none of the four seasons lasts forever. Some days are longer and some shorter. The moon waxes and wanes.

— *Weaknesses and Strengths*（*xu shi* 虚实）　　　　　　　　（林戊荪译）

（5）故不知诸侯之谋者，不能豫交；不知山林、险阻、沮泽之形者，不能行军；不用乡导者，不能得地利。故兵以诈立，以利动，以分合为变者也。故其疾如风，其徐如林，侵掠如火，不动如山，难知如阴，动如雷震。掠乡分众，廓地分利，悬权而动。先知迂直之计者胜，此军争之法也。

——《孙子兵法·军争篇》

（5）One who is not acquainted with the designs of his neighbors should not enter into alliances with them. Those who do not know the conditions of mountains and forests, hazardous defiles, marshes and swamps, cannot conduct the march of an army. Those who do not use local guides are unable to obtain the advantages of the ground. Now, war is based on deception. Move when it is advantageous and create changes in the situation by dispersal and concentration of forces. When campaigning, be swift as the wind; in leisurely marching, majestic as the forest; in raiding and plundering, be fierce as fire; in standing, firm as the mountains. When hiding, be as unfathomable as things behind the clouds; when moving, fall like a thunderbolt. When you plunder the countryside, divide your forces. When you conquer territory, defend strategic points. Weigh the situation before you move. He who knows the artifice of diversion will be victorious. Such is the art of manoeuvring.

— *Manoeuvring*　　　　　　　　　　　　　　　　　　　　　　（袁士槟译）

Unless you know the strategic intentions of the rulers of the neighbouring states, you cannot enter into alliances with them; unless you know the lay of the land — its mountains and forests, its natural hazards, its rivers and marshes — you cannot maneuver your troops on it; unless you employ local guides, you cannot turn the terrain to your advantage.

Now war is a game of deception. Move when it is advantageous, and disperse and concentrate as necessary to bring about changes in file military situation advantageous to your forces. When the army advances, it is as swift as the wind; when it is immobile, as still as the forest; when it attacks, as destructive as a fire; when it defends, as immovable as the mountain; when it conceals itself, it is as though hidden behind an overcast sky; and when it, strikes, it can be as sudden as a thunder bolt. When plundering the countryside, divide your forces; when extending your territory, distribute them to hold key points. Weigh the pros and cons before moving into action. He who masters the tactics of turning the tortuous into the direct will be the victor. That is the essence of the armed contest.

— *Contest to Gain the Initiative*　　　　　　　　　　　　　　（林戊荪译）

(6) 故三军可夺气，将军可夺心。是故朝气锐，昼气惰，暮气归。故善用兵者，避其锐气，击其惰归，此治气者也。以治待乱，以静待哗，此治心者也。以近待远，以佚待劳，以饱待饥，此治力者也。无邀正正之旗，勿击堂堂之阵，此治变者也。

——《孙子兵法·军争篇》

(6) Now, an army may be robbed of its spirit and its commander deprived of his confidence. At the beginning of a campaign, the spirits of soldiers are keen; after a certain period of time, they flag, and in the later stage thoughts turn towards home. And therefore, those skilled in war avoid the enemy when his spirit is keen and attack him when it is sluggish and his soldiers homesick. This is the control of the moral factor. In good order, they await a disorderly enemy; in serenity, a clamorous one. This is control of the mental factor. Close to the field of battle, they await an enemy coming from afar; at rest, they await an exhausted enemy; with well-fed troops, they await hungry ones. This is control of the physical factor. They do not engage an enemy advancing with well-ordered banners nor one whose formations are in impressive

array. This is control of the factor of changing circumstances.

— *Manoeuvring* （袁士槟译）

An entire army can be demoralized and its general deprived of his presence of mind. At the beginning of a campaign, file soldiers' morale is high, after a while it begins to flag and in the end it is gone. Therefore, he who is skilled in war avoids the enemy when file latter's spirit is high, and strikes when his spirit drains. This is how he copes with the question of morale. In good order, he awaits a disorderly enemy; with calm, he awaits a clamorous enemy. This is how he copes with self-possession. Being close to the battlefield, he awaits an enemy coming from afar; well rested, he awaits an exhausted enemy; with well-fed troops, he awaits hungry ones. This is how he copes with the question of strength. He does not intercept an enemy whose banners are in perfect array and refrains from attacking a powerful army in full formation. This is how he copes with changing circumstances.

— *Contest to Gain the Initiative* （林戊荪译）

（7）卒未亲附而罚之，则不服，不服则难用也。卒已亲附而罚不行，则不可用也。故令之以文，齐之以武，是谓必取。令素行以教其民，则民服；令不素行以教其民，则民不服。令素行者，与众相得也。

——《孙子兵法·行军篇》

（7）If troops are punished before their loyalty is secured, they will be disobedient. If not obedient, it is difficult to employ them. If troops have become attached to you, but discipline cannot be enforced, you cannot employ them. Thus, command them with civility but keep them under control by iron discipline, and it may be said that victory is certain. If orders are consistently carried out to instruct the troops, they will be obedient. If orders are not consistently carried out to instruct them, they will be disobedient.

If orders are consistently trustworthy and carried out, it shows that the relationship of a commander with his troops if satisfactory.

— *On the March* （袁士槟译）

If you punish soldiers for not being devoted to you, they will remain disobedient; and if they are disobedient, they will be difficult to use. But even when you have their devotion, if discipline is not enforced, you still cannot use them. Hence, you must win them over by treating them humanely and keep them in line with strict military discipline. This will ensure their allegiance.

If orders are consistently enforced in the training of soldiers, they will learn to obey; if orders are not enforced during training, they will not obey. When the authority of command is highly respected, then there is bound to be a harmonious relationship between the commander and his soldiers.

— *Deploying the Troops* （林戊荪译）

（8）是故不争天下之交，不养天下之权，信己之私，威加于敌，故其城可拔，其国可隳。施无法之赏，悬无政之令，犯三军之众，若使一人。犯之以事，勿告以言；犯之以利，勿告以害。投之亡地然后存，陷之死地然后生。夫众陷于害，然后能为胜败。故为兵之事，在于顺详敌之意，并敌一向，千里杀将，此谓巧能成事者也。

——《孙子兵法·九地篇》

(8) It follows that there is no need to contend against powerful combinations, nor is there any need to foster the power of other states. He relies for the attainment of his aims on his ability to overawe his opponents. And so he can take the enemy's cities and overthrow the enemy's state. Bestow rewards without respect to customary practice; publish orders without respect to precedent. Thus, you may employ the entire army as you would one man. Set the troops to their tasks without imparting your designs; use them to gain advantage without revealing the dangers involved. Throw them into a perilous situation and they will survive; put them in desperate ground and they will live. For when the army is placed in such a situation, it can snatch victory from defeat. Now, the crux of military operations lies in the pretence of following the designs of the enemy; and once there is a loophole that can be used, concentrate your forces against the enemy. Thus, even marching from a distance of a thousand li, you can kill his general. This is called the ability to achieve one's aim in an artful and ingenious manner.

— *The nine varieties of ground* （袁士槟译）

For this reason, you need not strive to form alliances with other states or foster your own forces within those states; when you pursue your own strategic intentions and bring your influences to bear on the enemy, you can take his cities and demolish his capital.

Confer extraordinary rewards and promulgate extraordinary regulations, and you can command the entire army as if it were one man. Assign the troops their tasks but do not reveal your plans, let them know the advantages but do not reveal the dangers. Only when you throw them into life-and-death situations will they fight to survive.

Only when you plunge them into places where there is no way out will they fight to stay alive. Only when the rank and file find themselves in a perilous situation will they turn defeat into victory. Therefore, the concern of a commander lies in carefully studying the designs of the enemy and concentrating his forces on the main thrust; then he can slay the enemy commander 1,000 li away. Thus, by using his ingenuity and skill, he can work wonders.

— *Nine Reigions* （林戊荪译）

（9）夫战胜攻取，而不修其功者凶，命曰费留。故曰：明主虑之，良将修之。非利不动，非得不用，非危不战。主不可以怒而兴师，将不可以愠而致战；合于利而动，不合于利而止。怒可以复喜，愠可以复悦；亡国不可以复存，死者不可以复生。故明君慎之，良将警之，此安国全军之道也。

——《孙子兵法·火攻篇》

(9) Now, to win battles and take your objectives but to fail to consolidate these achievements is ominous and may be described as a waste of time. And therefore, it is said that enlightened rulers must deliberate upon the plans to go to battle, and good generals carefully execute them. If not in the interests of the state, do not act. If you cannot succeed, do not use troops. If you are not in danger, do not fight a war. A sovereign cannot launch a war because he is enraged, nor can a general fight a war because he is resentful. For while an angered man may again be happy, and a resentful man again be pleased, a state that has perished cannot be restored, nor can the dead be brought back to life. Therefore, the enlightened ruler is prudent and the good general is warned against rash action. Thus the state is kept secure and the army preserved.

— *Attack by Fire* （袁士槟译）

To win battles and seize land and cities and yet fail to consolidate these achievements is fraught with dangers as it means a drain on your resources. Therefore it is said that a wide sovereign makes careful deliberations before launching a war and a good commander handles it with care. Do not go into battle if it is not in the interest of the state. Do not deploy the troops if you are not sure of victory. Do not send them into battle if you are not in danger. The sovereign should not start a war simply out of anger; the commander or general should not fight a battle simply because he is resentful. Take action only if it is to your advantage. Otherwise, do not. For an enraged man may regain his composure and a resentful person his happiness, but a state which has perished cannot be restored, nor can the dead be brought back to life.

Therefore, the enlightened sovereign approaches the question of war with utmost caution and the good commander warns himself against rash action. This is the way to keep the state secure and the army intact.

— *Attacking by Fire* （林戊荪译）

(10) 故三军之事，莫亲于间，赏莫厚于间，事莫密于间。非圣智不能用间，非仁义不能使间，非微妙不能得间之实。微哉！微哉！无所不用间也。间事未发，而先闻者，间与所告者皆死。

——《孙子兵法·用间篇》

(10) Of all those in the army close to the commander, none is more intimate than the spies; of all rewards, none more liberal than those given to spies; of all matters, none is more confidential than those relating to spy operations, He who is not sage and wise, humane and just, cannot use spies. And he who is not delicate and subtle cannot get the truth out of them.

Delicate, indeed! Truly delicate! There is no place where espionage is not possible. If plans relating to spy operations are prematurely divulged, the agent and all those to whom he spoke of them should be put to death.

— *Use of spies* （袁士槟译）

Of all those in the army close to the commander, none is more intimate than the agents; of all rewards, none more liberal than those given to agents; of all matters, none more confidential than those relating to secret operations. He who lacks wisdom cannot use agents; he who is not humane and generous cannot direct agents; he who is not sensitive and alert cannot get the truth out of them. So delicate and so secretive is espionage that there is nowhere you cannot put it to good use.

But if plans relating to secret operations are prematurely divulged, the agent and all those to whom he has leaked the secret should be put to death.

— *Using Spies* （林戊荪译）

(11) 故善用兵者，譬如率然；率然者，常山之蛇也。击其首则尾至，击其尾则首至，击其中则首尾俱至。

——《孙子兵法·九地篇》

(11) The skillful tactician may be likened to the shuai-jan. Now the shuai-jan is a snake that is found in the Chung Mountains. Strike at its head, and you will be attacked by its tail; strike at its tail, and you will be attacked by its head; strike at his

middle, and you will be attacked by head and tail both.

(Tr. Lionel Giles)

> The Skillful Warrior
> Deploys his troops
> Like the shuairan snake,
> Found on Mount Heng.（竹简作"恒山"）
> Strike its head,
> And the tail lashes back;
> Strike its tail,
> And its head fights back;
> Strike its belly,
> And both head and tail
> Will attack you.

(Tr. John Minford)

Therefore, those who are skillful in employing troops are like the snake found on Mount Chang. If you strike its head, its tail will come to help; if you strike at its tail, its head will come to help; and if you strike at its middle, both head and tail will come to the rescue.

（林戊荪译）

3. 比读感悟

翻译是一门跨文化交际的活动,这一活动不仅要译出源文的内容和思想,更要传达源语中特有的文化特质。

著作的翻译在做到忠实于原作的基础上更要保留和传达源文的文化特征。语义翻译要求忠实于原作,但也不能忽视向目标语读者传达源文的信息。通过分析对两种英译本《孙子兵法》中重点语句的翻译,可发现交际翻译在著作翻译中是一个可用又有效的策略,在介绍中国文学、传播思想文化方面作用显著。中文原文多用汉语中常见的四字句,读起来朗朗上口,意义明确。而翻译中常常对原作的某些部分用交际翻译,其余部分用语义翻译,二者结合使用,只是侧重和所用语境不同而已。袁士槟的译本(简称袁译)大部分采用了语义翻译的策略,而林戊荪的译本(简称林译)则运用了交际翻译结合脚注、解释说明等方式进行。

另外,读者不难看出,袁译常常对源文形式进行了一定的改变。比如在很多情况下,袁译删去了"孙子曰"几个字,译者将源文以第一人称翻译出来,而林戊荪的译文则是以第三人称翻译。

交际翻译的关键是传递信息,让读者去思考、去感受、去行动,为目标语读者"量体裁

衣",发挥了语言传达信息以及产生效果的功能。例如:

"亡国不可以复存,死者不可以复生,故明君慎之,良将警之。"

袁译:A state that has perished cannot be restored, nor can the dead be brought back to life.

Therefore, the enlightened ruler is prudent and the good general is warned against rash action. —— *Attack by Fire*

林译:A state which has perished cannot be restored, nor can the dead be brought back to life. Therefore, the enlightened sovereign approaches the question of war with utmost caution and the good commander warns himself against rash action. —— *Attacking by Fire*

"明君""良将"的翻译袁译使用"enlightened ruler"及"good general"是对源文中国君、将领的直译;而林译则使用"enlightened sovereign"及"good commander"这两个照顾西方读者思维的交际翻译的方法,向读者传达本句的内涵。

在解释和理解原作的时候,要避免对原作亦步亦趋,同时也应当避免超越作者的时代。比如源文中的"庙算"一词,各个译本处理各异。

源文:夫未战而庙算胜者,得算多也,未战而庙算不胜者,得算少也。多算胜,少算不胜,而况于无算乎! 吾以此观之,胜负见矣。

袁译忽视了"庙算"这个整体概念,而只是部分地翻译出了"算"的意义。他将之译为"estimate"。林译将之译为"makes full assessment of the situation at the pre-war council meeting in the temple",却是误解了"庙算"这个概念,误以为"庙"为"庙宇"的"庙"。事实上,此处的"庙"指的是"朝廷","庙算"即庙堂(太庙的明堂,古代帝王祭祀议事的地方)的策划,指的是朝廷议定的克敌谋略。又如:庙谋(朝廷的谋略)、庙朝(专指朝廷)、庙略(朝廷的谋略)、庙廊(朝廷;借指天子)等。"庙算"译得最好的是"makes many calculations in his temple"[莱昂内尔·贾尔斯(Lionel Giles 译)]。

军事著作中的术语最好要用目的语的军语术语来译,这是符合语域要求的,也是对于源语的意义、风格和形式的最好忠实或对等。

对于"曲制""官道"和"主用"这三个军事术语,贾尔斯、袁士槟和林戊荪的译本处理得都比较恰当。军事中的"法"也并不仅仅是"方法",不能用"method",因其并不是军事中的"法"。

总之,《孙子兵法》中所涉军事术语的翻译,既是一个语域问题,同时也是一个语体(style)问题,译者不应忽视。

五、练习与思考

1.分析题

(1)分析《计篇》两种译文的翻译手段,从奈达的功能对等理论出发,比较并指出林译和袁译的区别。

（2）仔细阅读"微乎微乎,至于无形;神乎神乎,至于无声。故能为敌之司命。进而不可御者,冲其虚也;退而不可追者,速而不可及也"的翻译,试分析译者使用了什么翻译策略,是如何体现出来的。

2. 实训题
翻译以下段落。
（1）孙子曰：凡用兵之法,将受命于君,合军聚众,交和而舍,莫难于军争。军争之难者,以迂为直,以患为利。故迂其途,而诱之以利,后人发,先人至,此知迂直之计者也。故军争为利,军争为危。举军而争利,则不及;委军而争利,则辎重捐。是故卷甲而趋,日夜不处,倍道兼行,百里而争利,则擒三将军,劲者先,疲者后,其法十一而至;五十里而争利,则蹶上将军,其法半至;三十里而争利,则三分之二至。是故军无辎重则亡,无粮食则亡,无委积则亡。

（2）孙子曰：凡处军相敌：绝山依谷,视生处高,战隆无登,此处山之军也。绝水必远水；客绝水而来,勿迎之于水内,令半济而击之,利；欲战者,无附于水而迎客；视生处高,无迎水流,此处水上之军也。绝斥泽,惟亟去无留；若交军于斥泽之中,必依水草而背众树,此处斥泽之军也。平陆处易而右背高,前死后生,此处平陆之军也。凡此四军之利,黄帝之所以胜四帝也。凡军好高而恶下,贵阳而贱阴,养生而处实,军无百疾,是谓必胜。丘陵堤防,必处其阳而右背之。此兵之利,地之助也。上雨,水沫至,欲涉者,待其定也。

3. 思考题
（1）什么情况下适合增译？请举例说明。
（2）你最喜欢《孙子兵法》的哪个译本？为什么？
（3）如果让你来翻译《孙子兵法》,你会采取哪些翻译策略？
（4）汉译英时常将汉语的流水句变为更紧凑的英语句,原因是什么？
（5）如何理解汉语的话题—说明结构？如何转化为英语的主谓结构？
（6）汉译英如何化简为繁？如何体现趋繁性？繁主要体现在何处？
（7）汉译英以动制静的核心因素是什么？如何表现？
（8）汉译英回译成汉语可以发现汉语的什么特点？
（9）如何理解翻译对汉语和英语都是一把双刃剑？
（10）为什么说汉英语言对比于翻译极其重要？

六、参考文献

［1］ 郭化若.孙子今译［M］.上海：上海古籍出版社,1978.

〔2〕 黄丽云.《孙子兵法》中古代文化负载词的理解和翻译探析[J].乐山师范学院学报,2013(3):84-87.

〔3〕 贾尔斯.孙子兵法[M].程郁,张和生,编译.长沙:湖南出版社,1993.

〔4〕 雷燕.从功能目的论视角看《孙子兵法·计篇》的两种译本[J].语言文字探索,2013(4):184-185.

〔5〕 林戊荪.孙子兵法,孙膑兵法[M].北京:外文出版社,2004.

〔6〕 吴海燕.从军事著作翻译看中国军事文化传播——交际翻译视角下《孙子兵法》两英译本的比较[J].外语教学与研究,2013(16):231-232.

〔7〕 张迎梅.从功能翻译理论视角看《孙子兵法》的两种译本[J].职业时空,2010(5):149-150.

〔8〕 Griffith, Samuel B.C. *Sun Tzu: The Art of War* [M]. London:Oxford University Press,1963.

〔9〕 Minford J. *The Art of War* [M]. New York:Penguine Books,2002.

第七课
唐诗译介赏析

> 唐诗是中国文化史上一颗耀眼的明珠,是我国古典文化艺术殿堂中的一块瑰宝。唐诗之所以成功首先是它题材完备,诸凡宇宙人生、羁旅晏游、民生国计、春花秋月、岭云塞草,无不可入诗。天地之广阔使诗人的眼界也变得十分开阔,使唐诗呈现一派多彩多姿的景象。同时,唐诗的形式多样。其基本形式包括古体诗与近体诗。唐代近体诗包括律诗与绝句两种,律诗与绝句也有五言与七言之分。唐诗的成就更是由于艺术上的自觉。短短四句或八句便能融时空、远近、高低、情景、现实与幻想于一炉,内容高度浓缩但又极其丰富。因此,唐诗无论在题材、形式,还是艺术性方面都达到了中国诗词巅峰。

一、翻译简介

国外译者早在 19 世纪末就已经开始英译唐诗。英国传教士湛约翰(John Chalmers)于 1872 年在《中国评论》(*The Chinese Review*)上发表的 15 首中国古诗的英译。理雅各(James Legge)、德庇时(John Francis Davis)、庞德(Ezra Pound)、翟理斯(Herbert Allen Giles)、弗莱彻(William John Bainbrigge Fletcher)等人在其后也陆续英译了部分唐诗,其中影响力最大的当属翟理斯的译作。翟理斯总共翻译了 101 首唐诗,多为李白、杜甫的作品。他把唐诗译为韵文,广受好评。英国作家斯特莱彻(Strachey)甚至认为翟理斯所译(以下简称"翟译")的唐诗是那个时代最好的诗。

20 世纪初英国学者韦利(Arthur Waley)认为翟译唐诗用韵虽美,但在表达原文的意义层面却有所损失。因此,韦利将唐诗译为散体诗(以下简称"韦译"),注重传递原文语义。总体来说,翟译重美,韦译重真。唐诗翻译中的韵体与散体、真与美之争由此展开并延续至今。

国内的唐诗英译始于清末民初。清光绪年间张棠资系统翻译了六百余首唐诗。改革开放后,国内唐诗英译迎来了高潮,其中影响较大的有吴钧陶的《杜甫诗英译一百五十首》、翁显良的《古诗英译》、张廷琛的《唐诗一百首》、徐忠杰的《唐诗二百首英译》、孙大雨的《英译唐诗选》、许渊冲的《唐诗三百首英译》等。

二、特殊概念的翻译

1. 叠字的翻译

叠字指由两个相同字组成的词语。中国古典诗歌中的叠字可追溯至《诗经》。因其韵律感强,朗朗上口,表达细腻,形象生动,唐诗中也大量出现。然而,译文要再现原文叠词的作用绝非易事。参看以下例种,不同译本对叠字的处理方式。

例1:

晴川历历汉阳树。——崔颢《黄鹤楼》

丰华瞻译:

Distant rows of trees along the creek in Hanyang shine in the sunlight.

许渊冲译:

By sunlit river trees can be counted one by one.

评析:此句写景。"历历"指景象清晰分明。丰华瞻译(以下简称"丰译")为"Distant rows",描绘了树木清晰分明的样子,译文再现原文语义。许渊冲译(以下简称"许译")为"one by one"既再现了原文树木清晰分明的情景,又与原文形式较为贴合,做到了形式与内容的统一。因此,笔者认为就此句而言,许译更胜一筹。

例2:

大弦嘈嘈如急雨,小弦切切如私语。——白居易《琵琶行》

杨宪益、戴乃迭译

The high notes wail like pelting rain,

The low notes whisper like soft confidences.

许渊冲译:

The thick strings loudly thrummed like the pattering rain,

The fine strings softly tinkled in a murmuring strain.

评析:《琵琶行》是唐代著名诗人白居易的不朽名作之一。本例中的两个叠词,"嘈嘈"形容沉重宏杂的声音,"切切"则形容尖细碎杂的声音。大弦沉着雄壮,宛若一阵急雨;小弦细促清幽,宛如一片私语。"嘈嘈""切切"两叠词此处拟声,描绘了弹奏琵琶曲的精微奥妙的音效及琵琶女高超的技艺。杨宪益与戴乃迭所译在处理这两个叠词时简洁地用了

"wail""whisper"对应原文"嘈嘈""切切",忠实地再现原文内容。然而,原文中"嘈嘈""切切"这种拟声的音乐性并未体现。而许译用"thrummed""tinkled"两个英语中的拟声词,同时以"loudly""softly"修饰,不仅忠实表达了原文意思,更再现了原文的韵律,使外国读者感受到此诗的音律之美,故不失为成功的译文。

2. 音韵的翻译

朱光潜在其《诗论》中曾说道:"诗是一种有韵律的纯文学","韵的最大功用在把涣散的声音联络贯串起来,成为一个完整的曲调。它好比贯珠的串子,在中国诗里这串子尤不可少。"音韵是唐诗的重要特点,也是其流传至今的缘由之一。唐诗中的音韵主要有尾韵、双声、叠韵等,而英语诗歌也讲求音韵,如头韵(alliteration)、尾韵(end rhyme)、中间韵(internal rhyme)、元音韵(assonance)、辅音韵(consonance)等。唐诗与英语诗歌不同的音韵给唐诗英译带来巨大的挑战,需要译者发挥主体性和创造力。

例1:

> 独坐幽篁里,
> 弹琴复长啸。
> 深林人不知,
> 明月来相照。
>
> ——王维《竹里馆》

宇文所安译:

> I sit alone in bamboo that hides me,
> plucking the harp and whistling long.
> It is deep in the woods and no one knows
> the bright moon comes to shine on me.

许渊冲译:

> Beneath the bamboo grove, alone,
> I seize my lute and sit and croon;
> No ear to hear me, save mine own;
> No eye to see me, save the moon.

评析:此诗是田园诗派代表王维的一首隔行押韵绝句。第一行中最后一字"里"与第三行最后一字"知"押韵;第二行最后一字"啸"与第四行最后一字"照"押韵。宇文所安的译本在第一行、第三行各有十个音节,第二行、第四行各有八个音节,可以说有一定的音律,但对原诗中押韵并未作处理。而许译将原诗译为每行八个音节。为了使译文押韵,许译将第一行"alone"与第三行"own"押韵,第二行"croon"与第四行"moon"押韵,加强了音韵的表现。

例2：

忽如一夜春风来，
千树万树梨花开。

——岑参《白雪歌送武判官归京》

宇文所安译：

All at once it seems in a single night
that breeze of spring has come；
On thousands of trees, on millions of trees
blossoms of pear appear.

许渊冲译：

As if the vernal breeze had come back overnight，
Adorning thousands of pear-trees with blossoms white.

评析：原诗中"来""开"两字押韵。就翻译而言，宇文所安的译本更倾向于在达意的同时忠实保留原文结构，但在音韵上有所损失。而许译故意破坏了英语语法结构，在达到意美的同时也追求押韵。一般而言，英语形容词置于名词之前，故"white blossoms"为正确的语法。但许渊冲为了与上一句最后一词"overnight"押韵，故意将"white blossoms"变为"blossoms white"，使国外读者也能身临其境感受此诗的音韵之美。

3. 典故的翻译

典故指诗文中引用的古代故事和有来历的词语。唐诗中典故一般来源于历史事件、民间传说、文学作品、神话、佛经等。由于大部分目标语读者对典故的来源知之甚少，故难以完全理解诗意及其价值观念，这也给唐诗的翻译带来了挑战。在大部分文学作品中，译者往往使用归化或异化的翻译策略处理典故翻译。归化（Domestication）指译者使用清晰流畅的语言使目标读者对外来文本的陌生感降到最低程度的翻译策略；异化（Foreignization）指译者通过保留原文中某些异国情调的内容来故意打破目标语表达习惯的翻译策略。因其译文相对于目标语读者不易接受，译者有时候要对原文中出现的文化现象进行补偿。在处理唐诗中典故翻译的时候，译者通常根据其对原作品的理解与对目标语读者接受程度的考虑选择不同的翻译策略。

例1：梨园子弟白发新。——白居易《长恨歌》

威特·宾纳（Witter·Bynner）译：

Her Pear-Garden Players became white-haired.

许渊冲译：

Actors, although still young, began to have hair grey.

评析：梨园本是唐代都城长安的一个地名。据史料记载，唐玄宗"选乐部子弟三百，教于梨园。声有误者,帝必觉而正之"。因唐玄宗李隆基在此地教演艺人,梨园后来就与戏曲艺术联系在一起,梨园子弟也成为曲艺演员的代名词。此处威特·宾纳的译本(以下简称"宾纳译本")采用异化的翻译策略,将"梨园子弟"译为 Pear-Garden Players,虽保留了源语言的文化特征,但对于目标语读者而言不免晦涩。许译采用归化的翻译策略,将其译为 Actors,虽更符合目标语读者的表达方式,更易为其接受,但剥夺了目标语读者了解中国梨园典故的机会,不免遗憾。

例2: 至今犹忆李将军。——高适《燕歌行》

威特·宾纳(Witter·Bynner)译:

We name to this day Li, the great General, who lived long ago.

许渊冲译:

Can they forget General Li sharing their weal and woe?

评析: 诗中"李将军"指西汉名将李广。其镇守边域,骁勇善战,使匈奴闻之色变,称其为飞将军。宾纳译本主要采用归化的翻译策略,同时用"great""who lived long ago",试图对"李将军"进行文化补偿。然而,这样只能让目标语读者知道李将军是个久远的历史人物,是个伟大的将军,未能再现原文中讽刺唐军临敌畏缩的内涵。而许译对李将军的形象补偿为"sharing their weal and woe",使李将军吃苦耐劳、骁勇善战的形象跃然纸上,对唐军的讽刺意味入木三分。因此,就此句而言,许译更胜一筹。

三、译文对比赏析

1. 经典诗句

(1) 几处早莺争暖树,谁家新燕啄春泥。

(1) Disputing for sunny trees, early orioles trill;
Pecking vernal mud in, young swallows come and go.

(许渊冲译)

Here and there first orioles contend in sunny trees;
To which households do new swallows wing, bearing their spring mud?

(张廷琛、魏博思译)

(2) 滕王高阁临江渚,佩玉鸣鸾罢歌舞。

(2) Near these islands a palace was built by a prince,
But its music and song have departed long since.

(翟理斯译)

By riverside towers Prince Teng's Pavilion proud;

No more ringing bells punctuate the dancers' refrain.

（许渊冲译）

(3) 昔日戏言身后事，今朝都到眼前来。

(3) What if one of us should die? We said for fun one day,
But now it has come true and passed before my eyes.

（许渊冲译）

In former years we chatted carelessly of death and what it means to die,
Since then it's passed before my very eyes.

（张廷琛、魏博思译）

(4) 苟能制侵陵，岂在多杀伤？

(4) It an invasion is repelled.
Why shed more blood unless compelled?

（许渊冲译）

If armed aggression could be curbed by an adequate military force,
What's the need for killing a lot of people?

（唐一鹤译）

(5) 锦瑟无端五十弦，一弦一柱思华年。

(5) Why should the sad zither have fifty strings?
Each string, each strain evokes but vanished springs.

（许渊冲译）

The richly painted zither somehow has fifty strings,
Each of which recalls a vanished year.

（张廷琛、魏博思译）

(6) 劝君莫惜金缕衣，劝君惜取少年时。

(6) Gather sweet blossoms while you may,
And not the twig devoid of flowers.

（许渊冲译）

When flowers bloom they need be plucked;
Wait not to grasp in vain at empty twigs.

（张廷琛、魏博思译）

(7) 东风不与周郎便,铜雀春深锁二乔。
(7) Had the east wind refused General Zhou a helping hand,
His foe'd have locked his fair wife on Northern shore.

（许渊冲译）

Had not the east wind given Zhou advantage,
The Qiao ladies would have been entombed
In the eternal spring of Cao Cao's pleasure palace!

（张廷琛、魏博思译）

(8) 回眸一笑百媚生,六宫粉黛无颜色。
(8) If she but turned her head and smiled, there were cast a hundred spells,
And the powder and paint of the Six Palaces faded into nothing.

（杨宪益、戴乃迭译）

Turning her head, she smiled so sweet and full of grace
That she outshone in six palaces the fairest face.

（许渊冲译）

2. 经典诗篇
(1) 写景抒怀

钱 塘 江 春 行
白居易

孤山寺北贾亭西,
水面初平云脚低。
几处早莺争暖树,
谁家新燕啄春泥。
乱花渐欲迷人眼,
浅草才能没马蹄。
最爱湖东行不足,
绿杨阴里白沙堤。

On Qiantang Lake in Spring
Bai Juyi

West of Pavilion Jia and north of Lonely Hill,
Water brims level with the bank and clouds hang low.
Disputing for sunny trees, early orioles trill,

Pecking vernal mud in, young swallows come and go.

A riot of blooms begins to dazzle the eye,

Amid short grass the horse hoofs can barely be seen.

I love best the east of the lake under the sky,

The bank paved with white sand is shaded by willows green.

（许渊冲译）

A Spring Outing by Qiangtang Lake
Bai Juyi

North of Gushan Temple, West of the Jia Pavilion,

Cloud most hug the newly brimming banks.

Here and there first orioles contend in sunny trees,

To which households do new swallows wing, bearing their spring mud.

Riotous flowers more and more dazzle the eyes,

The short grass walking on and on, east of the lake,

Where green willow shade the white sand banks.

（张廷琛、魏博思译）

(2) 赠别友人

芙蓉楼送辛渐
王昌龄

寒雨连江夜入吴,

平明送客楚山孤。

洛阳亲友如相问,

一片冰心在玉壶。

Farewell to Xin Jian at Lotus Tower
Wang Changling

A cold rain mingled with the Eastern Stream at night,

At dawn you leave the Southern hills lonely in haze.

If my friends in the North should ask if I'm all right,

My heart is free of stain as the ice in the crystal vase.

（许渊冲译）

Seeing Xin Jian off at Lotus Pavilion
Wang Changling

Last night the cooling rains from off the River swept through all of Wu.

At break of day I see you off, for the lonely peaks of Chu.

Should Luoyang friends and loved ones ask you how I am.
My heart's a piece of ice in a chalice carved of jade.

(张廷琛、魏博思译)

(3) 情爱相思

遣悲怀三首(其二)

元 稹

昔日戏言身后事，
今朝都到眼前来。
衣裳已施行看尽，
针线犹存未忍开。
尚想旧情怜婢仆，
也曾因梦送钱财。
诚知此恨人人有，
贫贱夫妻百事哀。

To my deceased wife

Yuan Zhen

What if one of us should die? We said for fun one day,
But now it has come true and passed before my eyes.
I can't bear to see your clothes and give them away,
I seal your embroidery lest it should draw my sighs.
Remembering your kindness, I'm kind to our maids,
Dreaming of your bounty, I give bounties as before.
I know there is no mortal but returns to the shades,
But a poor couple like us have more to deplore.

(许渊冲译)

Giving vent to sorrow

Yuan Zhen

In former years we chatted carelessly of death and what it means to die,
Since then it's passed before my very eyes.
I've given almost all your clothes away,
But cannot bear to move your sewing things.
Remembering your past attachments, I've been kind to maids you loved.
I've met your soul in dreams, and ordered sutras sung.
Certainly, I know this sorrow comes to all,

But to poor and lowly couples, everything life brings is sad.

（张廷琛、魏博思译）

(4) 边塞军旅

前出塞·其六

杜 甫

挽弓当挽强，

用箭当用长。

射人先射马，

擒贼先擒王。

杀人亦有限，

列国自有疆。

苟能制侵陵，

岂在多杀伤？

Song of the frontier

Du Fu

The bow you carry should be strong,

The arrows you use should be long.

Shoot before a horseman his horse,

Capture the chief to beat his force.

Slaughter shan't go beyond its sphere,

Each State should guard its own frontier.

In an invasion is repelled,

Why shed more blood unless compelled?

（许渊冲译）

Going Out of the Frontier Pass

Du Fu

The bow you draw should be strong,

The arrow you use should be long.

Shoot at his horse before the horseman,

Capture the brigand chief before his men.

There should be a limit to killing a lot of people,

States have their own boundaries they shouldn't go beyond.

If armed aggression could be curbed by an adequate military force,

What's the need for killing a lot of people?

（唐一鹤译）

(5) 人生感悟

锦　瑟

李商隐

锦瑟无端五十弦，
一弦一柱思华年。
庄生晓梦迷蝴蝶，
望帝春心托杜鹃。
沧海月明珠有泪，
蓝田日暖玉生烟。
此情可待成追忆？
只是当时已惘然。

The Sad Zeither

Li Shangyin

Why should the sad zither have fifty strings?

Each string, each strain evokes but vanished springs.

Dim morning dream to be a butterfly,

Amorous heart poured out in cuckoos cry.

In moon lit pearls see tears in mermaid's eyes,

From sunburnt jade in blue field let smoke rise,

Such feeling can not be recalled again,

It seemed lost even when it was felt then.

（许渊冲译）

The Ornate Zither

Li Shangyin

The richly painted zither somehow has fifty strings,

Each of which recalls a vanished year.

Dawn dreaming Zhuang Zi got mixed up with a butterfly,

King Wang lent tender feelings to the cuckoo's call.

In bright moonlit seas of blue, tears change to pearls,

The air above Lantian shimmers from the jade hidden within its hill.

These thoughts are not the stuff of recollection,

But what eludes our grasp as life itself unfolds.

（张廷琛、魏博思译）

(6) 人格境界

金 缕 衣

杜秋娘

劝君莫惜金缕衣，

劝君惜取少年时。

花开堪折直须折，

莫待无花空折枝。

The Golden Dress

Du Qiuniang

Love not your golden dress, I pray,

More than your youthful golden hours.

Gather sweet blossoms while you may,

And not the twig devoid of flowers.

（许渊冲译）

Cloth of gold

Du Qiuniang

I advise you not to cherish cloth of gold,

But to honor the days of youth.

When flowers bloom they need be plucked,

Wait not to grasp in vain at empty twigs.

（张廷琛、魏博思译）

(7) 咏史怀古

赤 壁

杜 牧

折戟沉沙铁未销，

自将磨洗认前朝。

东风不与周郎便，

铜雀春深锁二乔。

The Red Cliff

Du Mu

We dig out broken halberds buried in the sand,

And wash and rub these relics of an ancient war.

Had the east wind refused General Zhou a helping hand,

His foe's have locked his fair wife on Northern shore.

（许渊冲译）

Red Cliff

Du Mu

Uncorroded is the broken halberd, recovered from the sands,
Once washed, it proves a relic of Han.
Had not the east wind given Zhou advantage,
The Qiao ladies would have been been entombed,
In the eternal spring of Cao Cao's pleasure palace!

（张廷琛、魏博思译）

（8）永恒爱情

长恨歌（节选）

白居易

汉皇重色思倾国，
御宇多年求不得。
杨家有女初长成，
养在深闺人未识。
天生丽质难自弃，
一朝选在君王侧。
回眸一笑百媚生，
六宫粉黛无颜色。
春寒赐浴华清池，
温泉水滑洗凝脂。
侍儿扶起娇无力，
始是新承恩泽时。
云鬓花颜金步摇，
芙蓉帐暖度春宵。
春宵苦短日高起，
从此君王不早朝。
承欢侍宴无闲暇，
春从春游夜专夜。
后宫佳丽三千人，
三千宠爱在一身。
金屋妆成娇侍夜，
玉楼宴罢醉和春。
姊妹弟兄皆列士，
可怜光彩生门户。

遂令天下父母心，
不重生男重生女。
……
钗留一股合一扇，
钗擘黄金合分钿。
但教心似金钿坚，
天上人间会相见。
临别殷勤重寄词，
词中有誓两心知。
七月七日长生殿，
夜半无人私语时。
在天愿作比翼鸟，
在地愿为连理枝。
天长地久有时尽，
此恨绵绵无绝期！

A Song of Unending Sorrow
Bai Juyi

China's Emperor, craving beauty that might shake an empire,

Was on the throne for many years, searching, never finding,

Till a little child of the Yang clan, hardly even grown,

Bred in an inner chamber, with no one knowing her,

But with graces granted by heaven and not to be concealed,

At last one day was chosen for the imperial household.

If she but turned her head and smiled, there were cast a hundred spells,

And the powder and paint of the Six Palaces faded into nothing.

It was early spring. They bathed her in the FlowerPure Pool,

Which warmed and smoothed the creamy-tinted crystal of her skin,

And, because of her languor, a maid was lifting her

When first the Emperor noticed her and chose her for his bride.

The cloud of her hair, petal of her cheek, gold ripples of her crown when she moved,

Were sheltered on spring evenings by warm hibiscus curtains;

But nights of spring were short and the sun arose too soon,

And the Emperor, from that time forth, forsook his early hearings

And lavished all his time on her with feasts and revelry, His mistress of the spring, his despot of the night.

There were other ladies in his court, three thousand of rare beauty,

But his favours to three thousand were concentered in one body.

By the time she was dressed in her Golden Chamber, it would be almost evening;

And when tables were cleared in the Tower of Jade, she would loiter, slow with wine.

Her sisters and her brothers all were given titles;

And, because she so illumined and glorified her clan,

She brought to every father, every mother through the empire,

Happiness when a girl was born rather than a boy.

...

But kept one branch of the hairpin and one side of the box,

Breaking the gold of the hairpin, breaking the shell of the box;

"Our souls belong together," she said, "like this gold and this shell —

Somewhere, sometime, on earth or in heaven, we shall surely

And she sent him, by his messenger, a sentence reminding him

Of vows which had been known only to their two hearts:

"On the seventh day of the Seventh month, in the Palace of Long Life,

We told each other secretly in the quiet midnight world

That we wished to fly in heaven, two birds with the wings of one,

And to grow together on the earth, two branches of one tree."

Earth endures, heaven endures; some time both shall end,

While this unending sorrow goes on and on for ever.

（宾纳译）

THE EVERLASTING REGRET
Bai Juyi

The beauty-loving monarch longed year after year

To find a beautiful lady without peer.

A maiden of the Yangs to womanhood just grown,

In inner chambers bred, to the world was unknown.

Endowed with natural beauty too hard to hide,

One day she stood selected for the monarch's side.

Turning her head, she smiled so sweet and full of grace

That she outshone in six palaces the fairest face.

She bathed in glassy water of warm-fountain pool,

Which laved and smoothed her creamy skin when spring was cool.

Upborne by her attendants, she rose too faint to move,
And this was when she first received the monarch's love.
Flowerlike face and cloudlike hair, golden-headdressed,
In lotus-flower curtain she spent the night blessed.
She slept till sun rose high, for the blessed night was short,
From then on the monarch held no longer morning court.
In revels as in feasts she shared her lord's delight,
His companion on trips and his mistress at night.
In inner palace dwelt three thousand ladies fair;
On her alone was lavished royal love and care.
Her beauty served the night when dressed in Golden Bower
Or drunk with wine and spring at banquet in Jade Tower.
All her sisters and brothers received rank and fief
And honours showered on her household, to the grief
Of the fathers and mothers who'd rather give birth
To a fair maiden than any son on earth.

……

Keeping one side of the case and one wing of the pin,
She sent to her dear lord the other half of the twin.
"If our two hearts as firm as the gold should remain.
In heaven or on earth we'll sometime meet again."
At parting she confided to the messenger
A secret vow known only to her lord and her.
On seventh day of seventh moon when none was near,
At midnight in Long Life Hall he whispered in her ear,
"On high, we'd be two lovebirds flying wing to wing;
On earth, two trees with branches twined from spring to spring."
The boundless sky and endless earth may pass away,
But this vow unfulfilled will be regretted for aye.

(许渊冲译)

四、练习与思考

1. 分析题

(1) 分析"东风不与周郎便,铜雀春深锁二乔"这句中许渊冲译本与张廷琛、魏博思译本的不同翻译策略与技巧。

（2）比较分析《长恨歌》宾纳译本与许渊冲译本的特点。

2. 实训题

翻译以下篇目。

（1）
题都城南庄
崔 护

去年今日此门中，人面桃花相映红。

人面不知何处去，桃花依旧笑春风。

（2）
新嫁娘词
王 建

三日入厨下，洗手作羹汤。

未谙姑食性，先遣小姑尝。

（3）
无 题
李商隐

相见时难别亦难，东风无力百花残。

春蚕到死丝方尽，蜡炬成灰泪始干。

晓镜但愁云鬓改，夜吟应觉月光寒。

蓬山此去无多路，青鸟殷勤为探看。

3. 思考题

（1）唐诗翻译要注意哪些方面？

（2）你认为在唐诗翻译中该采用哪种翻译策略？归化还是异化？

（3）在唐诗翻译中，如何平衡意美、音美、形美？

（4）你更喜欢哪个《长恨歌》的译本？请解释原因。

五、参考文献

[1] 林月悦.译者主体性视域下的许渊冲及宇文所安唐诗英译对比研究[D].北京：北京外国语大学，2014.

[2] 罗忻晨.论许渊冲《唐诗三百首》中叠字的翻译方法[D].北京：北京外国语大学，2014.

[3] 孙雨竹.形式主义诗学与许渊冲英译唐诗中的节奏与声韵[J].成都理工大学学报（社会科学版），2016(04)：103－107.

[4] 吴可嘉.唐诗典故英译对比研究[D].大连海事大学，2012.

[5] 许渊冲.文学与翻译[M].北京：北京大学出版社，2016.

第八课
宋词译介赏析

> 词始于南朝，定形于中晚唐，盛行于宋朝，是宋朝最高文学成就的标志。其句子长短结合，配合音乐，以便于歌唱。每首词都有一个调名，叫作"词牌名"。因此，宋词又叫作曲子词、乐章等。
>
> 宋词按其文学风格可分为婉约派与豪放派。婉约派内容侧重儿女情长、离情别绪，注重音律，语言细腻圆润，柔美含蓄。其代表人物有李煜、柳永、周邦彦、李清照等。豪放派视野广阔，内容不拘泥于柳荫花下，山川河流、农舍阡陌皆可为词。其气势恢宏，不拘音律，有激扬豪迈之美，代表人物有苏轼、辛弃疾等。
>
> 在古代文学的阆苑里，宋词是一座芬芳绚丽的园圃，是继唐诗后中国古典文学又一个高峰。

一、翻译简介

相较于唐诗翻译而言，宋词翻译起步较晚，规模相对较小，对于宋词翻译史的研究也较为薄弱。西方最早出现宋词译本的出版物为1867年的法语图书《玉书》，书中翻译了6首李清照词。1926年我国著名文学家冰心女士在美国撰写的硕士论文《李易安女士词的翻译与编辑》中英译了李清照的26首词，这也是已知的最早由汉语英译的宋词作品。

宋词英译在20世纪30年代逐步发展。1933年，初大告在留英期间出版了译著《中华隽词》，内含50首唐诗宋词的英译。1938—1939年间，吴经熊等人在《天下月刊》中刊登了数十首英译宋词作品。

受到战火与时事变迁的影响,国内宋词翻译一度停滞不前。直至改革开放后,宋词翻译重新发展起来并日益繁荣,先后出版了胡云翼、黄宏荃、许渊冲等翻译名家的英译作品。其中,许渊冲的译作《唐宋词100首》是迄今为止影响力最大的宋词译作。

二、特殊概念的翻译

1. 词牌的翻译

同现代的歌词类似,词最初是伴曲而唱的。古人或按词制调,或依调填词,这些曲调名称就是词牌。词牌不是词的标题,只是根据乐曲对字数、句法、平仄和韵脚等做出规定的框架,所以大多数词的词牌与内容没有必然的联系。

尽管如此,词牌有其独特的文化内涵。不同译者鉴于对词牌文化特性的不同理解而产生不同的译文,词牌译名也一直无法统一。总体而言,词牌翻译有四种方法:直译法、意译法、音译法、音译加注法。

直译法按词牌的字面意思直接翻译,使原文的形式与内容都得以保留;意译则更注重挖掘词牌的文化内涵;音译法用汉语拼音的形式保留了原文的声音文化;音译加注法弥补了音译法有时候难以为外国读者接受的问题,通过对音译进行一定的解释,增加了译文的可读性。例如:

贺新郎:Congratulations to the Bridegroom(直译)

武陵春:Spring in Peach Blossom Land(意译,揭示了武陵人误入桃花源的典故)

一剪梅:To the Tune of Yi Jian Mei(音译)

念奴娇:Nien-nu Chiao (The Charms of Nien-nu)(音译加注)

每种译法都力图传递词牌的文化信息,但也都有不足之处。具体使用哪种译法取决于译者对词牌内涵的理解,包括了解其语言特点、词牌来源、是否包含历史典故等。以下两例供研读揣摩。

例1:望海潮

Watching the Tidal Bore(许渊冲译)

Watching the Sea Tide(卓振英译)

评析:词牌"望海潮",为北宋著名词人柳永所创,以柳永词《望海潮·东南形胜》为正体,相传柳永在钱塘江望潮时创此词。词牌中的三个字体现了这样的场景:观潮的人在钱塘江观潮。两位译者第一个字都用"watching"直译,强调观潮的时间较长。"海潮"许译为"Tidal Bore",卓译为"Sea Tide"。"Bore"一词在《牛津高级学习词典》中的定义为"a strong, high wave that rushes along a river from the sea at particular times of the yea",强调潮水汹涌澎湃。"Sea Tide"则无此意象。

例2:浣溪沙

Silk-Washing Stream(许渊冲译)

Bleaching Silk in the Stream(卓振英译)

评析:"浣溪沙"一作"浣溪纱",因春秋时期西施浣纱于若耶溪而得名。若将文本与场景相联系,"浣溪沙"的主体是人,尤指少女;其行为是浣纱;地点为溪边。许渊冲译(以下简称"许译")为"Silk-Washing Stream",其主体为"stream",即小溪,"Silk-Washing"修饰"stream",其译文的意思为洗纱的小溪,与原文意象明显不符;卓振英译(以下简称"卓译")为"Bleaching Silk in the Stream",其主体、行为、地点均与原文相符。可见,此处卓译较为贴切。

2. 典故的翻译

宋词中经常会出现典故,典故以其特定的文化背景与历史积淀使读者在品读时有时空穿梭之感,回味无穷。然而,宋词翻译也随之难上加难。在典故翻译中,译者需要了解典故的文化内涵,分析作者的写作背景及使用该典故所要表达的意图,同时要考虑目标读者对典故的接受程度,最好的翻译效果是让目标读者接受译文的同时留给其一定想象的空间。因此,宋词中典故的翻译并无固定的方法,生成译文时应结合多种因素综合考虑。

例1:英雄无觅,孙仲谋处。——辛弃疾《永遇乐·京口北固亭怀古》

As Sun Quan are not to be found again.(卓振英译)

But nowhere can be found

A hero like the king defending southern shore.(许渊冲译)

评析:该词为南宋著名词人辛弃疾所作。辛弃疾一生以恢复大宋江山为志,却因与主和派大臣韩侂胄不和而备受打压,壮志难酬。1205年,执政的韩侂胄将辛弃疾调离至镇江,将其排除于抗金大计之外。这首词为辛弃疾于在镇江上任知府时登上京口北固亭所作。该词借古讽今,表达了对苟且偷生者的愤慨及自己报效家国的决心和愿望。

此句中孙仲谋指三国时期孙吴开国皇帝孙权。孙权曾大败曹军,作者将此典故写入词中,既表达了对孙权的钦佩,又讽刺了主和派的不思进取。卓译采用直译的方式,将"孙仲谋"译为"Sun Quan"。由于国外读者对孙权的背景并不了解,无法将其与英明神武的开国皇帝相联系,故卓译忽略了典故翻译时的文化传递。许译将"孙仲谋"意译为"A hero like the king",并对孙权的形象信息补充为"defending southern shore",有效传递了该典故的历史文化信息,较为贴切。

例2:斜阳草树,寻常巷陌,人道寄奴曾住。——辛弃疾《永遇乐·京口北固亭怀古》

Behold the trees and grass in the dusk; it's said

that Jinu had lived in the commonplace lane.(卓振英译)

The slanting sun sheds its departing ray

O'er tree-shaded and grassy lane

Where lived the Cowherd King retaking the lost land.(许渊冲译)

评析：此句中寄奴是南朝宋开国皇帝刘裕的小名。刘裕自幼家境贫寒，仅依靠砍柴、种地、打渔和卖草鞋为生；后从军，屡立奇功，攻灭南燕，席卷关中，最终称帝。此处体现了刘裕金戈铁马，骁勇善战，同时讽刺当朝的妥协政策。卓译将"寄奴"直译为"Jinu"，目标语读者由于缺乏对刘裕文化背景的了解，对此未必能够接受。而许译用归化的策略，"寄奴"译为"Cowherd King"，同时对刘裕进行信息补偿"retaking the lost land"。虽说"Cowherd"与刘裕参军前的身份略有不符，但总体而言较好地传达了典故的文化信息。

3. 叠字的翻译

叠字指由两个或两个以上相同的字组成的词语。中国古典诗歌，尤其是宋词中大量使用叠字，具有较强的修辞功能。一般而言，宋词中叠字的作用主要包括以下三点：绘人绘物，形象生动；寓情于景，烘托意境；美化韵律，余音绕梁。正是由于叠字有这些功能，宋词对叠字的使用乐此不疲。宋词翻译中译者也应将作者使用叠字的艺术效果传达给目标语读者，但这也给翻译带来了极大的挑战。

例1：寻寻觅觅，冷冷清清，凄凄惨惨戚戚。——李清照《声声慢·寻寻觅觅》

林语堂译：

So dim, so dark,
So dense, so dull,
So damp, so dank,
So dead!

许渊冲译：

I look for what I miss,
I know not what it is,
I feel so sad, so drear,
So lonely, without cheer.

评析：《声声慢·寻寻觅觅》是宋代女词人李清照后期的作品。彼时北宋为金所灭，徽钦二帝被俘。李清照丈夫因病去世，她也因战乱流离失所，独自一人避难奔走，境况凄惨，无尽忧愁凝聚心头，于是便写下此不朽名作。该词通过描写残秋，抒发自己因国破家亡、沦落天涯而产生的孤寂落寞、悲凉绝望之感。

开篇"寻寻觅觅，冷冷清清，凄凄惨惨戚戚"尽现作者孤寂落寞、凄凉愁苦的心绪，同时完美地体现了音韵之美。因此，翻译时也要再现原文意境与声韵。林译使用了七个抑扬格，以七个"so"开头的两字短语与原文的一组叠字互为对应，同时巧妙地使用以"d"开头的七个单音节形容词压头韵，从最开始"dim"到最后"dead"，凄凉感层层递进。许译使用三音步抑扬格对应原词的音律，同时前两行"miss""is"押韵，后两行"drear""cheer"押韵；"so sad""so drear""so lonely"不仅压头韵，而且从三个角度将作者悲凉寂寞的意境体现得淋漓尽致。可以说，林译与许译都做到了意美、音美、形美，两者旗鼓相当,难分伯仲。

例2:梧桐更兼细雨,到黄昏、点点滴滴。——李清照《声声慢·寻寻觅觅》

林语堂译:

  And the drizzle on the kola nut

  Keeps on droning;

  Pit-a-pat, pit-a-pat!

许渊冲译:

  On parasol trees a fine rain drizzles, as twilight grizzles.

评析:林译先用"Keeps on droning"再现原诗意境:细雨绵绵,女子独自哀思,一筹莫展;后重复使用拟声词"Pit-a-pat, pit-a-pat"重现原词音律,与原词"点点滴滴"对应得恰到好处,堪称绝妙之笔。许译用"grizzles"(发出持续哭泣般的声音)一词,不仅与前文"drizzle"押韵,又模拟雨声,烘托了悲凉的氛围,给目标语读者描绘了一幅女子低声哭泣的意境。总体而言,两个译本各有千秋。

三、译文对比赏析

1. 经典词句

(1) 明月几时有?把酒问青天。不知天上宫阙,今夕是何年。

(1) How long will the full moon appear?

  Wine cup in hand, I ask the sky.

  I do not know what time of the year

  I would be tonight in the palace on high.

(许渊冲译)

  How rare the moon, so round and clear!

  With cup in hand, I ask of the blue sky,

  "I do not know in the celestial sphere

  What name this festive night goes by?"

(林语堂译)

(2) 舞低杨柳楼心月,歌尽桃花扇底风。

(2) The moon above, we danced the willows low

  Beneath my fan I felt a zephyr blow.

(赵彦春译)

  You danced till the moon hung low over the willow trees;

You sang until amid peach blossoms blushed the breeze.

（许渊冲译）

(3) 多情自古伤离别,更那堪,冷落清秋节!

(3) Lovers would grieve at parting as of old.
How could I stand this clear autumn day so cold!

（许渊冲译）

Since time immemorial, lovers have grieved at parting
Made more poignant in the fallow season of autumn.

（杨宪益、戴乃迭译）

(4) 绿杨烟外晓寒轻,红杏枝头春意闹。

(4) Beyond green willows morning chill is growing mild;
on pink apricot branches spring is running wild.

（许渊冲译）

Against the mist so cool the willows sway;
Upon the apricot twigs spring does play.

（赵彦春译）

(5) 大江东去,浪淘尽、千古风流人物。

(5) East flows the mighty river,
Sweeping away the heroes of time past;

（杨宪益、戴乃迭译）

The Great River eastward flows,
With its waves are gone all those
Gallant heroes of bygone years.

（许渊冲译）

(6) 满地黄花堆积。憔悴损,如今有谁堪摘?

(6) About the ground, chrysanthemums are bestrewn.
Gathering into heaps — bruised — withering soon.
With myself in utter misery and gloom,
Who cares to save them from their approaching doom?

（徐中杰译）

The ground is covered with yellow flowers,

　　Faded and fallen in showers.

　　Who will pick them up now?

(许渊冲译)

(7) 怒发冲冠,凭栏处、潇潇雨歇。

(7) Wrath sets on end my hair,

　　I lean on railings where

　　I see the drizzling rain has ceased.

(许渊冲译)

　　Hair on end and shoving my hat,

　　In wrath I lean on the balustrade,

　　While the rain leaves off its pitter-pat.

(王知还译)

2. 经典宋词

水 调 歌 头

苏　轼

明月几时有?把酒问青天。不知天上宫阙,今夕是何年。我欲乘风归去,又恐琼楼玉宇,高处不胜寒。起舞弄清影,何似在人间?

转朱阁,低绮户,照无眠。不应有恨,何事长向别时圆?人有悲欢离合,月有阴晴圆缺,此事古难全。但愿人长久,千里共婵娟。

Prelude to melody of flowing waters

Su Shi

　　How long will the full moon appear?

　　Wine cup in hand, I ask the sky.

　　I do not know what time of the year

　　would be tonight in the palace on high.

　　Riding the wind, there I would fly,

　　Yet I'm afraid the crystalline palace would be

　　Too high and cold for me.

　　I rise and dance, with my shadow I play.

　　On high as on earth, would it be as gay?

　　The moon goes round the mansions red

Through gauze-draped window soft to shed

Her light upon the sleepless bed.

Why then when people part, is the oft full and bright?

Men have sorrow and joy; they part or meet again;

The moon is bright or dim and she may wax or wane.

There has been nothing perfect since the olden days.

So let us wish that man

Will live long as he can!

Though miles apart, we'll share the beauty she displays.

（许渊冲译）

Prelude to melody of flowing waters

Sushi

How rare the moon, so round and clear!

With cup in hand, I ask of the blue sky,

"I do not know in the celestial sphere

What name this festive night goes by?"

I want to fly home, riding the air,

But fear the ethereal cold up there,

The jade and crystal mansions are so high!

Dancing to my shadow,

I feel no longer the mortal tie.

She rounds the vermilion tower,

Stoops to silk-pad doors,

Shines on those who sleepless lie.

Why does she, bearing us no grudge,

Shine upon our parting, reunion deny?

But rare is perfect happiness —

The moon does wax, the moon does wane,

And so men meet and say goodbye.

I only pray our life be long,

And our souls together heavenward fly!

（林语堂译）

鹧鸪天

晏几道

彩袖殷勤捧玉钟，
当年拼却醉颜红。
舞低杨柳楼心月，
歌尽桃花扇底风。

从别后，忆相逢，
几回魂梦与君同。
今宵剩把银釭照，
犹恐相逢是梦中。

The Partridge Sky

Yan Jidao

You proffered wine to me with easy grace.
I drank and was so drunk, a crimson face.
The moon above, we danced the willows low;
Beneath my fan I felt a zephyr blow.

How I wish we met, since you went away.
You several times came to my dream to stay.
Tonight I set the candle end aglow
For fear our tryst is but a passing show.

（赵彦春译）

The Partridge Sky

Yan Jidao

Time and again with rainbow sleeves you tried to fill
My cup with wine that drunk, I kept on drinking still.
You danced till the moon hung low over the willow trees;
You sang until amid peach blossoms blushed the breeze.

Then came the time to part,
But you're deep in my heart.
How many times have I met you in dreams at night!
Now left to gaze at you in silver candlelight,
I fear it is not you,
But a sweet dream untrue.

（许渊冲译）

雨　霖　铃
柳　永

寒蝉凄切,对长亭晚,骤雨初歇。都门帐饮无绪,留恋处、兰舟催发。执手相看泪眼,竟无语凝噎。念去去、千里烟波,暮霭沉沉楚天阔。

多情自古伤离别,更那堪,冷落清秋节！今宵酒醒何处？杨柳岸、晓风残月。此去经年,应是良辰好景虚设。便纵有千种风情,更与何人说！

Bells in the rain
Liu Yong

Cicadas chill

Drearily shrill.

We stand face to face in an evening hour.

Before the pavilion, after a sudden shower.

Can we care for drinking before we part?

At the city gate

We're lingering late,

But the boat is waiting for me to depart.

Hand in hand, we gaze at each other's tearful eyes

And burst into sobs with words congealed on our lips.

I'll go my way

Far, far away

On miles and miles of misty waves where sail the ships,

And evening clouds hang low in boundless Southern skies.

Lovers would grieve at parting as of old.

How could I stand this clear autumn day so cold!

Where shall I be found at daybreak

From wine awake?

Moored by a riverbank planted with willow trees

Beneath the waning moon and in the morning breeze.

I'll be gone for a year.

In vain would good times and fine scenes appear.

However gallant I am on my part,

To whom can I lay bare my heart?

(许渊冲译)

Bells in the rain
Liu Yong

Mournfully chirr the cicadas,

As the shower of rain stops

And we face the roadside pavilion at dusk.

We drink without cheer in the tent outside the city gate;

It is the moment we are loath to part

But the magnolia-wood boat beckons me on.

Hands clasped together we see our tears,

So overcome, unable to utter a single word.

Ahead lies a journey a thousand li of misty waves

And the vast sky of Chu hangs with heavy evening haze.

Since time immemorial, lovers have grieved at parting

Made more poignant in the fallow season of autumn.

What is this place where I have sobered from my drunken stupor?

"The riverside is strewn with willow trees,

The morning breeze wafts in with a waning moon."

Our parting will last for years,

Fine hours and scenes of beauty have no appeal

Even though my heart is filled with tender feelings,

But, with whom can I share them?

（杨宪益、戴乃迭译）

玉 楼 春
宋 祁

东城渐觉风光好,縠皱波纹迎客棹。绿杨烟外晓寒轻,红杏枝头春意闹。

浮生长恨欢娱少,肯爱千金轻一笑？为君持酒劝斜阳,且向花间留晚照。

Spring in jade pavilion
Song Qi

The scenery is getting fine east of the town;

the rippling water greets boats rowing up and down.

Beyond green willows morning chill is growing mild;

on pink apricot branches spring is running wild.

In our floating life scarce are pleasures we seek after.

How can we value gold above a hearty laughter?
I raise wine cup to ask the slanting sun to stay
and leave among the flowers its departing ray.

(许渊冲译)

The Jade Tower Spring

Song Qi

East Town feels the scene's the best;
The waves roll to meet the guest.
The mist cool, the willows sway;
Apricot twigs see Spring play.
Human life's too short a while;
The world loves gold than a smile!
To the Sun I raise my cup:
Why not light blooms, light them up?

(赵彦春译)

念 奴 娇

赤 壁 怀 古

苏 轼

大江东去,浪淘尽,千古风流人物。故垒西边,人道是,三国周郎赤壁。乱石穿空,惊涛拍岸,卷起千堆雪。江山如画,一时多少豪杰!

遥想公瑾当年,小乔初嫁了,雄姿英发。羽扇纶巾,谈笑间,樯橹灰飞烟灭。故国神游,多情应笑我,早生华发。人生如梦,一尊还酹江月!

Nian Nu Jiao

Memories of the Past at Red Cliff

Su Shi

East flows the mighty river,
Sweeping away the heroes of time past;
This ancient rampart on its western shore
Is Zhou Yu's Red Cliff of three Kingdoms' fame;
Here jagged boulders pound the clouds,
Huge waves tear banks apart,
And foam piles up a thousand drifts of snow;
A scene fair as a painting,

Countless the brave men here in time gone by!

I dream of Marshal Zhou Yu in his day

With his new bride, the Lord Qiao's younger daughter,

Dashing and debonair,

Silk-capped, with feather fan,

He laughed and jested

While the dread enemy fleet was burned to ashes!

In fancy through those scenes of old I range.

My heart overflowing, surely a figure of fun.

A man gray before his time.

Ah, this life is a dream,

Let me drink to the moon on the river!

（杨宪益、戴乃迭译）

Charm of a Maiden Singer
Memories of the Past at Red Cliff
Su Shi

The Great River eastward flows,

With its waves are gone all those

Gallant heroes of bygone years.

West of the ancient fortress appears

The Red Cliff. Here General Zhou won his early fame

When the Three Kingdoms were all in flame.

Jagged rocks tower in the air,

Swashing waves beat on the shore,

Rolling up a thousand heaps of snow.

To match the hills and the river so fair,

How many heroes brave of yore

Made a great show!

I fancy General Zhou at the height

Of his success, with a plume fan in hand,

In a silk hood, so brave and bright,

Laughing and jesting with his bride so fair,

While enemy ships were destroyed as planned

Like castles in the air.

Should their souls revisit this land,

Sentimental, his bride would laugh to say:

Younger than they, I have my hair all turned grey.

Life is but like a dream.

O moon, I drink to you who have seen them on the stream.

(许渊冲译)

声 声 慢

李清照

寻寻觅觅,冷冷清清,凄凄惨惨戚戚。乍暖还寒时候,最难将息。三杯两盏淡酒,怎敌他晚来风急?雁过也,正伤心,却是旧时相识。

满地黄花堆积。憔悴损,如今有谁堪摘?守着窗儿,独自怎生得黑?梧桐更兼细雨,到黄昏、点点滴滴。这次第,怎一个愁字了得!

Beats slowing down

Li Qingzhao

So dim, so dark,

So dense, so dull,

So damp, so dank,

So dead!

The weather, now warm, now cold,

Makes it harder.

Than ever to forget!

How can a few cups of thin wine

Bring warmth against

The chilly winds of sunset?

I recognize the geese flying overhead:

My old friends,

Bring not the old memories back!

Let fallen flowers lie where they fall.

To what purpose.

And for whom should I decorate?

By the window shut, Guarding it alone,

To see the sky has turned so black!

And the drizzle on the kola nut.

Keeps on droning: Pit-a-pat, pit-a-pat!
Is this the kind of mood and moment,
To be expressed by one word "sad"?

(林语堂译)

Beats slowing down
Li Qingzhao

I look for what I miss;
I know not what it is,
I feel so sad, so drear,
So lonely, without cheer.
How hard is it
To keep me fit
In this lingering cold!
By cup on cup
Of wine so dry,
Oh how could I
Endure at dusk the drift
Of wind so swift?
It breaks my heart, alas!
To see the wild geese pass,
For they are my acquaintances of old.

The ground is covered with yellow flowers,
Faded and fallen in showers.
Who will pick them up now?
Sitting alone at the window, how
Could I but quicken
The pace of darkness that won't thicken?
On plane's broad leaves a fine rain drizzles
As twilight grizzles.
O what can I do with a grief
Beyond belief?

(许渊冲译)

满 江 红

岳 飞

怒发冲冠,凭栏处、潇潇雨歇。抬望眼,仰天长啸,壮怀激烈。三十功名尘与土,八千里路云和月。莫等闲、白了少年头,空悲切。

靖康耻,犹未雪。臣子恨,何时灭! 驾长车,踏破贺兰山缺。壮志饥餐胡虏肉,笑谈渴饮匈奴血。待从头、收拾旧山河,朝天阙。

The River All Red

Yue Fei

Wrath sets on end my hair;

I lean on railings where

I see the drizzling rain has ceased.

Raising my eyes

Towards the skies,

I heave long sighs,

My wrath not yet appeased.

To dust is gone the fame achieved at thirty years;

Like cloud-veiled moon the thousand-mile land disappears.

Should youthful heads in vain turn grey,

We would regret for aye.

Lost our capitals,

What a burning shame!

How can we generals

Quench our vengeful flame!

Driving our chariots of war, we'd go

To break through our relentless foe.

Valiantly we'd cut off each head;

Laughing, we'd drink the blood they shed.

When we've reconquered our lost land,

In triumph would return our army grand.

(许渊冲译)

The River All Red

Yue Fei

Hair on end and shoving my hat,

In wrath I lean on the balustrade,

While the rain leaves off its pitter-pat.
Eyes fixed skyward, I sign long and loud.
A hero's fury fills my breast.
At thirsty, nothing achieved, unknown,
— but these to me are light as dust —
I've fought through eight-thousand li
Holding the field, under cloud and moon.
What I do mind, is not to let
My young head turn white in vain,
And be gnawed by empty sorrow then.

With the Jingkang Humiliation yet
Unavenged, unredressed,
How can a subject's grievance be
Ever effaced from memory?
I'll send war-chariots rough-shod
Through the gorges of Mt. Helan;
To quench my thirst, I'd drink the blood
Of Huns, while laugh and chat I can;
Heroic minded, to satiate hunger,
I would make Tartars' flesh my fare.
Till our lost land is all retrieved,
Then to the Imperial Palace, there
I'll make obeisance relieved!

（王知还译）

四、练习与思考

1. 分析题

（1）比较"靖康耻,犹未雪。臣子恨,何时灭"词句英译中许渊冲译本与王知还译本处理典故翻译的策略。

（2）分析《声声慢》两种译文的意境与音韵。

2. 实训题
翻译以下篇目。

昨夜雨疏风骤,浓睡不消残酒。

试问卷帘人,却道海棠依旧。

知否？知否？应是绿肥红瘦。

——李清照《如梦令·昨夜雨疏风骤》

3. 思考题

(1) 宋词词牌名称英译是否有必要统一？

(2) 在宋词翻译中如何传递典故的文化内涵？

(3) 宋词叠字翻译时如何兼顾意境与音律？

(4) 柳永《雨霖铃·寒蝉凄切》你更喜欢哪位译者的译本？请说明原因。

五、参考文献

[1] 龚晓斌,吴昊.宋词英译：回顾与展望[J].短篇小说(原创版),2013(11)：113-114.

[2] 潘雪雪.宋词典故英译分析——以辛弃疾的《永遇乐·京口北固亭怀古》为例[J].科教文汇(中旬刊),2017(2)：185-186.

[3] 孙芸珏.论《声声慢》叠词翻译中美学对等的再现[J].重庆邮电大学学报(社会科学版),2011(3)：129-133.

[4] 魏艳.毛泽东词作中词牌名英译研究——以辜正坤、许渊冲、黄龙译本为例[J].湖南第一师范学院学报,2017(3)：45-48+68.

[5] 张薇,李天贤.视觉化框架下宋词词牌名英译研究——以许渊冲和卓振英译本为例[J].现代语文,2017(9)：121-125.

第九课
《楚辞》译介赏析

> 《楚辞》是我国文学史上的第一部浪漫主义诗歌总集,可上溯至公元前3世纪。楚辞又称为"楚词",是一种骚赋诗体,由于诗歌形式是在楚国民歌基础上加工而成的,篇中又大量引用了楚地(今长江流域)的风物土产和方言词汇,遂得其名。它收录了战国后期以屈原、宋玉为代表的诗歌。作为我国古典文学史上划时代的作品,它也是全人类共同的文化遗产,对后世产生了广泛深远的影响。
>
> 该书以屈原的作品为主,其中《离骚》《九歌》《天问》等篇保存了较多的历史资料和神话传说。屈原(约前339—约前278),名平,战国时期楚国政治家,诗人,其作品中记载了他追求政治理想、忧国忧民的崇高情怀。屈原在20世纪曾被推举为"世界文化名人",得到广泛的纪念。

一、翻译简介

《楚辞》的翻译史已有130余年,迄今已经被译为包括英、法、日、德、意、俄等在内的多种语言,产生了越来越广泛的影响。

楚辞在19世纪中叶才传到欧美。目前,《楚辞》英译有32种,其中全译本7种,选译和节译25种。就译本而言,译者的兴趣点多在于屈原本人的诗作,尤其以《离骚》和《天问》的英译居多,目的主要是呈现中国远古的诗歌艺术,或通过翻译来研究屈原其人,或是通过从外部向内部观照的视角来对中国远古社会宗教、政治、文化进行历史人文探源。由于视角各异,产生的译本也各具特色。

1879年,英国学者庄延龄(Edward Harper Parker)翻译的《离骚》标志着《楚辞》开始进入英语世界；1895年，理雅各(James Legge)的《离骚及其作者》标志着《楚辞》在英语世界专门性研究的发端；亚瑟·韦利(Arthur Waley)通过英译《九歌》对远古中国进行了巫文化研究；霍克斯(David Hawkes)的《楚辞：南方的歌》从人类学角度介入《楚辞》研究。除此以外，欧美译家还有如翟理斯(Herbert Allen Giles)、鲍润生(Francis Xavier Biallas)、叶乃度(Eduard Erkes)、艾约瑟(Joseph Edkins)等赫赫有名的汉学家，他们分别从比较文学、人类学和心理学等不同角度来翻译和研究《楚辞》，对该作品在西方的译介传播起了奠基作用。

国内相对比较完整的英译本有：杨宪益、戴乃迭的《离骚及屈原的其他诗作》、许渊冲的《楚辞》、孙大雨的《英译屈原诗歌选》、卓振英的《楚辞》、海外华裔林文庆的《离骚，一首遭遇痛苦的悲歌》等。

二、书名翻译

和科技类文本不同的是，文学作品不仅是一种交流信息的手段，更是传情达意的工具。因此，在翻译文学作品时不仅要考虑到翻译的准确性，还要考虑到语音、语义、文化等其他因素，诗歌翻译尤其如此。总的来说，要辨其音，协其韵，还其形，传其神，解其意，化其境。

下面就几个典型的译名进行讨论。

1. Ch'u Tz'u：The Songs of the South，an Ancient Chinese Anthology，霍克斯，1959

1959年，霍克斯的《楚辞·南方的歌》在牛津大学出版社出版，这是迄今西方最完善的《楚辞》英译本。1985年企鹅公司对其进行了再版。

霍克斯对篇名的这一译法，同时采用了语音直译和语义直译两种方法来加以呈现。两种译文并行，相互印证，相互解释，将源语文化与目的语文化的距离相对拉近，既在音节上忠实于原文，同时在意义上又用注释延伸和补充原文内容，使读者更容易理解原文意义。

2. Elegies of the South，许渊冲，1994

1994年，湖南出版社出版了许渊冲英译（以下简称"许译"）的《楚辞》，包括屈原的全部诗作和宋玉的作品《九辩》等，共28首。该译本在前言中简略介绍了屈原的生平和作品，并对国内外的部分《楚辞》英译本作了简单评述。在英文译本后面还附有古文、白话文的对照。译者创造性地提出了"三美"原则，在翻译中尽量传达原诗的音美、意美和形美。译文采用了"abab, abcb"四步抑扬格诗体形式，并在句尾用"oh"来对应"兮"，原汁原味地呈现了中华文明的文学艺术。

由于译者本人的源语文化意识较强，对于中华文明的理解相较于一般西方译者更加本土化，因此，许译对书名的处理属于典型的语义直译。作品《楚辞》产生于长江流域，所表达的情感主要是悲愤、哀伤,译者将其译为"南方的哀歌"也就不足为奇了。

总体来讲,西方译者遵循"主流诗学"观念,翻译大多采用归化的方法,注重顺畅,在一定程度上有利于《楚辞》融入目的语社会语境。但由于译者在思维、行为和观察分析事物的视角方面的差异,译文对楚辞文化内涵的理解较为欠缺,对原作的真实思想诠释具有局限性。因此,在文化深度方面落后于原文,不能完全传达出文本所包含的思想意义。

国内译者多采用以弘扬民族文化为主要目的的"异化"翻译方法。因此,《楚辞》书名的翻译还有一些其他的译法,比如卓振英译为"The Verse of Chu"等。

三、特殊概念的翻译

《楚辞》是中国南方文化的源头活水,作品中出现了很多难以翻译的特殊概念,分析许渊冲和霍克斯对特殊概念的处理方式,可为译者带来一定的启示。

1. 语气助词"兮"

文学作品的艺术魅力和美学价值不仅源于其所表达的思想内容,还源于其语言文字的精心组织和运用所产生的以节奏和韵律为主要表现形式的音乐美。节奏和韵律也是作品思想内容和情感能够得到更好表现的重要途径。对文学文本来说,语言形式也具有意义,对作品主题意义和美学效果的表现具有重要的作用,因而译者应尽可能在译文中再现原文的语言形式。对于通过语言文字抒发的深意和情感,译者应在充分理解原文的基础上精心遣词造句,以最大限度地在译文中传递原文之情意。

在诗歌形式及音韵的处理上,"兮"字句的使用是《离骚》区别于其他诗歌体裁的一个不可忽视的特征,寄寓和抒发了作者复杂的思想情感,使诗歌富有音乐之美。而许译和霍克斯译本(以下简称"霍译")在这方面的处理大有不同,例如:

> 不抚壮而弃秽兮,
> 何不改乎此度?
> 乘骐骥以驰骋兮,
> 来吾道夫先路!

许译:Give up the foul while young and strong, oh!
Why won't you, my lord, change your style and way?
Ride your fine steed, gallop along, oh!
I'll go before you lest you stray.

霍译:Gather the flower of youth and cast out the impure!
Why will you not change the error of your ways?
I have harnessed brave coursers for you to gallop forth with:
Come, let me go before and show you the way!

评析：不难看出，对于语气词"兮"的处理，许渊冲巧妙地将其译为"oh"，并置于句末，做到了与原文形式上的对应，抒发了作者强烈的感情。而霍译没有把这个语气词翻译出来。另外，许译除了在句尾用"oh"来实现句尾押韵之外，在句末还用了"way"和"stray"构成尾韵修辞，借以传递原文之声音节奏，使得诗歌读来朗朗上口，富有音乐美。而霍译尽管在内容上忠实于原文，并且实现了与原文的对译，但在诗歌的美感上相对欠缺。

2. 文化负载词

典籍是用汉字记载的历代各领域的权威性著作，是中国历史的见证和华夏文化的重要载体，蕴含着中华民族特有的精神价值、思维方式、想象力和文化意识，体现了中华民族的生命力和创造力。在经济全球化的今天，传播华夏文化是增强文化软实力、让更多外国人了解中国的历史与未来的重要途径。而典籍作为人类文化多元系统的一个组成部分，积极参与到世界文化交流中去成为一种必然。因此，作为向海外传播华夏文化的桥梁，典籍翻译也就具有重要的意义。

2.1 翻译策略

翻译策略有直译（也叫对译）和意译之分。直译又分为语音直译、语义直译、字母＋语音直译或字母＋语义直译。意译指在形式改变不影响原文信息内容或作者意图的基础上，对原作语言单位的增、减、转、换、分、合。关于这两种译法，两位译者也各有不用的妙用。请看以下例子：

例1：一阴兮一阳，众莫知兮余所为。（《九歌·大司命》）

许译：Your life or death, oh! is in my hands.

霍译：A *yin* and a *yang*, a *yin* and a *yang*: None of the common folk know what I am doing.

评析：许译采用语义直译的方法，使读者一目了然，明确诗歌内容的思想所指，但由于舍弃了源语言的词汇本身，因此也顺带舍弃了源语言除表面意义之外更深层次的丰富的文化内涵；霍译采用语音直译的方法，虽然在音韵节奏上非常协调，但对于缺乏汉文化修养的读者来说，很难了解到"阴阳"这一特殊词汇所反映出的中国古代道家思想对立统一、相互转化的深刻哲学内涵，读者需要这一语汇信息的进一步补充说明。

例2：高阳（《离骚》中有"帝高阳之苗裔兮"）

许译：High Sunny King

霍译：the high lord Gao Yang

评析："高阳"一词在《辞海》中的解释是指颛顼，是我国上古时期一位氏族部落首领。因此"高阳"一词在中国文化中属于特有词汇，为保持其翻译的准确性，许渊冲和霍克斯都采取了直译的方法，但许译采用了语义直译的方法，更容易使人通过其字面意义了解其所指；而霍克斯采取了"不译之译"法，直接将其语音直译为 the high lord Gao Yang，这就需要读者在加注中进一步了解这个词的文化含义及其原有的文化内涵。

2.2 异化加注

对于出自中国历史典故、独具文化特色的内容,要想翻译成英文后让外国人理解或看得懂,用加注来介绍背景知识或特定的文化知识,就是一种必要的翻译补偿策略了。这种翻译方法可以为读者提供一种全新的视角,其生动性可以有效地帮助读者深入理解原文中的神话原型。中国独有的文化负载词汇、成语或者典故等在英文中找不到对应的词语时,采用这种方法可以向译文读者展示中国特有的背景文化、民俗、典故等内容,帮助读者更好地理解原作、体会原作的深意。但在注释的过程中需要注意的是,注释所用语言必须准确严谨、简明扼要、通俗易懂,同时还不能掺杂译者的主观思维和想象,必须按照原作者的写作目的来延伸和补充原文。《楚辞》中也出现了大量的文化负载词,请看以下例子:

例1:摄提(《离骚》中有"摄提贞于孟陬兮")

许译:Tiger's Day

霍译:She Ti,并加脚注:the name of a Chinese constellation made up of two groups of three stars to left the right of the bright star Arcturus in Bootes

评析:"摄提"是我国古代纪年的一个术语,全称摄提格,相当于今天所说的寅年。许译在形式上较为简洁,并且在句尾实现了诗歌的押韵,体现诗歌的美感,但同时也导致了一些文化信息的流失。霍译由于加入了注释,在翻译的准确性角度而言,补充了文化信息,使得外国读者更清楚地了解文化负载词的特殊含义。

例2:女娲(《天问》中有"女娲有体,孰制匠之")

许译:snake queen

霍译:Nu Wa,并加脚注:Nu Wa had a snake's tail instead of legs

评析:许译形象简洁,但对于西方读者来说,容易引发关于魔鬼撒旦的联想,因此对于深层次的文化含义,可能会引起误解误读。霍译采取语音直译和异化加注的补偿翻译方法,在形式上更忠实于原文,相对来讲也更符合中国神话原型,同时,随着译者对源文本理解的不断深入,也更易于不断改进加注。

例3:扶桑、若木(《离骚》中有"饮余马于咸池兮,总余辔乎扶桑。折若木以拂日兮,聊逍遥以相羊。")

许译:giant tree(大树),a branch(树枝)

霍译:Fu-sang tree,并加脚注:Mythical tree in the far east which the sun climbs up in his rising. According to one version of the myth, it had ten suns in its branches, one for every day of the week.

Jo-tree,并加脚注:In the far west. Its foliage gives off a red glow which illumines the earth below — presumably a mythological explanation of the sunset glow.

评析:许译采用了语义直译的方法,意象清晰,但没有体现出两种树木的神性意义,也没有表现出作者本人高洁的精神寓意。霍译保留了原诗的音韵和谐,同时在脚注中用神话意识对于两种树木进行了深层意象的阐释,带给读者丰富的文化内涵知识。

2.3 部分文化负载词翻译举例

中国是个具有五千多年历史的文明古国,中国的传统文化博大精深涉及中国传统文化的词汇在《楚辞》中有很多,先来了解一下部分传统文化的词汇的英文表达。

(1) 历史传说(人/神/地名)

高阳 the lord Gao Yang/High Sunny King

鲧　 the flood-fighter/Gun

夏启 the second king of Xia

羿　 The hunter/Yi

浇　 the traitor's sun/Jiao

夏桀 the last king of Xia

苍梧 the E'ergreen State

县圃 the Hanging Garden/the mountain's crest

灵琐 Fairy precincts/Celestial Gate

羲和 the driver of the sun

崦嵫 Holy Mountains

咸池 the Sun's Bath

望舒 Moon's Charioteer

飞廉 the Wind God/The curtain-rolling Winds

雷师 the Thunder God/The Lord of Thunder

帝阍 Heaven's Porter

白水 the white water/the Deathless Stream

阆风 Endless Peaks

春宫 House of Spring/Verhal Temple hall

宓妃 Fu fei/the Nymphean Queen

謇修 Lame Beauty/Lord of Dream

吕望 A butcher

周文 King Wen

宁戚 a cowherd/Ning Qi

齐桓 Duke Huan

天津 Heaven's Ford

西极 the world's western end

不周山 Mount Pillar Strong

孟陬 the first month of the year

东皇太一 the Great Unity，God of the Eastern Sky/The Almighty Lord of the East

玉饵 jade pendent

云中君 To the God of cloud

湘君 To the Lord of River Xiang

湘夫人 To the Lady of River Xiang

大司命 The Great Lord of Fate

少司命 The Young Goddess of Fate

东君 The God of the Sun

河伯 The God of the River

山鬼 The Goddess of the Mountain

(2) 其他重点词语

江离 selinea

辟芷 anglica

宿莽 sedges

申椒 pepper

菌桂 cassia/cinnamon

党人 partisans

九天 the Nine-fold Heaven/Ninth Heaven High

灵修 the Fair One/the Sacred One

留夷 sweet lichens/peonies

揭车 cart-halting flower

杜衡 asarums

芳芷 fragrant anglica

木兰 Magnolia

秋菊 chrysanthemum/aster

绳墨 the ruled line

鸷鸟 the eagle

兰皋 the marsh's orchid — covered margin

椒丘 Pepper Hill/the Hill of Pepper-trees

女媭 my sister

婵媛 Gently downcast

婞直 steadfast

菉葹 thorns and weeds/thorns, king grass, curly-ear

艾草 mugwort

3. 人称

对于诗歌的翻译，要求译者不能仅拘泥于原文的语义，而要在深入体会句子的形式和内容的基础上做出灵活处理,争取做到形神兼备,以便更好地传递原作者的思想感情。就《楚辞》而言,在传情达意上两位译者也各有不同,请看以下例子:

例1:
> 帝子降兮北渚,
> 目眇眇兮愁予。
> 嫋嫋兮秋风,
> 洞庭波兮木叶下。
>
> ——《九歌·湘夫人》

许译: Descend on northern isle, oh! my lady dear,
But I am grieved, oh! to see not clear.
The autumn breeze, oh! ceaselessly grieves
The Dongting waves, oh! with fallen leaves.

霍译: The child of God, descending the northern bank,
Turns on me her eyes that are dark with longing.
Gently the wind of autumn whispers;
On the waves of the Tung-t'ing Lake the leaves are falling.

评析: 在形式上,许译和霍译都压了尾韵,实现了音乐美。但是细看可以发现,两位译者在表情达意的处理上存在不同。在人称的处理上,尽管原文用的是第三人称"帝子",但许译采取了第一人称,以湘君的口吻,用"my lady dear"来直接表达其对湘夫人的思念之情,而霍译则采用了原文的第三人称,在表现力度上有所欠缺。

例2: 荃不察余之中情兮

——《离骚》

许译: To my loyalty you're unkind, oh!

霍译: But the Fragrant One refused to examine my true feelings

评析: 许译中"荃"字直接对应了第二人称"you",用对话的语气使读者明白其指是"人",读来似乎感觉到作者是在向对方直接发出抱怨批评,读者更难以想象"荃"其实是一种香草的名字,而且古人对此顶礼膜拜,所以此处可能指代身份高贵的君王,而非普通人。霍译创造性地使用了"the Fragrant One",并且使用了大写,联想到西方《圣经》中提到上帝时也常常在文中使用大写,因此这一第三人称的出现既表现出了植物具有香味的特性,同时也令读者可以联想到其深层含义喻指国君。

从以上例子的分析我们可以看出,在诗歌的翻译中要求译者不仅要正确理解原文的含义,而且要深刻领会作者的思想感情。

四、译文对比赏析

《楚辞》中有很多经典的句子和段落,译成英文之后不同版本的语言特点各不相同。

其英译本为数众多,各有千秋。下面分别选取了比较有影响力的许渊冲和霍克斯的译本来做对比赏析。

1. 诗歌篇名

屈原	许渊冲	霍克斯
《离骚》	Sorrow after Departure	On Encountering Sorrow (Li Sao)
《九歌》	The Nine Songs	The Nine Songs(Chiu Ko)
《山鬼》	The Goddess of the Mountain	The Mountain Goodness (Shan Kuei)
《国殇》	For Those Fallen for the Country	The Spirits of the Fallen (Kuo Shang)
《天问》	Asking Heaven	The Heavenly Questions (T'ien Wen)
《惜诵》	I Make My Plaint	Grieving I Make My Plaint (Hsi Sung)
《卜居》	Divination	Divination (Pu Chü)
《招魂》	Requiem	The Summoms of the Soul (Chao Hun)

2. 经典句子

吾令羲和弭节兮,望崦嵫而勿迫。

路曼曼其修远兮,吾将上下而求索。

——《离骚》

I bid the Driver of the Sun, oh!
To Holy Mountains slowly go.
My way ahead's a long, long one, oh!
I'll seek my Beauty high and low.
— *Sorrow after Departure*　　　　　　　　　　　　　　　　　　　　（许渊冲译）

I ordered Hsi-ho to stay the sun-steed's gallop,
To stand over Yen-tzǔ mountain and not go in.
Long, long had been my road and far, far was the journey;
I would go up and down to seek my heart's desire.
— *On Encountering Sorrow（Li Sao）*　　　　　　　　　　　　　　　（霍克斯译）

操吴戈兮被犀甲,车错毂兮短兵接。

旌蔽日兮敌若云,矢交坠兮士争先。

——《九歌·国殇》

We take our southern spears, oh! and don our coats of mail;
When chariot axes clash, oh! with daggers we assail.
Banner obscure the sun, oh! the foe roll up like cloud;
Arrows shower crisscross, oh! forward press our men proud.
— *The Nine Songs: For Those Fallen for the Country* （许渊冲译）

Grasping our great shields and wearing our hide armour,
Wheel-hub to wheel-hub locked, we battle hand to hand.
Our banners darken the sky; the enemy teem like clouds;
Through the hail of arrows the warriors press forward.
— *Chiu Ko: Kuo Shang*（*The Spirits of the Fallen*）: *Hymn to the Fallen*

（霍克斯译）

3. 经典段落
帝高阳之苗裔兮，
朕皇考曰伯庸。
摄提贞于孟陬兮，
惟庚寅吾以降。
皇览揆余初度兮，
肇赐余以嘉名。
名余曰正则兮，
字余曰灵均。
纷吾既有此内美兮，
又重之以修能。
扈江离与辟芷兮，
纫秋兰以为佩。
汩余若将不及兮，
恐年岁之不吾与。
朝搴阰之木兰兮，
夕揽洲之宿莽。

——《离骚》

Descendant of High Sunny King, oh!
My father's name shed sunny ray.
The Wooden Star appeared in spring, oh!
When I was born on Tiger's Day.

My father saw my birthday bright, oh!
He gave me an auspicious name.
My formal name was Divine Right, oh!
I was also called Divine Flame.
I have so much beauty inside, oh!
And add to it a style ornate.
I weave sweet grass by riverside, oh!
Into a belt with orchid late.
Like running water years will pass, oh!
I fear time and tide wait for none.
At dawn I gather mountain grass, oh!
At dusk I pick secluded one.

— *Sorrow after Departure* （许渊冲译）

Sicon of the High Lord Gao Yang,
Po Yung was my father's name.
When She T'i pointed to the first month of the year,
On the day *keng yin*, I passed from the womb.
My father, seeing the aspect of my nativity,
Took omens to give me an auspicious name.
The name he gave me was True Examplar;
The title he gave me was Divine Balance.

Having from birth this inward beauty,
I added to if fair outward adornment:
I dressed in selinea and shady andlica,
And twined autumn orchids to make a garland.
Swift I sped, as in fearful pursuit,
Afraid Time would race on and leave me behind.
In the morning I gathered the anglica on the mountains;
In the evening I plucked the sedges of the islets.

— *On Encountering Sorrow*（*Li Sao*） （霍克斯译）

帝子降兮北渚，
目眇眇兮愁予。
嫋嫋兮秋风，

洞庭波兮木叶下。
登白薠兮骋望，
与佳期兮夕张。
鸟何萃兮薠中，
罾何为兮木上？
沅有茝兮澧有兰，
思公子兮未敢言。
荒忽兮远望，
观流水兮潺湲。
麋何食兮庭中？
蛟何为兮水裔？
朝驰余马兮江皋，
夕济兮西澨。

——《九歌·湘夫人》

Descend on northern isle, oh! my lady dear,
But I am grieved, oh! to see not clear.
The autumn breeze, oh! ceaselessly grieves
The Dongting waves, oh! with fallen leaves.
I gaze afar, oh! 'mid clovers white
And wait for our tryst, oh! in the twilight.
Among the reeds, oh! can birds be free?
What can a net do, oh! atop a tree?
White clover grows, oh! beside the creek;
I long for you, oh! But dare not speak.
I gaze afar, oh! My beloved one
I only see, oh! Rippling waters run.
Could deer find food, oh! within the door?
What would a dragon do, oh! upon the shore?
At dawn by riverside, oh! I urge my steed;
Across the western stream, oh! at dusk I speed.
— *The Nine Songs: The Lady of River Xiang*

（许渊冲译）

The Child of God, descending the northern bank,
Turns on me her eyes that are dark with longing.
Gently the wind of autumn whispers;

On the waves of the Tung-t'ing lake the leaves are falling.

Over the white sedge I gaze out wildly;

For a tryst is made to meet my love this evening.

But why should the birds gather in the duckweed?

And what are the nets doing in the tree-tops?

The Yüan has its anglicas, the Li has its orchids;

And I think of my lady, but dare not tell it,

As with trembling heart I gaze on the distance

Over the swiftly moving waters.

What are the deer doing in the courtyard?

Or the water-dragons outside the waters?

In the morning I drive my steeds by the river;

In the evening I cross to the western shore.

— *Chiu Ko*:（d）*Hsiang Fu jen*（*The Lady of the Hsiang*）　　　　（霍克斯译）

皇天之不纯命兮，
何百姓之震愆！
民离散而相失兮，
方仲春而东迁。
去故乡而就远兮，
遵江夏以流亡。
出国门而轸怀兮，
甲之朝吾以行。
发郢都而去闾兮，
怊荒忽其焉极？
楫齐扬以容与兮，
哀见君而不再得。
望长楸而太息兮，
涕淫淫其若霰。
过夏首而西浮兮，
顾龙门而不见。

——《九章·哀郢》

Inconstant is Heaven on high. oh!

How people tremble far and nigh!

Scattered, all men are lost in woe; oh!

Just in mid-spring eastward I go.

I leave my home for far-off place; oh!

Exiled, along the stream I pace.

I pass through city gate with heavy heart, oh!

On the first day at dawn I part.

Leaving the capital of Chu, oh!

I am at a loss what to do.

In time we dip slowly the oar; oh!

My prince is not seen, I deplore.

Gazing on high trees, I heave sighs; oh!

Like sleet sad tears fall from my eyes.

Passing Summer Head, westward we float, oh!

The Dragon Gate can't be seen from my boat.

— *The Nine Elegies Lament for the Chu Capital* （许渊冲译）

High Heaven is not constant in its dispensations:

See how the country is moved to unrest and error!

The people are scattered, and men cut off from their fellows.

In the middle of spring the move to the east began.

I left my old home and set off for distant places,

And following the waters of the Chiang and Hsia, I travelled into exile.

I passed through the City gate with a heavy heart:

On the day *Chia*, in the morning, my journey began.

As I set out from the city and left the gate of my village,

An endless turmoil started in my mind.

And as the oars slowly swept in time,

I grieved that I should never look on my prince again.

I gazed on the high catalpa trees and heaved a heavy sigh,

And the tears in torrents, like winter's sleet, came down.

We passed the head of Hsia; and once, as we drifted westwards,

I looked back for the Dragon Gate, but I could not see it.

— *Chiu Chang:* （c）*Ai Ying* (*A Lament for Ying*) （霍克斯译）

曰：遂古之初，谁传道之？

上下未形，何由考之？

冥昭瞢暗,谁能极之?

冯翼惟象,何以识之?

明明暗暗,惟时何为?

阴阳三合,何本何化?

圜则九重,孰营度之?

惟兹何功,孰初作之?

——《天问》

Who could tell us at last

When did begin the past?

How could anyone know

The formless high and low?

Who knows where darkness did end

When light and shade blend?

How to imagine things

In air but not on wings?

How could darkness turn bright

When day divided from night?

How did light and shade strange

Originate and change?

Who did take measure of

The Ninth Heaven above?

Who built the firmament

Of such boundless extent?

— *The Song of the South: Asking Heaven* （许渊冲译）

Who was there to pass down the story of the beginning of things in the remote past?

What means are there to examine what it was like before heaven above and the earth below had taken shape?

How is it possible to probe into that age when the light and darkness were still undivided?

And how do we know about the chaos of insubstantial forms?

What manner of things are the darkness and light?

How did the *yin* and *yang* commingle?
How do they originate things, and how change them?

Who planned and measured out the round shape and ninefold gates of Heaven?
Whose work was this, and who first made it?
— *T'ien Wen*（*The Heavenly Questions*）　　　　　　　　　　（霍克斯译）

若有人兮山之阿，
被薜荔兮带女萝。
既含睇兮又宜笑，
子慕予兮善窈窕。
乘赤豹兮从文狸，
辛夷车兮结桂旗。
被石兰兮带杜衡，
折芳馨兮遗所思。
余处幽篁兮终不见天，
路险难兮独后来。
表独立兮山之上，
云容容兮而在下。
杳冥冥兮羌昼晦，
东风飘兮神灵雨。
留灵修兮憺忘归，
岁既晏兮孰华予。

——《九歌·山鬼》

In mountains deep, oh! looms a fair lass,
In ivy leaves, oh! girt with sweet grass.
Amorous looks, oh! and smiling eyes,
For such a beauty, oh! there's none but sighs.
Laurel flags spread, oh! over fragrant cars
Drawn by leopards, oh! dotted with stars.
Orchid as belt, oh! and crown above,
She plucks sweet blossoms, oh! for her dear love.
"The bamboo grove, oh! obscures the day;
I come too late, oh! hard is the way.
Standing alone, oh! on mountain proud,

I see below, oh! a sea of cloud.
"The day is dark, oh! as dark as night;
The east wind blows, oh! rain blurs the sight.
Waiting for you, oh! I forget hours.
Late in the year, oh! Who'd give me flowers?
— *The Nine Songs: The Goddess of the Mountain* （许渊冲译）

There seems to be some one in the fold of the mountain
In a coat of fig leaves with a rabbit-floss girdle,
With eyes that hold laughter and a smile of pearly brightness:
'Lady, your allurements show that you desire me.'
Driving tawny leopards, leading the striped lynxes;
A car of lily-magnolia with banner of woven cassia;
Her cloak of stone-orchids, her belt of asarum:
She gathers sweet scents to give to one she loves.
I am in the dense bamboo grove, which never sees the sunlight,
A Place of gloomy shadow, dark even in the daytime.
Solitary she stands, upon the mountain's summit:
So steep and hard the way is, that I shall be late.
The clouds' dense masses begin below me:
When the east wind blows up, the goddess sends down her showers.
Dallying with the fair One, I forget about returning.
What flowers can I deck myself with, so late in the year?
— *Chiu Ko*:（i）*Shan Kuei*（*The Mountain Goodness*） （霍克斯译）

五、练习与思考

1. 分析题

（1）分析《离骚》两种译文的翻译手段，说说许译和霍译的区别。

（2）比较"初既与余成言兮，后悔遁而有他。余既不难夫离别兮，伤灵修之数化"，两个译本之不同。

2. 实训题

翻译以下篇目。

（1）忽奔走以先后兮，及前王之踵武。

荃不察余之中情兮,反信谗而齌怒。
余固知謇謇之为患兮,忍而不能舍也。
指九天以为正兮,夫惟灵修之故也。
初既与余成言兮,后悔遁而有他。
余既不难夫离别兮,伤灵修之数化。

(2) 嗟尔幼志,有以异兮。独立不迁,岂不可喜兮。深固难徙,廓其无求兮。苏世独立,横而不流兮。闭心自慎,不终失过兮。秉德无私,参天地兮。

3. 思考题
(1) 什么情况下适合直译？请举例说明。
(2) 你最喜欢《楚辞》的哪个译本？为什么？
(3) 比较许译和霍译对《离骚》的翻译,谈谈各自有什么特点？
(4) 你认为诗歌翻译的形式与内容可以兼顾吗？
(5) 比较《离骚》中植物名的翻译,谈谈各自有什么特点？
(6) 汉译英如何化简为繁？如何体现趋繁性？繁主要体现在何处？
(7) 汉译英以动制静的核心因素是什么？如何表现？
(8) 汉译英再回译成汉语可以发现汉语的什么特点？
(9) 如何理解翻译对汉语和英语都是一把双刃剑？
(10) 为什么说汉英语言对比于翻译极其重要？

六、参考文献

[1] David Hawkes. Ch'u Tz'u, the Songs of the South, an Ancient Chinese Anthology[M]. Boston: Beacon Press, 1962.

[2] 王逸,洪兴祖.楚辞章句补注[M].长春:吉林人民出版社,2005.

[3] 许渊冲.楚辞:汉英对照[M].北京:五洲传播出版社,2012.

[4] 张娴.《楚辞》英译研究——基于文化人类学整体论的视角[M].北京:中国社会科学出版社,2018.

第十课
《红楼梦》译介赏析

> 《红楼梦》是四大名著之一,是我国古代小说史上最光彩夺目的篇章,也是现实主义创作的不朽丰碑。《红楼梦》展现了广阔的社会现实,集中表现了当时的社会矛盾。本书以贾宝玉和林黛玉的爱情悲剧为线索,通过描写以贾府为代表的封建大家族的衰亡,揭露了封建家族的腐朽和其败亡的必然命运。《红楼梦》描写了四百多个人物,塑造了独特、鲜活的人物形象,让人百读不厌。
>
> 《红楼梦》的体裁是长篇章回体白话小说,总体采用市井白话,同时存在大量诗词韵文、谚语俗语。语言通俗易懂,质朴自然,洗练准确;人物刻画光彩夺目,个性鲜明,栩栩如生;艺术结构宏大精致,众多事件彼此勾连,互为因果,浑然天成,呈现了广阔的社会历史图景,是中国古代小说艺术的顶峰。

一、翻译简介

《红楼梦》的翻译史已有200年。首个译本诞生于1800年前后,是韩文和中文对照全译抄本"乐善斋本"。《红楼梦》的早期译者主要是外交使节、传教士和留学生,被当作学习中国官话的启蒙读物而翻译成外文。其在20世纪30年代曾作为日本留学生学习标准北京话的课本。

《红楼梦》已被翻译成了英、法、德、日、韩、俄、泰、西班牙等语种的译本。20世纪70年代—80年代西方出现的全译本达20多种,其中日文、韩文译本占了大多数。《红楼梦》译本有摘译、节译、全译三种形式。摘译指译者挑出少量内容进行翻译,19世纪初海外出现过一大批此类译本,例如,罗伯特·汤姆(Robert Thom)的 *The Dreams of the Red*

Chamber(1846)就是《红楼梦》第六回的片段；伊·赫德生（E. Hudson）的 *An Old, Old Story* 则是将第四回译成英文。节译指翻译大部分内容，但删去了一些情节，比如大量删去诗词，还有的将原内容自行进行了编辑，总体规模多则相当于国内120回本的80回，少则只相当于40回—50回，但基本反映了《红楼梦》的故事情节。全译的两个代表性的译本一是杨宪益、戴乃迭夫妇所译，另一是霍克斯（David Hawkes）所译。两个译本采用了两种译法，杨戴夫妇的译本偏直译，霍译偏意译。这只是一般归纳，并非句句译法都完全如此。另外，还有黄新渠的简译本 *A Dream in Red Mansions*（*Saga of a Noble Chinese Family*）(《红楼梦(中国贵族家庭的传奇)》)等。

二、书名翻译

《红楼梦》属于章回小说，由民间说书而来，因此有着多个别名，如《石头记》《情僧录》《风月宝鉴》《金陵十二钗》《金玉缘》《大观琐录》《警幻仙境》等。《红楼梦》书名的翻译因此也呈现出多样性。例如：

Robert Thom（1846）：The Dreams of the Red Chamber

Edward Charles Bowra（1868）：The Dream of the Red Chamber

H. Bencraft Joly（1892）：Hong Lou Meng；The Dream of the Red Chamber, A Chinese Novel

王际真（1929）：Dream of the Red Chamber

Florence McHugh and Isabel McHugh（1958）：The Dream of the Red Chamber

David Hawkes（1973）：The Story of the Stone（前八十回），John Minford（1982）：The Story of the Stone（后四十回）

杨宪益、戴乃迭（1980）：A Dream of Red Mansions

下面就几个典型的译名进行讨论。

1. The Dream of the Red Chamber

这个翻译中最重要的是 chamber，词典上给 chamber 的定义是 a room in a house, especially a bedroom，因此 *The Dream of the Red Chamber* 即为"红色卧室的梦"，这个翻译不免有特指之嫌，例如，第五回贾宝玉神游太虚境的梦，但这个梦与主题思想不符。

2. A Dream of Red Mansions

词典上给 mansion 的定义是 a large, stately house，即宽敞而庄重的房子，体现了荣华富贵，正与原作主题相符。而红楼的"情"则通过 Red 隐含表现。

3. The Tale of the Stone, The Story of the Stone

这个翻译就是源自汉语《石头记》。

4. 其他

《情僧录》，杨宪益将其译为 Record of the Passionate Monk，而霍克斯将其译为 The

Tale of Brother Amor。

《风月宝鉴》,杨宪益将其译为 Precious Mirror of Love,而霍克斯将其译为 A Mirror for the Romantic。

《金陵十二钗》,杨宪益和霍克斯同译为 The Twelve Beauties of Jinling。

第五回宝玉梦中提及十二支仙曲名《红楼梦》,杨宪益将其译为 A Dream of the Red Mansions(即书名),霍克斯译为 A Dream of Golden Days,对梦进行了直译,而红楼采用意译或阐释。

总之,杨宪益在书名的翻译中多采用全译、重直译/异化的方式,简洁、平铺直叙。而霍克斯多采用改译、重意译/归化的方式,详实且生动活泼。

在影响力方面,已有的译本中主要是杨宪益、戴乃迭的 *A Dream of Red Mansions* 和霍克斯的 *The Story of the Stone* 具有较大的影响。在国内,两个译本平分秋色,但霍克斯的翻译在海外的影响远大于杨戴夫妇的译本。这其中原因很多,包括出版方面的不同。霍克斯的翻译出版于1973年,而杨宪益的出版时间是1978—1980年间。霍克斯的翻译是由赫赫有名的企鹅(Penguin)出版社出版,而杨宪益是国内的外文出版社出版,虽然外文出版社也是具有较高知名度的出版机构,但对国外读者来说,他们更认可的是他们熟知的企鹅社。另外,外国读者不懂原文,这便使他们趋于全盘接受霍克斯的翻译;而国内读者熟悉《红楼梦》原文本,读英文版的时候易于与原文本的对照,就发现杨戴夫妇的翻译更加贴近原文。

三、特殊概念的翻译

《红楼梦》具有博大精深的文化内涵,书中出现大量中国文化特有的概念和表达方式,比如人物对话中常出现历史信息、熟语、方言、土语,成了翻译的一大难点。分析杨戴夫妇(以下简称"杨译")和霍克斯(以下简称"霍译")对特殊概念的处理方式,可为译者带来一定的启示。

1. 历史文化信息

(林黛玉)心较<u>比干</u>多一窍,病如<u>西子</u>胜<u>三分</u>

杨译:

She looked more sensitive than Bi Gan, more delicate than Xi Shi. (Note)

霍译:

She had more chambers in her heart than the martyred Bi Gan; And suffered a tithe more pain in it than the beautiful Xi Shi.

评析:本句"一窍"指心房,"西子"指西施,"三分"是强化词、度量单位。在"心较比干多一窍"的翻译上,杨译采用"more sensitive",语言形式上并不是完全对等,但意义上却向原文趋近。霍译直接译出"more chambres"。杨译通过 note 补偿,霍译采用正文直接增译补偿。

商末纣王暴虐荒淫,横征暴敛,滥用重刑,从政多年的比干叹曰:"主过不谏非忠也,畏死不言非勇也,过则谏不用则死,忠之至也"。遂至摘星楼强谏三日不去。纣问"何以自恃",比干曰:"善行仁义所以自恃。"纣怒曰:"吾闻圣人心有七窍,信诸?"遂杀比干剖视其心。

对原文中的民族文化、历史文化信息,翻译时可采用加注或增译的方式,抑或选择翻译部分信息。

2. 熟语

这里的熟语是个广义的概念,它包括词组型的和句子型的,既有四字成语、俚语或土语,也有谚语、绝句等,这些语言形式的最大特点是具有强烈的民族文化内涵,有历史故事,有民族哲理。

例1:(鸳鸯:)如今都是<u>可着头做帽子了</u>,要一点富余也不能的。

杨译:

We have to <u>cut our coat according to our cloth</u>. Nowadays there's no margin at all.

霍译:

<u>Meals are made to measure nowadays</u>. We can't afford to be extravagant the way we used to be.

评析:"可着头做帽子"字面意义指"根据头的尺寸做帽子",比喻精打细算、恰到好处,不超出能力范围。两位翻译家都采用了较为朴素又直观易懂的方式,"cut our coat according to our cloth""meals are made to measure"都体现了原文的比喻义。二者的译文体现翻译没有定法,可以有多种可能的表达方式。

例2:(平儿:)咱二爷那脾气,<u>油锅里的还要捞出来花</u>呢。

杨译:

And being what he is, ready to <u>snatch money from a pan of scolding oil</u>, he'd start spending …

霍译:

And we all know what Master is like where money is concerned: he'd <u>spend the fat in the frying-pan if he could get it out</u>!

评析:"油锅里的还要捞出来花"意思是"为了抓到热油锅里的钱而不怕烫手",形容人吝啬、贪婪,为了钱而不怕冒风险。这是一句土话,译本要体现其土味。

两个译本在此用了不同方式表达"吝啬、贪婪"的含义。杨译的"snatch money from a pan of scolding oil",偏向直译,直白这句土语所指的意思。霍译采用"spend the fat in the frying-pan if he could get it out!"偏向意译,反映出了吝啬的程度以及原话的土味,再次体现语言的表征性,即"一句话百样说",一个道理可以用多种方式表达,而不改变其命题意义。

例3：（刘姥姥：）二十年前，他们看承你们还好；如今自然是拉硬屎，不肯去亲近他，故疏远起来。

杨译：

... and twenty years back they treated you not badly. Since then of course you've been too pig-headed to go near them, so that now you've drifted apart.

霍译：

Twenty years ago the Nanking Wangs used to be very good to you folk. It's only because of late years you have been too stiff-necked to approach them that they have become more distant with you.

评析：在这句话中，"拉硬屎"的命题意义是"瞎逞能，强充好汉，打肿脸充胖子，死要面子活受罪"。杨译采用的"pig-headed"和霍译采用的"stiff-necked"同是一种比喻，虽不是完全一样，但均接近原文。

翻译中很难在源语和目的语中找到完全对应的表达，这是因为不同语言体系对概念的切分、句法和对文化的表达方式不一样，选用何种东西作为比喻不会完全一样。

例4：兴儿道："这就是俗语说的'天下逃不过一个理字去'了。"

杨译：

"As the proverb says," he retorted, "everyone has to listen to reason."

霍译：

"It's like the proverb says: 'Three men with a carrying-pole can't shift Reason from its place.'"

评析：翻译谚语时，最佳方法是目标语也用谚语。在这句谚语的处理上，杨译短小精悍，霍译则将抽象的"reason"具体化。

例5：子兴道："依你说，'成则王侯败则贼'了。"

杨译：

"You are saying that such people may become princes or thieves, depending on whether they are successful or not."

霍译：

"You mean," Zi-xing interpreted, "Zhang victorious is a hero, Zhang beaten is a lousy knave."

评析："成则王侯败则贼"即"胜者为王，败者为寇"。在"王侯"和"贼"这一对立的概念上，杨译采用"princes"和"thieves"，其中"princes"指"the male ruler of a small country or state that has a royal family"；霍译用"hero"和"knave"表示对立概念。

例6：紫鹃道："姑娘身上不大好，依我说，还得自己开解着些。身子是根本，俗语说的，'留得青山在，依旧有柴烧。'"

234

杨译：

"You're so delicate, miss, I don't think you should worry so much. Health is what counts. As the saying goes, 'As long as the mountain's there, we shan't lack fuel.'"

霍译：

"You're not well, Miss. I think all this worrying is ruining your health. And good health is like the hill in the proverb: Keep the hill green, and you'll never lack fuel for winter again."

评析："留得青山在，依旧有柴烧"，可以用英语谚语"Where there is a will, there is a way"表示，也可以将"青山"和"柴"译出，就像杨译"As long as the mountain's there, we shan't lack fuel"。霍译"Keep the hill green, and you'll never lack fuel for winter again"加了"winter"，表示其他季节柴火比较容易获得，而冬季人们则需"keep the mountain green"，方能不缺柴。

例7：北静王又向贾政笑道："令郎乃龙驹凤雏，非小王在世翁前唐突，将来'雏凤清于老凤声'，未可量也。"贾政忙赔笑道："犬子岂敢谬承金奖。赖藩郡馀恩，果如所言，亦荫生辈之幸矣。"

杨译：

The prince turned to observe to Jia Zheng, "Your son is truly a dragon's colt or young phoenix. May I venture to predict that in time to come this young phoenix may even surpass the old one?"

"My worthless son does not deserve such high praise," replied Jia Zheng hurriedly with a courteous smile. "If thanks to the grace of Your Highness such proves the case, that will be our good fortune."

霍译：

The prince observed to Jia Zheng that "the young phoenix was worthy of his sire."

"I trust I shall not offend you by saying so to your face," he said, "but I venture to prophesy that this fledgling of yours will one day 'sing sweeter than the parent bird.'"

Jia Zheng smiled politely. "my son is doubtless unworthy of the compliment Your Highness is good enough to pay him. If, thanks to your encouragement, he turns out as you say, we shall count ourselves truly fortunate!"

评析：在处理"龙驹凤雏""雏凤清于老凤声"上，杨译偏向直译，将"龙驹"和"凤雏"的意象译了出来，霍译则更为自由，用意译的方式处理——"worthy of his sire"和"sing sweeter than the parent bird"，二者都表达出了原文中的恭维之意。

3. 金陵判词

《红楼梦》里的金陵判词预示着十位姑娘的命运，作为诗歌体，其中押韵、比喻等修辞丰富。

例1：（妙玉）欲洁何曾洁，云空未必空；可怜金玉质，终陷淖泥中。

杨译：

Chastity is her wish,

Seclusion her desire;

Alas, though fine as gold or jade,

She sinks at last in the mire.

霍译：

For all your would-be spotlessness

And vaulted other worldliness,

You that look down on common flesh and blood,

You yourself impure shall end up in the mud.

评析： 两个译文选择了不同的视角进行处理，杨译是直接按原文直译"洁""空""金""玉"，保留了原文二、四句押韵的韵体，而霍译采用的是叙述性的表达，描述了妙玉的命运，同时变换了原文的押韵方式，改用 AABB 偶韵体。

4. 流水句翻译

所谓的流水句，即为一连串的简单句组合在一起，以描写某个情节、某种情景，或某种心情等。

例1： 这个人打扮与众姑娘不同：彩秀辉煌，恍若神妃仙子。头上戴着金丝八宝攒珠髻，绾着朝阳五凤挂珠钗；项下戴着赤金盘螭璎珞圈；裙边系着豆绿宫绦双鱼比目玫瑰佩；身上穿着缕金百蝶穿花大红洋缎窄裉袄，外罩五彩刻丝石青银鼠褂，下罩翡翠撒花洋绉裙。一双丹凤三角眼，两弯柳叶吊梢眉。身量苗条，体格风骚，粉面含春威不露，丹唇未启笑先闻。

杨译：

Unlike the girls, she was richly dressed and resplendent as a fairy. Her gold-filigree tiara was set with jewels and pearls. Her hair-clasps, in the form of five phoenixes facing the sun, had pendants of pearls. Her necklet, of red gold, was in the form of a coiled dragon studded with gems. She had double red jade pendants with pea-green tassels attached to her skirt. Her close-fitting red satin jacket was embroidered with gold butterflies and flowers. Her turquoise cape, lined with white squirrel, was inset with designs in coloured silk. Her skirt of kingfisher-blue crepe was patterned with flowers.

She had the almond-shaped eyes of a phoenix, slanting eyebrows as long and drooping as willow leaves. Her figure was slender and her manner vivacious. The springtime charm of her powdered face gave no hint of her latent formidability. And before her crimson lips parted, her laughter rang out.

霍译：

Even as she wondered, a beautiful young woman entered from the room behind the one they were sitting in, surrounded by a bevy of serving women and maids. She was dressed quite differently from the others present, gleaming like some fairy princess with sparkling jewels and gay embroideries. Her chignon was enclosed in a circlet of gold filigree and clustered pearls. It was fastened with a pin embellished with flying phoenixes, from whose beaks pearls were suspended on tiny chains.

Her necklet was of red gold in the form of a coiling dragon. Her dress had a fitted bodice and was made of dark red silk damask with a pattern of flowers and butterflies in raised gold thread. Her jacket was lined with ermine. It was of a slate-blue stuff with woven insets in coloured silks. Her under-skirt was of a turquoise-coloured imported silk crepe embroidered with flowers.

she had, moreover, eyes like a painted phoenix, eyebrows like willow-leaves, a slender form, seductive grace; the ever-smiling summer face of hidden thunders showed no trace; the ever-bubbling laughter started almost before the lips were parted.

评析：汉语是一种意合的语言，即汉语语篇较少运用语言衔接手段标明语句之间的逻辑关系，主要靠语句所含意义实现语篇的连贯；相反，英语则是一种形合的语言，小句与小句之间需要一定的显性语言衔接手段以实现语篇的语义连贯。汉语的意合性造就大量流水句的运用。汉语流水句的突出特点就是小句与小句之间没有显性的语言衔接手段，但语篇的意义、连贯性和流畅性并不受影响。

抛开两个译文在其他语言层面选择上的差异，我们发现两者的共同之处就是按照各个小句子之间语意关系的密切度将原文长的流水句拆分成两个或四个句子，这样原文长句所包含的大量信息才能够在译文中讲清楚，且符合英语的行文规范。

四、译文对比赏析

1. 章回目录对比
（1）金寡妇贪利权受辱　张太医论病细穷源
（1）Widow Jin's self-interest gets the better of her righteous indignation; And Doctor Zhang's diagnosis reveals the origin of a puzzling disease

（霍克斯译）

Widow Jin Pockets Her Pride Because of Self-Interest Dr. Zhang Diagnoses

Keping's Illness

（杨宪益、戴乃迭译）

（2）王凤姐弄权铁槛寺，秦鲸卿得趣馒头庵

背景解释：

弄权：把握权力，操持朝政；凭借职位，滥用权力，即 manipulate power for personal ends。

馒头庵：即水月寺，离铁槛寺不远。因这庙里做的馒头好，故名馒头寺。

秦鲸卿：秦可卿的弟弟。秦鲸卿谐音"情经情"，也叫秦钟，暗指在贾宝玉的未来生活中播下了一粒"情种"。

得趣馒头庵：秦可卿去世后，秦钟和宝玉同时送殡至水月庵，与尼姑智能儿几次幽会缠绵。

(2) At Water-moon Priory Xifeng finds how much profit may be procured by the abuse of power;

And Qin Zhong discovers the pleasures that are to be had under the cover of darkness

（霍克斯译）

Xifeng Abuses Her Power at Iron Threshold Temple
Qin Zhong Amuses Himself in Steamed-Bread Convent

（杨宪益、戴乃迭译）

（3）王熙凤正言弹妒意　林黛玉俏语谑娇音

背景解释：

弹：批评，揭发(criticize; expose)，如：旌善以兴化，弹邪而矫俗。——《三国志·陶谦传》；仆常好人讥弹其文。有不善者，应时改定。——曹植《与杨德祖书》

相关词组：抨弹(抨击)；弹议(弹劾评议)；弹黜(弹劾罢黜)；弹文(弹劾官员过错的奏疏)；弹正(纠弹，纠正)；弹断(讥评)；弹激(激烈率直地予以抨击)

谑：取笑作乐(mock)如：

伊其相谑。——《汉书·地理志》。注："戏言也。"；调笑来相谑。——李白《陌上桑》；嗜酒善谑，而好为诗。——《宋史》

娇：撒娇(act like a pampered child)。如：

娇嗔(撒娇，故意作出生气的娇态)；娇懒(撒娇懒惰)

(3) Wang Xifeng castigates a jealous attitude with some forthright speaking; And Lin Daiyu makes a not unattractive speech impediment the subject of a jest

（霍克斯译）

Xifeng Reproves a Jealous Woman Daiyu Mocks a Prattling Girl

（杨宪益、戴乃迭译）

（4）诉肺腑心迷活宝玉　含耻辱情烈死金钏

白话文：因诉衷肠或表白宝玉感到迷惑,因含羞受辱金钏自杀了。

（4）Baoyu demonstrates confusion of mind by making his declaration to the wrong person; And Golden shows an unconquerable spirit by ending her humiliation in death

（霍克斯译）

An Avowal Leaves Baoyu Bemused Disgrace Drives Jinchuan to Suicide

（杨宪益、戴乃迭译）

（5）蒋玉菡情赠茜香罗　薛宝钗羞笼红麝串

背景解释：

宝玉初遇蒋玉菡,觉得彼此投缘,宝玉将自己的扇子坠送给蒋玉菡,蒋玉菡将北静王送的大红汗巾子送给宝玉,作为交换,宝玉将自己的松花色汗巾子解下送给他。

红麝串：红色的麝香串珠。宝玉看宝钗手上的红麝串和臂膀产生的种种幻想,被宝钗看出,于是宝钗害羞地将串子抛给宝玉,这场景恰巧被黛玉看到。

之所以"羞笼",是因为宝姐姐平时不喜弄装饰。如今这么出场,自然有些害羞,有些得意,有些要人看见又怕人看见。

（5）A crimson cummerbund becomes a pledge of friendship; And a chaplet of medicine-beads becomes a source of embarrassment

（霍克斯译）

Jiang Yuhan Gives a New Friend a Scarlet Perfumed Sash. Baochai Bashfully Shows Her Red Bracelet Scentd with Musk

（杨宪益、戴乃迭译）

（6）秋爽斋偶结海棠社　蘅芜苑夜拟菊花题

背景解释：

秋爽斋："斋",书房也。是贾探春在大观园的住所,充满了浓郁的书卷气息。贾母初宴大观园的地方。

海棠社：贾府处于兴盛之时最有名的一次结社,大家吟诗作赋尽显才情。

蘅芜苑：大观园中的建筑物,为薛宝钗在大观园里的居所。原名为蘅芷清芬,后被贾元春改为蘅芜苑。

菊花题：诗篇的雅号。

秋爽：秋日的凉爽之气。

海棠(Begonia)，也作思想草(Miss-grass)，蘅芜(Crab-flower)、菊花(Chrysanthemum)都是植物。

(6) A happy inspiration prompts Tanchun to found the Crab-flower Club; And an ingenious arrangement enables Baochai to settle the chrysanthemum poem titles

（霍克斯译）

Begonia Club Takes Form One Day in the Studio of Autumn Freshness. Themes for Poems on Chrysanthemums Are Prepared One Evening in Alpinia Park

（杨宪益、戴乃迭译）

(7) 变生不测凤姐泼醋　喜出望外平儿理妆

背景解释：

变生：有重大影响的突然变化；不测：意外。变故发生于突然之间。变生不测：诡变多端。

泼醋：产生嫉妒情绪，多指在男女关系上。同"拈酸吃醋"，即吃醋。

理妆：整理妆饰。

(7) Xifeng's jealousy is the object of an unexpected provocation; And Patience's toilet is a source of unexpected delight

（霍克斯译）

Xifeng, Taken by Surprise, Gives Way to Jealousy
Ping'er, Unexpectedly Gratified, Makes Her Toilet

（杨宪益、戴乃迭译）

(8) 薛小妹新编怀古诗　胡庸医乱用虎狼药

背景解释：

薛小妹：薛宝琴,薛姨妈的侄女,薛蟠、薛宝钗的堂妹。十分美貌,受贾母喜爱,夸她比画还好看,曾欲把她说给贾宝玉为妻。王夫人也认她为干女儿。她自幼读书识字,本性聪敏,在大观园里曾作《怀古绝句十首》。

虎狼药：又称虎狼之剂或狼虎之剂,词义是指病人经受不起的烈药。典故来源于《红楼梦》这一回。虎狼药对孕妇伤害极大,不能使用。

(8) A clever cousin composes some ingenious riddles; And an unskilful physician prescribes a barbarious remedy

（霍克斯译）

Baoqin Composes Poems Recalling the Past. An Incompetent Physician Prescribes

Strong Medicine

（杨宪益、戴乃迭译）

（9）强欢笑蘅芜庆生辰　死缠绵潇湘闻鬼哭

背景解释：

蘅芜：蘅芜苑。

生辰：薛宝钗的生日。

潇湘：潇湘馆，潇湘妃子的住所。"潇湘妃子"是指古代传说中舜妃娥皇、女英哭夫，而自投湘水，死后成湘水女神之称，在《红楼梦》里指林黛玉。

(9) A birthday party held for sister Allspice Necessitates a false display of jollity; And ghostly weeping heard at the Naiad's House provokes a fresh outburst of grief

（霍克斯译）

Baochai's Birthday Is Celebrated with Forced Mirth Baoyu, Longing for the Dead, Hears Ghosts Weeping in Bamboo Lodge

（杨宪益、戴乃迭译）

（10）甄士隐梦幻识通灵　贾雨村风尘怀闺秀

背景解释：

通灵：可以和死人的灵魂对话，或在梦中互通信息，这种现象就被叫作通灵。

风尘：比喻旅途的艰辛劳累，也比喻纷乱的社会或漂泊江湖的境况。

怀闺秀：贾雨村在落魄之际（风尘），竟然有闺中小姐（虽然是丫头）爱上他。

综述：这里指贾宝玉和林黛玉的来历。宝玉是石头下凡。这块石头因"无材补天"被女娲抛弃在青埂峰下，又四处游荡，到警幻仙子处做了神瑛侍者，遇见一株绛珠仙草，日日为她灌溉甘露，后来又被一僧一道携了投胎下凡做人，他就是贾宝玉。那株绛珠仙草也跟了石头下凡，她就是林黛玉。

(10) Zhen Shiyin makes the Stone's acquaintance in a dream; And Jia Yucun finds that poverty is not incompatible with romantic feeling

（霍克斯译）

Zhen Shiyi in a Dream Sees the Jade of Spiritual Understanding
Jia Yucun in His Obscurity Is Charmed by a Maid

（杨宪益、戴乃迭译）

（11）托内兄如海荐西宾　接外孙贾母惜孤女

背景解释：

托内兄：委托妻子的哥哥。

如海：人名，林如海，林黛玉之父。

西宾：旧时宾位在西，故称。常用为对家塾教师或幕友的敬称。

外孙和孤女：指同一人（林黛玉）。

（11）Lin Ruhai recommends a private tutor to his brother-in-law；And old Lady Jia extends a compassionate welcome to the motherless child

（霍克斯译）

Lin Ruhai Recommends a Tutor to His Brother-in-law
The Lady Dowager Sends for Her Motherless Grand-Daughter

（杨宪益、戴乃迭译）

（12）滴翠亭杨妃戏彩蝶　埋香冢飞燕泣残红

背景解释：

滴翠亭：大观园中一景。《释名》云："亭者，停也。所以亭憩游行也。"滴翠亭即为潇湘馆附近的一处水中之亭，四面俱是游廊回桥。

冢：高而大的坟。

埋香冢：葬花的地方。

（12）Beauty Perspiring sports with butterflies by the Raindrop Pavilion；And Beauty Suspiring weeps for fallen blossoms by the Flower's Grave

（霍克斯译）

Baochai Chases a Butterfly to Dripping Emerald Pavilion
Daiyu Weeps over Fallen Blossom by the Tomb of Flowers

（杨宪益、戴乃迭译）

2. 经典句段

（1）霁月难逢，彩云易散。心比天高，身为下贱。风流灵巧招人怨。寿夭多因毁谤生，多情公子空牵念。

（1）Seldom the moon shines in a cloudless sky,

　　And days of brightness all too soon pass by.

　　A noble and aspiring mind

　　In a base-born frame confined,

　　Your charm and wit did only hatred gain,

　　And in the end you were by slanders slain,

Your gentle lord's solicitude in vain.

(霍克斯译)

A clear moon is rarely met with,
Bright clouds are easily scattered;
Her heart is loftier than the sky,
But her person is of low degree.
Her charm and wit give rise to jealousy,
Her early death is caused by calumny,
In vain her loving master's grief must be.

(杨宪益、戴乃迭译)

(2) 枉自温柔和顺,空云似桂如兰,堪羡优伶有福,谁知公子无缘。

(2) What price your kindness and compliance,
Of sweetest flower the rich perfume?
You chose the player fortune favoured,
Unmindful of your master's doom.

(霍克斯译)

Nothing avail her gentleness and compliance,
Osmanthus and orchid with her fragrance vie;
But this prize is borne off by an actor,
And luck passes the young master by.

(杨宪益、戴乃迭译)

(3) 根并荷花一茎香,平生遭际实堪伤。自从两地生孤木,致使香魂返故乡。

(3) Your stem grew from a noble lotus toot,
Yet your life passed, poor flower, in low repute.
The day two earths shall bear a single tree,
Your soul must fly home to its own country.

(霍克斯译)

Sweet is she as the lotus in flower,
Yet none so sorely oppressed;
After the growth of a lonely tree in two soils
Her sweet soul will be dispatched to its final rest.

(杨宪益、戴乃迭译)

243

(4) 可叹停机德，堪怜咏絮才。玉带林中挂，金簪雪里埋。

(4) One was a pattern of female virtue,

　　One a wit who made other wits seem slow.

　　The jade belt in the greenwood hangs,

　　The gold pin is buried beneath the snow.

　　　　　　　　　　　　　　　　　　（霍克斯译）

　　Alas for her wifely virtue,

　　Her wit to sing of willow-down, poor maild!

　　Buried in snow the broken golden hairpin

　　And hanging in the wood the belt of jade.

　　　　　　　　　　　　　　　　　　（杨宪益、戴乃迭译）

(5) 二十年来辨是非，榴花开处照宫闱。

　　三春争及初春景，虎兕相逢大梦归。

(5) You shall, when twenty years in life's hard school are done,

　　In pomegranate-time to palace halls ascend.

　　Though three springs never could with your first spring compare,

　　When hare meets tiger your great dream shall end.

　　　　　　　　　　　　　　　　　　（霍克斯译）

　　For twenty years she arbitrates

　　Where pomegranates blaze by palace gates.

　　How can the late spring equal the spring's start?

　　When Hare and Tiger meet,

　　From this Great Dream of life she must depart.

　　　　　　　　　　　　　　　　　　（杨宪益、戴乃迭译）

(6) 才自精明志自高，生于末世运偏消。清明涕送江边望，千里东风一梦遥。

(6) Blessed with a shrewd mind and a noble heart,

　　Yet born in time of twilight and decay,

　　In spring through tears at river's bank you gaze,

　　Borne by the wind a thousand miles away.

　　　　　　　　　　　　　　　　　　（霍克斯译）

　　So talented and high-minded,

　　She is born too late for luck to come her way.

Through tears she watches the stream
   On the Clear and Bright Day;
   A thousand lithe east wind blows,
   But her home in her dreams is far away.

（杨宪益、戴乃迭译）

(7) 富贵又何为,襁褓之间父母违。展眼吊斜晖,湘江水逝楚云飞。

(7) What shall avail you rank and riches,
    Orphaned while yet in swaddling bands you lay?
    Soon you must mourn your bright sun's early setting.
    The Xiang flows and the Chu clouds sail away.

（霍克斯译）

   Nought avail her rank and riches,
   While yet in swaddling clothes an orphan lone;
   In a flash she mourns the setting sun,
   The river Xiang runs dry, the clouds over Chu have flown.

（杨宪益、戴乃迭译）

(8) 欲洁何曾洁,云空未必空。可怜金玉质,终陷淖泥中。

(8) For all your would-be spotlessness
    And vaunted otherworldliness,
    You that look down on common flesh and blood,
    Yourself impure, shall end up in the mud.

（霍克斯译）

   Chastity is her wish,
   Seclusion her desire;
   Alas, though fine as gold or jade
   She sinks at last in the mire.

（杨宪益、戴乃迭译）

(9) 子系中山狼,得志便猖狂。金闺花柳质,一载赴黄粱。

(9) Paired with a brute like the wolf in the old fable,
    Who on his saviour turned when he was able,
    To cruelty not used, your gentle heart

Shall, in a twelvemonth only, break apart.

（霍克斯译）

For husband she will have a mountain wolf,
His object gained he ruthlessly berates her;
Fair bloom, sweet willow in a golden bower,
Too soon a rude awakening awaits her.

（杨宪益、戴乃迭译）

3. 经典段落
(1) 宝黛初见

一语未了，只听外面一阵脚步响，丫鬟进来笑道："宝玉来了！"黛玉心中正疑惑着："这个宝玉，不知是怎生个惫懒人物，懵懂顽童？"——倒不见那蠢物也罢了。心中想着，忽见丫鬟话未报完，已进来了一位年轻的公子：头上戴着束发嵌宝紫金冠，齐眉勒着二龙抢珠金抹额；穿一件二色金百蝶穿花大红箭袖，束着五彩丝攒花结长穗宫绦，外罩石青起花八团倭缎排穗褂，登着青缎粉底小朝靴。面若中秋之月，色如春晓之花，鬓若刀裁，眉如墨画，面如桃瓣，目若秋波。虽怒时而若笑，即瞋视而有情。项上金螭璎珞，又有一根五色丝绦，系着一块美玉。黛玉一见，便吃一大惊，心下想道："好生奇怪，倒像在那里见过一般，何等眼熟到如此！"

While they were speaking, a flurry of footsteps could be heard outside and a maid came in to say that Bao-yu was back.

'I wonder,' thought Dai-yu, 'just what sort of graceless creature this Bao-yu is going to be!'

The young gentleman who entered in answer to her spoken question had a small jewel-encrusted gold coronet on the top of his head and a golden headband low down over his brow in the form of two dragons playing with a large pearl.

He was wearing a narrow-sleeved, full-skirted robe of dark red material with a pattern of flowers and butterflies in two shades of gold. It was confined at the waist with a court girdle of coloured silks braided at regular intervals into elaborate clusters of knotwork and terminating in long tassels.

Over the upper part of his robe he wore a jacket of slate-blue Japanese silk damask with a raised pattern of eight large medallions on the front and with tasselled borders.

On his feet he had half-length dress boots of black satin with thick white soles.

As to his person, he had:

a face like the moon of Mid-Autumn,

a complexion like flowers at dawn,

a hairline straight as a knife-cut,

eyebrows that might have been painted by an artist's brush,

a shapely nose, and eyes clear as limpid pools,

that even in anger seemed to smile,

and, as they glared, beamed tenderness the while.

Around his neck he wore a golden torque in the likeness of a dragon and a woven cord of coloured silks to which the famous jade was attached.

Dai-yu looked at him with astonishment. How strange! How very strange! It was as though she had seen him somewhere before, he was so extraordinarily familiar.

(霍克斯译)

The words were hardly out of her mouth when they heard footsteps in the courtyard and a maid came in to announce, "Baoyu is here."

Daiyu was wondering what sort of graceless scamp or little dunce Baoyu was and feeling reluctant to meet such a stupid creature when, even as the maid announced him, in he walked.

He had on a golden coronet studded with jewels and a golden chaplet in the form of two dragons fighting for a pearl. His red archer's jacket, embroidered with golden butterflies and flowers, was tied with a coloured tasselled palace sash. Over this he wore a turquoise fringed coat of Japanese satin with a raised pattern of flowers in eight bunches. His court boots were of black satin with white soles.

His face was as radiant as the mid-autumn moon, his complexion fresh as spring flowers at down. The hair above his temples was as sharply outlined as if cut with a knife. His eyebrows were as black as if painted with ink, his cheeks as red as peach-blossom, his eyes bright as autumn ripples. Even when angry he seemed to smile, and there was warmth in his glance even when he frowned.

Round his neck he had a golden torque in the likeness of a dragon, and a silk cord of five colours, on which hung a beautiful piece of jade.

His appearance took Daiyu by surprise. "How very strange!" she thought. "It's as if I'd seen him somewhere before. He looks so familiar."

(杨宪益、戴乃迭译)

(2) 晴雯撕扇

晴雯听了,笑道:"既这么说,你就拿了扇子来我撕,我最喜欢撕的。"宝玉听了,便笑着递与他。晴雯果然接过来,嗤的一声,撕了两半,接着嗤嗤又听几声。宝玉在旁笑着说:

"响的好,再撕响些!"正说着,只见麝月走过来,笑道:"少作些孽罢。"宝玉赶上来,一把将他手里的扇子也夺了递与晴雯。晴雯接了,也撕了几半子,二人都大笑。麝月道:"这是怎么说,拿我的东西开心儿?"宝玉笑道:"打开扇子匣子你拣去,什么好东西!"麝月道:"既这么说,就把匣子搬了出来,让他尽力的撕,岂不好?"宝玉笑道:"你就搬去。"麝月道:"我可不造这孽。他也没折了手,叫他自己搬去。"晴雯笑着,倚在床上说道:"我也乏了,明儿再撕罢。"宝玉笑道:"古人云,'千金难买一笑',几把扇子能值几何!"一面说着,一面叫袭人。袭人才换了衣服走出来,小丫头佳蕙过来拾去破扇,大家乘凉,不消细说。

'All right then,' said Skybright with a mischievous smile. 'Give me your fan to tear. I love the sound of a fan being torn.' Bao-yu held it out to her. She took it eagerly and — chah! — promptly tore it in half. And again — chah! chah! chah! — she tore it several more times. Bao-yu, an appreciative onlooker, laughed and encouraged her.

'Well torn! Well torn! Now again — a really loud one!'

Just then Musk appeared. She stared at them indignantly.

'Don't do that!' she said. 'It's wicked to waste things like that.'

But Bao-yu leaped up to her, snatched the fan from her hand, and passed it to Skybright, who at once tore it into several pieces. The two of them, Bao-yu and Skybright, then burst into uproarious laughter.

'What do you think you're doing?' said Musk. 'That's my fan you've just ruined.'

'What's an old fan?' said Bao-yu. 'Open up the fan box and get yourself another.'

'If that's your attitude,' said Musk, 'we might as well carry Out the whole boxful and let her tear away to her heart's content.'

'All right. Go and get it,' said Bao-yu.

'And be born a beggar in my next life?' said Musk. 'No thank you I She hasn't broken her arm. Let her go and get it herself.'

Skybright stretched back on the bed, smiling complacently. 'I'm rather tired just now. I think I shall tear some more tomorrow.'

Bao-yu laughed.

'The ancients used to say that for one smile of a beautiful woman a thousand taels are well spent. For a few old fans it's cheap at the price!'

He called to Aroma, who had just finished changing into clean clothes, to come outside and join them. Little Melilot came and cleared away the broken bits of fan, and everyone sat for a while and enjoyed the cool.

(霍克斯译)

"If that's so, get me a fan to tear up. I love ripping things apart."

With a smile he handed her his own. Sure enough, she ripped it in two, then tore it to pieces.

Baoyu chuckled.

"Well done! Try and make a bigger noise."

Just then along came Sheyue.

"What a wicked waste!" she cried. "Stop it."

Baoyu's answer was to snatch her fan from her and give it to Qingwen, who promptly tore it up and joined in his loud laughter.

"What's the idea?" demanded Sheyue. "Spoiling my fan — is that your idea of fun?"

"Just pick another from the fan case," Baoyu told her. "What's so wonderful about a fan?"

"You'd better bring the case out here then and let her tear the whole lot up."

"You bring it." Baoyu chuckled.

"I won't do anything of the sort. She's not broken her wrist, let *her* fetch it."

"I'm tired." Qingwen lay back laughing. "I'll tear up some more tomorrow."

"You know the ancient saying," put in Baoyu. "A thousand pieces of gold can hardly purchase a smile. And what are a few fans worth?"

He called for Xiren, who came out having just changed into clean clothes and got little Jia Hui to clear away the broken fans. Then they sat outside for a while enjoying the cool.

(杨宪益、戴乃迭译)

(3) 凤姐打趣黛玉

凤姐道:"前儿我打发了丫头送了两瓶茶叶去,你往那去了?"林黛玉笑道:"哦,可是倒忘了,多谢多谢。"凤姐儿又道:"你尝了可还好不好?"没有说完,宝玉便说道:"论理可倒罢了,只是我说不大甚好,也不知别人尝着怎么样。"宝钗道:"味倒轻,只是颜色不大好些。"凤姐道:"那是暹罗进贡来的。我尝着也没什么趣儿,还不如我每日吃的呢。"林黛玉道:"我吃着好,不知你们的脾胃是怎样?"宝玉道:"你果然爱吃,把我这个也拿了去吃罢。"凤姐笑道:"你要爱吃,我那里还有呢。"林黛玉道:"果真的,我就打发丫头取去了。"凤姐道:"不用取去,我打发人送来就是了。我明儿还有一件事求你,一同打发人送来。"

林黛玉听了笑道:"你们听听,这是吃了他们家一点子茶叶,就来使唤人了。"凤姐笑道:"倒求你,你倒说这些闲话,吃茶吃水的。你既吃了我们家的茶,怎么还不给我们家作媳妇?"众人听了一齐都笑起来。林黛玉红了脸,一声儿不言语,便回过头去了。李宫裁笑向宝钗道:"真真我们二婶子的诙谐是好的。"林黛玉道:"什么诙谐,不过是贫嘴贱舌讨人厌恶罢了。"说着便啐了一口。凤姐笑道:"你别作梦!你给我们家作了媳妇,少什么?"指宝玉道："你瞧瞧，人物儿，门第配不上，根基配不上，家私配不上？那一点还玷辱了谁呢？"

林黛玉抬身就走。宝钗便叫："颦儿急了，还不回来坐着。走了倒没意思。"

'I sent someone round to you the other day with two caddies-full of tea,' said Xi-feng, 'but you were out.'

'Yes,' said Dai-yu. 'I'm sorry: I forgot to thank you.'

'Have you tried it?' said Xi-feng. 'What did you think of it?'

'I wouldn't ask, if I were you,' said Bao-yu, chipping in. '*I* thought it was rotten. I don't know what the rest of you thought about it.'

'I thought the flavour was all right,' said Bao-chai. 'The colour wasn't up to much.'

'That was tribute tea from Siam,' said Xi-feng. '*I* didn't like it at all. I thought it wasn't as nice as the tea we drink every day.'

'Oh, I quite liked it,' said Dai-yu. 'Your palates must be more sensitive than mine.'

'If you really like it,' said Bao-yu, 'you're welcome to have mine.'

'I've still got quite a bit left,' said Xi-feng. 'If you really like it, you can have it all.'

'Thank you very much,' said Dai-yu. 'I'll send someone round to fetch it.'

'No, don't do that,' said Xi-feng. 'I'll send it round to *you*. There's something I want you to do for me. The person I send round about it can bring the tea as well.'

Dai-yu laughed mockingly:

'Do you hear that, everybody? Because she's given me a bit of her old tea, I have to start doing odd jobs for her.'

'That's fair enough,' said Xi-feng. 'You know the rule: "drink the family's tea, the family's bride-to-be".'

Everyone laughed at this except Dai-yu, who turned her head away, blushing furiously, and said nothing.

'Cousin Feng will have her little joke,' Li Wan observed to Bao-chai with a smile.

'Do you call that *a joke*?' said Dai-yu. 'It was a silly, idle remark, and very irritating.'

She gave a snort of disgust by way of reinforcement.

Xi-feng laughed:

'What's so irritating about it? Look at him!' — She pointed at Bao-yu — 'Isn't he good enough for you? Good looks, good family, good income. There are no snags that I can see. It's a perfect match!'

Dai-yu rose and fled.

'Oh, Frowner's in a rage! Come back Frowner!' Bao-chai called out after her. 'If you go, it will spoil all the fun.'

（霍克斯译）

"I sent you two canisters of tea the other day," interposed Xifeng. "Where were you?"

"Oh, it had slipped my mind. Thank you very much."

"How did you like it?" Xifeng asked.

"It's all right but I didn't care for it much," put in Baoyu. "I don't know how the rest of you found it."

"The flavour was quite delicate, but the colour wasn't too good," remarked Baochai.

"That was tribute tea from Siam," Xifeng told them. "Personally, I didn't find it as good as the kind we drink every day."

"I liked it," retorted Daiyu. "Different people have different tastes."

"In that case you can have mine," offered Baoyu.

"If you really like it I've plenty more," said Xifeng.

"Fine. I'll send a maid to fetch it," Daiyu promised.

"No need," rejoined Xifeng. "I'll have it sent round. I was going to send over to you tomorrow anyway to ask a favour."

"Listen to her!" cried Daiyu. "Just take a little tea from her and she starts ordering you about."

Xifeng chuckled.

"Asked a favour, you make such a fuss! Over drinking tea too. 'Drink our family's tea, a daughter-in-law to be'!"

As the whole party burst out laughing, Daiyu blushed and turned her head away, saying nothing.

Li Wan observed with a smile to Baochai, "Our second sister-in-law will have her joke."

"Joke?" Daiyu spat. "I call it disgustingly vulgar."

"Are you dreaming? What's wrong with being our daughter-in-law?" teased Xifeng, then pointed at Baoyu. "Look, isn't he handsome enough for you? Isn't his good enough for you? Isn't his family rich enough for you? Who could think it a bad match in any respect?"

Daiyu rose at once to go.

"You're offended," cried Baochai. "Come back, Daiyu! It'll spoil the fun if you go."

（杨宪益、戴乃迭译）

(4) 宝黛放风筝

一时丫鬟们又拿了许多各式各样的送饭的来，顽了一回。紫鹃笑道："这一回的劲大，姑娘来放罢。"黛玉听说，用手帕垫着手，顿了一顿，果然风紧力大，接过籰子来，随着风筝的势将籰子一松，只听一阵豁剌剌响，登时籰子线尽。黛玉因让众人来放。众人都笑道："各人都有，你先请罢。"黛玉笑道："这一放虽有趣，只是不忍。"李纨道："放风筝图的是这一乐，所以又说放晦气，你更该多放些，把你这病根儿都带了去就好了。"紫鹃笑道："我们姑娘越发小气了。那一年不放几个子，今忽然又心疼。姑娘不放，等我放。"说着便向雪雁手中接过一把西洋小银剪子来，齐籰子根下寸丝不留，咯登一声铰断，笑道："这一去把病根儿可都带了去了。"那风筝飘飘摇摇，只管往后退了去，一时只有鸡蛋大小，展眼只剩了一点黑星，再展眼便不见了。众人皆仰面睃眼说："有趣，有趣。"宝玉道："可惜不知落在那里去了。若落在有人烟处，被小孩子得了还好，若落在荒郊野外无人烟处，我替他寂寞。想起来把我这个放去，教他两个作伴儿罢。"于是也用剪子剪断，照先放去。

A maid came round offering them all sweets. Presently there was a cry from Nightingale：

'The wind's getting stronger, Miss. Do you want to release it now?'

Dai-yu made her handkerchief into a pad for her hand and tested the tension on the string. The wind was certainly pulling it with some force. She took over the winder from Nightingale and let it run free, so that the kite could pull itself away in the wind. There was a whirring noise as the last of the string ran out. Dai-yu asked the others if any of them would like to cut it for her.

'No, we've all got our own,' they said. 'You do yours first.'

'It's fun to see them fly away,' said Dai-yu, 'and yet it seems rather a pity.'

'But that's the main reason for flying kites,' said Li Wan, 'the pleasure of seeing them fly away. Not to mention the fact that it is supposed to get rid of your bad luck You of all people ought to let yours go, so as to get rid of your illness.'

'Come on, Miss, you've sent plenty of kites off in your time!' said Nightingale. 'Why be so stingy all of a sudden? If you won't cut it, I'll cut it for you.'

She snatched a little pair of West Ocean silver scissors out of Snowgoose's hand and snipped through the kite-string, an inch or so from the winder.

'Go away, kite!' she cried merrily. 'And take my mistress's illness with you!'

The kite began to swoop and soar. Soon it appeared no bigger than an egg. A few moments later and it was only a dot in the sky. Another moment and it had disappeared from sight altogether.

'Hurrah! Hurrah!' cried the cousins, as they watched it disappear.

'What a pity we don't know where she will land!' said Bao-yu. 'It would be nice if she landed somewhere where there are people and some little child were to find her. But suppose she lands in some uninhabited wilderness: how lonely she will be! I think I shall send my lady after her, to keep her company!'

He asked for the scissors and cut the string himself, and a second pretty lady went hurrying after the first one until it, too, disappeared.

（霍克斯译）

Then Zijuan exclaimed, "It's pulling hard now, miss. Won't you take over?"

Daiyu wrapped a handkerchief round her hand and pulled. Sure enough, the wind was blowing hard. She took the reel and paid out the cord. As the kite soared off, the reel whirred and all of a sudden the whole cord had run out. Then she urged the rest to let their kites drift away.

"We're all ready," they said. "You start first."

"Though it's fun to let it go, I haven't the heart to." she replied with a smile.

"Kite-flying is just for fun, that's why we call it 'sending off bad luck'," said Li Wan. "You should do this more often, and then you might get rid of that illness of yours. Wouldn't that be a good thing?"

"Our young lady's getting more and more stingy," put in Zijuan. "We always sent off a few kites every year, so why begrudge one today? If you won't do it, miss, I will." She took from Xueyan a pair of small silver Western scissors, and clipped the cord tied to the reel.

"There!" she said with a laugh. "That'll carry off her illness."

The kite drifted away until soon it seemed no bigger than an egg, then it dwindled to a speck like a black star and the next minute vanished from sight.

Watching with screwed-up eyes they cried, "What fun!"

"It's a pity we don't know where it'll land," observed Baoyu. "Let's hope it falls somewhere with people about and gets picked up by some children. If it falls in the wilderness where nobody lives, how lonely it will feel. I'd better send this one after it to keep it company.' He cut the cord of his kite and let it go too."

（杨宪益、戴乃迭译）

(5) 湘云醉酒

正说着，只见一个小丫头笑嘻嘻的走来，说："姑娘们快瞧，云姑娘吃醉了，图凉快，在山子后头一块青石板磴上睡着了。"众人听说,都笑道:"快别吵嚷。"说着,都走来看时,果见湘云卧于山石僻处一个石磴子上,业经香梦沈酣。四面芍药花飞了一身,满头脸衣襟上皆是红香散乱。手中的扇子在地下,也半被落花埋了,一群蜜蜂蝴蝶闹嚷嚷的围着。又用鲛帕包了一包芍药花瓣枕着。众人看了,又是爱,又是笑,忙上来推唤挽扶。湘云口内犹作睡语说酒令,嘟嘟嚷嚷说:"泉香酒冽,……醉扶归,宜会亲友。"众人笑推他说道:"快醒醒儿,吃饭去。这潮磴上还睡出病来呢!"湘云慢启秋波,见了众人,又低头看了一看自己,方知是醉了。原是纳凉避静的,不觉因多罚了两杯酒,娇娜不胜,便睡着了,心中反觉自悔。早有小丫头端了一盆洗脸水,两个捧着镜奁。众人等着,他便在石磴上重新匀了脸,拢了鬓,连忙起身,同着来至红香圃中。又吃了两杯浓茶,探春忙命将醒酒石拿来给他衔在口内,一时又命他吃了些酸汤,方才觉得好了些。

'Come and look, everyone!' — They were interrupted by a giggling young maid — 'Miss Yun must have been feeling drunk and gone out for some air. She's lying on the granite bench behind the rockery, fast asleep.'

'Let's be quiet and not waken her,' the others said amidst laughter, and followed her outside to have a look.

They found Xiang-yun where the maid had said, on a large stone bench in a hidden corner of the rockery, dead to the world. She was covered all over from head to foot with crimson petals from the peony bushes which grew round about; the fan which had slipped from her hand and lay on the ground beside her was half buried in petals; and heaped-up peony petals wrapped in a white silk handkerchief made an improvised pillow for her head. Over and around this petalled monstrosity a convocation of bees and butterflies was hovering distractedly. It was a sight that the cousins found both touching and comical. They made haste to rouse her and lifted her up into a half-sitting position on the bench. But Xiang-yun was still playing drinking games in her sleep and proceeded to recite the words of an imaginary forfeit, though her eyes were tightly closed.

'One. "The spring water being sweet, the wine is good." Two. "Pour me its liquid amber in a jade cup." Three. We'll drink till we see "The moon above the plum-tree bough". Four. Then, as we're "Rolling Home". Five. It will be "A good time to meet a friend."'

They shook her, laughing.

'Wake up! Wake up! Come and have something to eat. Lying on the damp stone like this you'll make yourself ill.' Xiang-yun … uplifted slowly then those orbs sereneand saw the faces of the cousins bending over her. Then she looked downwards and saw her own body and the place where she had been lying. She could remember escaping from the noise to rest for a few moments somewhere where it was cool and quiet. Evidently the wine from all those sconces she had been made to drink must have got the better of her and caused her to drop off. Ashamed to have been discovered in such a predicament, she struggled hastily to her feet and accompanied the others back to the summerhouse, where she rinsed her mouth out with water and drank two very strong cups of tea. Tan-chun made one of the girls fetch a piece of 'hangover rock' for her to suck. By the time she had sucked the rock for a bit and taken a few mouthfuls of hot, sour soup, she was feeling almost herself again.

(霍克斯译)

"Go and have a look quick, miss, at Miss Xiangyun," she cried. "She's drunk, and she's picked a cool spot on a stone bench behind the rockery to sleep it off."

The rest laughed to hear this.

"Let's not make a noise," they said.

With that they went out to look, and sure enough found Xiangyun lying on a stone bench in a quiet spot behind an artificial mountain. She was sound asleep and covered with peony petals, which had floated over from all sides to scatter, red and fragrant, over her face and clothes. Her fan, dropped to the ground, was half buried in fallen blossoms too, while bees and butterflies were buzzing and flitting around her. And she had wrapped up some peony petals in her handkerchief to serve as a pillow. They all thought she looked both sweet and comical. As they crowded round to wake her, Xiangyun was still mumbling lines for forfeits in her sleep:

Sweet the fountain, cold the wine

Gleaming like amber in a cup of jade;

The drinking lasts till the moon rises over the plum trees. Then the drunkards help each other back "An appropriate time to meet relatives and friends."

Laughing, they nudged her.

"Hurry up and wake up! We're going to eat. You'll make yourself ill if you sleep on this damp bench."

Xiangyun slowly opened her eyes then and saw them all, then looked down at herself and realized she was tipsy. She had come here in search of coolness and quiet, but as she had drunk so much wine by way of forfeits, overcome by dreamy inertia she had dozed off. Rather sheepishly, she hastily sat up, straightened her clothes and went back with the others to Red Fragrance Farm. There she had a wash and two cups of strong tea, and Tanchun sent for the "pebble to sober drunkards" for her to suck.

Presently she made her drink some vinegar soup too, after which Xiangyun felt better.

（杨宪益、戴乃迭译）

六、练习与思考

1. 分析题

（1）分析湘云醉酒这段文字两种译文的翻译手段，比较并指出霍译和杨译的区别。

（2）仔细阅读"子系中山狼，得志便猖狂。金闺花柳质，一载赴黄粱"的翻译，试分析译者使用了什么翻译策略？是如何体现出来的？

2. 实训题

翻译以下段落。

（1）宝玉听了，忙上前悄悄的说道："你这么个明白人，难道连'亲不隔疏，后不僭先'也不知道？我虽糊涂，却明白这两句话。头一件，咱们是姑舅姐妹，宝姐姐是两姨姐妹，论亲戚也比你远。第二件，你先来，咱们两个一桌吃，一床睡，从小儿一处长大的，他是才来的岂有个为他远你的呢？"黛玉啐道："我难道叫你远他？我成了什么人了呢？我为的是我的心！"宝玉道："我也为的是我的心。你难道就知道你的心，不知道我的心不成？"黛玉听了，低头不语，半日说道："你只怨人行动嗔怪你，你再不知道你怄的人难受。就拿今日天气比，分明冷些，怎么你倒脱了青肷披风呢？"宝玉笑道："何尝没穿？见你一恼，我一暴燥，就脱了。"黛玉叹道："回来伤了风，又该饿着吵吃的了。"

（2）二人正说着，只见湘云走来，笑道："爱哥哥，林姐姐，你们天天一处玩，我好容易来了，也不理我理儿。"黛玉笑道："偏是咬舌子爱说话，连个'二'哥哥也叫不上来，只是'爱'哥哥'爱'哥哥的。回来赶围棋儿，又该你闹'幺爱三'了。"宝玉笑道："你学惯了，明儿连你还咬起来呢。"湘云道："他再不放人一点儿，专会挑人。就算你比世人好，也不犯见一个打趣一个。我指出个人来，你敢挑他，我就服你。"黛玉便问："是谁？"湘云道："你敢挑宝姐姐的短处，就算你是个好的。"黛玉听了冷笑道："我当是谁，原来是他。我可那里敢挑他呢？"宝玉不等说完，忙用话分开。湘云笑道："这一辈子我自然比不上你。我只保佑着明儿得一个咬舌儿林姐夫，时时刻刻你可听'爱'呀'厄'的去！阿弥陀佛，那时才现在我眼里呢！"说的宝玉一笑，湘云忙回身跑了。

3. 思考题

（1）文学翻译要注意哪些方面？

（2）《红楼梦》的两个译本对人物名字是如何处理的？

（3）《红楼梦》的两个译本对于文化词语是如何翻译的？

（4）你喜欢哪位译者的译本？为什么？

第十一课
《西游记》评介赏析

> 《西游记》是我国明代著名的神魔小说之一,相传为吴承恩所作。书中融合了我国古代佛家、道家和释家的各种思想和学说,表现了惩恶扬善的古老主题。
>
> 《西游记》全书共 100 回,具体描写了孙悟空的出世和大闹天宫、唐僧的出世和取经缘由以及后来师徒四人历经九九八十一难,终于取得真经而归的故事。《西游记》的出现,开辟了神魔长篇章回小说这一新门类。书中将善意的嘲笑、辛辣的讽刺同严肃的批判巧妙结合起来,直接影响着讽刺小说的发展。在世界文学史上,它也具有重要地位。《美国大百科全书》认为它是"一部具有丰富内容和光辉思想的神话小说"。从 19 世纪起,《西游记》就被翻译为日、英、法、德、俄等十多种文字。

一、翻译简介

1758 年,日本小说家西田维财开始着手翻译《通俗西游记》,这被认为是对《西游记》作品最早的翻译,比西方的要早一个多世纪,而这一翻译工程直至 1831 年才完成。迄今为止,《西游记》已有了英、法、德、意、西、俄、日、朝、越等多国译本。

《西游记》的翻译也有片段翻译和文本翻译,最早将片段翻译成英文的是吴板桥(Samuel I. Woodbridge)的 *The Golden-Horned Dragon King ; or , The Emperor's Visits to the Spirit World*(《金角龙王,或称唐皇游地府》);亚瑟·韦利(Arthur Waley)于 1942 年翻译的 *The Adventures of Monkey* 成为西方影响最大的节译本;王际真翻译的《西游记》前七回被收入《中国智慧与幽默》(*Chinese Wit and Humor*),并于 1946 年出版;杨宪益、戴乃迭合译的《西游记》片段,也由《中国文学》杂志登出。

《西游记》最早的英译全本,由李提摩太(Timothy Richard)译出,名为 *A Mission to Heaven: A Great Chinese Epic and Allegory*(《天国之行:一个伟大的中国史诗与寓言》/《圣僧天国之行》);此后,海斯(Helen M. Hayes)、亚瑟·韦利(Auther Waley)、瑟内尔(George Theiner)等学者均出版过单行译本。余国藩则是第一位翻译《西游记》(*The Journey to the West*)全本的华人学者,此书于 2006 年出版时改名为 *The Monkey and the Monk*;谭力海于 1990 年也译出 *The Journey to the West* 全译本。而詹纳尔(W. J. F. Jenner)的 *Journey to the West*(《西游记》)是中国本土流行最广、影响最大的版本。

二、书名翻译

对《西游记》的英译名称,普遍译法为 Journey to the West,这点也得到了学界的认同。但在节译本中,研究者也会根据所翻译的情节而适当调整书名的译法,具体案例如下:

1. 杨宪益和戴乃迭(1978):Pilgrimage to the West

2. Samuel I. Woodbridge (1895):The Golden-Horned Dragon King; or, The Emperor's Visits to the Spirit World

3. 翟理斯(Herbert A. Giles)(1901):The Hsi Yu Chi, or Record of Travels in the West

4. Arthur Waley(1942):The Adventures of Monkey

5. 詹姆斯·韦尔(James Ware)(1905):The Fairyland of China

6. 倭纳(Edward Theodore Chalmers Werner)(1922):Myths and Legends of China

7. Timothy Richard(1913):A Mission to Heaven:A Great Chinese Epic and Allegory

8. 余国藩(2006):The Journey to the West,后改为 The Monkey and the Monk

9.《西游记》的其他译名:The Monkey King、White Monkey King、The Magic Monkey、The Monkey King:A Superhero Tale of China、Monkey:Folk Novel of China

在影响力方面,已有的译本中主要是余国藩的译本(以下简称"余译")和詹纳尔(以下简称"詹译")的译本最为突出。前者因为能够通读原文,在翻译中可以更好地结合本国文化习俗,从而达到传播中华文化的目的;而后者则更能从国外读者的视角出发,能做到使译文更好地贴近外国读者,因而也产生了巨大影响。

三、特殊概念的翻译

例1:"盖闻天地之数,有十二万九千六百岁为一元。将一元分为十二会,乃子、丑、寅、卯、辰、巳、午、未、申、酉、戌、亥之十二支也。每会该一万八百岁。"

詹译:"In the arithmetic of the universe, 129,600 years make one cycle. Each cycle can be divided into twelve phases: I, II, III, IV, V, VI, VII, VIII, IX, X, XI and XII, the twelve branches. Each phase lasts for 10,800 years."(endnote 1. "Represented also by twelve animals: mouse, bull, tiger, hare, dragon, serpent, horse, goat, monkey, cock, dog, and pig."）

余译："We heard that in the order of Heaven and Earth, a single period consisted of 129,600 years. Dividing this period into twelve epochs were the twelve stems of Tz, Chou, Yin, Mao, Chn, Ss, Wu, Wei, Shn, Yu, Hs, and Hai, with each epoch having to 10,800 years."

评析：中国的古代历法主要是用于记录时间，同时对应的有十二个不同的生肖，詹译本用十二个罗马数字来解释中国历法，虽然能看出是依次排列，但不足以让人联想到其背后蕴含的文化意义；而余译本直接采用音译的方法，对于本国读者而言能够做到一目了然，只是在面向外国读者时，需要加上注释才会更好。

例2：刘洪睁眼看见……真有个沉鱼落雁之容，闭月羞花之貌。

詹译：Liu Hong stared at... and her charms would have made fishes sink and wild geese fall from the sky, and her beauty put flowers and moon to shame.

余译：Liu Hong noticed that... Her features were striking enough to sink fishes and drop wild geese, and her complexion would cause the moon to hide and put the flowers to shame.

评析：对沉鱼落雁、闭月羞花这类成语的翻译，两者都采取了类似的方法，这样的做法也最能直接表现出这两个成语的基本含义。

例3：即去耳中擎出如意棒，迎风幌一幌，碗来粗细，依然拿在手中，不分好歹……

詹译：He took the as-you-will cudgel from his ear, and shook it in the wind till it was thick as a bowl, and once more created total chaos in the palace of Heaven, not caring the least of what he did ...

余译：Whipping the compliant rod out from his ear, he waved it once in the wind and it had the thickness of a rice bowl. Holding it in the hands, without regard for good or ill ...

评析：詹译本的"如意棒"似乎会让读者误解为是一根能够实现心愿的棍子，而余译本则直接简化为是顺人心意的棍子，在某种程度上能够使读者避免误解。

四、译文对比赏析

1. 经典句子

（1）盖闻天地之数，有十二万九千六百岁为一元。将一元分为十二会，乃子、丑、寅、卯、辰、巳、午、未、申、酉、戌、亥之十二支也。每会该一万八百岁。

——第一回 《灵根孕育源流出，心性修持大道生》

（1）In the arithmetic of the universe, 1,296,000 years make one cycle. Each cycle can be divided into twelve phases: I, II, III, IV, V, VI, VII, VIII, IX, X, XI and XII, the twelve branches. Each phase lasts 10,800 years.

(Represented by twelve animals: mouse, bull, tiger, hare, dragon, serpent, horse, goat, monkey, cock and pig)

— The Divine Root Conceives Spring Breaks Forth, As the Heart's Nature Is Cultivated, the Great Way Arises.

(詹纳尔译)

We heard that, in the order of Heaven and Earth, a single period consisted of 129,600 years. Dividing this period into twelve epochs were the twelve stems of Zi, Chou, Yin, Mao, Chen, Si, Wu, Wei, Shen, Yu, Xu, and Hai, with each epoch having 10,800 years.

— The Divine Root conceives, its source Revealed; Mind and nature nurtured, the Great Dao is born.

(余国藩译)

(2) 众猴又笑道:"大王好不知足！我等日日欢会,在仙山福地,古洞神州,不伏麒麟辖,不伏凤凰管,又不伏人间王位所拘束,自由自在,乃无量之福,为何远虑而忧也？"

——第一回 《灵根孕育源流出,心性修持大道生》

(2) The other monkeys laughed and said, "Your Majesty is being greedy. We have parties every day; we live in a mountain paradise, in an ancient cave in a divine continent. We are spared the rule of unicorns, the domination of phoenixes, and the restraints of human kings. We are free to do just as we like — we are infinitely lucky. Why make yourself miserable worrying about the future?"

— The Divine Root conceives, its source Revealed; Mind and nature nurtured, the Great Dao is born

(詹纳尔译)

The monkeys all laughed and said, "The Great King indeed does not know contentment! Here we daily have a banquet on an immortal mountain in a blessed land, in an ancient cave on a divine continent. We are not subject to the unicorn or the phoenix, nor are we governed by the rulers of mankind. Such independence and comfort are immeasurable blessings. Why, then, does he worry about the future?"

— The Divine Root Conceives Spring Breaks Forth, As the Heart's Nature Is Cultivated, the Great Way Arises.

(余国藩译)

(3) 那大圣闻言,暗笑道:"这如来十分好呆!我老孙一筋斗去十万八千里。他那手掌,方圆不满一尺,如何跳不出去?"

——第七回 《八卦炉中逃大圣,五行山下定心猿》

(3) When he heard this "offer the Great Sage smiled to himself and thought, This Buddha is a complete idiot. I can cover thirty-six thousand miles with a somersault, so how could I fail to jump out of the palm of his hand, which is less than a foot across?"

— *The Great Sage escapes from the Eight Trigrams Furnace ; The Mind Ape is Fixe Beneath Five Elements Mountain*

(詹纳尔译)

When the Great Sage heard this, he said to himself, snickering, "What a fool this Tathāgata is! A single somersault of mine can carry old Monkey one hundred and eight thousand miles, yet his palm is not even one foot across. How could I possibly not jump clear of it?"

— *From the Eight Trigrams Brazier the Great Sage escapes ; Beneath the Five Phases Mountain, Mind Monkey is still*

(余国藩译)

(4) 今日昧着惺惺使糊涂,只教我回去:"这才是'鸟尽弓藏,兔死狗烹!'罢!罢!罢!但只是多了那《紧箍儿咒》。"

第二十七回 《尸魔三戏唐三藏,唐僧恨逐美猴王》

(4) "'When these birds have all been shot. this bow is put away, and when the hares have all been killed the hounds are stewed'. Oh, well! If only you hadn't got that Band-tightening Spell."

— *The Corpse Fiend Thrice Tricks Tang Sanzang, The Holy Monk Angrily Dismisses the Handsome Monkey King*

(詹纳尔译)

That's how it is: When the birds vanish, the bow is hidden; when the hares perish, the hounds are eaten. All right! All right! There's only one thing left for us to settle, and that's the Tight-Fillet Spell."

— *The cadaver demon three times mocks Tripitaka Tang ; The Holy Monk in Spite Banishes Handsome Monkey King*

(余国藩译)

（5）清风暗道："这和尚在那口舌场中，是非海里，弄得眼肉胎凡，不识我仙家异宝。"

——第二十四回 《万寿山大仙留故友，五庄观行者窃人参》

（5）"This monk has developed eyes of flesh and a mortal body in the battlefield of mouths and tongues and the sea of disputation," thought Pure Wind, "and he can't recognize the treasure of this home of immortals."

On the Mountain of Infinite Longevity a Great Immortal Entertains an Old Friend; In the Wuzhuang Temple Monkey Steals Manfruit

（詹纳尔译）

"This monk," said Clear Breeze quietly to himself, "has been so corrupted by the fields of mouths and tongues, by the sea of strife and envy, that all he possesses are but two fleshly eyes and a worldly mind. That's why he can't recognize the strange treasures of our divine abode!"

At Long Life Mountain the Great Immortal detains his old friend; At Five Vilages Abbey, Pilgrim steals the Ginseng Fruit

（余国藩译）

2. 经典段落

（1）盖闻天地之数，有十二万九千六百岁为一元。将一元分为十二会，乃子、丑、寅、卯、辰、巳、午、未、申、酉、戌、亥之十二支也。每会该一万八百岁。且就一日而论：子时得阳气，而丑则鸡鸣；寅不通光，而卯则日出；辰时食后，而巳则挨排；日午天中，而未则西蹉；申时晡而日落酉；戌黄昏而人定亥。譬于大数，若到戌会之终，则天地昏蒙而万物否矣。再去五千四百岁，交亥会之初，则当黑暗，而两间人物俱无矣，故曰混沌。又五千四百岁，亥会将终，贞下起元，近子之会，而复逐渐开明。

——第一回 《灵根孕育源流出，心性修持大道生》

（1）In the arithmetic of the universe, 129,600 years make one cycle. Each cycle can be divided into twelve phases: I, II, III, IV, V, VI, VII, VIII, IX, X, XI and XII, the twelve branches. Each phase lasts 10,800 years. Now within a single day, the positive begins at the time I; At II the cock crows; at III it is not quite light; at IV the sun rises; V is after breakfast; and at VI one does business. VII is when the sun reaches noon; at VIII it is slipping towards the west; IX is late afternoon; the sun sets at X; XI is dusk; and at XII people settle down for the night. If you compare this with the big numbers, then at the end of Phrase XI Heaven and Earth became blurred and everything was in an inauspicious state. 5,400 years later came the beginning of Phrase

XII, when all was darkness and both human beings and inanimate things vanished from the world, for this reason it was called Chaos. Another 5,400 years later Phase XII was drawing to a close and a new cycle was about to begin. As Phase I of the new era approached, gradually there was light.

— *The Divine Root Conceives Spring Breaks Forth, As the Heart's Nature Is Cultivated, the Great Way Arises*.

（詹纳尔译）

We heard that, in the order of Heaven and Earth, a single period consisted of 129,600 years. Dividing this period into twelve epochs were the twelve stems of Zi, Chou, Yin, Mao, Chen, Si, Wu, Wei, Shen, Yu, Xu, and Hai, with each epoch having 10,800 years. Considered as the horary circle, the sequence would be thus: the first sign of dawn appears in the hour of Zi, while at Chou the cock crows; daybreak occurs at Yin, and the sun rises at Mao; Chen comes after breakfast, and by Si everything is planned; at Wu the sun arrives at its meridian, and it declines westward by Wei; the evening meal comes during the hour of Shen, and the sun sinks completely at Yu; twilight sets in at Xu, and people rest by the hour of Hai. This sequence may also be understood macrocosmically. At the end of the epoch of Xu, Heaven and Earth were obscure and all things were indistinct. With the passing of 5,400 years, the beginning of Hai was the epoch of darkness. This moment was named Chaos, because there were neither human beings nor the two spheres. After another 5,400 years Hai ended, and as the creative force began to work after great perseverance, the epoch of Zi drew near and again brought gradual development.

— *The Divine Root conceives, its source Revealed; Mind and nature nurtured, the Great Dao is born*

（余国藩译）

（2）美猴王享乐天真，何期有三五百载。一日，与群猴喜宴之间，忽然忧恼，堕下泪来。众猴慌忙罗拜道："大王何为烦恼？"猴王道："我虽在欢喜之时，却有一点儿远虑，故此烦恼。"众猴又笑道："大王好不知足！我等日日欢会，在仙山福地，古洞神州，不伏麒麟辖，不伏凤凰管，又不伏人间王位所拘束，自由自在，乃无量之福，为何远虑而忧也？"猴王道："今日虽不归人王法律，不惧禽兽威严，将来年老血衰，暗中有阎王老子管着，一旦身亡，可不枉生世界之中，不得久住天人之内？"众猴闻此言，一个个掩面悲啼，俱以无常为虑。

——第一回 《灵根孕育源流出，心性修持大道生》

(2) The Handsome Monkey King's innocent spirits could not, of course, last three or four hundred years. One day he suddenly felt depressed during a banquet with his monkey host, and he started to weep. The startled monkeys crowded around, bowed to him and asked, "What's the matter, Your Majesty?" "Although I'm happy now," the Monkey King replied, "I'm worried about the future. That's what getting me down." The other monkeys laughed and said, "Your Majesty is being greedy. We have parties every day; we live in a mountain paradise, in an ancient cave in a divine continent. We are spared the rule of unicorns, the domination of phoenixes, and the restraints of human kings. We are free to do just as we like — we are infinitely lucky. Why make yourself miserable worrying about the future?" To this the Monkey King replied, "Yes, we don't have to submit to the laws and regulations of human kings, and we don't live in terror of the power of birds and beasts. But time will come when we are old and weak, and the underworld is controlled by the King of Hell. When the time comes for us to die, we won't be able to go on living among the Blessed, and our lives will all have been in vain." All the monkeys covered their faces and wept as everyone of them thought about death.

— *The Divine Root Conceives Spring Breaks Forth*, *As the Heart's Nature Is Cultivated*, *the Great Way Arises*.

(詹纳尔译)

The Handsome Monkey King had enjoyed this insouciant existence for three or four hundred years when one day, while feasting with the rest of the monkeys, he suddenly grew sad and shed a few tears. Alarmed, the monkeys surrounding him bowed down and asked, "What is disturbing the Great King?" The Monkey King replied, "Though I am very happy at the moment, I am a little concerned about the future. Hence I'm distressed." The monkeys all laughed and said, "The Great King indeed does not know contentment! Here we daily have a banquet on an immortal mountain in a blessed land, in an ancient cave on a divine continent. We are not subject to the unicorn or the phoenix, nor are we governed by the rulers of mankind. Such independence and comfort are immeasurable blessings. Why, then, does he worry about the future?" The Monkey King said, "Though we are not subject to the laws of man today, nor need we be threatened by the rule of any bird or beast, old age and physical decay in the future will disclose the secret sovereignty of Yama, King of the Underworld. If we die, shall we not have lived in vain, not being able to rank forever among the Heavenly beings?" When the monkeys heard this, they all covered their faces and wept mournfully, each one troubled by his own impermanence.

— *The Divine Root conceives, its source Revealed; Mind and nature nurtured, the Great Dao is born*

（余国藩译）

（3）那大圣闻言，暗笑道："这如来十分好呆！我老孙一筋斗去十万八千里。他那手掌，方圆不满一尺，如何跳不出去？"急发声道："既如此说，你可做得主张？"佛祖道："做得！做得！"伸开右手，却似个荷叶大小。那大圣收了如意棒，抖擞神威，将身一纵，站在佛祖手心里，却道声："我出去也！"你看他一路云光，无形无影去了。佛祖慧眼观看，见那猴王风车子一般相似不住，只管前进。大圣行时，忽见有五根肉红柱子，撑着一股青气。他道："此间乃尽头路了。这番回去，如来作证，灵霄殿定是我坐也。"

——第七回 《八卦炉中逃大圣，五行山下定心猿》

(3) When he heard this offer the Great Sage smiled to himself and thought, "This Buddha is a complete idiot. I can cover thirty-six thousand miles with a somersault, so how could I fail to jump out of the palm of his hand, which is less than a foot across?" With this in his mind he asked eagerly. "Do you guarantee that yourself?" "Yes, Yes," the Buddha replied, and he stretched out his right hand, which seemed to be about the size of a lotus leaf. Putting away his as-you — will cudgel, the Great Sage summoned up all his divine powers, jumped into the palm of the Buddha's hand, and said, "I'm off." Watch him as he goes like a streak of light and disappears completely. The Buddha, who was watching him with his wise eyes, saw the monkey king whirling forward like a windmill and not stopping until he saw five flesh-pink pillars topped by dark vapors. "This is the end of the road," he said, "so now I'll go back. The Buddha will be witness, and the Hall of Miraculous Mist will be mine."

— *The Great Sage escapes from the Eight Trigrams Furnace; The Mind Ape is Fixe Beneath Five Elements Mountain*

（詹纳尔译）

When the Great Sage heard this, he said to himself, snickering, "What a fool this Tathāgata is! A single somersault of mine can carry old Monkey one hundred and eight thousand miles, yet his palm is not even one foot across. How could I possibly not jump clear of it?" He asked quickly, "You're certain that your decision will stand?" "Certainly it will," said Tathāgata. He stretched out his right hand, which was about the size of a lotus leaf. Our Great Sage put away his compliant rod and, summoning his power, leaped up and stood right in the center of the Patriarch's hand. He said simply, "I'm off!" and he was gone — all but invisible like a streak of light in the clouds. Training the eye of wisdom on him, the Buddhist Patriarch saw that the Monkey King was hurtling along relentlessly like a whirligig. As the Great Sage advanced, he suddenly saw five flesh-pink pillars supporting a mass of green air. "This must be the end of the road," he said. "When I go back presently, Tathāgata will be my witness and I shall certainly take up residence in the Palace of Divine Mists."

── From the Eight Trigrams Brazier the Great Sage escapes; Beneath the Five Phases Mountain, Mind Monkey is still

（余国藩译）

（4）行者道："师父错怪了我也。这厮分明是个妖魔,他实有心害你。我倒打死他,替你除了害,你却不认得,反信了那呆子谗言冷语,屡次逐我。常言道:'事不过三。'我若不去,真是个下流无耻之徒。我去! 我去! ——去便罢了,只是你手下无人。"唐僧发怒道："这泼猴越发无礼! 看起来,只你是人,那悟能、悟净,就不是人?"那大圣一闻得说,他两个是人,止不住伤情凄惨,对唐僧道声"苦啊! 你那时节,出了长安,有刘伯钦送你上路;到两界山,救我出来,投拜你为师,我曾穿古洞,入深林,擒魔捉怪,收八戒,得沙僧,吃尽千辛万苦;今日昧着惺惺使糊涂,只教我回去:这才是'鸟尽弓藏,兔死狗烹!'——罢! 罢! 罢! 但只是多了那《紧箍儿咒》。"

——第二十七回 《尸魔三戏唐三藏,唐僧恨逐美猴王》

（4）"You're wrong to hold it against me, master,"monkey replied,"as that wretch was obviously an evil monster set on murdering you. But so far from being grateful that I've saved you by killing it, you would have to believe that idiot's tittle-tattle and keep sending me away. As the saying goes, you should never have to do anything more than three times. I'd be a low and shameless creature if I didn't go now. I'll go, I'll go all right, but who will you have left to look after you?" "Damned ape," Sanzang replied, "you get ruder and ruder. You seem to think that you're the only one. What about Pig and Friar Sand? Aren't they people?" On hearing him say that Pig and Friar Sand were suitable people too, Monkey was very hurt. "That's a terrible thing to hear, Master," he said, "when you left Chang'an Liu Baoqin helped you on the way, and when you reached the Double Boundary Mountain you saved me and I took you as my master. I've gone into ancient caves and deep forests capturing monsters and demons. I won Pig and Friar Sand over, and I've had a very hard time of it. But today you've turned stupid and you're sending me back. when there birds have all been shot, this bow is put away, and when the hares have all been killed the hounds are stewed.' Oh, well! If only you hadn't got that Band-tightening Spell."

—— *The Corpse Fiend Thrice Tricks Tang Sanzang*, *The Holy Monk Angrily Dismisses the Handsome Monkey King*

（詹纳尔译）

"Master," said Pilgrim, "you have really wronged me. This is undeniably a monstrous spirit, bent on hurting you. I have helped you to ward off danger by killing her, but you can't see it. You believe instead those sarcastic and slanderous remarks of Idiot to such an extent that you try to get rid of me several times. The proverb says, 'Nothing can occur three times'! If I don't leave you, I'll be a base and shameless fellow. I'll go! I'll go! It's no big deal, in fact, for me to leave, but then you will have no man to serve you." Turning angry, the Tang Monk said, "This brazen ape is becoming even more unruly. So you think that you are the only man around here? Wuneng and Wujing, they are not men?" When the Great Sage heard this statement about the other two disciples, he was so deeply hurt that he could not but say to the Tang Monk, "O misery! Think of the time when Liu Boqin was your companion as you left Chang'an. After you delivered me from the Mountain of Two Frontiers and made me your disciple, I penetrated ancient caves and invaded deep forests to capture demons and defeat monsters. I was the one who, having experienced countless difficulties, subdued Eight Rules and acquired Sha Monk. Today, 'banishing Wisdom just to court Folly,' you want me to go back. That's how it is:

> When the birds vanish,
>
> The bow is hidden;
>
> When the hares perish,
>
> The hounds are eaten.

All right! All right! There's only one thing left for us to settle, and that's the Tight-Fillet Spell." The Tang Monk said, "I won't recite that again."

—— *The cadaver demon three times mocks Tripitaka Tang*; *The Holy Monk in Spite Banishes Handsome Monkey King*

（余国藩译）

（5）那长老见了，战战兢兢，远离三尺道："善哉！善哉！今岁倒也年丰时稔，怎么这观里作荒吃人？这个是三朝未满的孩童，如何与我解渴？"清风暗道："这和尚在那口舌场中，是非海里，弄得眼肉胎凡，不识我仙家异宝。"明月上前道："老师，此物叫做'人参果'，吃一个儿不妨。"三藏道："胡说！胡说！他那父母怀胎，不知受了多少苦楚，方生下。未及三日，怎么就把他拿来当果子？"清风道："实是树上结的。"长老道："乱谈！乱谈！树上又会结出人来？拿过去，不当人子！"

——第二十四回 《万寿山大仙留故友，五庄观行者窃人参》

（5）At the sight of the man fruit the monk recoiled some three feet, shaking with horror. "Goodness me!" he exclaimed. "How could you be so reduced to starvation in this year of plenty as to eat human flesh? And how could I possibly quench my thirst with a newborn baby?" "This monk has developed eyes of flesh and a mortal body in the battlefield of mouths and tongues and the sea of disputation," thought Pure Wind, "and he can't recognize the treasure of this home of immortals." "Venerable master," said Bright Moon, "this is what is called 'manfruit', and there is no reason why you should not eat one." "Nonsense, nonsense," said Sanzang, "They were conceived by their fathers and mothers and had to go through no ends of suffering before they were born. How can you treat them as fruit when they haven't been alive for three days yet?" "They really and truly grew on a tree," said Pure wind. "Stuff and rubbish," Sanzang replied. "Babies don't grow on trees. Take them away. It's very wicked."

On the Mountain of Infinite Longevity a Great Immortal Entertains an Old Friend; In the Wuzhuang Temple Monkey Steals Manfruit

（詹纳尔译）

When the elder saw the fruits, he trembled all over and backed away three feet, saying, "Goodness! Goodness! The harvest seems to be plentiful this year! But why is this abbey so destitute that they have to practice cannibalism here? These are newborn infants not yet three days old! How could you serve them to me to relieve my thirst?"

"This monk," said Clear Breeze quietly to himself, "has been so corrupted by the fields of mouths and tongues, by the sea of strife and envy, that all he possesses are but two fleshly eyes and a worldly mind. That's why he can't recognize the strange treasures of our divine abode!" Bright Moon then drew near and said, "Master, this thing is called ginseng fruit. It's perfectly all right for you to eat one." "Nonsense! Nonsense!" said Tripitaka. "Their parents went through who knows how much suffering before they brought them to birth! How could you serve them as fruits when they are less than three days old?" Clear Breeze said, "Honestly, they were formed on a tree." "Rubbish! Rubbish!" said the elder. "How can people grow on trees? Take them away! This is blasphemy!"

At Long Life Mountain the Great Immortal detains his old friend; At Five Vilages Abbey, Pilgrim steals the Ginseng Fruit

（余国藩译）

五、练习与思考

1. 分析题

（1）分析比较"经典句子（2）"中的两个译本，结合以上翻译策略部分，指出詹译和余译的不同。

（2）仔细阅读经典段落部分，指出其中习语翻译的不同，说说习语翻译需要注意的问题。

2. 实训题

翻译以下段落。

（1）却说那镇元大仙用手搀着行者道："我也知道你的本事，我也闻得你的英名，只是你今番越理欺心，纵有腾那，脱不得我手。我就和你讲到西天，见了你那佛祖，也少不得还我人参果树。你莫弄神通。"行者笑道："你这先生，好小家子样！若要树活，有甚疑难！早说这话，可不省了一场争竞？"大仙道："不争竞，我肯善自饶你？"行者道："你解了我师父，我还你一颗活树如何？"大仙道："你若有此神通，医得树活，我与你八拜为交，结为兄弟。"

（2）话说孙大圣得了金箍棒，打出门前，跳上高峰，对众神满心欢喜。李天王道："你这场如何"行者道："老孙变化进他洞去，那怪物越发唱唱舞舞的，吃得胜酒哩，更不曾打听得他的宝贝在那里。我转他后面，忽听得马叫龙吟，知是火部之物。东壁厢靠着我的金箍棒，是老孙拿在手中，一路打将出来也。"众神道："你的宝贝得了，我们的宝贝何时到手？"行者道："不难！不难！我有了这根铁棒，不管怎的，也要打倒他，取宝贝还你。"

3. 思考题

（1）结合换译的几种类型，讨论其使用的情况。
（2）你最喜欢《西游记》的哪个译本？为什么？
（3）词类换译的原因是什么？
（4）如果你来翻译《西游记》中的习语，你会采取哪些翻译方法？
（5）借助换译的以上分类，说说英汉语言的不同特点。
（6）习语翻译中直译和意译分别要注意哪些问题？
（7）做好习语翻译工作，译者要具备哪些素质？
（8）《西游记》的英译本传播情况如何？

六、参考文献

[1] 王卓.文化的西游[D].苏州：苏州大学,2011.

［2］ 黄小花.归化与异化：《西游记》英译研究［D］.福州：福建师范大学，2009.

［3］ 王丽娜.《西游记》外文译本概述［J］.文献，1980(4)：64-78.

［4］ 赵莲芬，戈玲玲.论幽默比喻的翻译方法——以《西游记》及其英译本为例［J］.海外英语，2018(1)：132-133.

［5］ 谢晓禅，丁宁.全球化语境下文学经典翻译传播的伦理探索——以《西游记》翻译为例［J］.淮海工学院学报（人文社会科学版），2018(1)：34-36.

第十二课
《三国演义》评介赏析

> 《三国演义》，全名为《三国志通俗演义》，是中国第一部长篇章回体历史演义小说，也是四大名著中唯一一本根据历史事实改编的小说，作者是元末明初小说家罗贯中。全书以史为据，以儒家思想为本，强调"忠义"，着重描写战争，讲述了从东汉末年到西晋初年之间近105年的历史风云，反映了三国时代的政治军事斗争和各类社会矛盾的转化，概括了这一时代的历史巨变，并塑造了一批叱咤风云的三国英雄人物。
>
> 自《三国演义》问世以来，各式各样的版本层出不穷，明代刻本有二十多种，清代刻本也有七十多种，在中国民间流传甚广。康熙二十八年(1689)，日僧湖南文山编译出版日文本《通俗三国志》之后，朝鲜、日本、印度尼西亚、越南、泰国、英国、法国、俄国等许多国家都对《三国演义》有本国文字的译本，并发表了不少研究论文和专著，对这部小说作出了极高的评价。

一、翻译简介

《三国演义》的英语全译本，国内学界公认比较受欢迎的有两个：一个是较早的邓罗（C. H. Brewitt-Taylor）英译的 Romance of The Three Kingdoms，1925年由上海别发洋行出版，共2卷；另一个是现在市面上比较流行的新译本，由美国汉学家罗慕士（Moss Roberts）翻译的 Three Kingdoms，1991年由美国加利福尼亚大学出版社及北京外文出版社联合出版，是目前译界最主要的研究文本。

本课选取《三国演义》中的五个经典片段，并以罗慕士和邓罗两位译者的译本为例，进行对比分析。

二、书名翻译

　　《三国演义》是中国古典文学中的鸿篇巨著，描写的是以 3 世纪的曹操、刘备、孙权为首的魏、蜀、吴三个政治、军事集团之间的矛盾和斗争，展示出那个时代尖锐复杂又极具特色的政治军事冲突。当今，许多企业将《三国演义》的方略运用到经营管理中。它是一部经过艺术构思和艺术加工的文学作品，成功地塑造了一个个个性鲜明、栩栩如生的艺术形象，生动地突出了人物的性格特征。《三国演义》被译成数十种文字，在世界多个国家广泛流传，尤其受到亚洲各国人民的喜爱。《三国演义》有两种英文译名，最早是 1925 年，邓罗将其翻译为 Romance of The Three Kingdoms。不难看出，译者是采取直译的方法，将"演义"译为"romance"。据《美国传统词典》，"romance"的解释为：A long, fictitious tale of heroes and extraordinary or mysterious events（传奇的故事，讲述英雄和不寻常的或神秘事件的长篇虚构故事）。应该说，该译名忠实原作，符合原意，能够真实反映三方之间的博弈场景，不失为一个对等翻译的佳作。但对读者尤其是亚洲读者来说，Romance 往往被理解为"浪漫史"。乍一看，读者以为该书描写的是三个王国的浪漫情调和深厚友谊，与故事中表现的那种惊心动魄、尖锐复杂的政治斗争大相径庭，容易使读者产生误解。文学作品更加讲究语言的精炼优美，由于两种语言表达方式不同，将译出语转为译入语时，常常可以删去或增添一些词。这样做并不损害原意，反而可以使译文更为通顺，语意更为清楚，表达更为准确。美国汉学家罗慕士将"三国演义"翻译成 Three Kingdoms，就是将原书名中的"演义"省略不译，以免产生歧义，符合翻译理论的原则。

三、特殊概念的翻译

　　《三国演义》可谓中国古典文学史上的一颗明珠，学习翻译不仅要掌握翻译的方法和技巧，还要饱读中外文学名著，提高自己的文学素养，下面我们就来学习一些与文学相关的词汇的翻译。

　　1. 文学类别
　　文学 literature
　　古典文学 classical literature
　　现代文学 contemporary literature
　　大众文学 popular literature
　　通俗文学 light literature
　　民间文学 folklore

长篇小说 saga (river) novel
中篇小说 short novel/long short story
短篇小说 short story
爱情小说 love story
侦探小说 detective story
怪诞小说 mystery story
推理小说 whodunit
幽默小说 humorous story
历史小说 historical novel
科幻小说 science fiction
随笔 essay
游记 book of travels
报告文学 reportage
评论 criticism
散文 prose
自传 biography
寓言 allegory
讽刺诗 satire

2. 文学修辞手法
比喻 figures of speech
对偶 antithesis
暗喻（隐喻）metaphor
明喻 simile
夸张 hyperbole
反语 irony
转喻（借代）metonymy
排比 parallelism
拟人 personification
拟物 synaesthesia
类比 analogy
含蓄陈述 understatement
委婉 euphemism
提喻 synecdoche
换喻 antonomasia

双关 pun
暗讽 innuendo
讽刺 sarcasm
矛盾修饰 oxymoron
渐进 climax
突降 anti-climax/bathos
头韵 alliteration
拟声 onomatopoeia
顿呼 apostrophe

3.《三国演义》重点词汇
豪杰 hero
太子 heir
梓宫 coffin
先主 the First Ruler
结义 to swear brotherhood
黄巾 the Yellow Scarves
正殿 main hall（in a palace or temple）
宦官/中涓 eunuch
太傅 Imperial Guardian
大将军 Regent Marshal
汉高祖 the Supreme Ancestor of Han Dynasty（Liu Bang）
卧龙先生 Master Sleeping Dragon
卧龙冈 Sleeping Dragon Ridge

四、译文对比赏析

《三国演义》"文不甚深，言不甚俗"，用的是半文半白的语言，形成简洁、明快而又通俗的语言特点。C. H. Brewitt-Taylor 和 Moss Roberts 两位译者在翻译这部小说时分别采用了不同的翻译手法与技巧，因而译文的风格不尽相同，各有千秋。下面我们就一些经典的句子和段落来进行对比赏析。

1.经典句子
(1) 天下大势，分久必合，合久必分。

——第一回 《宴桃园豪杰三结义，斩黄巾英雄首立功》

(1) The empire, long divided, must unite; long united, must divide. Thus it has ever been.

Chapter 1 Three Bold Spirits Plight Mutual Faith in the Peach Garden; Heroes and Champions Win First Honors Fighting the Yellow Scarves　（Tr. Moss Roberts）

Domains under heaven, after a long period of division, tends to unite; after a long period of union, tends to divide.

— *Chapter 1 Three Heroes Swear Brotherhood In The Peach Garden*; *One Victory Shatters The Rebels In Battlegrounds*

（Tr. C. H. Brewitt-Taylor）

(2) 不求同年同月同日生，只愿同年同月同日死。

——第一回　《宴桃园豪杰三结义，斩黄巾英雄首立功》

(2) We dare not hope to be together always but hereby vow to die the selfsame day.

Chapter 1 Three Bold Spirits Plight Mutual Faith in the Peach Garden; Heroes and Champions Win First Honors Fighting the Yellow Scarves

（Tr. Moss Roberts）

We ask not the same day of birth, but we seek to die together.

— *Chapter 1 Three Heroes Swear Brotherhood In The Peach Garden*; *One Victory Shatters The Rebels In Battlegrounds*

（Tr. C. H. Brewitt-Taylor）

(3) 皇天后土，实鉴此心，背义忘恩，天人共戮！

——第一回　《宴桃园豪杰三结义，斩黄巾英雄首立功》

(3) Let shining Heaven above and the fruitful land below bear witness to our resolve. May Heaven and man scourge whosoever fails this vow.

— *Chapter 1 Three Bold Spirits Plight Mutual Faith in the Peach Garden*; *Heroes and Champions Win First Honors Fighting the Yellow Scarves*

（Tr. Moss Roberts）

May Heaven, the all-ruling, and Earth, the all-producing, read our hearts. If we turn aside from righteousness or forget kindliness, may Heaven and Human smite us!

— *Chapter 1 Three Heroes Swear Brotherhood In The Peach Garden*; *One Victory Shatters The Rebels In Battlegrounds*

（Tr. C. H. Brewitt-Taylor）

(4) 淡泊以明志,宁静而致远。

——第三十七回 《司马徽再荐名士,刘玄德三顾草庐》

(4) Only through austerity and quiescence can one's purpose shine forth; only through concentration and self-control can one's distant goal be reached.

— Chapter 37 *Still Water Recommends Another Noted Scholar*; *Liu Xuande Pays Three Visits to Zhuge Liang*

(Tr. Moss Roberts)

By purity inspire the inclination; by repose affect the distant.

— Chapter 37 *Sima Hui Recommends A Scholar To Liu Bei*; *Liu Bei Pays Three Visits To The Sleeping Dragon Ridge*

(Tr. C. H. Brewitt-Taylor)

2. 经典段落

(1) 话说天下大势,分久必合,合久必分。周末七国分争,并入于秦。及秦灭之后,楚、汉分争,又并入于汉。汉朝自高祖斩白蛇而起义,一统天下,后来光武中兴,传至献帝,遂分为三国。推其致乱之由,殆始于桓、灵二帝。桓帝禁锢善类,崇信宦官。及桓帝崩,灵帝即位,大将军窦武、太傅陈蕃,共相辅佐。时有宦官曹节等弄权,窦武、陈蕃谋诛之,机事不密,反为所害,中涓自此愈横。

——第一回 《宴桃园豪杰三结义,斩黄巾英雄首立功》

(1) The empire, long divided, must unite; long united, must divide. Thus it has ever been. In the closing years of the Zhou dynasty, seven kingdoms warred among themselves until the kingdom of Qin prevailed and absorbed the other six. But Qin soon fell, and on its ruins two opposing kingdoms, Chu and Han, fought for mastery until the kingdom of Han prevailed and absorbed its rival, as Qin had done before. The Han court's rise to power began when the Supreme Ancestor slew a white serpent, inspiring an uprising that ended with Han's ruling a unified empire.

Two hundred years later, after Wang Mang's usurpation, Emperor Guang Wu restored the dynasty, and Han emperors ruled for another two hundred years down to the reign of Xian, after whom the realm split into three kingdoms. The cause of Han's fall may be traced to the reigns of Xian's two predecessors, Huan and Ling. Huan drove from office and persecuted officials of integrity and ability, giving all his trust to his eunuchs. After Ling succeeded Huan as emperor, Regent-Marshal Dou Wu and Imperial Guardian Chen Fan, joint sustainers of the throne, planned to execute the power-abusing eunuch Cao Jie and his cohorts. But the plot came to light, and Dou Wu and Chen Fan were themselves put to death. From then on, the Minions of the Palace knew no restraint.

— *Chapter 1 Three Bold Spirits Plight Mutual Faith in the Peach Garden*; *Heroes and Champions Win First Honors Fighting the Yellow Scarves*

(Tr. Moss Roberts)

Domains under heaven, after a long period of division, tends to unite; after a long period of union, tends to divide. This has been so since antiquity. When the rule of the Zhou Dynasty weakened, seven contending kingdoms sprang up, warring one with another until the kingdom of Qin prevailed and possessed the empire. But when Qin's destiny had been fulfilled, arose two opposing kingdoms, Chu and Han, to fight for the mastery. And Han was the victor.

The rise of the fortunes of Han began when Liu Bang the Supreme Ancestor slew a white serpent to raise the banners of uprising, which only ended when the whole empire belonged to Han (B.C. 202). This magnificent heritage was handed down in successive Han emperors for two hundred years, till the rebellion of Wang Mang caused a disruption. But soon Liu Xiu the Latter Han Founder restored the empire, and Han emperors continued their rule for another two hundred years till the days of Emperor Xian, which were doomed to see the beginning of the empire's division into three parts, known to history as The Three Kingdoms.

But the descent into misrule hastened in the reigns of the two predecessors of Emperor Xian — Emperors Huan and Ling — who sat in the Dragon Throne about the middle of the second century.

Emperor Huan paid no heed to the good people of his court, but gave his confidence to the Palace eunuchs. He lived and died, leaving the scepter to Emperor Ling, whose advisers were Regent Marshal Dou Wu and Imperial Guardian Chen Fan. Dou Wu and Chen Fan, disgusted with the abuses of the eunuchs in the affairs of the state, plotted the destruction for the power-abusing eunuchs. But Chief Eunuch Cao Jie was not to be disposed of easily. The plot leaked out, and the honest Dou Wu and Chen Fan were put to death, leaving the eunuchs stronger than before.

— *Chapter 1 Three Heroes Swear Brotherhood In The Peach Garden*; *One Victory Shatters The Rebels In Battlegrounds*

(Tr. C. H. Brewitt-Taylor)

（2）正饮间，见一大汉，推着一辆车子，到店门首歇了，入店坐下，便唤酒保："快斟酒来吃,我待赶入城去投军。"玄德看其人:身长九尺,髯长二尺;面如重枣,唇若涂脂;丹凤眼,卧蚕眉,相貌堂堂,威风凛凛。玄德就邀他同坐,叩其姓名。其人曰:"吾姓关,名羽,字长生,后改云长,河东解良人也。因本处势豪倚势凌人,被吾杀了,逃难江湖,五六年矣。今闻此处招军破贼,特来应募。"玄德遂以己志告之,云长大喜。同到张飞庄上,共议大事。飞曰:"吾庄后有一桃园,花开正盛;明日当于园中祭告天地,我三人结为兄弟,协力同心,然后可图大事。"玄德、云长齐声应曰:"如此甚好。"

——第一回 《宴桃园豪杰三结义,斩黄巾英雄首立功》

(2) As they drank, they watched a strapping fellow pushing a wheelbarrow stop to rest at the tavern entrance. "Some wine, and quickly — I'm off to the city to volunteer," the stranger said as he entered and took a seat. Xuande observed him: a man of enormous height, nine spans tall, with a two-foot-long beard flowing from his rich, ruddy cheeks. He had glistening lips, eyes sweeping sharply back like those of the crimson-faced phoenix, and brows like nestling silkworms. His stature was imposing, his bearing awesome. Xuande invited him to share their table and asked who he was.

"My surname is Guan," the man replied. "My given name is Yu; my style, Changsheng, was later changed to Yunchang. I am from Jieliang in Hedong, but I had to leave there after killing a local bully who was persecuting his neighbors and have been on the move these five or six years. As soon as I heard about the recruitment, I came to sign up." Xuande then told of his own ambitions, to Lord Guan's great satisfaction. Together the three left the tavern and went to Zhang Fei's farm to continue their discussion. "There's a peach garden behind my farm," said Zhang Fei. "The flowers are in full bloom. Tomorrow let us offer sacrifice there to Heaven and earth, and pledge to combine our strength and purpose as sworn brothers. Then we'll plan our course of action." Xuande and Lord Guan agreed with one voice: "So be it."

— Chapter 1 Three Bold Spirits Plight Mutual Faith in the Peach Garden; *Heroes and Champions Win First Honors Fighting the Yellow Scarves*

(Tr. Moss Roberts)

As they were drinking, a huge, tall fellow appeared pushing a hand-cart along the road. At the threshold he halted and entered the inn to rest awhile and he called for wine.

"And be quick!" added he. "For I am in haste to get into the town and offer myself for the army."

Liu Bei looked over the newcomer, item by item, and he noted the man had a huge frame, a long beard, a vivid face like an apple, and deep red lips. He had eyes like a phoenix's and fine bushy eyebrows like silkworms. His whole appearance was dignified and awe-inspiring. Presently, Liu Bei crossed over, sat down beside him and asked his name.

"I am Guan Yu," replied he. "I am a native of the east side of the river, but I have been a fugitive on the waters for some five years, because I slew a ruffian who, since he was wealthy and powerful, was a bully. I have come to join the army here."

Then Liu Bei told Guan Yu his own intentions, and all three went away to Zhang Fei's farm where they could talk over the grand project.

Said Zhang Fei, "the peach trees in the orchard behind the house are just in full flower. Tomorrow we will institute a sacrifice there and solemnly declare our intention before Heaven and Earth, and we three will swear brotherhood and unity of aims and sentiments. Thus will we enter upon our great task."

Both Liu Bei and Guan Yu gladly agreed.

— *Chapter 1 Three Heroes Swear Brotherhood In The Peach Garden; One Victory Shatters The Rebels In Battlegrounds*

(Tr. C. H. Brewitt-Taylor)

(3) 次日,于桃园中,备下乌牛白马祭礼等项,三人焚香再拜而说誓曰:"念刘备、关羽、张飞,虽然异姓,既结为兄弟,则同心协力,救困扶危;上报国家,下安黎庶。不求同年同月同日生,只愿同年同月同日死。皇天后土,实鉴此心,背义忘恩,天人共戮!"誓毕,拜玄德为兄,关羽次之,张飞为弟。祭罢天地,复宰牛设酒,聚乡中勇士,得三百余人,就桃园中痛饮一醉。

——第一回 《宴桃园豪杰三结义,斩黄巾英雄首立功》

(3) The next day the three men had a black bull, a white horse, and other offerings brought to the peach garden. Amid the smoke of incense they performed their ritual prostration and took their oath:

We three, though of separate ancestry, join in brotherhood here, combining strength and purpose, to relieve the present crisis. We will perform our duty to the Emperor and protect the common folk of the land. We dare not hope to be together always but hereby vow to die the selfsame day. Let shining Heaven above and the fruitful land below bear witness to our resolve. May Heaven and man scourge whosoever fails this vow.

So swearing, Xuande became the eldest brother; Lord Guan, the second; and Zhang Fei, the youngest. After the ceremonies they butchered the bull and spread forth a feast in the peach garden for the three hundred local youths they had recruited;

and all drank to their heart's content.

— *Chapter 1 Three Bold Spirits Plight Mutual Faith in the Peach Garden*; *Heroes and Champions Win First Honors Fighting the Yellow Scarves*

(Tr. Moss Roberts)

All three being of one mind, next day they prepared the sacrifices, a black ox, a white horse, and wine for libation. Beneath the smoke of the incense burning on the altar, they bowed their heads and recited this oath:

"We three — Liu Bei, Guan Yu, and Zhang Fei — though of different families, swear brotherhood, and promise mutual help to one end. We will rescue each other in difficulty; we will aid each other in danger. We swear to serve the state and save the people. We ask not the same day of birth, but we seek to die together. May Heaven, the all-ruling, and Earth, the all-producing, read our hearts. If we turn aside from righteousness or forget kindliness, may Heaven and Human smite us!"

They rose from their knees. The two others bowed before Liu Bei as their elder brother, and Zhang Fei was to be the youngest of the trio. This solemn ceremony performed, they slew other oxen and made a feast to which they invited the villagers. Three hundred joined them, and all feasted and drank deep in the Peach Garden.

— *Chapter 1 Three Heroes Swear Brotherhood In The Peach Garden*; *One Victory Shatters The Rebels In Battlegrounds*

(Tr. C. H. Brewitt-Taylor)

(4) 次日，玄德同关、张并从人等来隆中。遥望山畔数人，荷锄耕于田间，而作歌曰："苍天如圆盖，陆地似棋局；世人黑白分，往来争荣辱；荣者自安安，辱者定碌碌。南阳有隐居，高眠卧不足！"玄德闻歌，勒马唤农夫问曰："此歌何人所作？"答曰："乃卧龙先生所作也。"玄德曰："卧龙先生住何处？"农夫曰："自此山之南，一带高冈，乃卧龙冈也。冈前疏林内茅庐中，即诸葛先生高卧之地。"玄德谢之，策马前行。不数里，遥望卧龙冈，果然清景异常。

——第三十七回 《司马徽再荐名士，刘玄德三顾草庐》

(4) The next day Xuande, Lord Guan, and Zhang Fei went to Longzhong. On the hills men were carrying mattocks to their acres, singing:

The sky's a curving vault of blue,

The level earth a chessboard,

Where men their black and white divide,

Disgrace or glory to decide.

For the winners, peace and comfort,

For the losers, tiring toil.

In Nanyang someone lies secluded,

Securely sleeping. Stay abed!

Xuande reined in and asked who had composed the song. "Why, Master Sleeping Dragon," was the reply. "Where does he live?" Xuande asked. A farmer answered, "A short way south runs a high ridge called Sleeping Dragon Ridge. In front is a thin wood where you'll find the little thatched lodge that he's made his refuge." Xuande thanked the man and rode on. Soon the ridge came into view. It was a soothing scene of extraordinary peace ...

— Chapter 37 *Still Water Recommends Another Noted Scholar*; *Liu Xuande Pays Three Visits to Zhuge Liang*

(Tr. Moss Roberts)

Soon after the three brothers set out to find the abode of the wise man. When they drew near the Sleeping Dragon Ridge, they saw a number of peasants in a field hoeing up the weeds, and as they worked they sang:

"The earth is a checkered board,

And the sky hangs over all,

Under it humans are contending,

Some rise, but a many fall.

For those who succeed this is well,

But for those who go under rough.

There's a dozing dragon hard by,

But his sleep is not deep enough."

Liu Bei and his brothers stopped to listen to the song and, calling up one of the peasants, asked who made it.

"It was made by Master Sleeping Dragon," said the laborer.

"Then he lives hereabout. Where?"

"South of this hill there is a ridge called the Sleeping Dragon, and close by is a sparse wood. In it stands a modest cottage. That is where Master Zhuge Liang takes his repose."

Liu Bei thanked him and the party rode on. Soon they came to the ridge, most aptly named, for indeed it lay wrapped in an atmosphere of calm beauty.

— Chapter 37 *Sima Hui Recommends A Scholar To Liu Bei*; *Liu Bei Pays Three Visits To The Sleeping Dragon Ridge*

(Tr. C. H. Brewitt-Taylor)

（5）玄德乃辞二人，上马投卧龙冈来。到庄前下马，扣门问童子曰："先生今日在庄否？"童子曰："现在堂上读书。"玄德大喜，遂跟童子而入。至中门，只见门上大书一联云："淡泊以明志，宁静而致远。"玄德正看间，忽闻吟咏之声，乃立于门侧窥之，见草堂之上，一少年拥炉抱膝，歌曰："凤翱翔于千仞兮，非梧不栖；士伏处于一方兮，非主不依。乐躬耕于陇亩兮，吾爱吾庐；聊寄傲于琴书兮，以待天时。"

——第三十七回 《司马徽再荐名士，刘玄德三顾草庐》

（5）Xuande bade the drinkers good-bye and rode toward Sleeping Dragon Ridge. He dismounted at Kongming's farm and, finding the youth at the gate, asked, "Is your master in today?" "In the house reading," was the reply. Excitedly, Xuande followed the lad. Coming to the inner gate, they stopped before a couplet on the wall that read: "Only through austerity and quiescence can one's purpose shine forth; only through concentration and self-control can one's distant goal be reached." As Xuande was studying the words, he heard someone singing inside. Standing attentively by the door of the thatched house, he peered in and saw a young man with his arms about his knees, chanting:

The phoenix winging on the air

Will choose no tree

Except the wu.

The scholar keeping to his lair

Will have no lord

Except the true.

Oh, let me till these furrowed fields,

By this sweet home

That I call mine.

In books and song I place my dreams

And wait the time

The fates assign.

— Chapter 37 Still Water Recommends Another Noted Scholar; *Liu Xuande Pays Three Visits to Zhuge Liang*

(Tr. Moss Roberts)

So he remounted and went his way. He reached the little cottage, dismounted, and tapped at the door. The same lad answered his knock, and he asked whether the Master had returned.

"He is in his room reading," said the boy.

Joyful indeed was Liu Bei as he followed the lad in. In front of the middle door he saw written this pair of scrolls:

By purity inspire the inclination;

By repose affect the distant.

As Liu Bei was looking at this couplet, he heard someone singing in a subdued voice and stopped by the door to peep in. He saw a young man close to a charcoal brazier, hugging his knees while he sang:

"The phoenix dies high, O!

And only will perch on a magnolia tree.

The scholar is hidden, O!

Till his lord appear he can patient be.

He tills his fields, O!

He is well-content and loves his home,

He awaits his day, O!

His books and his lute to leave and roam."

— *Chapter 37 Sima Hui Recommends A Scholar To Liu Bei*; *Liu Bei Pays Three Visits To The Sleeping Dragon Ridge*

（Tr. C. H. Brewitt-Taylor）

五、练习与思考

1. 实训题

翻译以下段落。

（1）当夜五更时候，船已近曹操水寨。孔明教把船只头西尾东，一带摆开，就船上擂鼓呐喊。鲁肃惊曰："倘曹兵齐出，如之奈何？"孔明笑曰："吾料曹操于重雾中必不敢出。吾等只顾酌酒取乐，待雾散便回。"

却说曹寨中，听得擂鼓呐喊，毛玠、于禁二人慌忙飞报曹操。操传令曰："重雾迷江，彼军忽至，必有埋伏，切不可轻动。可拨水军弓弩手乱箭射之。"又差人往旱寨内唤张辽、徐晃各带弓弩军三千，火速到江边助射。比及号令到来，毛玠、于禁怕南军抢入水寨，已差弓弩手在寨前放箭；少顷，旱寨内弓弩手亦到，约一万余人，尽皆向江中放箭：箭如雨发。孔明教把船吊回，头东尾西，逼近水寨受箭，一面擂鼓呐喊。待至日高雾散，孔明令收船急回。二十只船两边束草上，排满箭枝。孔明令各船上军士齐声叫曰："谢丞相箭！"（选自第四十六回《用奇谋孔明借箭，献密计黄盖受刑》）

（2）正行时，军士禀曰："前面有两条路，请问丞相从那条路去？"操问："那条路近？"军士曰："大路稍平，却远五十余里。小路投华容道，却近五十余里；只是地窄路险，坑坎难行。"操令人上山观望,回报:"小路山边有数处烟起;大路并无动静。"操教前军便走华容道小路。诸将曰:"烽烟起处,必有军马,何故反走这条路?"操曰:"岂不闻兵书有云:虚则实之,实则虚之。诸葛亮多谋,故使人于山僻烧烟,使我军不敢从这条山路走,他却伏兵于大路等着。吾料已定,偏不教中他计!"诸将皆曰:"丞相妙算,人不可及。"遂勒兵走华容道。此时人皆饥倒,马尽困乏。焦头烂额者扶策而行,中箭着枪者勉强而走。衣甲湿透,个个不全;军器旗幡,纷纷不整:大半皆是彝陵道上被赶得慌,只骑得秃马,鞍辔衣服,尽皆抛弃。正值隆冬严寒之时,其苦何可胜言。(选自第五十回《诸葛亮智算华容,关云长义释曹操》)

2. 思考题

(1) 你认为 Taylor 将"逃难江湖"直译成"a fugitive on the waters"是否准确?为什么?

(2) 试比较分析直译与意译的优缺点。

六、参考文献

[1] 范仲英.实用翻译教程[M].北京:外语教学与研究出版社,1994.

[2] 鲁迅.中国小说史略(英文版)[M].杨宪益,戴乃迭,译.北京:外文出版社,1976.

[3] 鲁迅.鲁迅全集(第九卷)[M].北京:人民文学出版社,1991.

[4] 张今.文学翻译原理[M].开封:河南大学出版社,1987.

[5] 罗新璋.翻译论集[M].北京:商务印书馆,1984.

[6] 石欲达.中国古典小说书名英译中的得与失[J].外语研究,1996(2):20-25.

[7] 王平.文学翻译探索[M].长春:吉林人民出版社,2005.

[8] Danbmy, Conn. The Encyclopedia Americana[Z]. Americana Corp,1980.

[9] Grolier Academic Encyclopedia[Z]. Grolier International,1983.

第十三课
《水浒传》评介赏析

> 《水浒传》是我国四大古典名著之一,是一部以描写北宋末年农民起义为主题的长篇小说。书中描写以宋江为首的108位梁山好汉起义,以及聚义后接受招安,四处征战的故事。
>
> 《水浒传》是中国历史上最早用古白话文写成的章回小说之一。书中塑造了栩栩如生的人物形象,情节起伏跌宕,流传极广,脍炙人口,是一部在人民群众百年集体创作的基础之上进行整理、加工,创作出来的伟大作品,是我国古典文学的代表作之一。它具有丰富的民族文化内涵,对中国乃至东亚的叙事文学都有极其深远的影响,至今被翻译成多种文字在世界范围内流传。

一、翻译简介

《水浒传》是以白话文写成的明清章回小说,被后人归为中国古典四大文学名著之一。

其又名《京本忠义传》《忠义水浒传》,初名《江湖豪客传》,一般简称《水浒》,全书定型于明朝。

《水浒传》国内现存的简本以双峰堂刊本为最早。它的正式书名是《忠义水浒志传评林》,刊行于明万历甲午(1594)季秋月。

《水浒传》作者历来有争议,一般认为是施耐庵所著,而罗贯中则做了整理,金圣叹删节为七十回本。

以《水浒传》的回数区分,有一百回本、一百二十回本、七十回本、一百零四回本、一百一十回本、一百一十五回本、一百二十四回本等多种类型。

二、书名翻译

1. All Men Are Brothers

此为美国作家赛珍珠（Pearl S. Buck）1933 出版的 70 回译本，可能译自《江湖豪客传》。

2. Water Margin

此为英国学者 J. H. Jackson 1937 年出版的译本。

3. Outlaws of the Marsh

此为"中国翻译文化终身成就奖"获得者沙博理（Sidney Shapiro）于 1980 年出版的译本（100 回）。

4. The Marshes of Mount Liang

此为 John Dent-Young 和 Alex Dent-Young 父子于 1994 和 2002 年间由香港中文大学出版社出版的译本。

其中，在国际上影响最大的是赛珍珠版。2001 年 4 月 2 日《人民日报·海外版》评价布克夫人（中文名字为赛珍珠）翻译的《水浒传》是最好的译本，因为她精通中国文字，熟悉中国社会。

三、特殊概念的翻译

1. 中国古代官职

殿头官 the chief of ceremonies

参知政事 Deputy Minister

禁军教头 arm instructor of the Mighty Imperial Guards

学士 Court Scholar

都头 constable

老都管 the old chamberlain

提辖 Steward

府尹 prefect

步兵都头 infantry constable

马兵都头 cavalry constable

知县 the magistrate

保正 Ward chief

团练使 The District Garrison Commander

省院官 the Legal Office

文官 Civilian Commandant

武官 Military Commandant

蔡九知府 Prefect Cai the Ninth

太保 Deacon

2. 佛道语汇

太白金星 Great Star of White Gold

天师 Divine Teacher

禅杖 Buddhist stuff

智清禅师 Lucid Teacher

天罡地煞 stars of heavenly Spirits and Earthly Fiends

罗真人 Luo the Sage

紫虚观 Temple of the Purple Void

松鹤轩 the Hall of Pines and Cranes

法术 the magic

二仙山 Two Fairies Mountain

参禅 Consults the Seer

坐化 Expire in a Trance

3. 中国古代独特事物

翰林院 Hanlin Academy

待漏院 Hall of the Water Clock

伏魔殿 Suppression of Demons Hall

枢密院 Council of Military Affairs

大相国寺 the Great Xiangguo Monastery

金印 the golden print

六和塔 Six Harmonies Monastery

4. 中国古代习语

拨草寻蛇 separating the grass to find the snake

急来抱佛脚 a case of not burning incense in ordinary times, but embracing the idol's foot in a crisis

无巧不成书 Without coincidence there would be no story

远亲不如近邻 A close neighbor means more than a distant relative

捉奸见双,捉贼见赃,杀人见伤 For adultery catch the pair, for robbery find the root, for murderer produce the body

以眼还眼，以牙还牙 An eye for an eye, a tooth for a tooth
衣锦还乡 go home in one's official finery

5.《水浒传》重点人物
"及时雨"宋江 the Timely Rain
"玉麒麟"卢俊义 the Jade Unicorn
"智多星"吴用 the Wizard
"入云龙"公孙胜 the Dragon in Clouds
"神机军师"朱武 the Miraculous Strategist
"双枪将"董平 the General Two Spears
"小旋风"柴进 the Small Whirlwind
"扑天雕"李应 the Heaven-Soaring Eagle
"大刀"关胜 the Big Halberd
"豹子头"林冲 the Panther Head
"霹雳火"秦明 the Thunderbolt
"双鞭"呼延灼 the Two Rods
"小李广"花荣 the Lesser Li Guang
"金枪手"徐宁 the Mental Lancer
"青面兽"杨志 the Blue-Faced Beast
"急先锋"索超 the Urgent Vanguard
"没羽箭"张清 the Featherless Arrow
"美髯公"朱仝 the Beautiful Beard
"九纹龙"史进 the Nine Dragons
"没遮拦"穆弘 the Unrestrained
"镇三山"黄信 the Suppressor of Three Mountains
"病尉迟"孙立 the Sickly General
"丑郡马"宣赞 the Ugly Son in Law
"井木犴"郝思文 the Wild Dog
"百胜将"韩滔 the Ever-Victorious General
"天目将"彭玘 the Eyes of Heaven General
"圣水将"单廷珪 the Water General
"神火将"魏定国 the Fire General
"摩云金翅"欧鹏 the Golden Wings Brushing the Clouds
"火眼狻猊"邓飞 the Fiery-Eyed Lion
"锦毛虎"燕顺 the Elegant Tiger

"铁笛仙"马麟 the Elfin Flutist

"跳涧虎"陈达 the Gorge-leaping Tiger

"白花蛇"杨春 the White-Spotted Snake

"锦豹子"杨林 the Elegant Panther

"小霸王"周通 the Little King

"花和尚"鲁智深 The Tattooed Monk

"行者"武松 the Pilgrim

"赤发鬼"刘唐 The Red-Haired Demon

"插翅虎"雷横 the Winged Tiger

"黑旋风"李逵 The Black Whirlwind

"浪子"燕青 the Prodigy

"病关索"杨雄 the Pallid

"拼命三郎"石秀 the Rash

"两头蛇"解珍 the Two-Headed Snake

"双尾蝎"解宝 the Two-tailed Scorpio

"混世魔王"樊瑞 the Demon King Who Roils the World

"丧门神"鲍旭 the God of Death

"八臂哪吒"项充 the Eight-Armed Nezha

"飞天大圣"李衮 the Flying Divinity

"病大虫"薛永 the Sick Tiger

"金眼彪"施恩 the Golden-Eyed Tiger Cub

"小遮拦"穆春 the Slightly Restrained

"打虎将"李忠 the Tiger-Fighting General

"白面郎君"郑天寿 the Fair-Eyed Gentleman

"云里金刚"宋万 the Guardian of the Clouds

"摸著天"杜迁 The Skyscraper

"出林龙"邹渊 the Dragon from the Forest

"独角龙"邹润 the One-Horned Dragon

"花项虎"龚旺 the Flowery-Necked Tiger

"中箭虎"丁得孙 the Arrow-Struck Tiger

"没面目"焦挺 the Merciless

"石将军"石勇 the Stone General

"混江龙"李俊 the Turbulent River Dragon

"船火儿"张横 the Boat Flame

"浪里白条"张顺 the White Streak in the Waves

"立地太岁"阮小二 the Second Ferocious Giant

"短命二郎"阮小五 the Reckless Rash

"活阎罗"阮小七 the Devil Incarnate

"出洞蛟"童威 the Dragon from the Cave

"翻江蜃"童猛 the River Churning Clam

"小尉迟"孙新 the Junior General

"母大虫"顾大嫂 Gu the Tigress

"菜园子"张青 the Vegetable Gardener

"母夜叉"孙二娘 Sun the Witch

"旱地忽律"朱贵 the Dry-Land Crocodile

"鬼脸儿"杜兴 the Demon Face

"催命判官"李立 the Hill's Summoner

"活闪婆"王定六 The Lightening

"神行太保"戴宗 the Marvelous Traveler

"铁叫子"乐和 the Iron Throat

"鼓上蚤"时迁 the Flea on the Drum

"金毛犬"段景住 the Golden God

"白日鼠"白胜 the Daylight Rat

"小温侯"吕方 the Little Duke

"赛仁贵"郭盛 the Second Rengui

"毛头星"孔明 the Comet

"独火星"孔亮 the Fleming Star

"铁臂膊"蔡福 the Iron Arm

"一枝花"蔡庆 the Single Blossom

"矮脚虎"王英 the Stumpy Tiger

"一丈青"扈三娘 the Ten Feet of Iron

"圣手书生"萧让 the Master Hand

"铁面孔目"裴宣 the Ironclad Virtue

"玉幡竿"孟康 the Jade Flagpole

"神算子"蒋敬 the Magic Calculator

"玉臂匠"金大坚 the Jade-Armed Craftsman

"通臂猿"侯健 the Long-armed ape

"紫髯伯"皇甫端 the Purple Beard

"神医"安道全 the Skilled Doctor

"金钱豹子"汤隆 the Golden-Coined Spotted Leopard

"轰天雷"凌振 the Heaven-Shaken Thunder

"青眼虎"李云 the Black-Eyed Tiger

"操刀鬼"曹正 the Demon Craver

"铁扇子"宋清 the Iron Fan

"笑面虎"朱富 the Smiling Tiger

"九尾龟"陶宗旺 the Nine-tailed Tortoise

"险道神"郁保四 the Spirit of the Dangerous Road

6.《水浒传》重点词汇

好汉 true man

白虎堂 White Tiger Inner Sanctum

旌旗 military pennants

野猪林 Wild Roar Forest

开封府 Kaifeng government compound

山神庙 the Mountain Spirit Temple

草料场 the fodder depot

号箭 the signal arrow

水亭 the Lakeside Pavilion

梁山泊 Liangshan Marsh

落草 take to the hills/join the bandits

十八般武艺 eighteen forms of the fighting arts

凌迟处死 be executed by sliced to death

安平寨 Anping Stockade

快活林 Happy Grove

蒋门神 Jiang the Gate Guard Giant

玉环步鸳鸯脚 the jade-circle steps with duck and drake Feet

死囚牢 the condemned cell

飞云浦 Flying-Cloud Ponds

鸳鸯楼 Duck and Drake Bower

蜈蚣岭 Centipede Ridge

小鳌山 the Hill of Lanterns

清风寨 Clear Winds Fort

瓦砾场 a field of rubble

大汉 big fellow

三霸 three powers

天罗地网 heaven's mesh and earth's net

虎窟狼窝 a den of tigers and a lair of wolves

玉壶春酒 Springtime in Jade Bottles

吟反诗 recite a rebellious poem

传假信 send a false letter

城隍庙 the City Temple

辅国安民 defend the country and bring peace to the people

琼楼金阙 the fairyland's towers of gold and jade

报恩寺 the Grateful Retribution Monastery

翠屏山 Jade Screen Inn

祝家店 the Zhu Family Inn

连环计 a double linked plan

差拨 the head keeper

抄事房 the copying section

三路兵 A three-column army

连环马 an armored cavalry/the linked-up cavalry

军师 military advisor

钩镰枪 the barbed lance

摩拳擦掌 ground one's fists into palms

金铃吊挂 the golden hanging bell

降魔 defeat the Demon King

金沙渡 Golden Sand Crossing

翠云楼 the Jade Cloud Mansion

大名府 Daming City

忠义双全 complete loyalty and righteousness

四斗五方旗 four-dipper positions and five-pennant arches

九宫八卦阵 set troops in Nine Segments Within an Octagon

十面埋伏 lay ambush on all sides

阵列混天象 set up a zodiac deployment

颁恩降诏 bestow the emperor's pardon

破阵 crack the foe's deployment

双林渡 Double Woods Crossing

结义 pledge brotherhood

会垓 converse a large meeting

昱岭关 Yuling Pass

清溪洞 Clear Stream Cavern

7. 特殊表达的翻译

例1：王伦向林冲要<u>投名状</u>

赛珍珠译：formal application

沙博理译：membership certificate

评析：投名状是指加入某一组织表示忠心的保证书，翻译为"申请书"，并不合适。相比而言，沙博理的"membership certificate"更加合理。

例2：一百杀威棒

赛珍珠译：one hundred severe blows with bamboo

沙博理译：spirit breaking blows

评析：旧时为压倒犯人气焰，用棍棒打犯人，叫打杀威棒。这里，赛珍珠的"severe blows with bamboo"翻译比较片面，缺乏关键信息。

例3：三碗不过岗

赛珍珠译：If you drink three cups of wine, you will be unable to cross the mountain ridge.

沙博理译：Three bowls and you can't cross the ridge.

评析：赛珍珠的 cups 显得不够量，不够豪气。

例4：<u>透瓶香和出门倒</u>

赛珍珠译：the aroma penetrates the bottle, upon leaving the door you will fall down

沙博理译：seeps through the bottle fragrance, collaps outside the door.

评析：collapse 显然比 fall down 更传神。

例5：鲁智深在五台山出家后，不学坐禅，选了中间的禅床倒头便睡，<u>禅和子只得叹气道："善哉！"鲁智深便道："团鱼洒家也吃，甚么鳝哉！"禅和子道："却是苦也！"鲁智深便道："团鱼大腹，又肥甜了又好吃。那得苦也？"</u>

赛珍珠译：A priest exlaimed, "What a calamity!" Lu Ta shouted, "even a tortoise I shall eat; what calamity will there be?" The priest replied, "Of course there will be a calamity."

沙博理译："Evil!" exclaimed the monk. "What is this talk about eels."/"It's turtles I like to eat"/"Oh, bitter!"/"There is nothing bitter about them Turtle belly is fat and sweet. They make very good eating."

评析：赛珍珠译文有些费解，沙博理借用了 evil 和 eel 的谐音。

例6：京师大旱无雨，"<u>天下各州府雪片也似申奏将来。</u>"

赛珍珠译：A flood of petitions inundated the capital like heavy snow storm.

沙博理译：The court was snowed under with petitions for relief.

评析：赛珍珠译本"州府"的意义不准确

例7：这人吹弹歌舞，刺枪使棒，相扑玩耍，亦故胡乱学些诗书辞赋；若论仁义礼智，行信忠良，却是不会。

赛珍珠译：He could play well on wood and string instruments, but was no good at poetry or literature. If there was a discussion of benevolence, justice, propriety, wisdom or virtue he was unable to take part.

沙博理译：In addition to his skill with weapons, Gao Qiu could play musical instruments and sing and dance. He also learned a bit about poetry and versifying. But when it came to virtue and proper behavior, he did not know a thing.

评析：sense and reference 的处理，赛珍珠更重 sense，沙博理更重 reference。

例8："休要胡说！没地不还你钱，再筛三碗给我吃！"

赛珍珠译："Don't talk nonsense!" said Wu Sung, "I won't cheat you, so bring me three more cups of wine."

沙博理译："Poppycock! I am paying, aren't I? Pour me three more bowls."

评析：赛珍珠：文气，不豪气

例9：高俅要痛打王进，众头领求情。高俅便说："明天却和你理会！"

赛珍珠译：I will speak to you tomorrow

沙博理译：I will settle with you tomorrow.

评析：赛珍珠未能译出语气中的威胁。speak to you 的语气太柔。

例10：施恩见了武松，拜倒说："小弟久闻兄长大名，如雷贯耳，只恨云程阻隔，不能相见。"

赛珍珠译："I have long heard of your name like a crash of thunder." Said Shi En, "but unfortunately, we have ever been separated by impassable roads so that I couldn't meet you."

沙博理译：Elder brother's fame has long thundered in my ears. I hated the long distance that separated us.

评析：沙博理的译文简洁而不失忠实。

例11：郑关西强霸翠莲，鲁达听得郑大官人原来就是郑屠后道："呸！俺只道是哪个郑大官人，原来是杀猪的郑屠。这个腌臜泼才。投托着俺小种经略相公门下做个肉铺户，却原来这等欺负人！"

赛珍珠译："Bah! I know that fellow, he was previously a butcher and a filthy rascal. Some time ago he asked my help in getting the vice governor here to permit him to open his shop and this is how he cheats people."

沙博理译："Bah!" said Lu Da contemptuously. "So Master Zheng is only Zheng the pig-sticker, the dirty rogue who runs the butcher shop under the patronage of Young General Zhong, our garrison commander. And he cheats and bullies too, does he?"

评析：butcher 是中性词，pig-sticker 是俚语，含贬义

例 12：董将仕欲打发高俅回东京去，便假心假意对高俅说："小人家下萤火之光，照人不亮，日后恐误了足下。我转荐足下与小苏学士处，久后也得个出身，足下意内如何？"

赛珍珠译："Here we can offer you a little help. I will however recommend you to a certain Mr. Su, who may assist you in cutting you a fine career. What do you think of that?"

沙博理译："The light of my household is too feeble," he said, "it would only be holding you back to keep you here. I'm turning you over to Sun Junior, the Court Scholar. With him you'll be able to make a start. How does that sound?"

8. 双关语英语

例：西门庆道：王干娘，你这梅汤做得好，有多少在屋里？王婆笑道：老身做了一世媒，那讨一个在屋里？西门庆道："我问你梅汤，你却说做媒，差了多少！"——第二十三回《王婆贪贿说风情，郓哥不忿闹茶肆》

沙博理译：Ximen Qing said："You make very good sour plum drinks, godmother. Do you have a lot in stock?" Mistress Wang laughed, "I've been making mei all my life, but I don't keep any one here." "I was talking about sour plum drinks and you're talking about making matches! There's a big difference".

— *Chapter 24 For Money Mistress Wang Arranges a Seduction*；*In Anger Yunge Riots in the Tea-Shop*

杰克逊译：Ximenqing said punningly, "Gradma Wang, this plum juice is very nice. Have you any more in your establishment?" Grandma Wang laughed and said, "I have acted as a marriage matchmaker for a long time, but just at present I have no woman on hand in my house." "I asked you about 'mei'（plums）, and you replied about 'mei'（marriages）— there is a wide difference."

— *Chapter 23 Grandma Wang Being Covetous Spoke Seductively*；*Yu Ge Makes a Row in a Tea Shop*

9. 四字格翻译

例：长老道："遇林而起，遇山而富，遇水而兴，遇江而止。"——第五回《小霸王醉入销金帐，花和尚大闹桃花村》

沙博理译：The abbot intoned："Take action in the forest, prosper in the mountain, flourish amid the waters, but halt at the river."

— *Chapter 5 Drunk, the Little King Raises the Gold-spangled Bed Curtains*；*Lu the Tattooed Monk Throws Peach Blossom Village into Confusion*

杰克逊译：The abbot continued and said：

(1) "When you see a forest your lot will be improved;

(2) when you see a mountain you will become rich;

(3) when you enter a department(chou)you will move on; and

(4) when you see a river(chiang, also a man's name)you will stop.

— *Chapter 5 Little Tyrant When Drunk Goes Inside the Bed Curtains*; *LuDa, the Monk, Has a Fight at Tao Hua Village*

10. 文化词英译

例：(刘太公)他只有这个女儿养老送终，承祀香火，都在他身上。——第五回《小霸王醉入销金帐，花和尚大闹桃花村》

沙博理译：She is his only child.He needs her to look after him and <u>carry on his family line</u>. (In feudal China when a family had no sons, a son-in-law was sometimes adopted & at the time of marriage by the girl's parents. Instead of the girl going off with him, he moved into her father's household. Their children bore the girl's family name, and their sons were deemed continuers of her father's ancestral maleline).

— *Chapter 5 Drunk, the Little King Raises the Gold-spangled Bed Curtains*; *Lu the Tattooed Monk Throws Peach Blossom Village into Confusion*

杰克逊译：They all sat down and Lu Ta explained the position to ChouTung, advising him to break his engagement, and find a better girl.

— *Chapter 5 Little Tyrant When Drunk Goes Inside the Bed Curtains*; *LuDa, the Monk, Has a Fight at Tao Hua Village*

11. 直译和意译

例：史进喝道："汝等杀人放火，打家劫舍，犯着弥天大罪，都是该死的人！你也须有耳朵！好大胆！直来太岁头上动土！"——第二回 《王教头私走延安府，九纹龙大闹史家村》

沙博理译："You murder and burn, rob and plunder, your terrible crimes are all punishable by death," Shi Jin shouted. "Haven't you heard of me? Where do you get the gall to come and tweak the tiger's whiskers?"

— *Chapter 2 Arms Instructor Wang Goes Secretly to Tanan Prefecture*; *Nine Dragon Shi Jin Wreaks Havoc in Shi Family Village*

杰克逊译：Shi Jin spoke in a loud voice, "You kill people, set places on fire, rob with violence; your crimes fill the heavens, and you are all deserving of death. You ought to have ear; how dare you come to pouch the tiger's litter!"

— *Chapter 2 Drill Inspector Wang Goes Stealthily to Yanan Prefecture*; *Shi Jin Defends His Village*

四、译文对比赏析

《水浒传》中有很多经典的句子和段落,译成英文之后不同版本的语言特点各不相同。其英译本为数众多,良莠不齐而又各有千秋。本课选取了 J. H. Jackson 和 Sidney Shapiro 的译本来做对比赏析。

1. 经典句子

(1) 大虫见掀他不着,吼一声,却似半天里起个霹雳,振得那山冈也动,把这铁棒也似虎尾倒竖起来只一剪。

——第二十三回 《横海郡柴进留宾,景阳冈武松打虎》

(1) The tiger immediately turned around, and roared like thunder, so that the ridge almost quaked. The tiger was erect and stiff as a poker, and was slashed from side to side in rage.

— *Chapter 23 Squire Chai Detains a Guest*;*Wu Song Kills a Tiger*

(Tr. J. H. Jackson)

Both hungry and thirsty, the big animal clawed the ground with its front paws a couple of times, sprang high and came hurtling forward.

— *Chapter 23 Lord Chai Accomodates Guests in Henghai County*;*Wu Song Kills a Tiger on Jingyang Ridge*

(Tr. Sidney Shapiro)

(2) 这贩枣子的客人劝道:"你这个鸟汉子。他也说得差了,你也忒认真,连累我们也吃你说了几声。须不关他众人之事,胡乱卖与他众人吃些。"

——第十六回 《杨志押送金银担,吴用智取生辰纲》

(2) The date merchants intervened. "Stupid Oaf," they berated him. "What if that fellow said the wrong thing? You've even tried to take it out on us. Anyhow, it has nothing to do with these porters. Sell them some wine and be done with it."

— *Chapter 16 Yang Zhi in charge of the Convoy of Silver and Gold*;*Wu Yong Schemes How toGet the Birthday Presents*

(Tr. J. H. Jackson)

The man who was selling dates interposed and said, "You foolish fellow, That man (Yang Zhi) was wrong, but you are so particular and refused to sell us before, but I think you had better let them have a drink because they are not spoken against you."

— Chapter 16 Yang Zhi Escorts a Convoy of Precious Goods; Wu Yong by a Ruse Captures the Birthday Gifts

(Tr. Sidney Shapiro)

(3)智深道:"也是怪哉;歇一夜打甚么不紧,怎地便是讨死?"庄家道:"去便去,不去时便捉来缚在这里!"

——第五回 《小霸王醉入销金帐,九纹龙大闹史家村》

(3) "This is strange," replied Lu Da. "If I only stay for one night how shall I risk my life?" "Go away!" said the villagers. "If you do not go we shall tie you up."

— Chapter 5 Little Tyrant When Drunk Goes Inside the Bed Curtains; LuDa, the Monk, Has a Fight at Tao Hua Village

(Tr. J. H. Jackson)

"That's a strange talk. Why such a fuss about spending one night? Why so dangerous?" "Get going. Otherwise you're liable to be seized and bound."

— Chapter 5 Drunk, the Little King Raises the Gold-spangled Bed Curtains; Lu the Tattooed Monk Throws Peach Blossom Village into Confusion

(Tr. Sidney Shapiro)

(4)史进喝道:"汝等杀人放火,打家劫舍,犯着弥天大罪,都是该死的人!你也须有耳朵!好大胆!直来太岁头上动土!"

——第二回 《王教头私走延安府,九纹龙大闹史家村》

(4) Shi Jin spoke in a loud voice, "You kill people, set places on fire, rob with violence; your crimes fill the heavens, and you are all deserving of death. You ought to have ear; how dare you come to pouch the tiger's litter!"

— Chapter 2 Drill Inspector Wang Goes Stealthily to Yanan Prefecture; Shi Jin Defends His Village

(Tr. J. H Jackson)

"You murder and burn, rob and plunder, your terrible crimes are all punishable by death," Shi Jin shouted. "Haven't you heard of me? Where do you get the gall to come and tweak the tiger's whiskers?"

— Chapter 2 Arms Instructor Wang Goes Secretly to Tanan Prefecture; Nine Dragon Shi Jin Wreaks Havoc in Shi Family Village

(Tr. Sidney Shapiro)

(5) 林冲提着衮刀,对小喽啰道:"眼见得又不济事了!不如趁早——天色未晚——取了行李,只得往别处去寻个所在!"

——第十一回 《朱贵水亭施号箭,林冲雪夜上梁山》

(5) "It seems I'm out of luck again," said Lin. "I might as well go back while it's still early, pick up my luggage and start looking for another place."

— *Chapter 11 Zhu Gui Shoots a Whistling Arrow from an Arbor；Lin Chong Arrived at Liangshan Marsh in the Night During a Heavy Snowstorm*

(Tr. J. H. Jackson)

Lin Chong picking up his weapons spoke to his companion, "I see that I'm again unfortunate. I think I had better get my bundle, and set out for another place before it gets dark."

— *Chapter 11 Zhu Gui Shoot a Signal Arrow from the Lakeside Pavilion；Lin Chong Climbs Mount Liangshan in the Snowy Night*

(Tr. Sidney Shapiro)

2. 经典段落

(1) 那大虫又饿,又渴,把两只爪在地上略按一按,和身望上一扑,从半空里撺将下来。武松被那一惊,酒都作冷汗出了。说时迟,那时快;武松见大虫扑来,只一闪,闪在大虫背后。那大虫背后看人最难,便把前爪搭在地下,把腰胯一掀,掀将起来。武松只一闪,闪在一边。大虫见掀他不着,吼一声,却似半天里起个霹雳,振得那山冈也动,把这铁棒也似虎尾倒竖起来只一剪。武松却又闪在一边。原来那大虫拿人只是一扑,一掀,一剪;三般捉不着时,气性先自没了一半。那大虫又剪不着,再吼了一声,一兜兜将回来。

——第二十三回 《横海郡柴进留宾,景阳冈武松打虎》

(1) The tiger was both hungry and thirsty, and crouched on the ground ready for a spring. As the tiger sprang forward Wu Song was startled, and was covered with a cold sweat, but slipping to one side he escaped. The tiger immediately turned around, and roared like thunder, so that the ridge almost quaked. The tiger was erect and stiff as a poker, and was lashed from side to side in rage. Wu Song did not keep still, but kept moving about irregularly. In fact the tiger had only three methods of killing men, a crouch, a leap, and a blow with its tail. If these three failed, the tiger at once lost all courage or spirit. In such cases it always turned around, and gave a loud roar.

— *Chapter 23 Squire Chai Detains a Guest；Wu Song Kills a Tiger*

(Tr. J. H. Jackson)

Both hungry and thirsty, the big animal clawed the ground with its front paws a couple of times, sprang high and came hurtling forward. The wine poured out of Wu Song in a cold sweat. Quicker than it takes to say, he dodged, and the huge beast landed beyond him. Tigers can't see behind him, so as its front paws touched the ground it tried to side-swipe Wu Song with its body. Again he dodged, and the tiger missed. With a thunderous roar that shocks the ridge, the animal slashed at Wu Song with its iron tail. Once more he swiveled out of the way. Now this tiger has three methods for getting its victim — spring, swipe and slash. But none of them had worked, and the beast's spirit diminished by half. Again it roared, and whirled around

— Chapter 23 Lord Chai Accomodates Guests in Henghai County, Wu Song Kills a Tiger on Jingyang Ridge

(Tr. Sidney Shapiro)

（2）一日，正行之间，贪看山明水秀，不觉天色已晚，赶不上宿头；路中又没人作伴，那里投宿是好；又赶了三二十里田地，过了一条板桥，远远地望见一簇红霞，树木丛中闪着一所庄院，庄后重重叠叠都是乱山。鲁智深道："只得投庄上去借宿。"迳奔到庄前看时，见数十个庄家，急急忙忙，搬东搬西。鲁智深到庄前，倚了禅杖，与庄客唱个喏。庄客道："和尚，日晚来我庄上做甚的？"智深道："洒家赶不上宿头，欲借贵庄投宿一宵，明早便行。"庄家道："我庄今晚有事，歇不得。"智深道："胡乱借洒家歇一夜，明日便行。"庄家道："和尚快走，休在这里讨死！"智深道："也是怪哉；歇一夜打甚么不紧，怎地便是讨死？"庄家道："去便去，不去时便捉来缚在这里！"

——第五回 《小霸王醉入销金帐，九纹龙大闹史家村》

（2）One day he was enjoying the scenery of a mountain stream and did not notice it was evening, and that he had not found a place to sleep. The road was quite deserted. After he had gone thirty li more, he passed over a plank bridge, where he saw in the distance a red light emerging from a group of trees. It was a farmhouse in a wood with surrounding wild mountains rising one above the other. He went to the farmhouse and saw outside a dozen men who were very busy moving things about. He places his staff against the wall and spoke to the men to attract their attention. The villagers said, "Monk, why do you arrive so late at our farm?" "As I cannot find an inn near here," replied Lu Da, "I should like to stay at your farm tonight, and I will leave here early tomorrow morning." "We have some business here tonight so that you cannot stay." "However inconvenient it is, let me stay tonight", said Lu Da. "Monk, you'd better go at once, do not risk your life here." "This is strange," replied Lu Da. "If I only stay for one night how shall I risk my life?" "Go away!" said the villagers.

"If you do not go we shall tie you up."

— *Chapter 5 Little Tyrant When Drunk Goes Inside the Bed Curtains*；*LuDa, the Monk, Has a Fight at Tao Hua Village*

(Tr. J. H. Jackson)

As he was walking along one afternoon he became so absorbed in the beauty of the hills and streams that he failed to notice the lateness of the hour. Suddenly he realized that he'd never reach the next inn before dark, and he had no travelling companion. Where could he spend his night? He hastened on another twenty or thirty li. While crossing a wooden bridge he observed in the distance, shimmering beneath scarlet sunset clouds, a manor house in a grove of trees. Behind it rose massive tumbling mountains. "I'd better put up for the night in the manor," Lu said to himself. As he drew near, he saw scores of pheasants busily moving things from one place to another. At the entrance to the manor he rested his staff and hailed a few vassals. "What brings you to our manor this evening, monk?" They asked. "I couldn't reach an inn before dark," he replied. "I hope your manor will put me up for the night. I'll be moving on tomorrow morning." "We're busy tonight. You can't stay." "It's only for one night. Tomorrow, I'll leave." "Hurry along, monk. Don't hang around here if you want to live." "That's a strange talk. Why such a fuss about spending one night? Why so dangerous?" "Get going. Otherwise you're liable to be seized and bound."

— *Chapter 5 Drunk, the Little King Raises the Gold-spangled Bed Curtains*；*Lu the Tattooed Monk Throws Peach Blossom Village into Confusion*

(Tr. Sidney Shapiro)

(3) 陈达在马上看着史进，欠身施礼。史进喝道："汝等杀人放火，打家劫舍，犯着弥天大罪，都是该死的人！你也须有耳朵！好大胆！直来太岁头上动土！"陈达在马上答道："俺山寨里欠少些粮，欲往华阴县借粮；经由贵庄，假一条路，并不敢动一根草。可放我们过去，回来自当拜谢。"史进道："胡说！俺家现当里正，正要拿你这伙贼；今日倒来经由我村中过却不拿你，倒放你过去，本县知道，须连累于我。"陈达道："四海之内，皆兄弟也；相烦借一条路。"史进道："甚么闲话！我便肯时，有一个不肯！你问得他肯便去！"陈达道："好汉，叫我问谁？"史进道："你问得我手里这口刀肯，便放你去！"陈达大怒道："赶人不要赶上！休得要逞精神！"

——第二回 《王教头私走延安府，九纹龙大闹史家村》

(3) Chen Da paid his respect to Shi Jin by rising in his stirrups. Shi Jin spoke in a loud voice, "You kill people, set places on fire, rob with violence; your crimes fill the

heavens, and you are all deserving of death. You ought to have ear; how dare you come to punch the tiger's litter!" Chen Da replied from his horse, "We are short of grain at our mountain fortress and are going to borrow some grain at Huayin County. We have taken a short cut by passing your honorable village-but we will not disturb even a blade of grass here. Let us pass and on our return we will thank you." "Nonsense," replied Shi Jin, "I am the head of this village and I must arrest you. If I don't do so, I shall be implicated and the magistrate will blame me." "Within the four seas all men are brothers, so let us use your road," said Chen Da. "What meaningless talk!" said Shi Jin. "Even if I am willing, but there is one who is not, so you must have his content before you pass." "You are a hero. Tell me whom I must ask?" replied Chen Da. "You can ask the sword in my hand and if it is willing then you can pass," said Shi Jin. Chen Da spoke angrily, "You are trying to deceive me, but you should not be so presumptuous."

— *Chapter 2 Drill Inspector Wang Goes Stealthily to Yanan Prefecture; Shi Jin Defends His Village*

(Tr. J. H Jackson)

From their mounts, the two leaders looked at each other. Chen Da bowed in his saddle. "You murder and burn, rob and plunder, your terrible crimes are all punishable by death," Shi Jin shouted. "Haven't you heard of me? Where do you get the gall to come and tweak the tiger's whiskers?" "We hope to borrow some in Huayin. The road brings us by your honorable manor, but of course we wouldn't dare touch a blade of grass here. Let us pass. We'll thank you properly on our return." "Nonsense. I'm a ward chief. I've been meaning to go out after you bandits, but you've come to me. If I let you go and magistrate hears about it, I'll be implicated." "Within the four seas, all men are brothers." We'll trouble you to let us by. "Enough of idle chatter. Even if I were willing, there's another who won't agree. You'll have to ask him." "And who is that, good valiant?" "This sword in my hand!" Chen Da grew angry, "Don't push me too far. You'll force me to retaliate!"

— *Chapter 2 Arms Instructor Wang Goes Secretly to Tanan Prefecture; Nine Dragon Shi Jin Wreaks Havoc in Shi Family Village*

(Tr. Sidney Shapiro)

（4）时遇残雪初晴,日色明朗。林冲提着衮刀,对小喽罗道:"眼见得又不济事了! 不如趁早——天色未晚——取了行李,只得往别处去寻个所在!"小校用手指:"好了! 兀的不是一个人来?"林冲看时,叫声"惭愧"! 只见那个人远远在山坡下望见行来。待他来得较近,林冲把衮刀杆蓦了一下,蓦地跳将出来。那汉子见了林冲,叫声"阿也"!撒了担子,转身便走。林冲赶得去,那里赶得上;那汉子闪过山坡去了。林冲道:"你看我命苦么?来了三日,甫能等得一个人来,又吃他走了!"小校道:"虽然不杀得人,这一担财帛可以抵当。"林冲道:"你先挑了上山去,我再等一等。"小喽罗先把担儿挑出林去,只见山坡下转出一个大汉来。林冲见了,说道:"天赐其便!"只见那人挺着朴刀,大叫如雷,喝道:"泼贼!杀不尽的强徒!将俺行李那里去!酒家正要捉你这厮们,倒来拔虎须!"

——第十一回 《朱贵水亭施号箭,林冲雪夜上梁山》

(4) The last remnants of snow clouds had been swept away and the sky was a brilliant blue. "It seems I'm out of luck again," said Lin. "I might as well go back while it's still early, pick up my luggage and start looking for another place." "Over there!" The bandit said softly, pointing. "Someone's looking for another place." "At last!" Lin exclaimed. He saw a man walking towards them in the distance along the foot of the mountain. When he came close, Lin leaped out with a flourish of his halberd. "Aiya!" exclaimed the man. He cast down his laden carrying-pole, turned and fled. Lin gave chase, but the fellow was much too fast. He quickly vanished behind a rise. "Did you ever see such luck?" Lin fumed. "Three days I wait, and when one finally comes, I let him get away!" "Although you didn't kill anyone, that stuff he's left here ought to earn you some more time," said the bandit. "Take it up the mountain, I'll wait here a bit longer." Not long after the bandit had departed with a carrying-pole and its load, Lin saw a big fellow coming round the bend. "Heaven is merciful," he murmured. The man carried a halberd, and he was in a ranging fury, "Filthy rouges," he bellowed, "Where have you taken my luggage? Wait until I catch your varlets! I'll teach you to tweak the tiger's whiskers!"

— *Chapter 11 Zhu Gui Shoots a Whistling Arrow from an Arbor*; *Lin Chong Arrived at Liangshan Marsh in the Night During a Heavy Snowstorm*

(Tr. J. H. Jackson)

The snow had ceased falling, and there was a very clear bright sky. Lin Chong picking up his weapons spoke to his companion, "I see that I'm again unfortunate. I think I had better get my bundle, and set out for another place before it gets dark." His companion pointed with finger and said, "Fine! But is not that man coming?" Lin Chong looked in the direction pointed out, and said that he felt ashamed. In the distance he saw a man coming along by the foot of the mountain. He waited until the man got near, and then taking his halberd he struck it against the ground, and jumped out of the shade of the forest. The man upon seeing Lin Chong exclaimed "aiya", threw his load, and ran away. Lin Chong ran after him, but could not catch up to him. The man disappeared around the shoulder of the hill. Lin Chong spoke to his bandit companion who had followed him,"You see what bad luck I have! After waiting for three days the man who turns up ran away." The bandit replied,"Although you cannot kill the man you can seize the bundle of vegetables he has left behind instead." "You can carry the baggage up the mountain, but I will wait here for a little time more." A short time after the bandit had departed with the booty Lin Chong saw a tall man again coming along the road. Lin Chong said to himself,"Now Heaven is assisting me." The man was armed with a long bladed halberd, and upon getting near and seeing Lin Chong he shouted in a very loud voice,"You thief! I shall murder every bandit I can get hold of. Where is my baggage? I am going to arrest you as you have pulled the tiger's whiskers'."

—— *Chapter 11 Zhu Gui Shoot a Signal Arrow from the Lakeside Pavilion*；*Lin Chong Climbs Mount Liangshan in the Snowy Night*

(Tr. Sidney Shapiro)

3. 译本讨论

语用价值体现于全译的重构过程，要选用适于译语环境的表达式再现原作意图，确保读者对原作的正确理解。语用学是研究语言使用与理解的学问，它既研究说话人利用语言和外部语境表达意义的过程，也研究听话人对说话人的话语进行解码和推理的过程。语用学对翻译而言极具借鉴意义。在语用、语义、语形发生冲突时，我们要采取语用第一的原则。如"争取运动成绩和精神文明双丰收"这一句的翻译：

原译：For a good harvest both in sports and morals.

改译：For better athletic records and sportsmanship.

字面上看，原译似乎对原文"亦步亦趋"，每个字都对得上，但是"丰收"的英译太拘于原文的字面搭配。"精神文明"译成 morals，不是原文的本意，未能准确达义。本例表明语义与语用冲突时，语义让位于语用。在《水浒》的翻译中也有类似的例子：

史进喝道："汝等杀人放火，打家劫舍，犯着弥天大罪，都是该死的人！你也须有耳朵！好大胆！直来太岁头上动土！"

杰克逊译：Shi Jin spoke in a loud voice,"You kill people, set places on fire, rob with violence; your crimes fill the heavens, and you are all deserving of death. You ought to have ear; how dare you come to pouch the tiger's litter!"

沙博理译："You murder and burn, rob and plunder, your terrible crimes are all punishable by death," Shi Jin shouted. "Haven't you heard of me? Where do you get the gall to come and tweak the tiger's whiskers?"

对于"弥天大罪"的翻译,杰克逊(J. H. Jackson)和沙博理(Sidney Shapiro)的处理不同。在翻译的文化词语过程中,我们要充分考虑到源语所表达的形象是否能被译入语读者所理解和接受。杰克逊的译文采用了直译的方法,把"犯了弥天大罪"直译成"crimes fill the heavens",尽管在形式上做到了与原文一致,但是容易使读者不知所云。沙博理的译文采用了意译法,根据语用第一的原则,译为"terrible crimes",不仅准确传达了原文的意思,而且能使得译入语读者一目了然。

五、练习与思考

1. 分析题

(1) 分析以上两个版本的翻译,谈谈哪个版本的翻译更符合全译原则?

(2) 仔细阅读"智深道:'也是怪哉;歇一夜打甚么不紧,怎地便是讨死?'庄家道:'去便去,不去时便捉来缚在这里!'"的翻译,试分析译者使用了什么翻译策略?是如何体现出来的?

2. 实训题

翻译以下段落。

(1) 宋江便上梯来叫道:"你们且不要闹。我的罪犯今已赦宥,定是不死。且请二位都头进敝庄少叙三杯,明日一同见官。"赵能道:"你休使见识赚我入来!"宋江道:"我如何连累父亲兄弟?你们只顾进家里来。"宋江便下梯子来,开了庄门,请两个都头到庄里堂上坐下;连夜杀鸡宰鹅,置酒相待。那一百士兵人等,都与酒食管待,送些钱物之类;取二十两花银,把来送与两位都头做"好看钱。"当夜两个都头就在庄上歇了。

(2) 当时智深直打到法堂下,只见长老喝道:"智深!不得无礼!众僧也休动手!"两边众人被打伤了数十个,见长老来,各自退去。智深见众人退散,撇了桌脚,叫道:"长老与洒家做主!"此时酒已七八分醒了。长老道:"智深,你连累杀老僧!前番醉了一次,搅扰了一场,我教你兄赵员外得知,他写书来与众僧陪话;今番你又如此大醉无礼,乱了清规,打摊了亭子,又打坏了金刚,——这个且饶他,你搅得众僧卷堂而走,这个罪业非小!我这里五台山文殊菩萨道场,千百年清净香火去处。"

3. 思考题

(1) 什么情况下适合移译?请举例说明。
(2) 你最喜欢《水浒》的哪个译本?为什么?
(3) 如果让你来翻译《水浒》,你会采取哪些翻译策略?
(4) 汉译英时常将汉语的流水句变为更紧凑的英语句,原因是什么?
(5) 如何理解汉语和英语的语序差别?

(6) 汉译英文化移植要注意什么问题?

(7) 汉译英翻译口语化语篇要注意什么问题?

六、参考文献

[1] J. H. Jackson. Water Margin[M]. Shanghai：The Commercial Press，Ltd，1937.

[2] Sidney Shapiro. The Outlans of the Marsh[M]. Beijing：Foreign Language Press，1980.

[3] Venuti. L. The Translator's Invisibility：A History of Translation[M]. Shanghai：SFLEP，2004.

[4] 马特拉,阿芒(ArmandMattelart).世界传播与文化霸权——思想与战略的历史[M].陈卫星译,北京：中央编译出版社,2005.

[5] 施耐庵,罗贯中.水浒全传[M].北京：华夏出版社,1997.

[6] 孙建成.《水浒传》英译的语言文化[D].天津：南开大学,2007.

[7] 周振甫.文心雕龙今译[M].北京：中华书局,2005.

[8] 董琇.翻译风格的球体量化模型：基于《水浒传》英译本的翻译策略研究[J].外语电化教学.2014,(6)：12-17.

[9] 许燕.二十年来的《水浒传》英译研究[J].山东外语教学,2018.(2)：87-92.

[10] 白鹤,赵澍.浅析中外名著文体的不可译性[J].内蒙古农业大学学报,2004,(2)：123-124.

[11] 陈智淦.从《水浒传》的"吃"字翻译谈起[J].龙岩师专学报,2004,(2)：106-109.

[12] 郭梅,亦歌.《水浒》英译三种比较研究[J].长江学术,2006,(4)：91-96.

[13] 洪涛.论中国五大小说名著的不可译现象[J].唐都学刊,2003,(2)：26-30.

[14] 胡天赋.从人物的再现看赛译《水浒传》的后殖民主义色彩[J].河南大学学报,2006,(5)：79-83.

[15] 李林波.差异,对翻译意味着什么？[J].解放军外国语学院学报,2004,(6)：64-68.

[16] 李晶.翻译与意识形态——《水浒传》英译本不同书名成因探析[J].外语与外语教学,2006,(1)：46-49.

[17] 李军,王福英.文学翻译的文化误读——对 S. Shapiro 的英译本《水浒》的分析[J].语文学刊,2006,(7)：46-48.

[18] 王克友,任东升.叙述方式的转换与小说翻译效果——以《水浒传》第47回三个译文为例[J].外语教学,2005,(4)：77-80.

第十四课
《黄帝内经》译介赏析

> 《黄帝内经》简称《内经》，是中国传统医学四大经典之首，是我国现存最早的系统而完整的医学典籍，被公认为中医学的奠基之作。中医学作为一个学术体系的形成，即从《黄帝内经》开始。《黄帝内经》分《灵枢》《素问》两部分，前者重点论述病理，后者重点阐述经络穴位和针灸治疗。全书以生命为中心，从整体观上论述医学，呈现了自然、生物、心理、社会的"整体医学模式"，奠定了人体生理、病理、诊断以及治疗的认识基础，对中国传统医学影响极大。
>
> 《黄帝内经》成书于两千多年前的秦汉时期，是对中国上古医学的第一次总结，是仅存的战国以前医学的集大成之作。由于成书年代久远，其用词古奥生僻，语义、句法结构皆与现代汉语相差甚远，专业性强，加之竹简的错杂遗漏和反复抄写的人为误差，其思想内容难以把握。

一、翻译简介

《黄帝内经》自20世纪20年代起被介绍至海外，迄今已有18个英译版，包括节译本、编译本和全译本，译者背景各异，不乏医史学家、中医临床医师等专业人员。1925年，德国学者Percy Millard Dawson于 Annals of Medical History（《医学史年鉴》）上发表了一篇介绍《素问》的论文，节译了《素问》片段"Su-wen, the Basis of Chinese Medicine"，这是《内经》在海外的第一个译本。此后，美国医史学家威斯女士（Ilza Veith）选译《素问》前34章翻译的 The Yellow Emperor's Classic of Internal Medicine，于1949年出版，这是第一部公开出版的《素问》译本。这一阶段，《内经》的翻译主要为传播中国文化、介绍书中内容,未深究字句含义,误译较多。1978年吕聪明博士的《内经》译本出版,彼时,中医被广泛传播到世界各地。吕聪明强调尽力将原文内涵呈现出来以满足海外初学中医者的实际需求,故译本以直译为主,多为逐句对等英译。20世纪90年代后,《内经》译本大量出现,译者的翻译观普遍是重现中医医学价值。如旅美华人中医医师吴连胜、吴奇父子《内经》全译本以直译为主,采用音译加注释法按原文顺序将信息译出;美籍华人吴景暖中医师选译《灵枢》,译文的哲学和医学内涵并重,虽缺乏严格的术语标准,但贴近原文;德国医史学家 Paul U. Unschuld 的《素问》全译本,坚持从文化背景深入理解中医,将《素问》中的概念一一分解介绍,译著未采用任何现有的医学术语,全文翻译自成体系;李照国《内经》全译本是国内第一部英汉对照全译本,坚持"译古如古,文不加饰",基本概念以音译为主、释义为辅,篇章翻译以直译为主、意译为辅,最大限度保持原作写作风格和意义内涵。除上述提到的之外,另有罗希文《素问》前22章注解节译本等。

二、书名翻译

《黄帝内经》名简意丰,其书名英译主要有以下版本:

Ilza Veith (1949):The Yellow Emperor's Classic of Internal Medicine

黄雯(1950):Nei Ching, the Chinese Canon of Medicine

倪毛信(Maoshing Ni)(1995):The Yellow Emperor's Classic of Medicine:A New Translation of the Neijing Suwen with Commentary

吴奇、吴连胜(1997):The Yellow Emperor's Canon Internal Medicine

Paul U. Unschuld (2003):Huang Di Nei Jing Su Wen

李照国(2005):Yellow Emperor's Canon of Medicine

罗希文(2009):Introductory Study of Huangdi Neijing

《黄帝内经》译名较为一致,除少数直接音译;多数是将"黄帝"按约定俗成译为 Yellow Emperor,将"经"译为 Classic(经典)或 Canon(准则、规范,a generally accepted rule, standard or principle by which something is judged),用词贴切。

三、特殊概念的翻译

《黄帝内经》是中医学的奠基之作,是中国传统文化的重要组成部分。书中很多词汇,不仅是中国传统文化中的常用概念,更被赋予医学内涵。分析不同译者的处理方式,可带来一定启示。以下以李照国译本(以下简称"李译")、Ilza Veith 译本(以下简称"威译")和罗希文译本(以下简称"罗译")为例。

1. 中医医学术语

例1：六七，三阳脉衰于上，面皆焦，发始白。——《素问·上古天真论篇第一》

李译：

At the age of forty-two, as the three Yang Channels are deficient [in both blood and Qi], her countenance becomes wane and her hair begins to turn white.

威译：

When she reaches the age of forty-two, the pulse of the three [regions of] Yang deteriorates in the upper part (of the body), her entire face is wrinkled and her hair begins to turn white.

罗译：

Then when she is forty-two years old, the San Yang Channels become decrepit at the upper part, bringing on dull face and grey hair.

评析："三阳脉"是中医中的概念，意指太阳、少阳、阳明三经。李照国和罗希文皆将"经"译为 Channel，意为"a tubular passage or duct for liquid"。经络可以理解为气血运行的主要通道，在这点上，用 channel 达意。李译用小写 three，让读者明白这是三条经脉。罗译用大写 San Yang，是将其作为一整体的专业术语来处理，但此处的 San，却也让不懂之人不明所以。威译将"经"译为 pulse（脉搏），此为西医概念，与中医的经络完全不同，这种译法的根源在于对中医知识背景的不了解。

《正字通·系部》："经，凡织纵曰经，横曰纬"。"经"之本义为纵行之丝，后引申为南北纵形的干线。用 channel 仅能体现"通道"之意，无"纵形"内涵。现如今，在实际临床应用中，多使用 meridian 指代经络。meridian 本意为 a circle of constant longitude passing through a given place on the earth's surface and the terrestrial poles（经地球表面的某一点和极点的经线）。中医一直将人体与宇宙紧紧联系，认为人体是小宇宙。meridian 的经纬意向，恰与中医认为的经络纵形通道之意相仿。

对原文中的术语，可先理解原文中的民族文化、历史文化信息，翻译时可采用加注或增译，亦或选择翻译部分信息。

例2：天气通于肺，地气通于嗌，风气通于肝，雷气通于心，谷气通于脾，雨气通于肾。——《素问·阴阳应象大论篇第五》

李译：

Tianqi (Heaven-Qi) communicates with the lung, Diqi (Earth-Qi) communicates with the pharynx, Fengqi (Wind-Qi) communicates with the liver, Leiqi (Thunder-Qi) communicates with the heart, Guqi (Grain-Qi) communicates with the spleen and Yuqi (Rain-Qi) communicates with the kidney.

威译：

The heavenly climate circulates within the lungs, the climate of the earth circulates within the throat; <u>the wind</u> circulates within the liver, <u>thunder</u> penetrates the heart; <u>the air of a ravine</u> penetrates the stomach, <u>the rain</u> penetrates the kidneys.

罗本：

<u>Vital Energy in the Heaven</u> corresponds to the Lung, <u>Vital Essence on the Earth</u> corresponds to the Heart; <u>cereal Vital Energy</u> corresponds to the Spleen and <u>rain</u> corresponds to the Kidney.

评析："气"理论是中医学的核心之一，其所指非常广泛，类型也十分复杂。李译用音译加注释的方法，说明到底何为"气"。罗译将其意译成 Vital Energy/Essence，提升了文本的易读性，但却将"气"狭义化了——将"气"只是落点到"energy/essence"。威氏译成 climate（the typical conditions in a particular area），即气候，这里显然是原文化缺失的表现，对"气"的文化内涵不了解；且将"谷气"译成 the air of a ravine（山谷的空气）亦是误译，"谷"在此是"谷物"意，并非山谷。

"气"作为中华传统文化中的重要概念，本身具有多维性和抽象性特征，在外文中找不到对应词汇。对于此，可采取音译加注法。

例3：色味当五脏。——《素问·五藏生成篇第十》

李译：

The colors and the tastes correspond to <u>the Five Zang-Organs</u>.

威译：

Each color and flavor belongs to one of <u>the five viscera</u>.

罗译：

This is the correspondence of the five flavors to <u>the five Viscera</u>.

评析：脏象学说是中医学的核心内容。脏象，指人体内在脏腑的生理活动、病理变化反映于外的征象。脏象是一个动态的生理与病理概念，是生命本质与现象的统一。威译为 viscera（内脏，the large organs inside your body, such as heart, lungs and stomach），然而中医的"脏"远非内脏这么简单。所以此译法未传达出"脏"之内涵。

李译为"Five Zang-Organs"，首字母悉皆大写，表现出这是特殊术语，区别于西医的"脏器"概念。罗译方法类似，用大写的"Viscera"，以示区分。

2. 中医哲学概念词——以"道"为例

例1：夫<u>道</u>者，年皆百数，能有子乎？——《素问·上古天真论篇第一》

李译：

Could those who have mastered <u>the Dao（the art of preserving health）</u> have children when they are over one hundred years old?

威译：

Those who follow <u>Tao, the Right Way</u>, and thus reach the age of about a hundred years, can they beget children?

罗译：

Those who follow the Tao enjoy a long life of a hundred years. Can they produce offspring when they are a hundred?

评析：这句话意思是，懂得养生的人，年纪到了一百多岁，能生育子女吗？这里的"道"指的是养生之道。李本采用解释性信息加译法，将其译成"the Dao（the art of preserving health）"，读者读之即明白"道"在此的含义。威译策略基本相同，只是"the Right Way"还是意义模糊了些。罗译只是音译，意义并未清晰传达出来。

例2：非其人勿教，非其真勿授，是谓得道。——《素问·金匮真言论篇第四》

李译：

But do not teach these abstruse theories to anyone not eligible or unqualified to study them. This is the right way to pass on such valuable theories.

威译：

Not to teach it to the wrong person and never to tell or act a lie is called the achievement of Tao.

罗译：

Doctors who know the Tao will only pass on his skill to those who are the suitable to the study with the quintessence of the theory.

评析：这句话的意思是，不是愿为大众服务的人，切勿教也；不是有志于此的人，切勿传授。只有这样，才能真正继承医学的理论。句中的"道"是文化概念，意指，这样方是继承医学理论的正确之路。

李译和罗译依旧采用解释性信息进行翻译，让读者一目了然；威译的直译太为模糊。

例3：针石，道也。——《素问·汤液醪醴论篇第十四》

李译：

Zhenshi（needles and sharp stones）is the Dao（the therapeutic principle）.

威译：

This is the way of acupuncture.

罗译：

Acupuncture and stone-needles are treatments that ...

评析：这句话意为，针石治病，这不过是一种方法而已。这里的"道"是一种医学概念，指针石这种治病的方法。李译和罗译用解释性翻译，分别将其译为 the therapeutic principle 和 treatments。威译为 the way of acupuncture，倒也解释清楚了。

综上可见，"道"在不同语境中表达意不同，可能为哲学概念，亦可能为文化概念或医学概念。用解释性信息进行翻译可以更好传达文本含义。

3. 古汉语特有词汇

例1：彼春之暖，为夏之暑，彼秋之忿，为冬之怒。——《素问·脉要精微论篇第十七》

解释：春天的气候暖和，发展为夏天的气候暑热，秋天的劲急之气，发展为冬天的杀厉之气。

李译：

The warmth in spring [turns into] heat in summer, strong wind in autumn [develops into] ferocious cold in winter. （李译本将为句法结构的需要或为语义表达的需要而增加的词语置于[ ]中）

威译：

Those warm and genial days of Spring lead up to the heat of Summer, and the anger one might feel in Fall makes way to forgiveness and mercy which one feels in Winter.

罗译：

The mildness and warmth of the spring gradually grows into the blazing of the snmmer, which will gradually reduce its heat and evolve into the swiftness of the autumn, which again, will gradually stem into the severe cold of the winter.

评析："忿"与"愤"为古今字。在此意为"秋天的劲急之气"。李译和罗译分别为 strong wind 和 the swiftness，意义传达准确。威译在理解上有误，传达并不准确。

例2：中古之治病，至而治之。汤液十日。——《素问·移情变气论篇第十三》

解释：中古时候的医生治病，多在疾病一发生就能及时治疗，先用汤液十天。

李译：

[Doctors] in the middle ancient times usually treated diseases after they had already occurred. [They first used] Tangye (decoction) to treat for ten days.

威译：

When the medieval scholars treated diseases they used hot water and liquid treatment for ten days.

罗译：

In medieval times, treatment was given when diseases attacked. Decoctions were given for the first ten days to ...

评析："汤液"在古汉语中指的是中药汤剂。李译和罗译用 decoction（煎熬的药）来替代，表达准确。威译用 hot water and liquid treatment，明显理解有误。

例3：夜卧早起，广步于庭，被发缓形。——《素问·四气调神大论篇第二》

解释：人们应该入夜即睡觉，早一些起床，到庭院中散步，披开头发，舒缓形体。

李译：

[People may] sleep late in the night and get up early in the morning, taking a walk in the courtyard with hair running free to relax the body.

威译：

After a night of sleep people should get up early (in the morning); they should walk briskly around the yard; they should loosen their hair and slow down their movements (body).

罗译：

One should go to bed at late hours and get up early. He should stroll about the courtyard with his hair loosened and clothing unfastened.

评析："被"此为通假字，通"披"。李译和罗译很好的传达了文本含义：松开头发。三人译法，皆传达了此意。

通假字是中国古代的用字现象之一，指用读音相同或相近的字代替本字。因种种原因，未使用本字，而临时借用音同或音近的字来替代，故通假字本质上属于错字或别字，但这属于正常的文言现象。翻译时，需辨认出本字为何、含义为何，再作相应翻译。

例4：丈夫八岁，肾气实，发长齿更。——《素问·上古天真论篇第一》

解释：男子到了八岁，肾气开始充实，毛发长，牙齿更换。

李译：

For a man, at the age of eight, his Shenqi (Kidney-Qi) becomes prosperous and his teeth begin to change.

威译：

When a boy is eight years old the emanations of his testes (kidneys 肾) are fully developed, his hair grows longer and he begins to change his teeth.

罗译：

The kidney Vital Energy of an eight year old boy begins to develop. His hair grows long, his teeth change.

评析："丈夫"在此意为男子，今意缩小为与"妻子"相对。以上三人译法皆恰当。

4. 句法翻译

例1：发为白汗，调食和药，治在下俞。——《素问·经脉别论篇第二十一》

解释：大汗出，应注意饮食调养和药物的治疗，可选下腧位置进行针灸。

李译：

Whitish sweating due to retention of reverse flow of Qi. [It can be treated by] regulation of diet combined with the use of drugs. [At the same time,] the Acupoints located on the lower [limbs] can be medicines.

威译：

The breath becomes stagnant and dense and white perspiration is produced. In order to cure the trouble one should bring about a drainage in the lower part of the body and one must <u>blend the food with the medicines</u>.

罗译：

There will appear the symptoms of pains in the Heart with spontaneous perspiration caused by the conflict between the adverse vital Energy and the body Resistance. The patient should <u>be on diet and take medicine</u> Acupoints on the leg can also be punctured for a treatment.

评析：这个小分句中，"调食"与"和药"皆是动宾，二者间虽无衔接词，但放一起又是并列。李译和威译皆是用一个动词短语形式（动词＋介词＋宾语）将原文的动宾和并列结构统一呈现。罗译本则是用 and 连接两个动作来完成。

汉语为意合语言，较少用衔接语来明示逻辑关系，主要靠语句或词汇的本身的意义实现语篇的连贯。英语为形合语言，句子中则常用介词、连词等来衔接语言，明示句子结构。

例2：愿闻三阴。——《素问·阴阳离合论篇第六》

解释：原意再听你讲讲三阴的离合情况。

李译：

I'd like to know the ［separation and combination of］ three Yin.

威译：

I should like to know more about the three Yin.

罗译：

And what about the San Yin?

评析：原文中，信息未完整表达。威译和罗译采用直译。李译添加"the separation and combination of"，将缺失信息补全，更便于读者理解原文。

例3：观<u>权衡规矩</u>，而知病所主。——《素问·阴阳应象大论篇第五》

解释：诊查四时脉象的常变，即可知道疾病的方位。

李译：

［by］ examining ［whether］ <u>the pulse conditions ［in the four seasons are normal or not］</u>, ［one can］ know the location of the disease.

威译：

One should <u>examine irregularities which must be adjusted according to custom and usage</u>, and then the location where the disease prevails will become known.

罗译：

<u>Analyze the pulses in accordance with the seasons</u> so as to know the origin of disease.

评析：原文中的"权""衡""规""矩"分别是指秤锤、秤杆、圆规以及曲尺。这里用的是

借喻,用"权衡规矩"来借指不同季节脉象的变化。三个译本的处理方法,皆是跳出原来的比喻,直接译出所指意,只是威本的翻译有些理解错误。

例4:阴阳者,血气之男女也。——《素问·阴阳应象大论篇第五》

解释:以男女比喻血气的阴阳属性。

李译:

Yin and Yang symbolizes [the opposite properties] of blood and Qi.

威译:

Yin and Yang [the two elements in nature] create desires and vigor in men and women.

罗译:

the Yin and Yang make the male and female.

评析:原文中的"男女",指的是血气的阴阳属性,这里用的是隐喻。李译直截了当,将隐喻意直接译出,传达准确;威译和罗译理解上有差错。

四、译文对比赏析

1. 经典段落

(1) 昔在黄帝,生而神灵,弱而能言,幼而徇齐,长而敦敏,成而登天。

乃问于天师曰:"余闻上古之人,春秋皆度百岁,而动作不衰;今时之人,年半百而动作皆衰者,时世异耶? 人将失之耶?"

(1) Huangdi, or Yellow Emperor, was born intelligent. He was eloquent from childhood. He behaved righteously when he was young. In his youth, he was honest, sincere and wise. When growing up, he became the Emperor.

He asked Master Qibo, "I am told that people in ancient times all could live for one hundred years without any signs of senility. But people nowadays begin to become old at the age of fifty. Is it due to the changes of environment or the violation of the way [to preserve health]?"

(李照国译)

In former times there was Huang Di.

When he came to life, he had magic power like a spirit.

While he was [still] weak, he could speak.

While he was [still] young, he was quick of apprehension.

After he had grown up, he was sincere and skillful.

After he had matured, he ascended to heaven.

Now, he asked the Heavenly Teacher.

"I have heard that

The people of high antiquity,

In [the sequence of] spring and autumn, all exceeded one hundred years.

But in their movements and activities there was no weakening.

After one half of a hundred years, the movements and activities of all of them weaken.

Is this because the times are different?

Or is it that the people have lost this [ability]?"

(Tr. Paul U. Unschuld)

(2) 岐伯对曰:"上古之人,其知道者,法于阴阳,知于术数,食饮有节,起居有常,不妄作劳,故能形与神俱,而尽终其天年,度百岁乃去。今时之人不然也,以酒为浆,以妄为常,醉以入房,以欲竭其精,以耗散其真,不知持满,不时御神,务快其心,逆于生乐,起居无节,故半百而衰也。

夫上古圣人之教也,下皆为之。虚邪贼风,避之有时,恬淡虚无,真气从之,精神内守,病安从来?是以志闲而少欲,心安而不惧,形劳而不倦,气从以顺,各从其欲,皆得所愿。故美其食,任其服,乐其俗,高下不相慕,其民故自朴。是以嗜欲不能劳其目,淫邪不能惑其心,愚、智、贤、不肖,不惧于物,故合于道,所以能年皆度百岁而动作不衰者,以其得全不危故也。"

(2) Qibo answered, "The sages in ancient times who knew the Dao (the tenets for cultivating health) followed [the rules of] Yin and Yang and adjusted Shushu (the ways to cultivate health). [They were] moderate in eating and drinking, regular in working and resting, avoiding any overstrain. That is why [they could maintain a desirable] harmony between the Shen (mind or spirit) and the body, enjoying good health and a long life. People nowadays, on the contrary, just behave oppositely. [They] drink wine as thin rice gruel, regard wrong as right, and seek sexual pleasure after drinking. [As a result,] their Jingqi (Essence-Qi) is exhausted and Zhenqi (Genuine-Qi) is wasted. [They] seldom [take measures to] keep an exuberance [of Jingqi] and do not know how to regulate the Shen (mind or spirit), often giving themselves to sensual pleasure. Being irregular in daily life, [they begin to] become old even at the age of fifty."

When the sages in ancient times taught people, they emphasized [the importance of] avoiding Xuxie (Deficiency-Evil) and Zeifeng (Thief-Wind) in good time and keep the mind free from avarice. [In this way] Zhenqi in the body will be in harmony, Jingshen [Essence-Spirit] will remain inside, and diseases will have no way to occur.

[Therefore people in ancient times all lived] in peace and contentment, without any fear. They worked, but never overstrained themselves, making it smooth for Qi to flow. [They all felt] satisfied with their life and enjoyed their tasty food, natural clothes and naive customs. [They] did not desire for high positions and lived simply and naturally. That is why improper addiction and avarice could not distract their eyes and ears, obscenity and fallacy could not tempt their mind. Neither the ignorant nor the intelligent and neither the virtuous nor the unworthy feared anything. [Such a behavior quite] accorded with the Dao (the tenets for cultivating health). This is the reason why they all lived over one hundred years without any signs of senility. Having followed the tenets of preserving health, [they could enjoy a long life free from diseases].

（李照国译）

Qi Bo responded:
"The people of high antiquity,
those who knew the Way,
they modeled [their behavior] on yin and yang and
they complied with the arts and the calculations.
[Their] eating and drinking was moderate.
[Their] rising and resting had regularity.
They did not tax [themselves] with meaningless work.
Hence,
They were able to keep physical appearance and spirit together,
and to exhaust the years [allotted by] heaven.
Their life span exceeded one hundred years before they departed.
The fact that people of today are different is because
They take wine as an [ordinary] beverage,
And they adopt absurd [behavior] as regular [behavior].
They are drunk when they enter the [women's] chambers.
Through their lust they exhaust their essence,
Through their wastefulness they dissipate their true [qi].
They do not know how to maintain fullness and
They engage their spirit when it is not the right time.
They make every effort to please their hearts, [but]
They oppose the [true] happiness of life.
Rising and resting miss their terms.

Hence,

it is [only] one half of a hundred [years] and they weaken.

Now,

When the sages of high antiquity taught those below,

they always spoke to them [about the following].

The depletion evil and the robber wind,

There are [specific] times when to avoid them.

Quiet peacefulness, absolute emptiness

The true qi follows [these states].

When essence and spirit are guarded internally,

Where could a disease come from?

Hence

The mind is relaxed and one has few desires.

The heart is at peace and one is not in the fear.

The physical appearance is taxed, but is not tired.

The qi follows [its appropriate course] and therefrom results compliance:

everything follows one's wishes;

in every respect one achieves what one longs for."

(Tr. Paul U. Unschuld)

(3) 春三月,此谓发陈,天地俱生,万物以荣,夜卧早起,广步于庭,被发缓形,以使志生,生而勿杀,予而勿夺,赏而勿罚,此春气之应,养生之道也。逆之则伤肝,夏为寒变,奉长者少。

(3) [In] the three months of spring, all things on the earth begin to grow. The natural world is resuscitating and all things are flourishing. [People may] sleep late in the night and get up early in the morning, taking a walk in the courtyard with hair running free to relax the body and enliven the mind. [Such a natural resuscitating process should be] activated instead of being inhibited, promoted instead of being deprived and encouraged instead of being destroyed. This is what adaptation to Chunqi (Spring-Qi) means and this is the Dao (the principle) for Yangsheng (cultivation of health). Any violation of this rule may impair the liver and result in cold diseases in summer [due to] insufficient supply for growth [in summer].

(李照国译)

The three months of spring,

they denote effusion and spreading.

Heaven and earth together generate life;

the myriad beings flourish.

Go to rest late at night and rise early.

Move through the courtyard with long strides.

Dishevel the hair and relax the physical appearance,

thereby cause the mind [to orient itself on] life.

Give life and do not kill.

Give and do not take.

Reward and do not punish.

This is correspondence with the qi of spring and

it is the Way to nourish life.

Opposing it harms the liver.

In summer, this causes changes to cold, and

there is little to support growth.

(Tr. Paul U. Unschuld)

(4) 夏三月,此谓蕃秀,天地气交,万物华实,夜卧早起,无厌于日,使志无怒,使华英成秀,使气得泄,若所爱在外,此夏气之应,养长之道也。逆之则伤心,秋为痎疟,奉收者少。

(4) The three months of summer is the period of prosperity. Tianqi (Heaven-Qi) and Diqi (Earth-Qi) have converged and all things are in blossom. [People should] sleep late in the night and get up early in the morning, avoiding any detestation with longer hot daytime and anxiety in life, trying to delight themselves and enabling Qi to flow smoothly. [Such an attitude toward life in summer] is just like the outward manifestation of a cheerful state of mind. This is what adaptation to Xiaqi (Summer-Qi) means and this is the Dao (principle) for Yangsheng (cultivation of health). Violation [of this rule] may impair the heart and result in Jienue (malaria) in autumn and severe disease in winter [due to] insufficient supply for astringency [in autumn].

(李照国译)

The three months of summer,

They denote opulence and blossoming.

The qi of heaven and earth interact and

the myriad beings bloom and bear fruit.

Go to rest late at night and rise early.

Never get enough of the sun.
Let the mind have no anger.
Stimulate beauty and have your elegance perfected.
Cause the qi to flow away,
as if that what you loved were located outside.
This is correspondence with the qi of summer and
it is the Way to nourish growth.
Opposing it harms the heart.
In autumn this causes jie and malaria, and
there is little to support gathering.
Multiple disease [develops] at winter solstice.

(Tr. Paul U. Unschuld)

(5) 黄帝问曰:"六化六变,胜复淫治,甘苦辛咸酸淡先后,余知之矣。夫五运之化,或从天气,或逆天气,或从天气而逆地气,或从地气而逆天气,或相得,或不相得,余未能明其事。欲通天之纪,从地之理,和其运,调其化,使上下合德,无相夺伦,天地升降,不失其宜,五运宣行,勿乖其政,调之正味,从逆奈何?"

(5) Huangdi asked, "I've already known [the normal] transformation and [abnormal] changes of the six kinds of Qi, [the disease caused by] Predomination and Retaliation [of Qi] and the therapeutic [principles as well as] the transforming sequence of sweetness, bitterness, pungency, saltiness, sourness and blandness. [But] I am still unclear about the transformation of the Wuyun (Five-Motions) [which sometimes] follows Tianqi (Heaven-Qi), [sometimes] abides by Tianqi (Heaven-Qi) but violates Diqi (Earth-Qi), [sometimes] follows Diqi (Earth-Qi) but violates Tianqi (Heaven-Qi), [sometimes] follows [the Qi that is in the Spring] but [sometimes] violates [the Qi that is in the Spring]. What [should I do if I] want to abide by the law of the heavens, to follow the principle of the earth, to harmonize the Motion [of Qi] and to adjust the transformation [of Qi] so as to balance the Upper and the Lower, to prevent violation, [to normalize] the ascending and descending [activities] of the heavens and the earth to avoid abnormal changes, [to smooth] the movement of the Wuxing (Five-Elements) to prevent deviation and to apply the five flavors [according to] the normal and abnormal [Motions of Qi]?"

(李照国译)

Huang Di commented, "I would like to hear further details on each of the various circuit years, its ruling influences, and its excess, harmonious, and deficient states."

(Tr. Maoshing Ni)

(6) 岐伯曰:"先立其年以明其气,金木水火土运行之数,寒暑燥湿风火临御之化,则天道可见,民气可调,阴阳卷舒,近而无惑,数之可数者,请遂言之。"

(6) Qibo said, "[The Tiangan (Heavenly Stems) and Dizhi (Earthly Branches) of] a year should be decided first [in order to understand] the dominations of Metal, Wood, Water, Fire and Earth in motion [as well as] the transformations of Cold, Summer-Heat, Dryness, Dampness, Wind and Fire [when they govern the heavens and are in the Spring]. [Based on such an understanding,] the law of the heavens is cognizable, [the activity of] Qi in the human [body] can be regulated, the flexion and extension of Yin and Yang are understandable. The ways of Qi-Motion can be analyzed. Please allow me to explain it [for You]."

(李照国译)

Qi Bo replied, "First of all one needs to determine the elemental phase, the yearly and seasonal primary and secondary ruling atmospheric influences of the circuit year. Then ascertain the excess or deficient nature of the ruling influence in relation to the various cycles of the five elemental phase law. Once this information is secured, one will be able to estimate the meteorological and epidemiological tendencies of the year. Utilize herbs that would counteract the effects of the pathogenic influences. Restrain the excess while fortifying the deficient. Take preventive measures by living a healthy, balanced life and consume appropriate foods corresponding to the seasonal needs."

(Tr. Maoshing Ni)

(7) 黄帝问曰:"天元九室,余已知之,愿闻气交,何名失守?"

(7) Huangdi asked, "I have already known the nine [states of] stagnation of Tianyuan (Heaven-Qi). I still want to know [what is] Qijiao (Qi-Convergence) and what is [called] Shishou (loss of position)."

(李照国译)

HUANG DI asked, "What circumstances constitute a lapse in the cyclical intercourse between the heavenly and the earthly energies?"

(Tr. Maoshing Ni)

(8) 岐伯曰:"谓其上下升降,迁正退位,各有经论,上下各有不前,故名失守也。是故气交失易位,气交乃变,变易非常,即四时失序,万化不安,变民病也。"

(8) Qibo answered, "It refers to ascent and descent [of the intermediate Qi at the right and left sides as well as maintaining in] the due position and abdication [of Qi dominating the heavens and in the Spring which are discussed] respectively in the canons. [Since there are abnormal changes of the intermediate Qi at the right and left sides], it is called loss of position. Because Qi-Convergence becomes abnormal and has changed its position, extraordinary abnormal changes occur [at the period of] Qi-Convergence. [This indicates that] the normal order of the four seasons is broken, [leading] to unsmooth transformation of all things and occurrence of diseases."

(李照国译)

Qi Bo replied, "What you asked is in reference to the primary and the secondary ruling influences that appear in a preset sequential way. When the atmospheric influences form heaven appear as they should at the correct yearly and seasonal interval, there is harmony. A lapse occurs when the influences are off track: that is, they either do not depart on time or appear on time; the result is then instability in nature and disease in human beings."

(Tr. Maoshing Ni)

(9) 帝曰:"升降不前,愿闻其故,气交有变,何以明知?"

(9) Huangdi said, "I want to know the reasons of abnormal changes of ascent and descent. How could I know that Qi-Convergence has changed?"

(李照国译)

Huang Di inquired, "Can you elaborate on the mechanism behind these lapses?"

(Tr. Maoshing Ni)

(10) 岐伯曰:"昭乎问哉!明乎道矣。互气交有变,是为天地机,但欲降而不得降者,地窒刑之。又有五运太过,而先天而至者,即交不前,但欲升而不得其升,中运抑之,但欲降而不得其降,中运抑之。于是有升之不前,降之不下者,有降之不下,升而至天者,有升降俱不前,作如此之分别,即气交之变,变之有异,常各各不同,灾有微甚者也。"

(10) Qibo answered, "What an excellent question [Your Majesty] have asked! The principles involved must be made clear. [The reason responsible for] the changes of Qi-Convergence [lies in] the mechanism [of the movement] of the heavens and the earth. [The reason that Qi] should descend but simply cannot descend [lies in the fact

that it is] inhibited by stagnation [of Earth-Qi]. The other [reason is] the excess of the Wuyun (Five-Motions) [which] arrives early, [making] Qi-Convergence impossible to accomplish. [When Year-Qi] should ascend but cannot ascend, [it is] inhibited by the Middle-Motion; [when it] should descend but cannot descend, [it is] obstructed by the Middle-Motion. That is why [sometimes Qi] cannot ascend, [sometimes Qi] cannot descend, [sometimes Qi] ascends to the heavens [instead of] descending [to the earth], [sometimes Qi] is unable [to perform the activities of both] descending and ascending. [The reason to] make such a differentiation [is that] the changes [occurring at the period of] Qi-Convergence are various. So the calamities [caused] are [sometimes] slight and [sometimes] severe."

(李照国译)

Qi Bo responded, "The primary ruling influence represents the influential heavenly energy that dictates the meteorologic trends of the first half of a year, while the secondary ruling influence represents the native earthly energy that dictates the last half of a year. When the secondary ruling influence is excess, it could inhibit the arrival of the succeeding primary ruling influence. Further, when the yearly elemental phase circuit is excess, it could also dominate the current year's ruling influences. The interference of the normal cycles will result in differing degrees of damage, depending on the cause."

(Tr. Maoshing Ni)

五、练习与思考

1. 分析题
(1) 比较李译本和威译本,分析各自用了什么翻译手段和策略。
(2) 仔细阅读李译本和 Maoshing Ni 译本,分析各自特点是什么。

2. 实训题
翻译以下段落。
(1) 秋三月,此谓容平,天气以急,地气以明,早卧早起,与鸡俱兴,使志安宁,以缓秋刑,收敛神气,使秋气平,无外其志,使肺气清,此秋气之应,养收之道也。逆着则伤肺,冬为飧泄,奉藏者少。

(2) 冬三月,此谓闭藏,水冰地坼,无扰乎阳,早卧晚起,必待日光,使志若伏若匿,若有私意,若已有得,去寒就温,无泄皮肤,使气亟夺,此冬气之应,养藏之道也。逆之则伤肾,春为痿厥,奉生者少。

3. 思考题

（1）医学专著翻译要注意哪些方面？

（2）《黄帝内经》的三个译本对于文化词语是如何翻译的？

（3）你喜欢哪位译者的译本？为什么？

六、参考文献

[1] 李照国.Yellow Emperor's Canon of Medicine[M]. Xi'an：World publishing Corporation，2005.

[2] Ilza Veith. The Yellow Emperor's Classic of Internal Medicine[M]. Taipei：South Material Center. Inc.，1982.

[3] Ni Maoshig. THE YELLOW EMPEROR'S CLASSIC of MEDICINE：A New Translation of the NEIJING SUWEN with Commentary[M]. Berkeley：University of California Press，1949.

[4] Paul U. Unschuld，Hermann Tessenow，Zheng Jinsheng. Huang Di nei jing su wen：An Annotated Translation of Huang Di's Inner Classic-Basic Questions[M]. Los Angeles：University of California Press，2011.

[5] 罗希文.Introductory Study of Huangdi Neijing[M].北京：中国中医药出版社，2009.

[6] 闫方园.衔接视域下《黄帝内经·素问》英译对比研究——以《四气调神大论》部分篇章为例[D].北京：北京中医药大学，2019.

[7] 秦元刚.学术期刊中《黄帝内经》书名英译版本探析[J].中国中医药现代远程教育 2018(9)：47－49.

参考答案

第一课 《诗经》译介赏析

1. 分析题

(1) 许渊冲和理雅各翻译的"悠悠苍天,曷其有极"分别如下:

  O gods in boundless, endless sky,

  Can all these end before I die?

（许渊冲译）

  O thou distant and azure Heaven!

  When shall (our service) have an end?

（理雅各译）

原文是感叹句和疑问句,译文分别用"O"和感叹号表示感叹,从而体现了原文的句式。

(2)《诗经·卫风·木瓜》使用了赋和兴的手法。

以许渊冲译文为例,为了避免重复,分别用 quince, peach, plum 代指木瓜、木桃、木李。前两段的第二句都相同:"Not in return, you see, But to show acquaintance made",第三句变成了"Not in return, you see, But to show love fore'er"。而理雅各全部用了"Not as a return for it, But that our friendship might be lasting",可见不同译者对形式的处理稍有不同。

2. 实训题

(1)
      FOU YI

  We gather and gather the plantains;

  Now we may gather them.

  We gather and gather the plantains;

  Now we have got them.

  We gather and gather the plantains;

Now we pluck the ears.
We gather and gather the plantains;
Now we rub out the seeds.
We gather and gather the plantains;
Now we place the seeds in our skirts.
We gather and gather the plantains;
Now we tuck out skirts under our girdles.

(2) BO ZHOU

It floats about, that boat of cypress wood,
There in the middle of the He.
With his two tufts of hair falling over his forehead,
He was my mate;
And I swear that till death I will have no other.
O mother, O Heaven,
Why will you not understand me?

It floats about, that boat of cypress wood,
There by the side of the He.
With his two tufts of hair falling over his forehead,
He was my only one;
And I swear that till death I will not do the evil thing.
O mother, O Heaven,
Why will you not understand me?

3. 思考题
略

第二课 《三字经》译介赏析

1. 分析题
略

2. 实训题
(1) Then Kuang Wu arose

and founded the Eastern Han dynasty.
It lasted four hundred years
and ended with the Emperor Hsien.

（翟理斯译）

With Guang Wuh began
The Eastern Han.
Th' four hundredth year,
Han Hsian died drear.

（赵彦春译）

(2) Wei, Shu, and Wu,
fought for the sovereignty of the Hans.
They were called the Three Kingdoms,
and existed until the two Chin dynasties.

（翟理斯译）

Shuh, Woo, Weigh
Struggled their way;
Three kingdoms reared;
Two Jins appeared.

（赵彦春译）

3. 思考题
略

第三课 《论语》译介赏析

1. 分析题
略

2. 实训题

(1) The Master said, 'Only common people wait till they are advanced in ritual and music [before taking office]. A gentleman can afford to get up his ritual and music later on.' Even if I accepted this saying, I should still be on the side of those who get on with their studies first.

(2) The Master said, my adherents in Ch'ên and Ts'ai were none of them in public service.

Those who worked by moral power were Yen Hui, Min Tzuch'ien, Jan Kêng and Jan Yung. Those who spoke well were Tsai Yü and Tzu-kung. Those who surpassed in handling public business was Jan Ch'iu and Tzu-lu; in culture and learning, Tzu-yu and Tzu-hsia.

(3) The Master said, Hui was not any help to me; he accepted everything I said.

(4) The Master said, Min Tzu-ch'ien is indeed a very good son. No one can take exception to what his parents or brothers have said of him.

(5) Nan Jung in reciting the Song repeated the verse about the scepter of white jade three times. (In consequence of which) Master K'ung gave him his elder brother's daughter to marry.

(6) K'ang-tzu of the Chi Family asked which of the disciples had a love of learning. Master K'ung replied, There was Yen Hui. He was fond of learning, but unfortunately his allotted sapan was a short one, and he died. Now there is none.

(7) When Yen Hui died, his father Yen Lu begged for the Master's carriage, that he might use it to make the enclosure for the coffin. The Master said, Gifted or not gifted, you have spoken of your son and I will now speak of mine. When Li died he had a coffin, but no enclosure. I did not go on foot in order that he might have an enclosure. I did not go on foot in order that he might have an enclosure; for I rank next to the Great Officers and am not permitted to go on foot.

(8) When Yen Hui died, the Master said, Alas, Heaven has bereft me, Heaven has bereft me!

(9) When Yen Hui died the Master wailed without restraint. His followers said, Master, you are wailing without restrain! He said, Am I doing so? Well, if any man's death could justify abandoned wailing, it would surely be this man's!

(10) When Yen Hui died, the disciples wanted to give him a grand burial. The Master said it would be wrong to de so; nevertheless they gave him a grand burial. The Master said, Hui dealt with me as though I were his father. But I have failed to deal with him as though he were my son. The fault however is not mine. It is yours, my friend!

(11) Tzu-lu asked how one should serve ghosts and spirits. The Master said, Till you have learnt to serve men, how can you serve ghosts? Tzu-lu then ventured upon a question about the dead. The Master said, Till you know about the living, how are you to know about the dead?

(12) When Min Tzu-ch'ien stood by the Master's side in attendance upon him his attitude was one of polite restraint. That of Tzu-lu was one of impatient energy; that

of Jan Ch'iu and of Tzu-kung was genial and affable. The Master was pleased.

[The Master said], A man like Yu never dies in his bed.

(13) When the men of Lu were dealing with the question of the Long Treasury, Min Tzu-ch'ien said, What about restoring it on the old lines? I see no necessity for rebuilding it on a new plan. The Master said, That man is no talker; but when he does say anything, he invariably hits the mark.

(14) The Master said, Yu's zither has no right to be in my house at all. Where upon the disciples ceased to respect Tzu-lu. The Master said, The truth about Yu is that he has got as far as the guest-hall, but has not yet entered the inner rooms.

(15) Tzu-kung asked which was the better, Shih or Shang. The Master said, Shih goes too far and Shang does not go far enough. Tzu-kung said, If that is so, Then Shih excels. The Master said, To go too far is as bad as not to go far enough.

(16) The head of the Chi Family was richer than the Duke of Chou; but Ch'iu, when entrusted with the task of collecting his revenues for him, added to them and increased the yield. The Master said, He is no follower of mine. My little ones, you may beat the drum and set upon him. I give you leave.

(17) [The Master said], Ch'ai is stupid, Shên is dull-witted, Shih is too formal; Yu, too free and easy.

(18) The Master said, Hui comes very near to it. He is often empty. Ssu (Tzu-kung) was discontented with his lot and has taken steps to enrich himself. In his calculations he often hits the mark.

(19) Tzu-chang asked about the Way of the good people. The Master said, He who does not tread in the tracks cannot expect to find his way into the Inner Room.

(20) The Master said (of someone), That his conversation is sound one may grant. But whether he is indeed a true gentleman or merely one who adopts outward airs of solemnity, it is not so easy to say.

3. 思考题
略

第四课 《道德经》译介赏析

1. 分析题
略

2. 实训题

(1)　　When your power of perception
penetrates every corner,
Are you capable of knowing nothing?
Giving all things life and propagation
Without claiming to be their owner,
Benefiting them without claiming
to be their benefactor,
And being their head without ruling them,
All these are called
the most intrinsic Teh (virtue).

（辜正坤译）

(2)　　I try my best to be in an extreme
emptiness of mind;
I try to keep myself in a state of stillness.
From the vigorous growth of all things
I perceive the way they move
in endless cycles.
All things, full of vitality,
Finally return to their own roots.
Returning to roots means stillness.
Also means a return to destiny.
A return to destiny is known
As the law of eternity.
To understand the law is known
as enlightening.

（辜正坤译）

3. 思考题
略

第五课 《庄子》译介赏析

1. 分析题
略

2. 实训题

There is a limit to our life, but to knowledge there is no limit. With what is limited to pursue what is unlimited is a perilous thing. When knowing this, we still seek to increase our knowledge, the peril cannot be averted. In doing what convention considers as good, eschew fame. In doing what convention considers as bad, escape disgrace or penalty. Always pursue the middle course. These are the ways to preserve our body, to maintain our life, to support our parents, to complete our terms of years.

Prince Wen Hui's cook was cutting up a bullock. Every blow of his hand, every heaven of his shoulder, every tread of his foot, every thrust of his knee, every sound of the rending flesh and every note of the movement of the chopper were in perfect harmony — rhythmical like the dance of "The Mulberry Grove" simultaneous like the chords of the "Ching Shou."

"Ah, admirable," said the prince, "that your art should become so perfect!"

The cook laid down his chopper and replied: "What your servant loves is *Tao*, which is more advanced than art. When I first began to cut up bullocks, what I saw was simply whole bullocks. After 3 years' practice, I saw no more bullocks as wholes. At present, I work with my mind, but not with my eyes. The functions of my senses stop; my spirit dominates. Following the natural veins, my chopper slips through the great cavities, slides through the great openings, taking advantage of what is already there. I did not attempt the central veins and their branches, and the connectives between flesh and bone, not to mention the great bones. A good cook changes his chopper once a year, because he cuts. An ordinary cook changes his chopper once a month, because he hacks. Now my chopper has been in use for 19 years; it has cut up several thousand bullocks; yet its edge is as sharp as if it just came from the whetstone. At the joints there are always interstices, and the edge of the chopper is without thickness. If we insert that which is without thickness into an interstice, there is certainly plenty of room for it to move along. Nevertheless, when I came to a complicated joint, and see that there will be some difficulty, I proceed anxiously and with caution. I fix my eyes on it. I move slowly. Then by a very gentle movement of my chopper, the part is quickly separated, and yields like earth crumbling to the ground. Then standing with the chopper in my hand, I look all round, with an air of triumph and satisfaction. Then I wipe my chopper and put in in its sheath."

"Excellent," said the prince, "from the words of this cook, I learned the ways of cultivating life."

When Kung Wen Hsien saw the Master of the Right, he was startled and said: "Who is he? How is it that he has but one foot? Is this due to nature or due to man?"

"This is due to nature, not to man," said the Master of the Right. "Nature produces the foot and causes it to be this one only. The appearances of man are well balanced. From this I know it is due to nature, not to man."

The pheasant of the marshes gets a peck once in ten steps, a drink once in a hundred. Yet it does not want to be fed in a cage. In the marshes, its spirit is heathy, and consequently it forgets health.

When Lao Tzu died, Chin Shih went to mourn over him. He uttered three yells and went out.

A disciple asked him, saying, "Were you not a friend of the master?"

"Yes, I was," replied Chin Shih.

"If so, is it proper to offer your mourning merely in the way you have done?"

"Yes," said Chin Shih. "At first, I thought the other mourners were his [Lao Tzu's] men; now I know they are not. When I went in to mourn, there were old persons weeping as if for the loss of their children; and the young ones, as if for that of their mother. These persons assembled there, uttered words, and dropped tears, which are not to be expected. This is to violate the principle of nature and to increase the emotion of man, forgetting what we have received from nature. These were called by the ancients the penalty of violating the principle of nature. When the Master came, it was because he had the occasion to be born. When he went, he simply followed the natural course. Those who are quiet at the proper occasion and follow the natural course cannot be affected by sorrow or joy. They were considered by the ancients as the men of the gods, who were released from bondage."

The fingers may not be able to supply all the fuel. But the fire is transmitted, and we know not when it will come to an end.

（冯友兰译）

3. 思考题

略

第六课 《孙子兵法》译介赏析

1. 分析题

(1) 以《计篇》第一段为例,《孙子兵法》原文为:

孙子曰:兵者,国之大事,死生之地,存亡之道,不可不察也。

袁士槟译:

War is a matter of vital importance to the state; a matter of life or death, the road either to survival or to ruin. Hence, it is imperative that it be studied thoroughly.

林戊荪译:

Sunzi said:

War is a question of vital importance to the state, a matter of life and death, to road to survival or ruin. Hence, it is a subject which calls for careful study.

读者不难看出,袁译对原文形式进行了一定的改变。原文多用汉语中常见的四字句,读起来朗朗上口,意义明确。

袁士槟的译文删去了"孙子曰"几个字,译者将原文以第一人称翻译出来,而其他三种译文均是以第三人称翻译。袁士槟的译文是在参考了前人译本的基础之上而成的,加上译者对原文的理解也较国外译者准确,所以总的来说还是一种不错的译文。

(2) 译者使用了增译的手段来译"微乎微乎,至于无形;神乎神乎,至于无声"。袁士槟的译文将其译为:"How subtle and insubstantial, that the expert leaves no trace. How divinely mysterious, that he is inaudible."林戊荪的译文为:"So subtle is the expert that he leaves no trace, so mysterious that he makes no sound."两者都加了"expert"这个对象,来使源文意思更加具体和完整。

2. 实训题

(1) Sunzi said: Generally in war, the commander receives his mandate from the sovereign. In the process of assembling his troops, mobilizing the population and taking up positions against the enemy, nothing is more difficult than troop maneuvering to gain the initiative in war. What is involved here is to turn the tortuous into the direct and to turn adversity into advantage. You render tile enemy's route tortuous by luring him with inducements of easy gains, and as a result, you may set out after he does but arrive at the contested battlefield before him. To be able to do so is to have understood the method of turning the tortuous into the direct.

Troop maneuvering can be a source of both advantage and disaster. If you throw in the army with all its equipment and supplies to contend for some advantage, you will not arrive in time; if you abandon them, your equipment and supplies will be lost. For this reason, if an army stores away its amour and sets off in haste, not stopping for days and nights and marching at double speed for 100 li to gain the advantage, some of its generals might be captured by file enemy, its strongest men might get there first but the exhausted ones would lag behind, and in that case, only one tenth of the army would reach the destination. In a forced march of 50 li to contend for advantage, the commander of the advance unit might be defeated, and as a rule only half of the army would reach its destination. But were it to travel 30 li at such a pace to contend for advantage, then two-thirds of the army would reach its destination. It must be remembered that an army which is without its equipment, food and fodder, and material reserves cannot survive.

(2) Sunzi said: Generally, in positioning your troops and assessing the enemy, you should pay attention to the following:

While passing through mountains, stay close to the valleys and pitch camp on high ground facing the sun; if the enemy is on high ground, avoid fighting an uphill battle. So much for positioning an army when in the mountains.

After crossing a river, move to distance yourself from it; when the advancing enemy is crossing the river, do not meet him in the river; it is to your advantage to wait until he is halfway across, and then strike; if you are ready for a decisive battle, do not position your troops near the water to confront your enemy; when encamping in such a region, take up a position on high ground facing the sun; do not take up a position that is downstream from the enemy. So much for positioning an army when near a river.

When crossing salt marshes, get through them quickly and without delay; if you encounter the enemy in the middle of a marshland, you must take a position close to reeds and water with trees to your rear. So much for positioning an army in marshland.

On flatlands, position yourself on open ground, with the main flank backed by high ground; that way the dangerous ground is in front of you and the safe ground is behind you. So much for positioning an army on flatlands.

It was such advantageous positioning of his troops in these four different situations that enabled the Yellow Emperor to defeat his four opponents.

Generally speaking, a maneuvefing army prefers high, dry ground to low, wet ground; it prizes the, sunny side and shuns the shady side, so that food and water would be readily available and remain in ample supply and men and horses may rest and restore their strength and be free of diseases. These conditions will guarantee victory./All armies prefer high ground to low, and sunny places to dark. If you are careful of your men, and camp on hard ground, the army will be free from disease of every kind, and this will spell victory. (Giles)/Generally speaking, an army prefers high ground and dislikes the low, prizes the sunny side and shuns the shady side, seeks a place in which food and water are readily available and ample to supply its needs, and wants to be free of the numerous diseases. These conditions mean certain victory. (Ames)

When encountering hills, embankments and dikes, the army must be positioned on the sunny side with the main flank backed against the slope. These measures are beneficial because they help to exploit whatever the terrain affords. When it is raining upstream and foaming waters descend, do not try to cross immediately; wait for the water to subside.

3. 思考题
略

第七课 唐诗译介赏析

1. 分析题
略

2. 实训题

(1) **Written in Village South of the Capital**
Cui Hu
In this house on this day last year a pink face vied
In beauty with the pink peach blossom side by side.
I do not know today where the pink face has gone,
In vernal breeze still smile pink blossom full blown.

(许渊冲译)

(2) **A Bride**
Wang Jian
Married three day, I go shy-faced
To cook a soup with hands still fair.
To meet my mother-in-law's taste,

I send to her daughter the first share.

（许渊冲译）

(3)   **To One Unnamed**

Li Shangyin

It's difficult for us to meet and hard to part；
The east wind is too weak to revive flowers dead.
Spring silkworm till its death spins silk from love-sick heart；
A candle but when burned out has no tears to shed.
At dawn I'm grieved to think your mirrored hair turns grey；
At night you would feel cold while I croon by moonlight.
To the three fairy hills it is not a long way.
Would the blue birds oft fly to see you on the height?

（许渊冲译）

3. 思考题
略

第八课　宋词译介赏析

1. 分析题
略

2. 实训题

Last night the wind blew hard and rain was fine.
Sound sleep did not dispel the aftertaste of wine.
I ask the maid rolling up the screen.
"The same crab-apple tree," she says, "is seen."
"But don't you know,
O don't you know,
The red should languish and the green must grow?" (Like A Dream by Li Qingzhao)

（许渊冲译）

3. 思考题
略

第九课 《楚辞》译介赏析

1. 分析题

(1) 初既与余成言兮,后悔遁而有他。

   余既不难夫离别兮,伤灵修之数化。

霍译:There once was a time when he spoke with me in frankness;

   But then he repented and was of another mind.

   I do not care, on my own count, about this divorcement,

   But it grieves me to find the Fair One so inconstant.

许译:The word you've given still remains, oh!

   But you go back on it and stray.

   Departure causes me no pains, oh!

   Of your fickleness what to say?

分析:诗歌原文中没有用到人称代词,两位译者都采用了意译的方法,增译了人称代词。一、二句霍译用了人称代词 he,采取的是陈述的语气,三、四句霍译依照原文的陈述句句式翻译;许译用了人称代词"you",采用的是直接的对话语气,且把三、四句改译为反问句,更直接地抒发了作者的情感,增加了诗歌的表现力。

2. 实训题

(1) 'I hurried about your chariot in attendance,

   Leading you in the tracks of the kings of old.'

   But the Fragrant One refused to examine my true feelings:

   He led ear, instead, to slander, and raged against me.

   How well I know that loyalty brings disaster;

   Yet I will endure: I cannot give it up.

   I called on the ninefold heaven to be my witness,

   And all for the sake of the Fair One, and no other.

   There once was a time when he spoke with me in frankness;

   But then he repented and was of another mind.

   I do not care, on my own count, about this divorcement,

   But it grieves me to find the Fair One so inconstant.

   I run before it and behind, oh!

   I wish you would follow your sire.

337

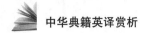

　　　　To my loyalty you're unkind, oh!
　　　　You heed slander and burst in fire.
　　　　With frank advice you won't comply, oh!
　　　　I endure and cannot have done.
　　　　Be my witness, Ninth Heaven High, oh!
　　　　I've done all for you Sacred One.
　　　　The word you've given still remains, oh!
　　　　But you go back on it and stray.
　　　　Departure causes me no pains, oh!
　　　　Of your fickleness what to say?

（2）Oh, your young resolution has something different from the rest!
　　　　Alone and unmoving you stand; how can one not admire you?
　　　　Deep-rooted, hard to shift; truly you have no peer!
　　　　Alter to this world's ways you hold your ground,
　　　　unyielding against the vulgar tide.
　　　　You have scaled your heart;
　　　　you guard yourself with care;
　　　　have never fallen into error;
　　　　Holding a nature free from bias, impartial even as Heaven and Earth are.
　　　　While young, you aspire and as you please,
　　　　Quite different from other trees, oh!
　　　　Grown up, independent you stand.
　　　　How you're admired in southern land！oh!
　　　　You're too deep-rooted to transplant;
　　　　Seeking nothing, you're so exuberant, oh!
　　　　You stand alone in this world wide,
　　　　Unyielding to the vulgar tide, oh!
　　　　You seal your heart and act with care;
　　　　You've done nothing wrong elsewhere, oh!
　　　　So selfless, you have virtues high,
　　　　And become one with earth and sky, oh!

　　3. 思考题
　　略

第十课 《红楼梦》译介赏析

1. 分析题
略

2. 实训题

（1）"'Old friends are best friends and close kin are kindest,'" said Bao-yu, coming over to where she sat and speaking very quietly. 'You're too intelligent not to know that. Even a simpleton like me knows that much! Take kinship first: you are my cousin on Father's side; Cousin Bao is only a mother-cousin. That makes you much the closer kin. And as for length of acquaintance: it was you who came here first. You and I have practically grown up together — eaten at the same table, even slept in the same bed. Compared with you she's practically a new arrival. Why should I ever be any less dose to you because of her?'

'Whatever do you take me for? Do you think I want you to be any less close to *her* because *of me*? It's the way I feel that makes me the way I am.'

'And it's the way I feel,' said Bao-yu, 'that makes me the way I am! Do you mean to tell me that you know your Own feelings about me but still don't know what my feelings are about you?'

Dai-yu lowered her head and made no reply. After a pause she said:

'You complain that whatever you do people are always getting angry with you. You don't seem to realize how much you *provoke* them by what you do. Take today, for instance. It's obviously colder today than it was yesterday. Then why of all days should you choose today to leave your blue cape off?'

Bao-yu laughed.

'I didn't. I was wearing it this morning the same as usual; but when you started quarrelling just now, I got into such a sweat that I had to take it off.'

'Next thing you'll be catching a cold,' said Dai-yu with a sigh, 'and then Heaven knows what grumblings and scoldings there will be!'

（霍克斯译）

Baoyu stepped to her side and said softly, "Someone of your intelligence should know that distant relatives can't come between close ones, and new friends can't take the place of old. Dense as I am, I know that. Look, you're the daughter of my father's sister, while Baochai's a cousin on my mother's side — you're more closely related to me than she is. Besides, you came here first, we've eaten at the same table, slept in the same bed and grown up together, while she has only recently arrived. How could I be less close to you because of her?"

"Do I want you to be less close to her? What do you take me for? It's just that my feelings are hurt."

"And it's your feelings that concern me. Do you only know your own heart and not mine?"

Daiyu lowered her head and was silent. After a pause she said:

"You blame other people for finding fault with you, without realizing how provoking you can be. Take today, for example. Why leave off your fox-fur cape when it's turned so cold?"

Baoyu laughed.

"I was wearing it till you grew angry. Then I got so hot and bothered that I took it off."

"Well," she sighed, "if you catch cold there'll be the devil to pay."

（杨宪益、戴乃迭译）

(2) Just then Xiang-yun burst in on them and reproved them smilingly for abandoning her:

'Couthin Bao, Couthin Lin: you can thee each other every day. It'th not often I get a chanthe to come here; yet now I have come, you both ignore me!'

Dai-yu burst out laughing:

'Lisping doesn't seem to make you any less talkative! Listen to you: "Couthin!" "Couthin!" Presently, when you're playing Racing Go, you'll be all "thicktheth" and "theventh"!'

'You'd better not imitate her,' said Bao-yu. 'It'll get to be a habit. You'll be lisping yourself before you know where you are.'

'How you do pick on one!' said Xiang-yun. 'Always finding fault. Even if you are tho perfect yourthelf, I don't thee why you have to go making fun of everyone elthe. But I can show you thomeone you won't dare to find fault with. I shall certainly think you a wonder if you do.'

'Who's that?' said Dai-yu

'If you can find any shortcomings in Cousin Bao-chai', said Xiang-yun, 'you must be very good indeed.'

'Oh *her*,' said Dai-yu coldly. 'I wondered whom you could mean. I should never dare to find fault with *her*.'

But before she could say any more, Bao-yu cut in and hurriedly changed the subject.

'I shall never be a match for you as long as I live,' Xiang-yun said to Dai-yu with a disarming smile. 'All I can thay ith that I hope you marry a lithping huthband, tho that you have "ithee-withee" "ithee-withee" in your earth every minute of the day. "Ah, Holy Name I think I can thee that blethed day already before my eyeth!'

Bao-yu could not help laughing; but Xiang-yun had already turned and fled.

（霍克斯译）

They were interrupted by Xiangyun's arrival.

"Why, *Ai* Brother and Sister Lin!" she cried cheerfully. "You can be together every day, but it's rarely I have a chance to visit you; yet you pay no attention to poor little me."

"The lisper loves to rattle away," said Daiyu with a laugh. "Fancy saying *ai* instead of *er* like that. I suppose, when we start dicing, you'll be shouting one, love, three, four, five...."

"If you copy her long enough, you'll soon be talking the same way," Baoyu teased.

"How you do pick on one!" cried Xiangyun. "Always finding fault! Even if you are better than all the rest of us, there's no need to go making fun of everyone else. But I know someone you'd never dare find fault with. If you do, I'll really respect you."

"Who's that?" Daiyu promptly asked.

"Dare you pick fault with Cousin Baochai? If so, good for you. I may not be up to you, but you've met your match in *her*."

"Oh, *her*." Daiyu snorted. "I wondered whom you meant. How could I ever presume to find fault with her?"

Baoyu tried to stop them, but Xiangyun rattled on:

"Naturally I'll never come up to you in this lifetime. I just pray that you'll marry a husband who talks like me, so that you hear nothing but 'love' the whole day long. Amida Buddha! May I live to see that day!"

That set everyone laughing, and Xiangyun turned and ran out.

（杨宪益、戴乃迭译）

3. 思考题

略

第十一课 《西游记》评介赏析

1. 分析题

（1）詹纳尔译：The monkeys all laughed and said, "The Great King indeed does not know contentment! Here we daily have a banquet on an immortal mountain in a blessed land, in an ancient cave on a divine continent. We are not subject to the unicorn or the phoenix, nor are we governed by the rulers of mankind. Such independence and comfort are immeasurable blessings. Why, then, does he worry about the future?"

余国藩译：The other monkey laughed and said: "Your Majesty is being greedy. We have parties every day; we live in a mountain paradise, in an ancient cave in a divine continent. We are spared the rule of unicorns, the domination of phoenixes, and the restraints of human kings. We are free to do just as we like — we are infinitely lucky. Why make yourself miserable worrying about the future?

两个译本"不伏麒麟辖，不伏凤凰管"的翻译各有不同。詹译使用了被动语态"be subject to"，余译把动词结构换译为名词"the rule of unicorns, the domination of phoenixes"，化动为静，更加符合英语的表达习惯。

（2）略

2. 实训题

（1）We were telling you about the Zhenyuan Great Immortal, who grabbed Pilgrim and said, "I know your abilities, and I have heard of your reputation. But you have been most deceitful and unscrupulous this time. You may indulge in all sorts of wizardry, but you can't escape from my hands. I'll argue with you all the way to the Western Heaven to see that Buddhist Patriarch of yours, but you won't get away from having to restore to me the Ginseng Fruit Tree. So stop playing with your magic!" "Dear Sir!" said Pilgrim, laughing. "How petty you are! If you want the tree revived, there's no problem. If you had said so in the first place, we would have been spared this conflict." "No conflict!" said the Great Immortal. "You think I would let you get away with what you have done?" "Untie my master," said Pilgrim, "and I'll give you back a living tree. How's that?" "If you really possess the power," said the Great Immortal, "to make the tree alive again, I'll go through the proper ceremony of 'Eight Bows' with you and become your bond-brother."

（2）We were telling you about the Great Sage Sun, who recovered his golden-hooped rod and fought his way out of the door. He was filled with delight as he leaped up to the tall summit to face the various gods. "How did you do this time?" asked the Devarāja Li. "By his transformation," said Pilgrim, "old Monkey managed to get inside the cave. That fiend and his subordinates were all singing and dancing, drinking their victory wine. I did not succeed in detecting where he put his treasure, but when I went to the rear of the cave, I heard horses neighing and dragons whining and I knew that they had to be the belongings of the fire department. The golden-hooped rod was leaning against the east wall; old Monkey picked it up and fought his way out." "You got your treasure," said the deities, "but when could we get back ours?" "It's easy! It's easy!" said Pilgrim. "When I have this iron rod, I'll strike him down and recover your treasures for you, no matter what."

3. 思考题
略

第十二课 《三国演义》评介赏析

1. 实训题

(1) The little fleet reached Cao Cao's naval camp about the fifth watch, and Zhuge Liang gave orders to form line lying prows west, and then to beat the drums and shout.

"But what shall we do if they attack us?" exclaimed Lu Su.

Zhuge Liang replied with a smile, "I think their fleet will not venture out in this fog. Go on with your wine, and let us be happy. We will go back when the fog lifts."

As soon as the shouting from the river was heard by those in the camp, the two admirals, Mao Jie and Yu Jin, ran off to report to Cao Cao, who said, "Coming up in a fog like this means that they have prepared an ambush for us. Do not go out, but get all the force together and shoot at them."

He also sent orders to the ground camps to dispatch six thousand of archers and crossbowmen to aid the marines.

The naval forces were then lined up shooting on the bank to prevent a landing. Presently the soldiers arrived, and ten thousand and more soldiers were shooting down into the river, where the arrows fell like rain. By and bye Zhuge Liang ordered the boats to turn round so that their prows pointed east and to go closer in so that many arrows might hit them.

Zhuge Liang ordered the drums to be kept beating till the sun was high and the fog began to disperse, when the boats got under way and sailed down stream. The whole twenty boats were bristling with arrows on both sides.

As they left, Zhuge Liang asked all the crews to shout derisively, "We thank you, Sir Prime Minister, for the arrows!" (Extracted from *Chapter 46 Using Strategy, Zhuge Liang Borrows Arrows; Joining A Ruse, Huang Gai Accepts Punishment*, translated by C. H. Brewitt-Taylor)

(2) As they were going, the soldiers said, "There are two roads before us. Which shall we take?"

"Which is the shorter?" asked Cao Cao.

"The high road is the more level, but it is fifteen miles longer than the bye road which goes to Huarong Valley. Only the latter road is narrow and dangerous, full of pits and difficult."

Cao Cao sent men up to the hill tops to look around.

They returned, saying: "There are several columns of smoke rising from the hills along the bye road. The high road seems quiet."

Then Cao Cao bade them lead the way along the bye road.

"Where smoke arises there are surely soldiers," remarked the officers. "Why go this way?"

"Because the 'Book of War' says that the hollow is to be regarded as solid, and the solid as hollow. That fellow Zhuge Liang is very subtle and has sent people to make those fires so that we should not go that way. He has laid an ambush on the high road. I have made up my mind, and I will not fall a victim to his wiles."

"O Prime Minister, your conclusions are most admirable. None other can equal you," said the officers.

And the soldiers were sent along the bye road. They were very hungry and many almost too weak to travel. The horses too were spent. Some had been scorched by the flames, and they rode forward resting their heads on their whips. The wounded struggled on to the last of their strength. All were soaking wet and all were feeble. Their arms and accouterments were in a deplorable state, and more than half had been left upon the road they had traversed. Few of the horses had saddles or bridles, for in the confusion of pursuit they had been left behind. It was the time of greatest winter cold, and the suffering was indescribable. (Extracted from *Chapter 50 Zhuge Liang Foresees The Huarong Valley Episode; Guan Yu Lifts His Saber To Release Cao Cao*, translated by C. H. Brewitt-Taylor)

2. 思考题

略

第十三课 《水浒传》评介赏析

1. 分析题

(1) 略

(2) 智深道:"也是怪哉;歇一夜打甚么不紧,怎地便是讨死?"庄家道:"去便去,不去时便捉来缚在这里!"

杰克逊译:"This is strange," replied Lu Da. "If I only stay for one night, how shall I risk my life?" "Go away!" said the villagers. "If you do not go we shall tie you up."

沙博理译:"That's a strange talk. Why such a fuss about spending one night? Why so dangerous?" "Get going. Otherwise you're liable to be seized and bound."

杰克逊将句子直译为"If I only stay for one night, how shall I risk my life?",而沙博理采用了有形移译的方法,依照英语表达习惯把中心语"why such a fuss"移到了句首。

2. 实训题

(1) Songjiang mounted the ladder and called:"Quite down, out there. Leniency to my crime has already been declared. It's no longer a capital offence. If you two constables will come into our humble manor and have a few cups of wine with us, I'll go with you to the magistrate tomorrow." "You're not going to get us in there with any of your tricks," Zhao Neng exclaimed. "Would I implicate my own father and brother? Come in. You don't have to worry." Song Jiang came down from the ladder, opened the manor gate, and invited the two constables into the guest hall. That night they were wined and dined on chicken and goose. The hundred or more soldiers were also given food and drink, and each some money. Bars of silver worth twenty ounces were presented to the two constables as "thanks for their kindness."

(2) Right to the door or the preaching hall the battle raged. Then the voice of the abbot rang out:"Sagacious, stop that fighting; You, too, you monks!" The attackers have suffered, several dozen injured. They were glad to fall back when the abbot appeared. Lu threw down his table legs. "Abbot, help me," he cried. By now he was eight-tents sober. "Sagacious, you're giving me too much trouble," said the cleric, "The last time you got drunk and raised a rumpus I wrote your sponsor squire Zhao about it and he sent a letter of apology. Now you've disgraced yourself again, upset

your pure way of life, wrecked the pavilion and damaged two idols. All this we can overlook, but you drove the monks from the meditation room, and that's a major crime. Wenshu Buddha meditated when our monastery stands today. For centuries hollow grounds have known only tranquility and the fragrance of incense. It's no place for a dirty fellow like you. The next few days you stay with me in the abbot's hall. I'll arrange for you to be transferred elsewhere."

3. 思考题
略

第十四课 《黄帝内经》译介赏析

1. 分析题
略

2. 实训题

(1) The three months of autumn is the season of Rongping (ripening). In autumn it is cool, the wind blows fast and the atmosphere is clear. [People should] sleep early in the night and get up early in the morning just like Ji (hens and roosters). [They should] keep their mind in peace to alleviate the soughing effect of autumn, moderating mental activity to balance Qiuqi (Autumn-Qi) and preventing outward manifestation of sentiments to harmonize Feiqi (Lung-Qi). This is what adaptation to Qiuqi (Autumn-Qi) means and this is the Dao (principle) for Yangshou (cultvation of health and regualtion of daily life). Any violation [of this rule] will impair the lung and leads to Sunxie (diarrhea) with undigested food in it in winter [due to] insufficient supply for storage [in winter].

(李照国译)

The three months of autumn,
they denote taking in and balance.
The qi of heaven becomes tense.
The qi of the earth becomes bright.

Go to rest early and rise early,
Get up together with the chicken.
Let the mind be peaceful and tranquil, so as

to temper the punishment carried out in autumn.

Collect the spirit qi and

cause the autumn qi to be balanced.

Do not direct your mind to the outside and

cause the lung qi to be clear.

This is correspondence with the qi of autumn and

it is the Way to nourish gathering.

Opposing it harms the lung.

In winter this causes outflow of [undigested] food and

there is little to support storage.

(Tr. Paul U. Unschuld)

(2) The three months of winter is the season for storage. The water freezes and the earth cracks. [Cares must be taken] not to disturb Yang. [People should] sleep early in the night and get up late in the morning when the sun is shining, physically maintaining quiet just like keeping private affairs or as if having obtained [what one has desired]. They should guard themselves against cold and try to keep warm, avoiding sweating so as to prevent loss of Yangqi. This is what adaptation to Dongqi (Winter-Qi) means and this is the Dao (principle) for Yangcang (cultivating health and promoting the storing functions of the body). Any violation will impair Shenqi (Kidney-Qi) and reduce the energy for the following season, leading to Weijue (dysfunction, weakness and coldness of the limbs) in spring due to insufficient supply for growth [in spring].

(李照国译)

The three months of winter,

they denote securing and storing.

The water is frozen and the earth breaks open.

Do not disturb the yang [qi].

Go to rest early and rise late.

You must wait for the sun to shine.

Let the mind enter a state as if hidden,

{as if shut in}

as if you had secret intentions,

as if you already had made gains.

Avoid cold and seek warmth and
do not [allow sweat] to flow away through the skin.
This would cause the qi to be carried away quickly.

This is correspondence with the qi of winter and
it is the Way of nourishing storage.
Opposing it harms the kidneys.
In spring this causes limpness with receding [qi], and
there is little to support generation.

(Tr. Paul U. Unschuld)

3. 思考题

略